The Gifford Lectures, 1951, First Series

NATURAL RELIGION
AND
CHRISTIAN THEOLOGY

NATURAL RELIGION
AND
CHRISTIAN THEOLOGY

THE GIFFORD LECTURES 1951

FIRST SERIES:
Science and Religion

BY

CHARLES E. RAVEN
D.D., D.Sc., F.B.A.

Regius Professor Emeritus of Divinity,
University of Cambridge

CAMBRIDGE
AT THE UNIVERSITY PRESS
1953

PUBLISHED BY

THE SYNDICS OF THE CAMBRIDGE UNIVERSITY PRESS

London Office: Bentley House, N.W.1
American Branch: New York

Agents for Canada, India, and Pakistan: Macmillan

Printed in Great Britain by The Carlyle Press, Birmingham, 6

CONTENTS

To the memory of
my friend and Chancellor
JAN CHRISTIAAN SMUTS

PREFACE

THESE two volumes represent in slightly longer and less informal shape the lectures delivered under the title 'Religio Medicorum' in the Martin Hall, New College, Edinburgh in May 1951 and 1952. The audacity of attempting to treat so large and necessarily detailed a theme and the consciousness of the gaps in my own equipment for it made the prospect of their delivery an ordeal. The generosity and encouragement of the University and of the audience have transformed it in retrospect into a singularly happy remembrance. To express gratitude to all who were kind to me would involve a long list of friends old and new: to single out any is liable to be ungracious. Sir Edward Appleton, Principal of the University and Principal John Baillie of New College will, I hope, consent to represent their colleagues and guests. To them and to all concerned both in the preparation and the delivery of the lectures I can only say: Thank you with all my heart.

C.E.R.

INTRODUCTORY:
RELIGION AND NATURE

IT is customary, and perhaps even desirable, for anyone who has the honour to be invited to deliver lectures on Lord Gifford's foundation to say something of the conditions on which the lectureship was constituted. This is the more necessary at the present time when Natural Religion is temporarily under a cloud and when certain of the recent lecturers have not concealed their belief that for the Christian it is, if not a contradiction in terms, at least a heresy which he is bound to renounce and castigate. If nature is what Saint Augustine proclaimed it to be, a mere *massa perditionis*, then obviously no other course is possible.

It need not be argued that for such an attitude there is a reasonable defence. Natural religion is a phrase that came into existence in an atmosphere of conflict and as a challenge to the prevailing supernaturalism of traditional orthodoxy. At its best it was significant of the attempt to deliver Christendom from its thousand years' captivity to the belief in a rigid antithesis between the secular and the sacred, and of the conviction of the best seventeenth century thought that the order of nature not only proceeded from the same source but revealed the same quality as the order of grace. But dualism was too deeply ingrained in Catholic and Protestant theology for the phrase to be sympathetically considered: it threatened the Catholic separation of reason from faith not less than the Protestant doctrines of the universal effect of the Fall: it savoured of Spinozism and, curiously enough, of the rationalistic deism which was its opposite: it infringed the dearest prerogatives both of ecclesiastics and of Calvinists: if there were any such thing as natural religion, then the uniqueness of Christ, the certainty of hell, the necessity for *sola fides*, indeed the whole structure of conventional apologetic were threatened. The denunciations called out by so conciliatory and orthodox a treatise as Sir Thomas Browne's *Religio Medici* show how inveterately hostile were the Churches of Western Europe to any attempt to formulate 'a religion for the scientist'.

The effect of such hostility was inevitable. The phrase became a slogan—to its opponents a synonym for laxity, almost for paganism, to its upholders not only a repudiation of the miraculous and supernatural as these were commonly understood, but a protest against any experience which could not be explained and even demonstrated by the scientific reason. So long as this reason was given the large scope and meaning which it held for Whichcote or Cudworth, for Bishop Butler or for William Law, natural religion could be welcomed and acclaimed. When reason was made equivalent to mathematics and the universe was given the character of a mere machine, the phrase became less acceptable. It may easily be argued that when Lord Gifford used it he did so with a desire to exclude the supernatural quite as much as to expound the natural.

If this was in fact his intention, it is manifest that it has been widely ignored by very many of those who have accepted appointment under his trust. For me as for them it would be impossible to conform to his will in such terms; indeed my whole contention is that nature and supernature belong together and that to divorce them, as is, alas, so freely done by our neo-orthodox theologians, is to come perilously near to the most notorious of all the early heresies. If nature is so corrupted as to be the antithesis of grace, then the Creator must be, as the Arians supposed, of a different substance from the Redeemer—unless of course He has, as some suggest, ceded His control of the world to the successful rebellion of the devil. If grace is radically contrasted with the beauty and truth and goodness of the natural order, then any belief in a real Incarnation is impossible—unless the Christ be, as the Gnostics maintained, and their modern followers admit, a divine intruder totally other than mankind. If God is God, and God is manifested in Christ, then Creation, Redemption and Sanctification must be identical in origin and fundamentally also in character. It was the chief purpose of the Nicene Creed in its original form to maintain that this is the case.

If natural religion is a phrase open to objection as implying the exclusion of everything that cannot properly be assigned to the order of nature as normally understood, dislike of it has certainly been increased by the identification of nature with the realm of science, and science with the technique of weight and measurement. Many of us who insist upon the continuity of nature and supernature cannot approve, indeed strongly resent, the process which has first abstracted from the natural world certain elements in it susceptible to quantitative study and mechanistic interpretation, and then has proceeded to claim that these elements do in fact constitute the whole of the natural order. This matter is so important in itself and so germane to the subject of these lectures as to demand a fuller examination.

Nature in the sense in which it will be used in these lectures includes the whole of man's physical and terrestrial environment, earth and sky, land and sea, plants and animals, everything from the structure of the atom to the composition of the galaxy, and from the non-filterable viruses to the saints and sages of mankind. It is convenient to speak of the values discernible in this environment and of the quality of our spiritual and mystic insight into it as supernatural: but this does not imply that they contradict or are antithetical to the natural order—merely that they represent a higher level of our experience of it. It does not lie within the scope of these lectures to inquire into the special problem of man's dual relationship to nature: obviously he is not only, like the animals, himself a part of nature 'rolled round in earth's diurnal course with rocks and stones and trees', but, unlike them, he is also capable of a sense of detachment from it which at once involves a capacity to contemplate and criticize and also to feel solitary and self-conscious: in this regard it may be legitimate to call him 'the great Amphibium'—though the phrase has been gravely misused.

But it is clear that he has this double attitude, and highly probable that here is the distinction which gives him his special status. That the power of contemplation and of conscious selfhood alike spring out of a basic sense of awe, and that in consequence man may properly be distinguished as 'a worshipping animal' 'made in the image of God', is perhaps a legitimate inference from the evidence. If so, it would indicate how intimately connected are the dual aspects of religion, the awareness which has its culmination in ecstasy and the shame which involves penitence and self-abasement.

From the earliest days of our species man's relationship to nature shows this twofold quality. He derives from nature not only the sustenance of his physical being but the imagery and setting of his emotional and intellectual life. But he is from the first never able merely to accept and enjoy it: he must always be discovering from it affinities and animosities, mysteries which fascinate and terrify, objects that possess magic properties, haunts of ancient dread, presences that arouse imagination, problems that stimulate thought. It is at once a work of art—and we are artists before we are scientists or moralists—a school for curiosity and its satisfaction, and a home for growth in character and fellowship.[1] In it all is what Rudolf Otto has taught us to call the holy, the *mysterium tremendum et fascinans*. Totem and fetish, tabu and code, myth and folk-tale are gradually developed; and the apparatus of religion, cultus and ethic and doctrine, appears in embryo.

How a vague and undifferentiated animism, appropriate to the great god Pan, passed into a polytheism suited to man's growing ability to differentiate, analyse and estimate his surroundings; how this in turn gave him material for a varying valuation of the universe and so fixed the broad types of religious ethos—world-renouncing or world-accepting, dualist or pantheist; and how, thus, experience of the natural suggested and coloured the interpretation of the quality and meaning of man's life; these questions will always deserve the closest attention[2] even when, as at

[1] The subject is developed in my book, *The Creator Spirit*, pp. 105-31.

[2] I would acknowledge my debt to J. Oman, *The Natural and the Supernatural*, the most profound treatment of this subject known to me, and a book that has received less attention than it deserves.

present we can only see them in broad and often fragmentary
outline.

At a very early stage the problem of number, unity and plurality,
the significance of particular numbers and sequences, had begun
to attract attention; and speculations about it are an important
factor in the growth of human thought. The starry heavens, the
phases of the moon, the appearances of the planets, and their
possible influence upon earthly happenings and human destiny,
these played a part (though, relatively to other mysterious phenomena which bore more directly upon human prosperity, an
unimportant part) in shaping man's reaction to his world. But it
is with rain and sun, seed-time and harvest, the ways of beast and
bird, the fertility of cattle, the procuring of food and shelter and
the management of domestic and tribal affairs that his days were
principally occupied. The organic life around him, human, animal
or vegetable, was always the primary stimulus alike to his activities
and to his speculations.

Even when the age of intellectual inquiry was in its splendid
springtime in Greece there is little evidence that abstract and
numerical problems or even those of motion and its transmission
took a prominent place or made a large contribution. The
Pythagoreans like the priests of Egypt and the magians of Persia
observed and counted, measured and speculated with real accuracy
and insight: mathematics began to be a valuable part of man's
equipment and to stimulate and guide his ingenuity and inventive-
ness: machinery of a simple sort was constructed and used: but it
is with himself and human society, with plants and animals and
with the significance and interpretation of nature that thought is
chiefly concerned; and when Aristotle, the first of scientists, set
out his teaching, though he raised and discussed the question of the
mover and the moved, it was with the natural order in the full
sense rather than with science in its modern quantitative aspect that
he fills his books.[1] It is the total reaction to the order of nature, and

[1] Those like Professor B. Farrington who interpret Greek science in Marxist terms are
reduced to denigration of its greatest minds and to a wholly unhistorical estimate of the
scientific and social concern of the Ionic and Atomist schools. For a devastating exposure of
their case, cf. F. M. Cornford, *The Unwritten Philosophy*, pp. 117-37.

not merely the mathematical or industrial manipulation of it, that is to him, as to most of us, the important consideration.

It is with man's attitude to nature as a whole—an attitude out of which has developed at particular periods, and notably since the seventeenth century, the scientific movement strictly so called —that the student of religion is primarily concerned. The study of nature is indeed a perennial obligation for all mankind: we live with it and by it; and our general valuation of it, a valuation so deep-seated as to be largely unconscious, has a profound influence upon our whole life and thought. Hence the relation of religion towards nature, as Dr John Oman has proved, supplies a fundamental source of study for those who would appreciate the true character of a religious system; it is a matter far larger and more significant than the familiar business of religion and science. For science itself, as at present limited in scope and competence, only includes particular elements of the natural order; and these have been selected less for their intellectual and philosophic than for their practical and utilitarian interest. Indeed it is largely out of the misunderstanding between the order of nature and the field of science that our controversies have arisen. Instructed scientists are fully aware that they are only concerned with certain special aspects of nature, aspects appropriate to the scope of a particular research and patient of a special and technical manipulation. But the ordinary person, and indeed often the less thoughtful scientist, assumes that science has taken the whole of nature into its purview, that what it does not include is either unimportant or illusory, and that hypotheses valid for particular data are laws of universal application. Students of the subject who are familiar with the detailed history of any scientific development will easily recall examples of the ignoring and indeed the suppression of evidence which did not happen to be compatible with current scientific convictions.

This is not, of course, a defect peculiar to scientific research. In some degree every specialist must limit the field of his studies and select from it the evidence immediately relevant to his inquiry. That he should afterwards check his results, by testing their appropriateness to related problems and where possible by considering their bearing upon knowledge as a whole, is plainly desirable. But in these days of increasing departmentalism, and when no generally approved philosophy supplies a criterion, he cannot be expected to do so with any completeness. In fact even in the closely related fields of botany and zoology it is not difficult to find signs of a lack of co-ordination.

Such a defect only becomes important when, as has happened in this case, hypotheses based upon admittedly selected evidence are put forward as if they not only covered the whole order of nature but could be used to exclude any other data from consideration. To the historian, for example, nothing is more evident than that the era of modern science was initiated by a new enthusiasm for investigation and classification and speculation and by a new method of observation and experiment; and that in its early stages the movement owed far more to the biologists than to the mathematicians, far more to the anatomists and herbalists, the gardeners and explorers than to the astronomers. To represent the history of science, as is done in almost all the text-books, as a papal succession, Copernicus, Kepler, Galileo, Newton, with Boyle and Hooke and a few others wedged into the series, is only possible on the assumption that the important contributions are those which led up to the dominant mechanism and determinism of the late nineteenth century, and that the astonishing achievements of zoologists and botanists in the sixteenth and seventeenth centuries can be ignored. Historians of science have, until recently, committed the same error as historians of the early Church in the fourth and fifth centuries: they have written as if the only events of importance in the previous period were those which directly anticipated and promoted the current orthodoxy of their own day.

This is a matter of such importance, and the claim just made is so far new, that it requires illustration. In the histories of science —almost all written by scientists who have had no training in historical research and little acquaintance with general history—it is almost invariably assumed that the work of Copernicus was at once the starting-point and the epoch-making event of the scientific movement. Vesalius's work in anatomy, Gilbert's contribution on magnetism, Harvey's discovery of the circulation of the blood are the only universally recognized achievements outside the field of astronomy. Of biologists before Linnaeus there is usually no mention: Gesner scarcely appears in their indexes; Ray receives a page or two of commendation; Stensen and Redi, and even Malpighi and Swammerdam are hardly better recognized. Yet, from the point of view of the knowledge of nature, no single work is of more importance as initiating a new era than Gesner's *Historia Animalium*, which not only was the first book to summarize, criticize, and dismiss the age-old fables and legends of Aesop, Philologus, and the Bestiaries, but by its provision of accurate descriptions, notes of habits and distribution, and quite admirable illustrations founded the scientific study of zoology and exerted an unequalled influence upon its development. So too in the realm of particular discoveries it may well be argued that the overthrow of spontaneous generation, the universal belief, authorized alike by Scripture[1] and the Classics,[2] that bees were generated from putrefying flesh, lice from human sweat, caterpillars from cabbages and the London Rocket from wood-ash,[3] was an achievement as necessary, as difficult, and in its effects at least as influential as that of Copernicus; and hardly less notable is the rejection of the equally widespread belief in the transmutation of species.[4] Yet Francesco Redi's experiments, Swammerdam's demonstrations and Ray's lifelong advocacy have never been recognized as accomplishing anything of fundamental and revolutionary value. No one will wish to diminish the honour due to astronomers and mathematicians; but historically the origin of modern science is traceable to a much wider movement, to a wholly new approach to the order of nature, and to the simultaneous development of new knowledge in a very wide field of exploration, study and research. It was as part of this wider move-

[1] Judges xiv. 8, 9.   [2] Vergil, *Georgics* IV, 281-314.

[3] One of the last arguments for spontaneous generation was the sudden abundance of this plant, *Sisymbrium irio*, on the ruins of London after the Great Fire of 1666.

[4] For its persistence cf. Note 1 below, pp. 204-5.

ment that the specialized work of astronomers and mathematicians grew into prominence and gradually established an almost exclusive claim. Newton's great achievement,[1] coming at a time when the original impulse of the New Philosophy had almost spent itself, ushered in a new era, but must not be allowed to occlude the brilliance of the previous period or to distort its significance.

That the biological sciences which had in fact made such remarkable progress in the seventeenth century should have had to mark time, in spite of the physiological studies of Malpighi and Grew and later of Stephen Hales, was plainly inevitable.[2] So long as physics was committed to the doctrine of the four elements and chemistry still entangled with alchemy and white magic there could be no full exploration of the processes and functioning of the living organism. It was unfortunate that the vast but inflated reputation of Linnaeus (whose claim to high distinction depends solely upon his work in identification and nomenclature)[3] and the speed and utility of the developments in applied mathematics, physics and engineering should have fostered a distorted interpretation of the origin of modern science and given an exaggerated importance to mechanistic analogies. By the close of the eighteenth century the machine had become the symbol and instrument of the whole scientific movement; the attempt to see nature as a whole was abandoned; and the study of the living organism was being forced on to physical and chemical lines. In consequence we may note that the sort of questions which Harvey suggested in his *De Generatione*[4] and Ray propounded for investigation in *The Wisdom of God in the Works of Creation*[5] were ignored for nearly two centuries by professional biologists. Science had produced industrialism and transformed civilization—and the countryside. It was natural that utility should become its objective, and that it

[1] The attempt by B. Hessen in *Science at the Cross Roads* to interpret Newton in terms of economic determinism is fully answered by Dr G. N. Clark, *Science and Social Welfare in the Age of Newton*.

[2] A good illustration is Ray's failure to carry through satisfactorily his book on respiration.

[3] As a systematist his classification of plants was inferior to that of Ray or even Cesalpino, as a scientist he contributed chiefly collections and binomial names; cf. below Chap. VIII.

[4] E.g. with regard to the courtship and egg-laying of birds.

[5] Cf. my *John Ray*, pp. 464-76.

should concern itself with the means of livelihood rather than with life.

It is hardly surprising that religion which in Britain had given a warm welcome and valuable help to science in the seventeenth century should have found the partnership much more difficult in the nineteenth. For in fact materialism, 'the categories of weight and measurement', having sufficed to accomplish immense results in physics and chemistry, extended its claims to cover the domination of the animate realm and even of man. When Descartes in the seventeenth century had argued that all the rest of the animal kingdom were mere automata, he was met by sharp and in fact unanswerable criticism from Henry More, John Ray and many others, who were quick to point out in the language of their own day that a creature self-impelled, self-fuelling, self-repairing, self-reproducing, self-controlling, self-surrendering and, at the human level, self-conscious could not, except by gross misuse of language, be described as a machine; and in any case Descartes had specially exempted man from the robot class. But the biologists of two hundred years later, even if they did not explicitly assert that man was a mere animal, yet made it plain that science could only deal with the living organism as with a piece of complicated machinery. And when the camp-followers of the sciences went on to assert that science was the only source of verifiable knowledge, the outlook for artist and poet, moralist and saint was not very inviting. By the first decade of the present century the frontier between science and religion had become almost an iron curtain: it was hard for an honest and intelligent youngster to keep a footing in both worlds.

For this estrangement the scientists can hardly be held to blame. The concentration upon physics and chemistry at the close of the seventeenth century was an essential phase in the development of the whole movement; and its technological and industrial consequences were a proper and valuable outcome. That 'pure' and 'applied' science go together, and that the basic motive in scientific progress is far more often curiosity and the passion for truth than economic or commercial advantage, are convictions which the historian can hardly dispute. But it was certainly unfortunate that success in the use of quantitative methods and mechanical analogies should have narrowed down the content of 'natural philosophy' and banished from the field of science the organic and holistic categories which the best minds of the seventeenth century had insisted upon employing. For it meant that attempts to study the living organism in its own proper functioning and environment were dismissed as vitalistic, Lamarckian or teleological and as in any case outside the proper sphere of the scientist. There were times when it seemed that biology had forfeited all right to its name, since it was concerned not with the study of life but with dead organisms dissected and analysed in a laboratory.

But it must be acknowledged that the champions of religion during this critical period carry a large responsibility for the estrangement. When Sir Thomas Browne wrote his *Religio Medici* he was speaking in broad agreement with the outstanding scientists and theologians of his day. It seemed then that the work of Boyle and Wilkins, Ray and Willughby and Grew, Sydenham and Bentley and Newton supported by that of Whichcote and More and Cudworth, Worthington and Compton and Tillotson would succeed in giving to the world an interpretation of the Christian religion in accordance alike with the early theology of the Greek Fathers and with the findings of contemporary science. Indeed we may well argue that it was because our galaxy of men of genius found in Britain what they could not have found elsewhere, a climate of opinion in churches and universities wholly favourable to their work, that they brought this country so rapidly to a position of eminence.[1] For a little time the new philosophy and the reformed religion went hand in hand.

Unfortunately, just when science was becoming increasingly mathematical, religion became first over-intellectualized, then controversial, then reactionary and in consequence lethargic and corrupt. Bishop Butler's complaint in the preface of his *Analogy*

---

[1] When Comenius came to Britain in 1641, we had no scientists of eminence to meet him; fifty years later Malpighi from Italy and Leeuwenhoek from Holland sent their best work to London as the great centre for publication.

is familiar and true; and though the work of the Wesleys was neither anti-scientific nor unscholarly, its evangelism tended to establish a contrast between the world of nature and the world of grace and to overemphasize the hereafter at the expense of the here. Before the awakening had become effective Tom Paine had associated liberal theology with republican politics; the churches had recoiled into conservatism; and a century of conflict, Genesis and geology, the origin of species, the problem of miracle, the higher criticism, had begun. From the effects and indeed the recurrence of these conflicts we are still suffering.

In these lectures we shall be concerned not so much with the well-worn theme of the relation between religion and science in the narrow sense of that word as with the chief phases in the history of man's knowledge, interpretation and religious valuation of the order of nature; and we shall confine our study to Western thought during the Christian era. It is a subject hardly mentioned in popular histories, whether secular or ecclesiastical, apart from occasional paragraphs upon the development of science or occasional accounts of episodes like the treatment of Galileo and Servetus or the rise of deism or the Darwinian controversy. That it throws an interesting light upon the movement of thought and in some respects discloses the general outlook of ordinary folks more clearly than can be done by political, military or ecclesiastical records, and that it is therefore of value to the general historian, would, I believe, be readily granted. But it is more obviously significant for the study of religion, and specifically of Christianity, since man's reaction to nature is intimately connected with and powerfully influences his concept of God, and in Christendom belief in 'the Word made flesh' commits its upholders to a profound appreciation of the physical realm and makes Christianity the most materialistic of the world's great religions.

In such a survey of history the development of modern science can be set in its perspective; and the special phase of it which has given us the industrial age and the astonishing achievements of the past century can be seen as vastly influential but by no means isolated, as revolutionary but also as temporary, as an episode in a universal and age-long human activity. Now that its extreme mechanistic period is passing, and it is no longer regarded by any of us as omnicompetent, we ought to be in a position to consider more clearly its contribution to the general life and thought of man and especially to his religion. Though at present, in reaction against the exaggerated and often arrogant claims made for it a generation ago, we are momentarily prone to summarize its effects in terms of bigger bombs and deeper dug-outs, and though the attempts of its advocates to discover in it sanctions for human morality, and encouragements for human hope do not seem very promising,[1] yet, once the idea that by its quantitative techniques it can answer any of the perennial questionings of mankind is abandoned, we can not only recognize its true significance for philosophy and theology but also employ it as a pointer and a purge. In these respects a study of its findings will illuminate much that religion needs to know about the creative process, about human character and potentialities, and about the scope and validity of our experiences, and will also eliminate many of the traditional accretions and speculations which have for centuries distorted the doctrine of the Churches.

For such a study the time is hardly yet ripe; for in two of the most important fields, philosophy and psychology, there is still a manifest obscurity. Though, in the former, Logical Positivism no longer dominates the scene and, having done a useful work of destructive *elenchus*, cannot now prevent a return to matters of wider and more general importance, there is still no clear agreement as to the form that this return will take.[2] In the latter, though the upheavals, conflicts and exaggerations of the past thirty years are yielding to saner and more stable researches, we have still to wait for any adequate exposition of comparative psychology and have to depend too largely upon results drawn from human

[1] Cf. the discussion opened by Dr C. H. Waddington in *Science and Ethics* or Dr J. Huxley's Romanes lecture.

[2] Moreover the methods of traditional thought and the symbols of ordinary speech are inadequate for the presentation and discussion of the range of ideas disclosed by modern mathematical physicists. It may be that as light waves were unable to show us the non-filterable viruses so our present language cannot portray this new field, and we must wait for the appropriate 'electronic microscope' to reveal it.

infants and invalids. But while any attempt to assess and restate can only be tentative, yet the matter is at once so important and so urgent as to excuse what would otherwise be premature. Anything that enables us to carry on with the essential business of promoting a truer understanding of the good life and of encouraging closer co-operation between the disciples of science and of religion will (however ineffective it may be) at least be aimed in the right direction. For without such understanding and co-operation there can be little prospect either of progress or of peace.

Nevertheless although it would be easier if the problems of epistemology and meaning were less obscure, there is much in the present situation to foster a research into the history of natural religion and its proper effects upon Christian theology. The radical change—to be examined in detail later—which has recently taken place in the attitude of scientists following upon the breakdown of the doctrine of the closed universe, upon the new concept of law and upon the enlargement of the field of scientific research, has not yet been met by a similar change on the part of theologians. But it is now becoming clear that neo-orthodoxy, biblical theology, Barthianism, or whatever the movement is best called, has done its work, that its defective character is becoming manifest not only from its origins but from its effects, and that it has merely shelved the problems which its noisier advocates have claimed that it had solved. There is indeed plenty of evidence that the tasks interrupted by it (which are in fact fundamental for Christianity and concerned with our present subject) are now being resumed, and that the liberalism, which alone can undertake those tasks, in spite of the premature announcements of its death, is rising again with vigour and returning to them.

It is indeed evident that any theology which set itself to expound a reasonable faith, following the succession of the earliest Greek Christians and of the Christian Platonists of the third and of the seventeenth centuries and committed to the belief that the universe like the Incarnation reveals the nature of God, had a peculiarly difficult time in the first decade of the present century. For its advocates were bound to ask and were right in asking questions as to the nature of the physical world, as to the possibility of miracle, and as to the authenticity of the Biblical records to which at that period a science dominated by determinist and mechanist principles could only give negative answers. As a consequence those who were not content to be obscurantists or to keep faith and reason in separate compartments were bound to put forward tentative and minimizing statements and to expose themselves to charges of unorthodoxy if not of heresy. They asked the right questions of the experts; they could not find the right answers. But to condemn on that ground the intention or the methods of their inquiry is only justifiable if indeed orthodoxy is synonymous with ignorance. It is not unfair to add that in fact the most contemptuous of their critics are men whose qualifications are not of a very high order.

With the change in the scientific outlook from an almost arrogant confidence to an almost despairing hesitation about the possibility of reaching real knowledge there has come an opportunity for reopening the quest and a good prospect that the problems will no longer prove unanswerable. We shall not see a return to the old orthodoxies; three centuries of scientific study have profoundly altered our whole understanding of the order of nature: but at least we shall conduct our inquiry in a spirit of goodwill and under a sense of the gravity and urgency of the task. And if experience of such adventure is any guide, we shall find as we proceed that the problems of the scientist and the theologian are not, in fact, dissimilar; that the student of evolution has to face issues dealing with creative causation, with survival value, with adaptation to environment, with the emergence of individual and social aptitudes and even with what J. H. Fabre called 'a sublime law of sacrifice',[1] issues which are analogous if not identical with those familiar in Christian doctrine and ethics; and that to form the habit of surveying subjects like love and power, evil and pain, from the double standpoints both of the study of the universe and of the records of Christ is to discover how each illuminates and is illuminated by the other. We are still very far from the time when

---

[1] Cf. his *Oubreto Prouvençalo. Le Semeur*, quoted by C. V. Legros, *Fabre, Poet of Science*, pp. 234-5.

15

a stereoscopic picture will emerge; but enough is now visible to make the attempt after it interesting and hopeful. A new 'Analogy' on a far more vast and satisfying scale than Butler ever dreamed of may yet be presented to us; for, whereas he knew little of the order of nature and studied both it and religion from the rationalistic standpoint of his age, we have a vastly larger mass of attested evidence to consider and can study both nature and supernature with primary emphasis upon conation rather than cognition, personality rather than intelligence.

It is perhaps allowable for one who began the study of Christian theology under F. C. Burkitt and of Mendelian genetics under W. Bateson in the same term in 1907—and when neither the subjects nor the teachers had anything in common—to express at the close of these introductory remarks the conviction which has been borne in upon him after a lifetime of attention to it. He has become increasingly sure of the continuity of biological and historical studies, that the story of evolution is in series with that of humanity, and that, if the whole record down to and including Christ is accepted as covering a single process, it discloses a remarkable coherence and can be interpreted consistently in terms of what St Paul declared to be its end, 'the manifestation of the sons of God'. That there are immense difficulties in such an explanation, that it involves a radical transvaluation of our deep-seated ideas and ambitions, that the result is very far from the usual picture of comfortable security and of rewards and punishments, and that here as elsewhere our reach exceeds our grasp, is only what any such claim would involve. But the current objection, that science deals only with the general and history deals especially with the particular, is only arguable if we ignore the fact that the whole record is concerned with individuation, discloses as each new level is reached an increasing measure of particularity, and prepares for the completion of the individual in a rich and diversified community. Properly viewed, the urge of the living organism from its primitive origin at the unicellular level to its present culmination in the saint can be seen as the attainment, under similar conditions and with increasing range, of the fullness of life appropriate to it; and if the organism remains sensitive and responsive, this urge is capable of manifesting new and unforeseeable possibilities. There is no such thing as inevitable or mechanical progress; the whole is worked out in terms of the interaction of organism and environment; it manifests at every stage adventure and sacrifice; it is often side-tracked, blocked, blind-alleyed; but it moves. And on earth we are its present growing-point—at a very critical phase of our growth.

But if the whole process of nature and history is continuous, then it is appropriate to interpret it continuously and in terms suited to its fullest development. Hitherto science has begun its exposition from the earliest pages of the story, using the obvious physical and inanimate categories; it has then gone on to apply these to stages in the tale to which they are manifestly inadequate, and has attempted to explain even the human chapters by mechanistic and behaviourist imagery, although by doing so humanity is reduced to the level of the robot and the interest and significance of the record are destroyed. If it is argued that such procedure is justifiable, since along with continuity of process there is also the emergence of novelty and that therefore we must introduce at particular points in the story vital, intellectual and spiritual elements with which science is not concerned, this is to abandon the attempt at a single coherent interpretation and to admit that science cannot adequately discuss the living organism. We must surely make the effort to explain the whole not from its origin but from its present end, to formulate categories which will do justice to the whole nature of man, and to see whether these cannot be applied so as to bring the complete process from first to last within the scope of a single and consistent exposition. If we can get rid of the habit of thinking of the stages as antithetical and abandon the familiar contrasts between inorganic and organic, physical and psychic, bodily and spiritual—as the whole trend of recent thought is constraining us to do—we shall be able to maintain both continuity and novelty and avoid the extravagances both of materialism and of panpsychism.

It is perhaps too much to expect that scientists, who are only just beginning to move outside their self-imposed techniques of weight and measurement and are still scared by any suggestion of teleological or vitalistic interpretations, should be ready to approve or initiate such an undertaking. Philosophers have been attempting it in a variety of ways and with a considerable measure of success—though when, like Bergson, they have had the necessary combination of knowledge with imagination they have been regarded by the more old-fashioned scientists as poets rather than thinkers. Perhaps indeed for such a task the poet is still the appropriate agent: certainly the great speech in Browning's *Paracelsus* and large parts of Bridges's *Testament of Beauty*, like the work of Lucretius and of Goethe, give a more satisfying vision of the order of nature than can be found in neo-Darwinian doctrines of evolution; and A. N. Whitehead whose thought will probably have more influence upon the future than that of any recent philosopher may well be right in his insistence that the poets are our true guides. But a poet with the necessary knowledge in science, history, philosophy and religion would be hard to find.

In default of such qualifications there are still certain suggestions that can be made. Mechanism and teleology, though usually regarded as alternatives and even opposites, are plainly not irreconcilable. Dr Agnes Arber in her very interesting treatment of the philosophy of plant-form[1] has examined them in relation to the problem of causation and shown that so considered there need not be any antagonism between them. In each case there is manifest purpose, the adaptation of means to ends, of form to function; and though, as currently employed, mechanism is taken to mean design but not a designer, yet the whole essence of a machine consists in its being exactly framed and fitted to serve a particular purpose.[2] Thus when Dr Julian Huxley[3] ridicules Bergson's *élan vital* by saying that its use is as absurd as it would be to say that a steam-engine was driven by an *élan locomotif*, he is ignoring both formal and final causes and arguing either that the engine is 'a fortuitous coincidence of atoms' or that 'the impulse

[1] *The Natural Philosophy of Plant Form* especially pp. 199-211.
[2] Cf. C. S. Sherrington, *Man and his Nature*, p. 187, 'A machine preaches to us of purpose all the time'.　　　　　　[3] Cf. his *Evolution: the Modern Synthesis*, p. 458.

to achieve steam-traction' is not a fair summary of the purpose which inspired its design: obviously a machine which in every plate and rivet reveals the object for which it exists is teleological through and through and could hardly be better described than as a manifestation of the *élan locomotif*, the final cause determining its particular type of adjustment to the special function that it will serve, and the formal cause being related to its place in human transport, in civilization and in contemporary history. If in artifacts the element of purpose is external, whereas in organisms it is inward and vital, this indicates nothing more than a warning that the old teleology of watch and watchmaker is inadequate, and that creation is not so much an operation from without by a transcendent demiurge as an impulse from within, operating in terms of process and growth rather than of plan and manufacture. For the Christian such an account of evolution will not seem inconsistent with St Paul's picture of the Spirit of God co-operating actively but imperceptibly with the creature in the age-long travail which will one day bring to birth the children of God.[1]

For religion and for theology (its intellectual interpretation), an account of the creative process which regards it as the manifestation and, in some sense, the embodiment of the divine Spirit would seem more satisfying and, from the Christian standpoint, more consistent than the traditional view which sees God and the Universe in terms of the Maker and his work or of the King and his realm; for this has always carried the suggestion that the creation, when once brought into being, runs 'of itself' under the supervision and, on occasion, with the intervention of God, and that His energy is expressed by special acts to initiate new stages in its history or to correct defects in its working. No doubt the picture of a deity thus external to his world would not now be regarded by most of us as adequate, indeed would be generally seen to be defective. But the language of Scripture, the background of Christian hymns, prayers and preaching, and on occasion the pronouncements of ecclesiastical authority still endorse and too often insist upon it; and those who protest find themselves

---

[1] Rom. viii. 18 ff.

regarded either as dangerously pantheistic or at least as falling short of the biblical faith in a living God. We have not yet fully reached the level of Charles Kingsley's welcome of the *Origin of Species* or realized that, having got rid of the Master-magician, we must now choose 'between the absolute empire of accident and a living, immanent, ever-working God'.[1] For those who think that this leaves them an open option it will be well to add a couple of pregnant sentences from the last essay by that brilliant and sensitive thinker, F. M. Cornford. Defending Plato against the atomists he writes: 'It seemed to him that a theory which reduced all reality to little bits of dead, impenetrable body, moving chaotically in a void, could not account for an ordered universe or for the phenomena of life, including our own minds with their thoughts and feelings. And, whatever materialists may have believed a century ago, no one, I suppose, now holds that all these phenomena can be satisfactorily explained in terms of an unlimited number of billiard balls, banging about and colliding in empty space.'[2] That is an admirable description of 'the absolute empire of accident'; and it cannot be evaded by reference to the change in our concept of the structure of the atom or by meaningless talk about 'pseudo-teleology'.

If it is possible to sum up the situation in a few sentences I would do so by recalling a conversation that I had some thirty years ago with Dr William Temple. We had been discussing the change of outlook that was coming over theology as a result of the development of science and the changes in the social order. I put to him that, whereas Christendom down to and including our immediate predecessors like Bishop Gore had regarded the Universe as the theatre on the stage of which was played out the drama of Man's Fall and Redemption, our generation, taking evolution seriously, must see the theatre not as a mere setting, itself subsidiary and irrelevant, but as an integral and essential part of the play; and that this must in fact enlarge our whole concept of the scope and character of religion. It is the purpose of the chapters that follow to examine and elucidate this conviction.

[1] *Life of Charles Kingsley*, II, p. 171.   [2] *The Unwritten Philosophy*, p. 123.

II

THE BIBLICAL ATTITUDE
TOWARDS NATURE

IF, as we have suggested, man's attitude towards nature has an intimate and most powerful influence upon his religion, then it may safely be said that Christianity was singularly congruous with the natural philosophy of the folk among whom it took its origin. Those who delighted in tracing the *Preparatio evangelica* might well have demonstrated that, alone among the peoples of the ancient world, Jew and Greek, who contributed the religion of the Old Testament and the philosophy of Hellenism, were qualified to sponsor belief in an Incarnation, since they alone saw the Order of Nature as at once the creation and the manifestation of deity. That nature is in every part of it alive, that it is sustained and controlled by the living God, that it expresses and reveals His character, and that it is at once the scene and the condition of human history, are convictions common both to Hebrew and to Greek thought. For each of them its beauty and order and worth are witnesses to the splendour, proofs of the wisdom, and incentives to the service of its Creator.

It is important to stress this broad agreement between the two great cultures which shaped western Christendom in its early days, because in recent years and under the influence of the new orthodoxy Protestant theologians have been concerned to set Jew and Greek in contrast. Interpreting the Old Testament from the standpoint of Luther and Calvin, and ignoring the deeper teachings of Plato and the tragedians, such theologians have ascribed to the Jew an almost morbid sense of guilt and of the corruption of humanity and nature and to the Greek a shallow and childish confidence in his own cleverness and destiny. That Hebrew thought focused attention rather upon the moral, and Greek upon the intellectual task of mankind, that the former stressed penitence while the latter stressed illumination, and that the practicality and austerity of Israel can easily be contrasted with the factiousness and artistry of Hellas, may be true enough. But that even before Alexander they had very much in common is as plain as is their very intimate contact during the three centuries before Christ.

The Jewish attitude towards nature has been so fully discussed by Dr H. Wheeler Robinson in his posthumous book *Inspiration and Revelation in the Old Testament* that it may well seem unnecessary for one who has little claim to speak on the subject to spend time upon it. But the present misunderstanding of the whole matter has so strong and so disastrous an effect upon present religion that it is important to examine it in some detail. Failure to appreciate his Jewish heritage has been mainly responsible for the perversion of St Paul's teaching and for the assigning of a scriptural authority to doctrines of the total depravity of the world and of the radical antithesis of nature and grace.

The delight in the physical universe, the appreciation of the majesty of desert and mountain and of the manifold beauty of valley and woodland have never been more perfectly expressed than in the diverse library of Hebrew writings which constitute the Old Testament. From the poem of creation in the first chapter of Genesis with its climax 'And, behold, it was very good' through the long detail of the books of the Law, through the histories and the writings of the prophets to its fullest expression in the psalms, there is perpetual evidence of a concern for and joy in the world of nature both as the living symbol of God's power and care and as the effective instrument of His revelation and purpose. That a knowledge of the creation 'from the cedar tree that is in Lebanon even unto the hyssop that springeth out of the wall'[1] should be an essential part of the wisdom of Solomon, and a

---

[1] I Kings iv. 33.

perpetual joy for all devout minds, is appropriate for a people living in a small, beautiful and diversified country where a livelihood can never have been easy.[1] That their study of the works of the Lord should be associated with a high regard for personal and social hygiene and with moral standards which have preserved Jewry through every kind of persecution is testimony to the integrity and consistency of their way of life.

This love of nature comes out both in the most secular and in the most religious of Old Testament writings. The Song of Songs, that charming series of love-poems whose allegorical interpretation is typical of the Jewish belief that nature has value not only in itself but as emblem and parable, is full of illustrations from plants and animals accurately observed and joyously remembered. As is natural for a people forbidden to make 'graven images' and notably less graphic in their visualizing than ourselves, there is an emphasis upon hearing, the singing of birds and the voice of the dove, and especially upon scents, the fragrance of flowers and fruits, which suggests how much we of the Greek tradition have lost by our concentration upon sight at the expense of other senses. But this is fully in keeping with the range and quality of the poet's sensitiveness. The Book of Job, the most profound religious and speculative document in the Old Testament, lays even more stress upon the order of nature. Here, when the problem of unmerited suffering which is the book's theme proves insoluble and the reader seems faced with the dilemma that God is either powerless or unjust, it is to the majesty and mystery of the universe that the author directs attention in order to rebuke man's intellectual pride and to encourage his faith—'Though He slay me, yet will I trust in Him'.[2] With this end God answers Job by an account of earth and sea, wind and rain, the stars in their splendour and their order, and of the animal creation in its variety of form and habit, the lion crouching for its prey, the mountain goat and its calving, the Onager and the Aurochs,

---

[1] Even if the climate has been changed by the stripping of the forests, the hill country must always have been 'stony ground' for the farmer.

[2] Job xiii. 15.

the Ostrich with its eggs set in the sand, the Lesser Kestrel migrating to the south, and the Vulture spying corpses from afar.[1]

Similar passages occur in Psalm civ and indeed elsewhere in the Psalter; in Proverbs (xxx. 19) the 'things too wonderful for me', the way of the eagle in the air, and the serpent on the rock, of the ship in the sea and of a man with a maid; in Jeremiah (viii. 7) the migration of the Storks, the Turtle-dove, the Crane and the Swift;[2] and, though less significantly, in most parts of the Old Testament. They are not, in the usual sense of the word, scientific: if Solomon spoke of trees, 'also of beasts, and of fowl, and of creeping things, and of fishes',[3] it is probable that he too did so in proverb and fable[4] rather than with the objectivity and exactitude of a biologist: but there is evidence not only of interest but of real insight, of curiosity and accuracy of observation, and above all of that reverence and wonder which is man's proper acknowledgment of God's majesty and of man's own creaturehood. Although the stark immensity of wilderness and sea is never far off, nature to the Jew is primarily God's good gift for the service and the advancement of man; it fulfils this purpose not only in the physical realm but by being itself the responsive instrument of God's messages and revelations. God's spirit moves over chaos in the beginning;[5] His breath creates;[6] His Word brings into being;[7] in it He works His signs, portents and wonders; the glow of fire, the radiance of light, the convulsion of storm and earthquake, these are the normal accompaniments of His presence: but all things are at His command; there is nothing that cannot happen if He wills it.

> Earth's crammed with heaven,
> And every common bush afire with God;
> But only he who sees, takes off his shoes,
> The rest sit round it and pluck blackberries.[8]

[1] Job xxxviii–xxxix. These chapters show clearer acquaintance with nature than the descriptions of Behemoth and Leviathan (hippopotamus and [?] crocodile) in xl–xli. For the Ostrich cf. H. B. Tristram, *Fauna and Flora of Palestine*, p. 139.

[2] Cf. Tristram, *op. cit.* p. 82 for this identification.   [3] I Kings iv. 33.

[4] Cf. Jehoash's message to Amaziah, II Kings xiv. 9; II Chron. xxv. 18-19; and the parable of Jotham, Judges ix. 8-15.

[5] Gen. i. 2. H. W. Robinson, *op. cit.* p. 11, states that this reference stands alone, since elsewhere the Spirit is associated with activity in and through humanity.

[6] Ps. civ. 30.   [7] Ps. xxxiii. 9 etc.   [8] *Aurora Leigh*, Bk. VII.

Mrs Browning's familiar lines are fully in keeping with the Old Testament's attitude to nature, even though the Jew, until he came into contact with Greek thought, had no clear idea as to the extent or mode of the divine indwelling. Nature drew its order from God and, as monotheism prevailed, the unity of the Godhead gave to that order a coherence and wholeness impossible on other terms. And this in biblical Judaism as in the New Testament is not disturbed by any dualistic emphasis upon the devil or by any doctrine of the consequences of the Fall. It is not that Hebrew thought ignores the fact of evil or refuses to face the problems arising from it. But, difficult as these proved to be, they are always in the Scriptures conditioned by the basic certainty that, under all circumstances and despite all evidence to the contrary, God reigns and beside Him there is none else.

The characteristic feature of this Jewish outlook is that, although nature in whatever shape is never regarded as illusory or inanimate, it is on the other hand never identified with deity nor treated as perfect. The pantheism of much Indian thought is as remote as the optimism often ascribed to the Greeks. The world is God's world, shaped by His wisdom and obeying His law, the home of His people, the scene of His marvellous acts: but it is also a place of darkness and cruel habitations in which the righteous does not always flourish and his seed seems sometimes to be forsaken. The problem thus raised, underlined as it was by the constant disasters and disappointments of His people, haunted Jewish thought continually. God was God; Israel was His folk; His power was sufficient—else were He not divine: and yet Israel suffered repeatedly and inescapably. It must be that the Judge of all the earth is at once righteous and mighty; yet if so why did He allow the defeat of His worshippers and refuse to be propitiated and to forgive? Known transgressions must of course be punished; secret sins might account for further punishment: but even so too often it appeared that He had cast them off and they were helpless to understand the reason for their affliction. Even when, with the last and greatest of the prophets, there were indications that suffering was not always proof of the sufferer's guilt, and, if vicarious, might have atoning value, there was no satisfactory answer to the problem of unmerited calamity. The adoption after the exile of a dualistic outlook together with demonology and the growth of belief in rewards and punishments after death were attempts to solve it; but like most of such hypotheses they only removed the difficulty to realms in which it became less easy to study.

One chief reason for the failure of Hebrew thought to provide a theodicy arose out of its lack of an adequate doctrine of divine immanence. God's relationship to the world was represented as external and transcendental. He sustained it continually and intervened on special occasions in its affairs; and His activity is recognized alike in the normal processes of nature and in the catastrophic events which intrude into and seemingly contradict it. But it is not until Greek influence begins to be felt that there is clear sign of an indwelling deity or any development of the idea of God's Wisdom as His agent and representative; and even then it is only in such a passage as Wisdom vii, with its obvious use of Stoic ideas and language, that we find a clear equivalent to the Hellenic concept of Nous or Logos.

In its origin the Greek valuation of nature differed widely from the Jewish. The Bible starts with 'In the beginning God created' and this, though not itself an ancient utterance, is typical of the Hebrew approach. The Greek on the other hand finds himself in a world of wonder and interest, listens eagerly to its manifold voices, asks innumerable questions, and devises a tale of its beginning and evolution. 'In the beginning Chaos; and then the Egg; and then the hatching from it of Heaven and Earth and Eros, and the wedding of the two by the third, and their progeny'—so the Orphic pattern seems to have run;[1] and it is only later that deities appear. There is in fact no tale of a Creation until the *Timaeus* of Plato: before that time some variant of the evolutionary pattern had been accepted; and in all its forms the urge to fuller development had been from within not from without. Dryads and nymphs dwelling in the woodlands and the seas, personifications of love and strength, wisdom and power, deities appropriate

---

[1] Cf. W. K. C. Guthrie, *Orpheus and Greek Religion* (London, 1935).

to the various aspects of the natural order—popular religion fills the earth with them. For the philosopher the search for unity in this endless multiplicity, for the real and permanent within the ebb and flow of phenomena, and the consequent tendency to discount the world of sense-perception when the ideas discernible through it had been disclosed, followed a similar course. Yet though this might lead to the theory that the body was a tomb and the earth a prison-house, the Greek in as full measure as the Jew and with a richer artistic enjoyment rejoiced in the loveliness of his land and found in it a constant stimulus to his curiosity, encouragement to his imagination and satisfaction to his aspirations. For him also nature pulsed with joyous life.[1]

In consequence the Greek develops a scientific interest in nature very easily; for he is more conscious of diversity than of unity, and perhaps more concerned with the thing in itself than with its significance and relationships; and his intensely graphic imagination makes him quick to distinguish differences and to classify. It is as difficult to picture a Jew writing Aristotle's *Historia Animalium* as a Greek giving us the first chapter of Genesis. Both of them delight in nature; both indulge in fables and draw analogies from it; both think it important to observe and study it for the sake of appreciating and interpreting what lies beyond it. But, whereas the Jew finds in nature lessons about God which confirm what he has already learnt elsewhere, the Greek approaches it in the spirit of the artist or the pioneer in order to see some new thing and to explore its general significance.[2] Yet even so we must add that often, as in the case of Plato, when he has discovered the meaning he is ready to ignore the emblem that has disclosed it.

Thus it is that though the Greeks did little in the way of mechanical invention they raised the problem of movement which was to become so important in relation to the history of modern science. It is obvious that the difference between rest and motion

[1] The most famous example, perhaps unique in its degree, is Aeschylus, *Prometheus Vinctus*, 88-96; and cf. Homer, *Iliad* II, 459-63, etc.

[2] Cf. Seneca, *Nat. Quaest.* VII, ch. 31, with its thoroughly Greek picture of the vast scale of God's 'secrets' in nature and of the length of man's research into them; cf. Note II below, pp. 205-6, on the supposed pessimism of the Greeks.

is one of the most noticeable of criteria; and that it was from the first a chief distinction between the dead and the living, between things and persons. Yet when Aristotle developed his philosophy of the mover and the moved, he did little more than adapt concepts derived from primitive animism to data observable by common sense, and assume that where there was movement there must be ultimately, if not immediately, a living agent responsible. In popular myth Aeolus and the cave of the winds, Poseidon the earth-shaker, Apollo and the chariot of the sun were familiar; and the principle appropriate to a world of demons and magic was universal enough to postpone any serious discussion. With the deity as the first mover and His agents and creatures transmitting His initiative, the questions which Kepler and Galileo investigated by rolling marbles down inclined planes or dropping lead and feathers from the Leaning Tower, and for which in Newton's case the fall of an apple gave a clue, were hardly asked and certainly not investigated. It was not until the discovery of gunpowder and the study of ballistics, the use of hydraulic power and of machines for mill and mine in the fourteenth and fifteenth centuries, that new ideas of the source and nature of impetus were formulated. Neither Greek science nor Roman technology contributed much towards them.

It is of course impossible to summarize in a paragraph or two the complex and seminal influences that Western civilization and religion owe to the Greeks. In art and letters, in medicine and science, in philosophy and politics they are 'our founders and principal benefactors', the source from which we derive the criterion by which we estimate our achievements. Plato, Aristotle, Plotinus; Hippocrates, Dioscorides, Galen; Archimedes, Euclid, Ptolemy: to recite their names is enough. Suffice it to say that the present tendency to minimize the value of our debt, particularly in religion, by setting Greek and Jew in contrast, and to suggest that Christendom owes everything to the Jew, is marked by distortion both as to facts and as to the inferences from them. We have already seen how closely the two agree in their appreciation of nature: as we turn from the Old Testament to the New we shall discover how this affinity was ripened into an intimate and fruitful union by the events of the three hundred years before Christ.[1]

It is one of the most serious defects in the traditional understanding of Christian origins that we still ignore the significance of the interval between the time of Nehemiah and that of John the Baptist. Treating the Bible as a single inspired record we pass from Malachi to St Matthew as if the momentous events which changed the character and faith of the Jewish people had never taken place. We have already hinted at the influence of the Persian period in fostering dualistic ideas of the powers of evil, a new concern with life after death and an insistence upon exclusiveness and moral rigidity—an influence which became immensely important for Judaism and for Christianity in the early centuries of the Christian era. But these were less far-reaching than those which followed upon the conquests of Alexander and his policy of racial intermixture—the foundation of Alexandria, the hellenizing of Syria and Egypt, the dispersion of the Jews, and the great developments effected by the synagogue and the Septuagint. By these Israel was not only committed to a world-wide expansion but was equipped with unique and universal instruments for its religious observances and the exposition of its faith. It only needed the persecution of Antiochus Epiphanes, disclosing the primacy, urgency and splendour of this faith, and the intrusion of Pompeius bringing Palestine into the sphere of the Roman dominion, to complete the preparation for the coming of Jesus.

It is of course obvious that the events thus briefly listed are the essential background for any appreciation of the New Testament or of the unique event which gave rise to it. It is equally obvious that modern scholarship has been fully acquainted with them for three generations. But it remains true that both religion and theology, while accepting Jewish separatism and Jewish eschatology, have been very unwilling to admit the influence of Greek thought either in its philosophy or in its mysteries. With the latter, evident as it appears to be in regard to the development of the

---

[1] For a remarkable example dating from *c.* 100 B.C. cf. *Testament of the XII Patriarchs,* Naphtali ii. 8-10.

Eucharist and of ecclesiasticism, we are not here concerned. With the former, affecting profoundly not only the subsequent interpretation of the Incarnation but the whole life and thought of Jesus and His contemporaries, any student of the relationship between natural religion and Christianity is immediately and vitally implicated. Unfortunately in spite of its scope and importance it is a subject on which a large amount of work still requires to be done. The debt of Stoic ethics to Judaism both in the early days at Tarsus and in the case of Seneca, the Hellenistic influence in the Wisdom literature, the extent and character of the liberal synagogues in the Dispersion and in Jerusalem at the time of our Lord, the position and number of Greek-speaking Jews and of proselytes, the adoption of Greek words and ideas into Aramaic, the Platonic and Stoic influence upon St Paul, and above all the provenance, Greek or Hebrew, of the Fourth Gospel, such questions may be unanswerable; that they can be asked indicates how absurd it is to regard the two strains as pure and distinct. In fact at the beginning of the Christian era they were very closely intermingled.[1]

The result of the fusion is to maintain and enrich the Old Testament insistence upon the worth of the natural order, both in itself and as the symbol and instrument of the divine, by linking these two, the physical and the spiritual, organically and inseparably. Whereas previously there had been reference rather to particular creatures in respect of their salient qualities, the speed of the horse and the strength of the aurochs, there is in the usage of Jesus emphasis rather upon the elemental and universal, the colour and texture of the flowers, the germination and vicissitudes of the seed-corn, the natural fertility of the soil,[2] the secret working of

---

[1] A striking example of this is given by D. Daube, *Rabbinic Methods of Interpretation and Greek Rhetoric* (in *Hebrew Union Coll. Annual* XXII, pp. 239-64). He proves that Hillel (*c.* 30 B.C.) derived his rules for Talmudic interpretation from teachers trained in Alexandria and that they were based upon the rules of Greek rhetoric.

[2] Mark iv. 28; the point of this brief but important parable is not the secrecy of growth but the fact that the earth is so constituted as to bear fruit. The attempt to lay all the stress upon the harvest (e.g. C. H. Dodd, *The Parables of the Kingdom*, pp. 176-80) makes meaningless the crucial word and clause αὐτομάτη ἡ γῆ καρποφορεῖ—*of its own nature* the earth is fruitful.

the leaven in the dough. Instead of the 'special providences' of the King who works from without for His favourites, there is the perpetual operation of the Father who sends His rain upon the just and unjust alike. Unlike most of His predecessors Jesus gives no suggestion that man by his own merits can command God's benefits or 'bargain for His love': we are always and at our best 'unprofitable servants', and rewards and punishments are nothing more than the consequences of our own actions. God's judgment is not something over and above; it is always personal and to be interpreted in terms of broken or restored relationship.[1] Indeed there is throughout all His teaching an avoidance of abstract and theological language, of argument and discussion. Jesus does not lecture about nature or mankind or the deity: He conveys an immediate experience of our relationship to the world and to one another and to God, using the method of the poet rather than that of the mathematician, the sociologist or the philosopher; and the result is to make the hearer aware of this relationship with a wholeness of response and a realism of appreciation which any student of the Gospels will recognize as characteristic.

Moreover—and this for our subject is a consideration of great significance—Jesus breaks away from the general tendency of religion at His time, and, instead of concentrating upon the abnormal or clothing His message in the language of the demonic and supernatural, bases His teaching upon the ordinary and the commonplace. Jewish literature since the Maccabean wars, when not frankly under Hellenistic influence, had reacted against Hellenism into the borderland of fantasy and extravagance characteristic of the Book of Daniel and of the apocalyptic tradition. Such imagery, as we know from the Epistles to the Thessalonians, was congenial to the elements in the pagan world which were agog for portent and prodigy, and liked their religion presented in violently catastrophic form. The Apocryphal Gospels, Acts and Apocalypses show us how easy Christians found it to pander to this craving; and there are passages in the New Testament which show signs of

---

[1] Even in the Synoptists where the language of legal justice is occasionally used, the meaning is consistent with the definition of judgment in John iii. 19.

a similar concession.[1] But Jesus Himself teaches not by transforming the world into a battlefield of devils and angels or displaying God in earthquake and cataclysm but by bidding men consider the lilies and the birds, by setting a child in the midst, by telling tales of sowers and fishermen, of women baking bread and merchants seeking pearls. The background of His discourse is nature not supernature and He aims not at turning our eyes and minds away from the natural order but at enabling us to discover in it and through it the manifestation of deity.

So stated it might seem that 'all was for the best'; that the hard facts of evil and pain were being ignored; and that earth was still an Eden. But in fact no teacher has more fully recognized the perversity and distortion of the world or the folly and wickedness of mankind. The soil of the earth is shallow and stony; thistles and tares grow up among the wheat and choke it; evil beasts devour and ravage; evil thoughts and passions, deeds of violence and fraud, deliberate rebellion against God, deliberate cruelty towards men defile and destroy humanity. Indeed it is the primary condition of life that it should advance through sacrifice: 'He that loveth his life shall lose it; and he that hateth his life in this world shall keep it unto life eternal'[2]—that is, shall here and now learn to live truly and perennially. Those who refuse thus to live condemn themselves to destruction and involve others in their ruin;[3] for the world is so ordered that only if God's will is known and obeyed can its capacity for promoting fullness of life be realized.[4] Jesus here as always does not philosophize or argue about evil. He uses the language of His day in ascribing it not only to human sin but to a personified power of evil, Satan, the devil, the adversary, whose influence is manifest in the imperfection of the natural order and the disease and malice of mankind. But

[1] Notably the so-called 'Little Apocalypse' inserted in Mark xiii and from it in Matt. xxiv and Luke xxi; and a few shorter sayings and glosses chiefly in the First Gospel.

[2] John xii. 25. For variants of the same saying cf. Matt. x. 39; xvi. 25. Mark viii. 35; Luke ix. 24; xvii. 33.

[3] In a few passages, e.g. Matt. xxiii. 15 etc. the language is appalling in its severity. These are mostly in the First Gospel alone, and may therefore be doubtfully authentic. For the problem raised by them cf. F. A. M. Spencer, *The Theory of Christ's Ethics*, pp. 179–84.

[4] Cf. Matt. vi. 33.

though the deadly character of evil is strongly stressed, there is never a suggestion that it is invincible or that there are circumstances under which it cannot be overcome. Indeed there are hints not only that it is always subject to God's control but even that in some sense it ministers to His glory.[1]

Although any full description of the mode by which Jesus dealt with the evil of the world lies beyond our scope, the subject is so vital, so misunderstood, and so important in relation to His attitude towards nature that it cannot be omitted. In the crisis of His life, when the inevitable clash with ecclesiastical tradition and secular authority came, two lines of action were open to Him: He could have met force by force, or He could have gone into hiding. He did neither. Rather He put His own teaching into practice: He refused to give way to anxiety or fear, and living from moment to moment or as theologians call it 'eschatologically'[2] let His enemies work their will with Him. The prediction in which Plato[3] and the Second Isaiah[4] foretell the fate of the righteous was fulfilled; and the Cross became the universal symbol of Christendom. Any serious student of the creative process may find reason to believe that it is as appropriate a sign of creation as of redemption.

That the attitude of Jesus towards nature, like that of His Hebrew and Greek forerunners, has nothing in common with the pessimism of Augustine and Calvin may perhaps suggest that the contrast between His teaching and that of St Paul is as great as some scholars and very many critics of Christian orthodoxy have suggested. Saul of Tarsus,[5] Pharisee of the Pharisees, pupil of Gamaliel, persecutor of Christians, might well have been a rigorist and puritan. In fact he was the chief agent in the liberation of the new religion from legalism, the protagonist of the revolutionary

---

[1] Cf. e.g. John ix. 3 and perhaps Matt. xiii. 38-42.

[2] I.e. in the realm not of means but of ends, or as St Paul puts it 'in the heavenlies'.

[3] Cf. *Republic* II, 361e, 'The righteous man will be scourged, racked, bound and at last crucified'.   [4] Isa. liii. 3-9.

[5] I cannot follow Dr J. Knox, *Chapters in a life of Paul*, in dismissing the evidence of Acts as to Paul's birthplace. In any case he was a townsman. Some of us will not forget W. R. Maltby's saying, 'He had never seen a cow; or he couldn't have said "God careth not for oxen".'

idea of God as Love, the example and the teacher of the primacy of personal relationship ('faith') in ethics and doctrine, and the first to propound a coherent scheme of creative evolution. It is one of the ironies of history and a chief cause of the cleavage between religion and science that certain relatively subordinate elements in his teaching should have been isolated from their contexts, given an emphasis quite inconsistent with their true meaning, and made the foundation of the Paulinism of traditional theology. It is indeed remarkable that the elements in St Paul's teaching which have had the largest influence upon Christendom, the doctrines of the Fall and of predestination and of the divine authority of the State (to name but three), should occupy so small and incidental a place in his actual writings.

The first of these, the doctrine of the Fall, with its sequel, the infection and total corruption of nature, is so relevant to our theme and has had such a far-reaching effect in estranging Christendom from an interest in science that it deserves fuller treatment. The Apostle in his exposition of the life-giving work of Christ expanded his first presentation of this, as a deliverance from Jewish legalism, into a comparison between Adam, whose sin according to Genesis ii. 17, and iii. 19 brought death upon mankind, and Jesus, whose victory restored to us life. The comparison between the first and the second Adam is certainly an important contribution to the interpretation of the good news: it illustrates for men familiar with the story of the Fall the magnitude and relevance of the redemption. Its significance both in Catholic and Protestant theology, its familiarity through John Milton's great epic, its association with the art and cultus and doctrine of Christendom give it a cardinal place in the popular understanding of the faith. Yet to St Paul it is by no means a fundamental concept. When he is dealing with the guilt and the need of humanity in his great indictment both of the pagan and of the Jewish world in Romans i-iii, he never suggests that they, like all mankind, are corrupted by Adam's sin but argues that the pagans ignored the manifest evidence of God's presence and character provided by His work in the creation, degraded their concept of deity and therefore of man, exploited one another sexually and so corrupted all their relationships; and that the Jews though they knew God and proclaimed His Law yet had themselves signally failed to keep that Law and so had brought contempt upon it and upon themselves. Only in one short passage (Romans v. 12-14) does he introduce the fall of Adam which he had previously mentioned in connexion with the resurrection of Christ in I Corinthians xv. 21 and 22 and 45-9. These two allusions are the only references to the matter by St Paul or indeed in the New Testament except the sentence in I Timothy ii. 13, 14 which is probably not Pauline and in any case refers to the primary guilt of Eve rather than to the abiding effects of the Fall.

Moreover in the crucial passage itself (Romans v. 12-14) it is by no means certain that the Apostle's language enforces the belief that Adam's sin tainted his posterity. St Paul makes it clear that death, when once introduced as punishment for Adam's disobedience, became universal: but he explicitly states first that until the giving of the Law there cannot be sin in the full sense and secondly that even those who did not sin as Adam had done were still subject to death. It is hard to believe that such ambiguous language would have been used if St Paul had held strongly or clearly the traditional doctrine of the Fall: certainly he did not teach that by the Fall all subsequent mankind lost its sense of responsibility and became wholly corrupt. Nor, as we can see from a later passage, is his account of the Fall reconcilable with that of the tradition. When, in the great passage Romans viii. 18-39 in which he completes his account of the 'scheme of salvation' by relating it to the whole cosmic process, he speaks of the created universe as subject to frustration, incomplete, stultified, he explicitly states that this is not due to any wilful act of its own, but solely to the purpose and decree of God who has imposed this condition upon it with a view to its ultimate deliverance, when the travail of the ages at length brings to birth God's own family. St Paul is far too good a theist, far too close a student of the Old Testament,[1] to believe that the imperfection of

---

[1] The crucial passage is Gen. iii. 17-18.

creation is due to any act of devil or man: only God is in control of His world. Nor because still imperfect is that world deprived of the power to strive and agonize and yearn for that which is to come. With the active assistance of God's indwelling Spirit the creation gropes its way forward in hope.[1]

There is nothing here, or indeed anywhere in the New Testament, to suggest that on earth no progress can in fact take place or that God's will cannot be done. Indeed St Paul constantly asserts that life 'in Christ',[2] in the Spirit,[3] in the heavenlies[4] is the present obligation of mankind and that he and his followers can attain it. We shall have to discuss the whole question of eschatology later; for our present knowledge of the age, extent and duration of this earth and of the physical universe is so vastly different from Biblical ideas that it is difficult to interpret those ideas intelligibly and impossible to regard them as authoritative. Meanwhile we need only note that there is no Scriptural warrant for denying the fact of progress, and very much for affirming it; that Dean Inge's famous *jeu d'esprit* on the subject proceeds rather from his Tory politics than from his Liberal theology; and that the whole evidence of scientific studies demonstrates that life on this earth has developed from lowly beginnings to the human level, is still developing, and in spite of dangers and set-backs is capable of further and unforeseeable progress in the ages that lie ahead. Such progress has perhaps never been what could properly be called automatic; certainly at the level of organic existence it is always conditional: each increase of capacity brings its own hazards. But the 'travail' is not fruitless. *E pur si muove.*

St Paul himself, if at an early stage of his thought he expected an early 'end of the age',[5] transformed his message of a physical or literal Second Coming of Christ into a gradual and spiritual return to be achieved as mankind became united in the community which embodied His Spirit and carried on His work. He looked in his later Epistles not to the dramatic irruption of the

---

[1] Dr K. Barth, *Romans* (tr. E. C. Hoskyns), p. 310, adds 'of a future which never can be in time!'   [2] Gal. ii. 20 etc; and so, increasingly, 'in Christ' is his watchword.   [3] Gal. v. 16-25 etc.   [4] Phil. iii. 20.   [5] Cf. I Thess. i. 10, ii. 19, iv. 15-17.

glorified Christ but to the building up of His body as new cells were added to it and new activities made possible. Even if the classic description of this process in Ephesians iv. 4-16 is by another hand, its whole substance is foreshadowed in indisputably authentic passages like I Corinthians xii. 4-27, Romans xii. 4, 5, and Colossians ii. 19. The Apostle proclaimed and expected a period of progressive development culminating in the fulfilment of the purpose and agony of the creation.

Whether this culmination is to be described as happening in or outside of time is a subject rather of current controversy than of serious significance. It is, of course, a commonplace that human imagination can picture neither an end to the series of events nor a series (in any real sense) which does not lead up to an end. Those who argue that the 'end of the age' cannot come in history presumably mean that it is not just one happening among others, that it puts an end to transitoriness and the experience of succession, and that thereafter those who survive live 'eternally'. Those who dispute this say that this is a very crude way of envisaging the relationship of temporal and eternal; that 'eternal life' is not a condition following upon the finish of the time-sequence but an experience realizable here and now; and that whatever is, be it temporary or permanent, if it affects living entities, is matter for history. That there is real progress towards a real goal is important: as to the date or character of that goal we need not attempt to be wiser than Jesus.[1]

In any case it is abundantly plain that St Paul, following the Jewish conviction of the worth of nature as God's creation and reinterpretating its character in the light of Christ's revelation of the Creator, succeeded by his insistence that God was not primarily power or wisdom but love[2] in throwing light upon the problems of suffering and sin which had so perplexed the sages of the Old Testament. When at Corinth, schooled by his experiences at Thessalonica and Athens, he came to see Christ crucified as the true interpretation of the universe, he made it possible to answer the problems of its meaning and purpose in a fashion which

[1] Cf. Mark xiii. 32.   [2] I Cor. i. 22-4.

confirmed the new concept of God and established the new community among men.[1]

There is one further point to be raised to complete the picture of the New Testament attitude towards nature. In the Fourth Gospel we see made explicit a conviction and an experience thoroughly in keeping with the best both of Jewish and of Greek thought, namely, that the natural order and particular events in it can and do enable men in some sense to 'live eternally'. The theophanies of the Old Testament whereby in and through physical objects God makes contact with His servant, the 'mysteries' whereby the initiate is *renatus in aeternum*, and the principle of conforming to the harmony of nature in the Pythagorean philosophers—all these hint at the knowledge that time and space are capable of being modes of the realization of eternity. When the Fourth Evangelist represents Jesus as saying 'This is life eternal, that they might know thee the only true God, and Jesus Christ, whom thou hast sent',[2] he plainly does not refer to an immortality that is attained after death, but to a relationship here and now which does not change or pass away. He is, in fact, uttering what poets and mystics have always said, that in and through the transient is expressed and realized the permanent. If this be true—and there is a mass of testimony to it—then the antithesis between nature and super-nature becomes absurd, and the total corruption of the natural must be abandoned: nature and grace become sacramentally related as outward to inward, and an incarnation of the divine is in keeping with the whole character of the physical world, since 'God so loved it'.[3]

There is thus to be found in the Biblical attitude to nature that same duality of terror and fascination, ecstasy and abasement which we saw to be characteristic of man's earliest experience. Since Rudolf Otto first drew attention to the *mysterium tremendum et fascinans* in man's apprehension of the holy,[4] Professor J. Hempel[5]

---

[1] II Cor. xiii. 14.   [2] John xvii. 3.

[3] John iii. 16. It is highly significant that Augustine, *In Joh. Tract.* XII, wholly omits this verse.   [4] Cf. his *The Idea of the Holy*.

[5] In his *Gott und Mensch im Alten Testament* (Stuttgart, 1936): I owe this reference to H. W. Robinson, *op. cit.* p. 52.

has pointed out that this same contrast is found in the concept of man's relations with God in the Old Testament and represents not a contradiction but the poles of a single religious experience. The New Testament, still more deeply concerned with the twin facts of illumination and abasement, demonstrates by example and precept that it is the vision of God which brings acknowledgement of sin and that conversely it is the self-emptying in penitence that enables the gift of the Spirit and the integration of the individual into the society. The whole process as it affects the order of nature is nowhere more fitly described than in the three great sayings in the Fourth Gospel: 'I am come that they might have life, and that they might have it more abundantly' (x. 10); 'He that loveth his life shall lose it; and he that hateth his life in this world shall keep it unto life eternal' (xii. 25); 'And this is life eternal, that they might know thee the only true God, and Jesus Christ, whom thou hast sent. . . . That they all may be one' (xvii. 3 and 21). So to the followers of Christ out of the inspiration of their discipleship and the humiliation of their betrayal was born the community of the Church.

III

NATURE IN THE EARLY CHURCH

THAT the Graeco-Roman world in the early years of Christianity should have developed a serious scientific movement might well have been expected. Aristotle had laid a firm foundation; explorers, technicians, farmers, doctors, mathematicians and astronomers had developed his work;[1] there was leisure, wealth and interest to sustain it. The great Museum at Alexandria had drawn east and west into a fruitful partnership. The Roman republic, illiterate even after its triumph over Carthage, had conquered and been conquered by the Greeks; and Lucretius had shown the splendid possibilities of the resulting partnership. Imperial Rome, not so long after, had opened up land and sea for travel, and was ransacking the world for food-stuffs for its banquets and animals for its arena. The Augustan age might well have fulfilled Vergil's dream in the Fourth Eclogue of peace and prosperity, of culture and science.

Whatever be the verdict upon the writers of the classical period, whether Vergil be as Dryden claimed the greatest poet of all time or as others would have it a Roman Tennyson, it is obvious that after it in the Silver and later ages there was no Latin writer or artist or thinker of more than the second grade between Tacitus and Augustine. Men of letters in great numbers were producing treatises on agriculture and architecture, geography and natural history, medicine and engineering, philosophy and religion: the result was an unrivalled output of mediocrity. In these fields Rome was almost wholly imitative; and what she imitated she

[1] Cf. for example the development and application of science in Egypt under the Ptolemies in M. Rostovtzeff, *Social and Economic History of Hellenistic World*, pp. 351-80.

vulgarized. Her genius, pre-eminent in organization and display-ing a remarkably military, political, legislative and administrative efficiency, was not distinguished by intellectual, artistic or religious qualities. *Tu regere imperio populos, Romane, memento.* Empire was her prerogative; and all the rest could go. It is significant that in the great reredos of St Peter's the throne is set above the Cross.

If anyone is disposed to regard this criticism as too severe, let him consider as an example the achievements of Greece and Rome respectively in the field of zoology. Aristotle with little help from predecessors or locality, and on evidence mainly provided by the good offices of Alexander, produced the *Historia Animalium*, the *De Partibus* and the *De Generatione;* and these are not only the first scientific treatises on the subject in Europe but outstandingly the best until Conrad Gesner's work in the sixteenth century. Augustus boasted that he had given the Romans the spectacle of some 3500 African animals killed in the circus; his successors kept up the tale; yet out of all this lavish material we have only Pliny's scientifically worthless tomes. Now that Mr G. Jennison has published his admirable records[1] of the beasts and birds sent to Rome during the empire we have got evidence of the vast and varied collections from Asia and Africa available for study in the city—or at least for slaughter in its hunting-shows. Yet after Pliny (few of whose comments are independent or of interest) there is nobody but a fabulist like Babrius or a copyist like Solinus.

But in the little communities of Christians a higher view of nature and of history, a deeper concern with the physical universe, was not only an essential element in their double inheritance but an inevitable consequence of their principal conviction. If in Christ the invisible had been made manifest and the hidden been unveiled, if in Him 'God had visited and redeemed His people', then nature, this world of flesh and blood, this humanity of ours, must be in some sense *capax deitatis.* The world was not only as the Old Testament had always declared God's world, but it was, if indeed 'His Word had been made flesh and dwelt among us',

[1] *Animals for Show and Pleasure in Ancient Rome* (Manchester, 1937); and see Mr H. Nicolson upon it in *Spectator,* 17 March 1950.

41

organic to Him in the most intimate fashion. An integrated and harmonious exposition of the universe was a necessary part of any Christian theology.

Towards its formulation a long step had been taken in the New Testament writings. We have seen how St Paul with an astonishing originality worked out the changes in the character of God and consequently of the creative process necessitated by the acknowledgment of Christ, and how the Fourth Evangelist set the gospel-story in this climate and scenery. But it was by the employment of the term Logos—the divine Word and Reason—that the clearest guide to the new outlook was attained; and of this the Prologue of the Fourth Gospel is perhaps the earliest example.[1] In this term the two strains, Jewish and Greek, were combined—on the one side, the Word that God spake in creation and to His servants and the Wisdom which was 'the beginning of His works'; and on the other side the Reason which was the governing element in man and the universe, the Thought of which all things are the expression, the Mind which controls and inspires. In the Logos both the transcendent and the immanent energy of the Godhead were represented. To expand and illustrate and apply its full meaning was to set out the outline of a complete Christian theology in a form easily intelligible to students whether of the Scriptures or of contemporary pagan philosophies. The Logos was at once the divine agent in the giving of the Torah and the inspiration of the prophets, the rational principle whose guidance could be traced in the cosmos and in the ways of the animal creation, the reason which distinguished man from the irrational beasts, the Son of God incarnate for us in Jesus and thus made Man, and the indwelling Spirit by whose presence the body of the Church was constituted. The simplest of all theologies, belief in a transcendent and 'wholly other' Deity manifested by an ever-present all-sustaining cosmic Representative was thus brought to the service of the Christian gospel. For the Jews, Philo of Alexandria had already offered a similar translation of Hebrew religion into these terms, commending it to the Graeco-Roman

[1] It would hardly be accurate to claim for it an originating influence.

world and initiating the idea of its superior antiquity and authority.[1] For the pagans, Cicero in his *De Natura Deorum* and Seneca in his *Naturales Quaestiones* represent a sort of *lingua franca* in philosophy, part Stoic part Platonic, in which a theistic interpretation of the universe as an intelligible order established for man's benefit and encouraging him to progress in virtue was expounded with abundant reference to the astronomy and biology of the period.[2] For the Christian, therefore, it was only necessary to add the special claim made in the Prologue of the Fourth Gospel in order to become possessed of a complete and appropriate apologetic.

The succession of Greek Apologists, beginning with the un-named writer of the beautiful letter to Diognetus, including Athenagoras, Theophilus and Tatian and best represented by Justin Martyr, shared this method of presenting their case and gave us the so-called Logos-theology. Justin in his two *Apologies* to the pagan world and in his *Dialogue with Trypho* works out the system for a Greek and a Jewish audience respectively. In the former he affirms that a seed of Logos is implanted in the whole human race[3] and claims that those who lived according to this Logos, like Socrates and Heracleitus among the Greeks and Abraham and Elijah and many others among the 'barbarians', were Christians before Christ;[4] and then develops an account of the teaching of Jesus and the character of His Church so as to prove that here indeed is the perfect Logos. In the latter he demonstrates from prophecy (on occasion without complete fidelity to the text)[5] the argument that Jesus is the fulfilment of the Word spoken of old and reproduces many of the familiar Testimonia with their interpretations. His work is naïve and fresh and his general line of argument at once clear and com-prehensive. It was expanded both on its philosophical and on its moral side by Clement of Alexandria, and formed the framework

---

[1] That Plato was 'Moses speaking Greek' was argued both by Philo and by Clement of Alexandria.

[2] Mainly from Aratus of Soli whose astronomical poem Cicero translated and from Aristotle; Seneca has a few points, e.g. on colour and the chamaeleon (*N.Q.* I, 5, 7) which seem to be original.

[3] *Apol.* II, 8.   [4] *Apol.* I, 46.

[5] Cf. for example *Dial.* LXVII quoting Isa. vii. 14.

upon which Origen built the first complete system of Christian scholarship and doctrine.

Clement of Alexandria's work is from first to last an exposition of the Logos-theology; and few scholars have been better equipped than he for the task of demonstrating that the whole world, Greek and Jew alike, 'has had as its teacher Him who filled the Universe with His energy in creation, salvation, beneficence, lawgiving, prophecy, teaching and indeed all other instruction'.[1] For Clement with his very wide knowledge of literature could escape from too great a concentration upon Testimonia from the Scriptures and succeeded in showing more effectively than any other how wide was the foreshadowing of Christ and how universal the fulfilment by Him of man's highest aspirations.[2] Moreover, though primarily a scholar and man of letters, Clement avoids the error of over-intellectualization. He places the emphasis upon the love of God and of the Teacher for mankind,[3] and insists that teaching, because more akin to healing than to imparting information, aims at wholeness of life rather than mere wisdom.[4] Sound learning is essential if we are to be His pupils; but character as disclosed by deeds is of more value than correctness of opinion or cleverness of speech.[5] Details of conduct, ranging from the trivial to the intimate, form a large part of his subject matter, and he treats them frankly and with common sense. His final picture of the Gnostic or fully instructed Christian lays stress upon knowledge, but only as contributory to godliness,[6] and, as a protest against the esoteric lore and ascetic virtue of the followers of Valentinus and the self-styled Gnostic schools, is both effective and attractive.

It is disappointing that Clement who has so clear a sense of the wholeness of creation and of the loving purpose of God towards it does not develop a fuller exposition of the order of nature. He is too good a Christian to despise the body or to deprecate the study of science[7] but he is also too much a Platonist to think it of high importance. At least we can say that he refuses to accept

---

[1] *Protrept.* XI.   [2] Cf. for example *Strom.* VI, 17 and 18.   [3] *Paed.* I, 8.
[4] *Protrept.* XI and *Paed.* I, I.   [5] *Paed.* I, 9 and 10.   [6] *Strom.* VI, 7-10.
[7] Cf. for example *Strom.* VIII, 4.

fables from it; for the most famous of them all, that of the Egyptian phoenix, must have been known to him both from Herodotus[1] and from his namesake Clement of Rome[2] whose *Epistle* he quotes freely and fully; and yet he never mentions it anywhere.

In Origen there is more evidence of a profound interest in nature and of a considerable amount of scientific information.[3] The broad lines of his theology are similar to those of Clement, but he has a larger vision of its scope and sees all the knowable as integral to and integrated by the knowledge of God. Though his primary interest is pastoral and his chief task the exposition of the Bible by critical, allegorical and theological methods, he constantly calls contemporary science to his aid and reveals not only the extent and variety of his acquaintance with it but his sympathy with its subject and his sense of its value. The man who could put on record his hope that after this life is over he will be able to explain the reason for the manifold diversity of the natural world and particularly for the special properties of different plants,[4] was one who, given other circumstances, would have made a great scientist.

As such he is obviously sceptical as to the phoenix,[5] just as in another book he declares the griffin of Leviticus to be non-existent.[6] Similar and of greater significance, in view of his reverence for the Scriptures, is his frank criticism of the creation narrative in Genesis i: 'What man of intelligence will believe that the first, and second, and third day, and evening and morning existed without the sun and moon and stars?'[7] And with this we can compare his rejection of a literal acceptance of this chapter in *Contra Celsum*, vi, 60 and the *Commentary on St Matthew*, xiv, 9, and of the story of the Fall (Genesis ii) in *Contra Celsum*, iv, 40 where Adam is regarded not as a historical personage but as a type or symbol of humanity. Perhaps the clearest example of Origen's

---

[1] *Hist.* ii, 73.   [2] *Ep.* i, 25.

[3] Cf. A. von Harnack, *Texte und Unters.* xlii, 4, pp. 100 ff. I am indebted for help in this subject to my friend, the Rev. H. Chadwick.

[4] *De Princ.* ii, 11, 5.   [5] *C. Cels.* iv, 98.

[6] *De Princ.* iv, 1, 17; he refers to Lev. xi. 13.   [7] *De Princ.* iv, 1, 16.

scientific outlook is his treatment of Celsus' attack upon the Virgin-birth of Jesus[1] in the latter's story of the Virgin's adultery with a soldier, Panthera. Origen in reply appeals to the physiognomists Zopyrus, Loxus and Polemon, who maintain that there is a real correlation between soul and body, and argues that if so then it is unthinkable that so pure a soul could have dwelt in a body so basely born.

That a tradition of the importance of nature was a vital part of the great legacy which Origen bequeathed to the Church is clear from the work of the last great Origenist to attain high ecclesiastical dignity, Basil of Neo-Caesarea. He and his friend, Gregory of Nazianzus, at a time when Origen's memory had not yet been defamed,[2] had published the *Philocalia*, an interesting and very valuable selection from his theological writings. Basil, who like his brother, Gregory of Nyssa, was something of a naturalist, gave proof of his genuine knowledge of nature, both from literature and from observation, in his very attractive series of addresses on the Work of Creation, the *Hexaemeron*. These, delivered extempore in Lent and to an audience of working-folk, give a good impression of contemporary science adapted for popular consumption and show that a great Christian leader still maintained the value of the lessons to be drawn from the 'works of the Lord' and had not accepted fable as a substitute for fact. He is not always accurate, even in his versions of Aristotle or Pliny; and his own observations are not free from distortion by anthropomorphic presuppositions. But in the main he strives to be objective and to give his hearers an adequate picture, avoiding allegories and exhortations and the discovery of moral lessons, and content to let nature speak for itself. 'To me' he writes in Discourse IX, i, 'grass is grass; plant, fish, wild beast, domestic animal, I take them all in their literal meaning'; and in Discourse V (the most interesting of the discourses) 'I want creation to thrill you with such

---

[1] *C. Cels.* I, 33.

[2] It is sufficient evidence of the corruption of the Church in the fifth and sixth centuries that Origen, the most learned and saintly of the Alexandrians, was vilified by Jerome and condemned by Justinian; and that Cyril, theologically dishonest and guilty of intrigue, violence and bribery, was canonized.

wonder that everywhere every tiny plant may remind you of its Maker' and 'A single blade of grass is enough to occupy your whole mind as you contemplate the skill that produced it'.[1] And along with such general remarks are passages like v, 7 where he describes the double sex of the date-palm and how the husbandmen shake over the drooping female 'the seeds, so to say, of the male which they call "psen"';[2] and then goes on to tell the similar process of 'caprification' in figs where the wild fig is planted next to the cultivated; or like that in the next section, 'Amber is the crystallized sap of plants; as is evidenced by the bits of straw and little insects caught up in it'.[3]

These discourses reveal their author's knowledge and insight most plainly when they are compared with the Latin imitation of them by Ambrose of Milan. His *Hexaemeron* is based upon that of Basil but with some few additions derived from Pliny[4] and with much added edification. Thus in the passage *Hex*. III, 7, parallel to Basil's sayings about the worth of a blade of grass, he interpolates a discourse on the text 'All flesh is grass' (Isaiah xl); and later, in III, 13, he makes a long digression on osiers binding the vine like the love of Christ binding us. It seems clear that Ambrose had no personal knowledge of, or indeed interest in, the subject; he merely uses it as an allegory and preaches a sermon upon it. In this respect Basil represents the last of the old outlook: Ambrose is typical of that which was already taking its place.

For unfortunately the Logos doctrine and its magnificent expansion into the Origenistic theology was not able to stand up against the influences which were changing the whole attitude of Western man towards the order of nature and confronting Christendom with the situation which Dr W. Temple in his younger days described as 'the bankruptcy of Chalcedon'. To analyse in

---

[1] For a close parallel cf. B. Whichcote, *Works* (ed. 1751), III, p. 176.

[2] See Note III below, p. 206.

[3] Probably Basil got this from Pliny, *N.H.* XXXVII, 33-46. He mentions this proof that it is a gum; so does Tacitus, *Germania* LV. Herodotus, *Hist*. III, 115, and Dioscorides, I, 110 and II, 100 have no such record.

[4] E.g. *Hex*. v, 9 (on the sea-urchin) from *N.H.* IX, 51; *Hex*. v, 23 (silkworms) from *N.H.* XI, 26; *Hex*. VI, 22 (birds' feet) from *N.H.* x, 13; and *Hex*. VI, 22 (swan song) from *N.H.* x, 32.

full the causes which led to the degradation of nature and history, to the establishment of the antithesis between secular and sacred, and to the replacement of science and factual record by fable and hagiology is a task too lengthy to be fully repeated here.[1] The obvious cause was no doubt the fact that 'the days were evil'. Christianity though it prolonged and also preserved the grandeur of Rome was not able to prevent the economic, political and moral decline of Rome's Empire. With the closing in of the dark ages faith became a creed, hope an escapism, and love a snare; to contrast the transient with the supernatural, to flee from the world rather than to convert it, and to order this life so as to secure the bliss of heaven became the object of Christian endeavour. But these changes arose not only out of the pessimism of the period: they had begun soon after the close of the Apostolic age and were due rather to the excellence with which the Church undertook its work than to any weakness or failure. Indeed, here as so often in human affairs, distortion is seen to accompany not our wickedness but our virtues: at the best we are unprofitable servants.

Put briefly the main causes of distortion were these. Firstly the Church was commissioned to evangelize a world that was bored and blasé; to attract attention it was natural to concentrate upon the miraculous and sensational elements in the gospel, even though these were the matters which Jesus charged men to keep secret. The Apocryphal Gospels, the arguments from prophecy and from thaumaturgy, and the insistence upon the vested interests of the orthodox in miracles testify to the contempt for the ordinary and the normal. The age craved excitement: Christianity had marvels to show and too often mistook the abnormal for the profound. Nature became despised as 'common and unclean'.

In the second place the Church had to confront an age of widespread moral corruption. The Christian Apologists have no hesitation in describing and denouncing it; and the contemporary evidence alike of Petronius and of Pompeii bears out their charges. They did a great antiseptic and ennobling work, but at the familiar cost of becoming to a sad extent sex-obsessed and puritanical.

[1] For an account in some detail cf. my book, *The Gospel and the Church*, pp. 59–165.

Tertullian, Jerome and in his last phase even Augustine reveal a 'horror of the flesh' which is incompatible with any high valuation of nature.

In the third place the Church was exposed to persecution; its chief glory was the heroic courage with which its martyrs faced the lions. Martyrs might forgive their enemies: but in others' eyes sufferings here must be justified by rewards and for the persecutors torments hereafter. To the pagan world such ideas were familiar.[1] Even in the Apocalypse Hades had become a place of torture;[2] and by the time of Tertullian's *De Spectaculis* the *dies irae* with all its sadism was a recognized part of Christian orthodoxy. Man's doom in the hereafter became a matter of overwhelming importance; insurance against hell-fire was the primary obligation of a prudent Christian. This world was only an examination hall, and the order of nature its furniture.

For in addition to these practical causes there was another arising out of a theological necessity. The Church had inherited the Old Testament and must needs explain the contradictions between it and the New and the significance of its less edifying episodes. As early as in the Epistle of Barnabas such passages were treated as allegorical—a method already familiar to the interpreters of Homer and freely adopted by Philo. Clement and Origen had employed it with a fertile ingenuity to reconcile inconsistencies and disclose hidden meanings until it came to be granted that the records had a double value, as plain tale for the simple and as esoteric lore for the initiate. So facts became symbols, history a shell to be thrown aside when its kernel had been abstracted and nature an emblem only valuable for what it could be supposed to signify.

With this debasement of the value of the creation came the changes which produced the antithesis between God as immortal, changeless, impassible and man as mortal, transient, suffering; which made the unity of God and man in Christ a contradiction in terms; which led to the tearing asunder of the Church by

[1] E.g. in the Orphic beliefs, the Pseudo-Platonic *Axiochus* and Vergil, *Aeneid* vi.
[2] Cf. Rev. xiv. 9-11.

unedifying and largely unintelligible controversies, Apollinarian, Nestorian, Eutychian, Chalcedonian, Monophysite; which destroyed the most venerable sees of Christendom and exposed the Churches of Palestine and Syria, Mesopotamia and Egypt to the assaults of Mohammed. It is impossible to survey these changes in full detail:[1] but, for their importance in determining the attitude of Western culture towards nature for the ensuing millennium and indeed until the present time, they deserve some exposition.

Theologically what took place in consequence of the devaluation of nature is obvious and was perhaps inevitable. The Logos doctrine had provided a simple and satisfying concept of the person of Christ. If all men possessed as their human birth-right (were they not made 'in the image of God?')[2] what Justin called seeds of Logos or if, to put it otherwise, Jesus Christ was the archetype of mankind, then He stood to us as the 'perfect round' to the 'broken arcs'; and however vast and fundamental the difference between the absolute and the relative there was no total disparity between His nature and ours. On such terms a real Incarnation was apprehensible. Similarly if the Logos was both Word and Reason, the functions of the Holy Spirit as the indwelling spark or seed of deity in us and in the world were given an adequate place in theology: all through the creative process there was evidence of an element of reason, of purpose and guidance, at work; and in man this element was not only recorded in the Scriptures but manifested in contemporary folks by the love, joy, peace and fortitude which were 'His fruits'. When the concept of Logos was abandoned, the divinity of Christ as Son of God became at once separated from any 'image 'of itself in man; and as the natural order sank into contempt it became almost blasphemy to suggest that man's nature could ever be really united with God's—by definition the two were opposite. Yet if God and man were one Christ, the opposites must somehow be conjoined. In effect the manhood was absorbed, being defined as impersonal;[3]

[1] The account of them in my *Apollinarianism* (Cambridge, 1923) has not (I think) been superseded or seriously criticized.   [2] Gen. i. 26-7.

[3] It is not easy to attach any meaning to this, since personality is the essential character of manhood.

and the Incarnation became a theophany. Similarly, when the Holy Spirit was separated from the Logos, no attempt was made to define His relationship to the Word or the particular character and sphere of His activities. In the Nicene Creed of A.D. 325 no such definition was attempted. When, in the later phase of the Arian controversy (*circa* A.D. 360), debate about the status of the Spirit arose, His consubstantial Deity was asserted by analogy with that of the Son, but the matter was never adequately argued. As a result the Spirit, whose indwelling had been regarded as the essential and constitutive element in the life of the Church and the source of all value and virtue, became restricted in His operation implicitly if not expressly to certain ecclesiastical rites, baptism, confirmation, ordination and the like, which it was the privilege of the hierarchy to bestow.

How inevitably these theological changes were accompanied by a separation of the secular from the sacred and a restriction of religion to ecclesiastical and almost to monastic areas can be seen most clearly in Augustine's last great treatise, *De Civitate Dei*.[1] It may be true, as has been urged, that he was striving to achieve some sort of synthesis of the two world-views, the pagan with its conviction of the worth of the present order and its hesitation as to that order's permanent value, and the Christian which, starting from the belief that the present order had had its true nature and meaning disclosed by Christ's teaching, cross and resurrection, was now increasingly interpreting this disclosure in terms of the intrusion of another and sacred order which condemned the present as incurably corrupt and only redeemed it by withdrawing from it, into the ark of the sacred, those who were destined for rescue. If so, it is plain that in fact he merely adopted the second in its contemporary form. The two states are radically distinct: those who belong to the terrestrial, be they the best of men like Plato, have their reward in the honours and fame that earth can bestow: they may prepare for the City of God, but have no part nor lot in it. Unless before it is too late these pagans take refuge in the

---

[1] Finished in A.D. 426, four years before his death and representing the last stage of his thought.

supernatural ark of the Church they will perish everlastingly. Here in his most influential writing is the logic which led him to deny all virtue to the unbaptized and to return at the end of his life, in his writings against Julian, to a view of the physical world hardly distinguishable from the Manichaeism of his youth; the same spirit which in his exposition of the Fourth Gospel constrained him to omit altogether the great saying 'God so loved the world'. There can be no high valuation of nature when the whole secular realm is so totally condemned.

The effect of this interpretation of history, which virtually reduced the meaning of Providence to the protection and guidance of the Church, was to empty belief in progress of any reference to the world of nature and of secular affairs.[1] In place of the universalism which had been openly advocated by Origen and implicitly by the Greek Apologists who preceded him there was a reversion to the belief that the world was steadily degenerating. *Aetas parentum peior avis* had been characteristic of the Roman world into which Christianity came; for a few centuries Christendom had lived up to its own good news of the coming of the Kingdom of God. Now with the breakdown of civilization hope had been transferred from the world to the Church and from this world to the next: when the Kingdom came it would be by miracle and with fire: the earth and all that it contained would be utterly consumed.

In view of the tragic circumstances of the time and of the far-reaching changes in the ethos and presentation of the Christian Gospel it is not surprising that Augustine and the Churchmen of Western Christendom thus reject the order of nature as a *massa perditionis*, totally corrupt and doomed to destruction. But while we live in the world and depend upon it for our livelihood we cannot wholly ignore it. *Naturam expellas furca; tamen usque recurret* is not only true of weeds in the garden. What was the man of the fourth and fifth and sixth centuries to say of God's world?

[1] This opinion, characteristic of orthodoxy until long after the Renaissance and restated very powerfully by the great Bossuet in 1681 in his much lauded book, *Discours sur l'Histoire Universelle*, was not seriously challenged until the rediscovery of the worth of nature in the sixteenth century.

Fortunately an answer to that question, compatible with the outlook of the time, had long been in preparation. There existed and had been collected from very early times folk-tales concerning animals and plants, monsters and monstrosities which we know best in the fragmentary writings ascribed to Physiologus, 'the 'Naturalist',[1] and represented by translations into very many languages. These deal with sirens and hydras, the panther and the elephant, the dragon and the asp-turtle,[2] and are furnished with appropriate texts from Scripture and with moral lessons valuable to preachers. The longest and most familiar of them is the long epic of Reynard the Fox. These and the somewhat similar stories about plants formed the nucleus of the medieval bestiaries and herbals. They are assimilated to and amalgamated with the fables which, in the ancient days of Greece when Solon and the Sages flourished and Croesus ruled in Lydia, a certain Aesopus is said to have invented and written. Of Aesop nothing reliable or contemporary is known; and the stories of him are improbable and unilluminating. Plato[3] and a few others[4] allude to 'Aesopian tales'; and indeed the fashion, whether due to him or not, became immensely popular as table-talk and to pass the time. Linking up with the folk-tale on the one side and with the parable on the other they represent a type of story which has been universally told since men dressed up in horns and masks for dances or painted bison and deer on their caves.

But although so familiar that the characteristics of the principal birds and beasts had long become stereotyped, these fables already collected and circulated did not win a secure place in literature until early in the third century after Christ. Then Babrius,[5] probably a native of Italy, but writing choliambic verses in Greek, produced a hundred and forty in two volumes in the reign of Alexander Severus; and these like the earlier collections were used

[1] Apparently committed to writing in Greek and at Alexandria, perhaps in the second century A.D. There is an almost equally old Latin version.

[2] Or whale, the sea-monster mistaken by sailors for an island; cf. H. Hermannsson *Icelandic Physiologus*, pp. 10-11 and Plate B. 8, and A. S. Cook, *Old English Physiologus*, pp. 12-21.

[3] E.g. *Phaedo* 60 d.   [4] Cf. Herodotus, *Hist.* II, 134-5; Aristophanes, *Wasps* etc.

[5] Cf. Introduction to his works by W. G. Rutherford (London, 1883).

in schools as the first step in the teaching of literature (rhetoric). Children thus became acquainted at an early age with the *dramatis personae* of the fable—lion, bear, fox, sheep, mouse, eagle, crane, tortoise, frog and the rest. From the schools the characteristics attached to the several animals became common knowledge and were absorbed into the various digests and encyclopedias like Solinus's *Polyhistor*, Isidore of Seville's *Origines*,[1] or Hraban of Mainz's *De Universo*.[2] This not only imposed upon the animals a temperament and habits which often had little relation to reality, but imputed to them traditional actions which, even if not assumed to have happened, yet coloured the whole popular opinion of the creature in question. Verifiable observations like those recorded by Aristotle were thus either ignored if they contradicted the fable, or transformed into congruity with it. A great mass of lore was developed; and this wholly replaced the authentic evidence so that each beast became a heraldic emblem of a particular virtue or vice. Some of these identifications have been forgotten: some still survive and even in this scientific age are generally accepted.

This widely familiar attitude towards the animal kingdom, and to a less extent also towards the vegetable kingdom, commended itself to the Church as being in keeping with the symbolism of the sacramental system and also as providing a fertile source of edification for teachers and preachers. Very early in Christian history Clement of Rome had fastened upon the phoenix as a type of the risen Christ: not long after the 'pelican in its piety'[3] became a still more elaborate symbol of Him. Allegorical interpretations were already applied to the Old Testament as they had been to Homer: it was natural to adapt a similar sort of explanation to the world of nature, forcing the characteristics and behaviour of plants and animals into a shape in which they would illustrate the moral and

---

[1] Isidore is a man of some small originality. Thus in *Orig.* xii, 7 he writes of birds: 'some are migratory returning at a fixed time like Storks and Swallows; others are gregarious in flight like Starlings and Quails'; and of the bat (classed as a bird) 'it flies sustained by the delicate membranes of its arms, an animal like the mice'.

[2] Hardly deserving mention: what he says in Bk. viii is copied from Isidore.

[3] Isidore, *Orig.* xii, 7 queries the truth of the tale.

religious convictions of the day, and either by example or warning drive home the appropriate lesson.

The Aesopic or animal fable was freely combined with the Lycian fables about gods or men; and these too furnished patterns which helped to bring about a transformation of history into hagiology parallel to that which took place in regard to nature. Legends of an edifying and supernatural sort were attached to a few outstanding figures in history, Alexander the Great or the poet Vergil, and with lavish generosity to the martyrs and saints of the Church. Many, indeed the majority, of the most popular of these, St Veronica, St Margaret, St Giles, for example, had no verifiable historical existence; others like our own St George were bare names even if historically identifiable; others were actual persons whose characters were in fact quite different from their 'acta'. We have lately seen one such legend raised to the status of a dogma of the Roman Church; and anyone familiar with Catholic lives of the recently canonized like St Thomas More or even of prominent converts like G. K. Chesterton will know that hagiology is still being practised.

Of the growth of such legends examples can easily be found. An attractive and typical specimen[1] is that of the Crocodile bird which originates in an observation reported by Herodotus (II, 68) of the plover (*Hoplopterus spinosus*), which collects insects round the crocodiles as they rest on the mudbanks of the Nile and on occasion has been seen to enter an open mouth and pick bits of food from its teeth. This story, combined with a tall tale adjoining it in Pliny (*H.N.* VIII, 37) of how the ichneumon (which does in fact eat crocodile eggs) runs down the open gullet of its enemy and tears his belly, had yielded by the time of Alexander Neckam[2] a fusion of the two and a complete illustration for the preacher of the working of vice. For sin like the bird first soothes its victim by gentle tickling of its lips; then ventures into its opened mouth; then feeds; then lulls the beast to sleep; and finally runs down the gullet to the heart and works death.

Of the far-reaching and long-continued influence of such fables

---

[1] For fuller detail, cf. my *English Naturalists*, pp. 18-19. [2] *De Nat. Rerum* I, 57.

an admirable instance is preserved by John Strype, abridging the Chronicle.[1] It describes how James I when in the summer of 1609 he began to find the mantle of the great Elizabeth and his own divine right to wear it hard to sustain and was much troubled by signs of dissatisfaction among his nobles, decided to preach them a sermon of warning in the shape of an acted fable. Aesop had related how the King of Beasts had dealt as judge and executioner with a refractory subject, the Bear. There was in the menagerie of the Tower a magnificent lion sent to him by the Sultan of Morocco: there was also a bear that had broken loose from the bear-pit at Southwark and killed a child. James ordered a cage to be built on Tower Green in the shape of a law-court, and round it thrones for himself and seats for his troublesome nobles. The scene was set; the lion was placed on the judgment-seat; then the bear was admitted to the dock. But at that point Aesop proved unreliable: the lion fled whimpering to a corner of the cage; the bear, inured to mastiffs, saw no reason to pick a quarrel; and the intended demonstration of royal justice developed into a farce.

It was not until the latter part of the seventeenth century that this attitude towards nature disappeared from the region of the supposedly factual. Even in 1670 Ray in the preface to Willughby's *Ornithology* had to explain that he had rigidly excluded from the book all 'hieroglyphics, emblems, morals, fables, presages or ought else pertaining to Divinity, Ethics, Grammar or any sort of humane learning'. But by this time the collections of fables and emblems, now regarded as such, had been formed and had established a short-lived literary convention.[2] Emblem books were freely published during the latter part of the century; and manuscript productions complete with pictures, verses, epigrams and a moral were a regular part of the occupation of persons of culture.[3] In this way the great flood of fabulous lore gathered during a thousand

---

[1] Cf. Strype, *Survey of London* (ed. 1764), I, p. 123.

[2] Cf. Dr R. Freeman, *The English Emblem-books;* and the huge collections by G. P. Valeriano, *Hieroglyphica* (Lyons, 1626) and F. Picinelli, *Mundus Symbolicus* (Cologne, 1695).

[3] A beautifully bound and executed specimen by Richard Waller, Secretary to the Royal Society, 1687, was presented to me by Dr A. B. Cook.

and more years was drawn off from the fields of natural history; the area was cleared for biology; and religion could return to a truer appreciation of nature. There is as yet little sign of a similar abandonment of hagiology.

IV

ST ALBERT AND THE MIDDLE AGES

WHEN out of the darkness and upheavals of the close of the first Christian millennium scholarship and philosophy began to revive, their growth was at every stage conditioned by belief in the radical disparity between the world and the Church, the natural and the supernatural. In Western Catholicism the heritage of the Roman Empire gave to the Papacy a responsibility for secular affairs and a temptation to set up a theocracy which on the one hand saved it from the complete dualism of Cathari and Albigenses and on the other, because the segregation of the secular from the sacred was universally acknowledged, embroiled it in constant struggles with the Emperors and such kingdoms as had the will and power to resist its demands. It is proof of the extent to which the doctrine of the two swords was fundamental to contemporary thought that even Hildebrand never ventured to assert a totalitarian claim for the Church's authority and indeed that those who most strongly pressed the universality of spiritual obligations did so by denying the worth and even the reality of the whole physical realm. Even in the greatest period of medieval civilization there were very few who had any appreciation of the wholeness of experience or any hesitation in affirming as fundamental the contrast between the two worlds.

This contrast is nowhere more evident than in the fields of nature and of history. We can see from the development of architecture, from the records of agriculture and from the realistic treatment of flowers and foliage by artists and sculptors that sound knowledge and close observation were not lacking. Mankind lived in a world of real beasts even if they wrote about them in terms of legend and allegory. But when we look for some evidence of understanding whether of the principles of building or of the flora and fauna of the countryside or of the characters and events of the human scene, we find a literature of magic and fable and hagiology. Clerks like our own Alexander Neckam or Bartholomew the Englishman, who wrote on the nature of things, fill their pages with the fantastic emblems of heraldry, with wonderful tales of plant and bird and beast derived ultimately from some record of Pliny or Physiologus furbished and moralized by generations of preachers and troubadours. Monographs like Odell Sheppard's *Lore of the Unicorn* or Heron-Allen's *Barnacles in Nature and Myth* could be multiplied almost indefinitely; and the legends became so familiar as to defy centuries of disproof.

It is obvious to anyone who considers the amazing skill and science which designed and executed the timber-work of the great lantern in Ely Cathedral or the wide stone vaulting of its Lady Chapel that these architects of the fourteenth century were masters not only of technical skill but of sound rules of construction and imaginative audacity in adventuring upon new experiments. They plainly had behind them a mass of properly tested experience if not of theoretical principles, such as could have been easily developed into a science of engineering. Similarly the artists who carved the roof-bosses of the same Lady Chapel or the still more excellent Chapter-house at Southwell,[1] and who filled the borders of missals or the foregrounds of pictures with flowers,[2] obviously knew the form and habit of growth of the plants which they rendered so sensitively. This is not heraldry but observation, and as different from the stereotyped and unrecognizable illustrations of the *Ortus Sanitatis* as a gazelle is from a yale or a rhinoceros from a unicorn. Why is it that when we get to the writers, to the clerks and scholars who ought to share the craftsman's knowledge, we

---

[1] For an admirable collection of pictures cf. C. J. P. Cave, *Roof Bosses in Medieval Churches* (Cambridge, 1948), and for a discussion of their source and character, N. Pevsner, *The Leaves of Southwell.*

[2] Cf. Joan Evans, *English Art, 1307-1461* and W. Blunt, *The Art of Botanical Illustration*, pp. 18-44.

so seldom find anything but the reproduction of traditional fables?[1]

That this is the case can be verified by reference to almost every writing that professed to deal with nature until the beginning of the sixteenth century. In the very popular work of Bartholomew, the *De Proprietatibus Rerum*, which was written in the mid-thirteenth century and printed in 1491 by Wynkyn de Worde, and which in its last edition in 1582 became Shakespeare's natural-history book, there is hardly a sign of any single piece of first-hand knowledge except in his description of the domestic cat: even he failed to make an emblem out of the creature that slept on his hearthrug. But elsewhere even in animals almost equally familiar he rehearses conventional tales which have been the commonplace of every writer since Solinus and Isidore and moralizings which first appear as far back as the *Hexaemeron* of St Ambrose. The royalty of the lion, the cunning of the fox, the chastity of the elephant, the piety of the pelican these have become the common property of mankind. We are still 'licked into shape' like the bear's cubs in our youth, and privileged to utter a 'swan song' in our old age. But, though the influence of fable be granted, we can only give an answer to our question by a more detailed survey of the period in which the possibility of attaining an integrative and satisfying philosophy was most nearly realized.

Such integration was indeed plainly experienced by St Francis and his first followers. Their ecstatic joy in the universal manifestation of the divine, though it was accompanied by a strong element of asceticism and renunciation, was a new expression of the scriptural confidence that the earth is the Lord's and of the New Testament witness that humanity here and now can live with Christ in the heavenlies. How far the full quality of St Francis' joy in nature and joy in suffering could have been presented in terms of a philosophy which would have successfully challenged the contemporary antithesis between natural and supernatural must remain open to question; for St Bonaventure who is the best

---

[1] The question why medieval civilization never produced a scientific movement is discussed below, cf. pp. 71-3.

interpreter of the Franciscan experience into a philosophic system did not share his master's profound experience of suffering. But it is clear from Dr Etienne Gilson's learned and sympathetic exposition[1] that here, as a sequel to St Francis and from a pupil of Alexander of Hales, is a type of Christian philosophy that restates, as against the new Aristotelianism of St Albert,[2] the Platonist doctrine of man's kinship with the divine and so escapes that sharp contrast between reason and faith which is characteristic of the great Aristotelians, St Albert and St Thomas. It might seem therefore that here was a system which could see life steadily and see it whole as illuminated by the Light that lighteth every man that cometh into the world. St Bonaventure was himself too good an Augustinian to attach sufficient worth to the study of the creation. But that such a philosophy might properly have been combined with a true scientific outlook is clear from the achievements of the two great Franciscans of Oxford, Robert Grosseteste and his pupil, Roger Bacon.

Among the manifold interests of his vigorous and challenging intellect Grosseteste fastened upon the value of geometry, the knowledge of 'lines, angles and figures',[3] and developed it by a series of experiments which were of real value. To claim him as the founder of modern science is an exaggeration, but there seems a clear case for regarding him as one of the very first to appreciate the value of accurate measurement and to examine physical phenomena with a view not only to description but to explanation. The titles of his works on light, the tides, the rainbow, comets, and the movements of the heavenly bodies, on colour and on sound reveal the general character of his interests; and study of them discloses evidence of real originality, careful observation and shrewd inference. He paid little heed to the medical and biological studies which usually play a large part in the activities

[1] *The Philosophy of St Bonaventure* (London, 1938).

[2] Gilson, *op. cit.* pp. 7-10 demonstrates that he knew and rejected St Albert's views; cf. especially his account of Bonaventure's doctrine of the creation of animals and its difference from that of St Thomas (pp. 294-302).

[3] Cf. A. E. Taylor in *European Civilisation*, III, p. 826. For the authenticity of the *De Lineis* and his other writings, cf. S. Harrison Thomson, *The Writings of R. Grosseteste* (Cambridge, 1940).

of the early scientists; and this may be partly due to his acquaintance with Aristotle's *Physica* (from which, however, he did not hesitate to depart) rather than with the *Historia Animalium*, translations of which were unknown to him. But as a pioneer in the field of physics and especially of optics, perspective and lenses, and as a great educator and inspirer of research he deserves more credit than he has received. Roger Bacon's homage, the tribute of a man not given to praise of others, is plain proof of his real eminence. Considering his absorption in the practical affairs of church and kingdom, his achievement is very remarkable.

Besides his direct researches, Grosseteste influenced the learning of his time by his insistence upon the use of accurate versions of the classical and biblical authorities and the duty of tracing wherever possible all knowledge back to its original sources. His own efforts to obtain good translations from Greek and Hebrew and his encouragement to Jewish and other scholars gave to the University of Oxford a real rebirth, and initiated a movement which bore much fruit in the century that followed. Indeed in this respect as in his scientific work he is in some sense a forerunner of the Renaissance.

His immediate influence found its fullest expression in his pupil and fellow-Franciscan, Roger Bacon. Coming to Oxford while 'the Lord Robert' was at the zenith of his fame as a teacher, Bacon learnt from him a love of experiment, an interest in mathematics, and a zeal for the accurate study of languages; and he had the alertness and the leisure to make full use of his lessons. Unfortunately the details of his life are still far from clear. He taught in Paris for some years, 1245-51. He returned thence to Oxford, but was recalled to Paris in 1257 and there spent ten years in ill health and relative inaction. On the election of Guy de Foulques as Pope Clement IV he was instructed to send a full statement of his opinions to Rome and in consequence, in 1266-8, wrote and submitted the *Opus Maius* and other treatises as part of the *Scriptum Principale* which he had planned on an encyclopedic scale but never in fact completed. The result was negligible and apparently he went back to Oxford and wrote the *Compendium*

Studii Philosophiae. In 1277 he was condemned by the chapter of Franciscans in Paris on account of suspected novelties, thrown into prison, and kept there for some fourteen years. He was released and allowed to return to Oxford just before his death in 1292 and was then writing his last book, the *Compendium Studii Theologiae.* This outline of events seems tolerably certain. But even the recent publication of all his writings has not yet given occasion for a full study of his history and achievements.[1]

It seems indeed plain that unlike any other of his contemporaries he had a real sense of the unity of all experience, of the need to begin with an exact study of the data whether physical or philological, and of the importance of breaking down the barriers between the several departments of learning and of technical skill. His immense care to determine the precise meaning of words as illustrated by his efforts to identify correctly the birds and animals of Scripture[2] is on a par with his enthusiasm for Peter Peregrinus de Maricourt[3] who had gathered from workers of all sorts their knowledge of metals and agriculture, of engineering and warfare, of handicrafts and medicine. Out of all this assembly of knowledge he wished to formulate an interpretation of nature which should not only enable practical advances in civilization but should illuminate and support Christian ethics and theology. Commencing with the detailed study of language,[4] a revised form of the traditional *trivium,* and continuing with mathematics and the *quadrivium,* he proposed to proceed to optics, astronomy and geography, alchemy, agriculture including both plants and animals, and medicine, the whole being treated experimentally; and from this to go on to metaphysics and moral philosophy. That he had a real appreciation of the homogeneity of all knowledge and of the

---

[1] The three full-length studies of his work by R. Carton in vols. II, III and V of *Études de Philosophie Médiévale* (Paris, 1924) lead only to the conclusion that Bacon remains an enigma. [2] For examples cf. my *English Naturalists,* pp. 10-12.

[3] Author of a letter on the magnet, printed at Augsberg in 1558 and described by Dr G. Sarton as 'one of the greatest monuments of experimental research in the Middle Ages', *Introd. to History of Science,* II, pt. 2, p. 1031.

[4] 'Bacon held that the knowledge of languages was the first gate that led to the acquisition of wisdom', S. A. Hirsch in *R. Bacon: Commemoration Essays,* p. 103, referring to *Opus Tertium* XXVIII, 102. Bacon produced the first Greek grammar.

continuity of all progress so that there was no room for a duality of reason and faith or of the secular and the sacred, distinguishes him from other Christian thinkers of his period, and makes it hardly surprising that they regarded him with suspicion. Unfortunately his extreme readiness to point out the follies and the corruptions of his time, and to ridicule and abuse the scholars whose mistakes he wished to correct, raised up inevitably a number of enemies who could give vent to personal antipathy under the pretext of condemning speculations and vindicating tradition.

If it is said of him, as it is said with justice of his later namesake who so remarkably resembled him, that his speculations led to little concrete result and that he talked much of experiment while doing little, the answer is plain. His improvements of the calendar, his comments upon gunpowder, his study of magnetism, his confidence that the globe could be circumnavigated, his conviction that, 'of the three ways of acquiring knowledge—authority, reasoning and experience—only the last is effective',[1] and indeed the whole quality of his mind can be cited against it. He had the real scientific spirit, combining it with a sense of the wholeness and coherence of the universe; and this sets him in a class apart. Moreover, he alone perceived what the great Dominicans, his contemporaries, strenuously denied, that, as A. E. Taylor has put it, 'there is at bottom no difference between natural and supernatural knowledge. His serious theory is that all certain knowledge is experimental, but experiment is of two kinds, experiment made on external nature, the source of certainty in natural science, and experimental acquaintance with the work of the Holy Spirit within the soul, the source of the knowledge of heavenly things which culminates in the vision of God'.[2] Dr G. Sarton in his monumental *Introduction to the History of Science* says of him that 'the majority of modern scientists feel more genuinely attracted to him than to any other medieval personality'[3] and 'Bacon was not a philosopher, but he was one of the greatest thinkers of all ages'.[4]

[1] *De Erroribus Medicorum*, quoted by E. Withington in *R. Bacon: Commemoration Essays*, p. 357.　[2] In *European Civilisation*, III, p. 827.　[3] *Op. cit.* II, pt. 2, p. 954.　[4] *Ibid.* p. 960.

It is a sad pity that his contemporary and ecclesiastical superior had none of his concern with mathematics or science. St Bonaventure had certainly a strong belief in the liberality of the grace of the Holy Spirit and shared with St Francis a readiness to find it in all men and in some measure in the whole creation. But he had also a sense of the sharp contrast between pagan and Christian. Aristotle[1] for example was to him a philosopher in darkness—one whose whole teaching, learned and impressive as it was, could not be reconciled with the heavenly wisdom. This as Gilson proves[2] is not due to his ignorance of the recovered scripts of Aristotle or even of their use by Albert the Great. It is a deliberate conviction that a Christian philosophy cannot be combined with anything so manifestly defective in its theology. If he cavilled principally at the Aristotelian doctrine of the eternity of the world, this was only one point in a wholesale condemnation. In consequence his own attitude towards nature and such studies of it as Grosseteste and Bacon or Aristotle and Albert had developed became critical and suspicious. And his suspicions were increased by his Augustinianism: for him as for Augustine the World was tainted by the Fall. St Francis had mortified himself to share its pain and had done so joyously. Bonaventure could only condemn and escape. Instead of joining in the salutation of the Song of the Sun he was compelled to resist belief in the value of the creatures for their own sake and to turn away from study and observation to the well-worn tradition of analogy and symbol. There is in him no real integration of reason and faith or of the natural and the revealed: there is no room for science in any true sense of the word.

Bonaventure was not by interest or training qualified to develop a philosophy which could deal seriously with the world of nature and history. But among his contemporaries there was one who had both the ability and the opportunity. Albert of Cologne, later known as Albert the Great, and now canonized as the patron

[1] The changing attitude to Aristotle in Paris, from his condemnation in 1209 to the condemnation of his opponents in 1624, is a theme of much interest; so is the story of the various translations of his works.   [2] Cf. above.

saint of science, had a remarkable flair for the observation and study of flora and fauna, a taste for experiment, and a mind of great activity. Born at Bollstadt in Swabia and brought up in a noble house where horse and hound and falcon were familiar to him, he finished his education in Venice and Padua where he decided to enter the Order of Preachers. After ordination he was employed in teaching, spent some time in Paris, and at Cologne received the young Thomas of Aquinum as one of his pupils. Becoming possessed of the Latin versions of most of Aristotle's works,[1] being familiar with the writings of Maimonides and Avicenna (Ibn Sina), and realizing the impossibility of neglecting or condemning Aristotelianism, the two Dominicans set themselves to christianize Aristotle's position and to use it as the main source of their philosophy. Albert along with a multitude of other writings produced a series of massive books on animals and on plants[2] in which his own observations, the teachings of Aristotle and the tradition inherited from bestiaries and herbals were set out in the form of a commentary and catalogue. Consideration of the best and final books of his *De Animalibus* in which he deals separately with the mammals, birds, fishes, serpents and worms will illustrate his quality as a naturalist and enable us to gauge the strength of the tradition which frustrated all his efforts.

Of the animals he has a good account of the Beaver and its houses, of the Stag shedding its horns, of the Badger which he had often watched, of the Marmot storing food for the winter, of the white Hares in the Alps, of the Otter and one that was tamed for hunting fish, and of the Squirrel and its drey. In all these cases and several others he is plainly writing with first-hand knowledge and genuine desire to be accurate. Of course on creatures unknown to him or fabulous he recounts the traditional tales of Pliny and Solinus and Isidore and Jorach;[3] but even so he is critical and on several occasions states roundly that the story is

---

[1] The great work of William of Moerbeke was not begun till 1268, but much had been done in versions both from Greek and Arabic since Grosseteste's complaints.

[2] Sarton's considered opinion is that these represent his best work, but that even so it is uncritical and uncreative; cf. *op. cit.* II, pt. 2, pp. 935, 938-9.

[3] For this obscure Jew cf. Sarton in *Isis*, xv, 171.

false. He includes three unicorns—the Monoceros, a strange composite which may reflect rumours of the Rhinoceros, the Onager, a wild ass with a horn in its forehead, and the Unicornis which he declares that Pompey took in triumph to Rome. He includes other fabulous creatures, the Leoncophona, the Manticora, the Onocentaurus, the Pegasus. He talks of the 'Aloy' and ascribes to it Caesar's account of the Elk which has no joints to its legs—a story which he assigns to Pliny. He asserts that the Mouse and the Mole are spontaneously generated from soil, and that mice have fallen in rain in Egypt. But, for all that, he is quite clearly convinced that what he has seen and knows is worth recording, and in recording it he stakes out a claim for observation as against tradition, for fact to replace fable.

When he deals with birds the evidence that he was a real naturalist is still more plain. Beginning with the Eagle as the king of birds and including some of the traditions about it he claims that he has collected good evidence of its habits and corrects Jorach on the strength of his personal knowledge. He then rejects all belief in the Harpy in spite of Adelinus, Solinus and Jorach; and in connexion with the tale of a one-eyed Heron roundly accused Pliny of telling many great lies. Even of the Phoenix, which ever since the days of Clement of Rome had been a sacred emblem, he writes with evident scepticism, closing his brief summary of the legend by quoting from Plato 'we must not calumniate what is written in sacred literature'. So too of the hardly less venerable tale of the Pelican he concludes with the words 'these matters are rather read in histories[1] than proved as natural by experiment'.[2]

His own most famous achievement is the rejection of the legend of the Barnacle Goose. As 'the fourth kind of Goose' he describes it, says that it is popularly supposed to be born of a tree, but adds that 'with us, a goose of this kind paired with a domestic goose and reared chickens'.[3] Under a later heading, the Barliates or Boumgans, he gives the barnacle legend in full detail and says

---

[1] He regularly uses *hystoriae* to denote fables; cf. his account of Gryphons, *De Animal.* XXIII, 46.   [2] *De Animal.* XXIII, 90 (ed. H. Stadler, II, p. 1506).   [3] *De Animal.* XXIII, 6.

'This is altogether absurd as I and many of my friends have seen them pair and lay eggs and hatch chicks'.[1] But this example of his accuracy does not stand alone. He has an admirable account of the Bittern, its immobility, its dangerous habit of attacking an intruder, and its booming—though he declares that to produce it the beak is plunged into mud. Still better is his record of the Stork, the White, which nests on buildings, and the Black which avoids them for marshes and solitude. He describes the feeding of its young, how it swallows, digests and then regurgitates the food, and its 'clappering' with its beak thrown back on to its shoulders. Yet here also he mars his story by denying that Storks migrate and insisting that in the winter they hide in caverns. So too, though he knows that Cuckoos lay in other birds' nests and that the foster parents feed the intruder gladly, he affirms that the bird winters in hollow trees, and recites the belief that, if a man when he hears the Cuckoo for the first time digs up the soil under his right foot, he will find it fatal to fleas. His descriptions when first-hand are usually excellent: the Woodcock 'roding' at dawn and dusk; the Cormorant diving for fish, nesting in trees and killing them, and sitting in the sun with its wings open; the Oriole building its nest of wool and slinging it at the end of slender branches; the Partridge feigning injury and luring intruders from its nest—'many birds large and small do this';[2] the House Sparrow which has a grey crown to its head and nests in buildings and the Tree Sparrow with a reddish-brown crown nesting in hollow branches; and the Vulture gorging itself so that it can hardly rise from the ground and hunting its prey by its sense of smell—this last an error shared by the saint's devoted follower, Charles Waterton.[3]

Along with these it must be admitted that he often repeats absurdities without protest: the Osprey is stated to have one foot

[1] *De Animal.* XXIII, 19 (Stadler, II, p. 1646). This rejection had no effect even upon scholars; thus J. C. Scaliger in his book on the *De Plantis* (Paris, 1556), p. 125, gives the barnacle legend as illustrating transmutation, and repeats it in his attack on Cardano (Paris, 1557). Cf. for the whole subject E. Heron-Allen, *Barnacles in Nature and Myth* (Oxford, 1928).

[2] As noted by Albert's contemporary, the Emperor Frederick II; cf. C. H. Haskins, *Studies in the History of Mediaeval Science*, pp. 321-2.

[3] Cf. his *Essays on Natural History* (London, 1838), pp. 17-48.

webbed and the other armed with talons; the Crane, to safeguard the flock, sets a sentinel which holds a stone in its claw to keep it awake; the 'Caladrius' predicts the course of disease, turning its head towards a sick man if he is to recover and away if he is to die. Like his contemporaries, he includes the Bat among the birds.

His other books on fishes, serpents and 'Worms'—the last a miscellaneous collection including frogs, fleas and slugs—are less impressive, being, in the main, lists copied from Avicenna, Galienus and others. In *De Aquatilibus* he notes the two Whales captured in his time, one in Friesland near Stavoren and the other in Holland beyond Utrecht, records a number of facts which he claims to have collected, and states that he is passing over what was written by men of old time because it does not agree with the evidence (XXIV, p. 1525). He had seen and handled a freshly killed Swordfish and gives a good description of it. He notes that the Pike if it catches a Perch or other scaly fish can only swallow it head first and that the Salmon bends its body till head and tail meet before it leaps, and describes how a companion touching an Electric Ray with his finger could hardly get back sensation into his arm for six months. On Serpents he notes under the Salamander (XXV, 46) that he has tried experiments with Spiders in fire. On Worms he describes very accurately (XXVI, 17) the metamorphoses of a caterpillar—egg, larva, resting period, winged state; but under Butterfly (XXVI, 28) he seems to believe that the eggs produce at once winged insects. He also gives a good account of spiders and bees, of ants and the ant-lion, but accepts the spontaneous generation of lice, fleas and clothes moths.

It is plain that he was a man with a remarkable appreciation of nature and a real delight in recording accurately what he had observed. Moreover, he had the courage to challenge tradition and reject authority. Since his canonization his memory is in real danger of being injured by the exaggerated eulogies of Catholic propagandists,[1] who ignore the plain fact that he was in most

---

[1] Thus, e.g. H. Wilms, *Albert the Great* (London, 1933), p. 14, attacks belief in evolution as proof that 'the modern scientific temper' is not only 'inimical to the faith' but 'at a level far lower than the much abused Middle Ages'.

respects a good traditionalist and strive to present him as an anticipator of modern biological discoveries. But this must not be allowed to create prejudice against him.

For indeed he was, except when his own observations compelled him to originality, a man of his own time, and prepared to accept its basic beliefs, however absurd. To study his work on plants is to realize this. The seven books are a monument to his industry; but the sixth, some two hundred and fifty pages in length, which contains his alphabetical descriptions of trees and plants, is a disappointing compilation, most of it being medical and derived from Avicenna's *Canon* II. There is very little evidence of first-hand knowledge or of the readiness to dismiss legend so manifest in his zoological work; indeed on occasion he distorts his authorities, for instance, when dealing with the date-palm he describes the female as embracing and clinging to the male branches and receiving from them not pollen but vigour.[1] The remaining books deal at length and discursively with various general questions relating to plants. Occasionally there are interesting suggestions: his note of the connexion between galls and insects on the oak,[2] and his treatment of the structure of seeds;[3] but in the main the ideas are traditional and wholly unscientific. For example, he sets out at length (in V, 7, pp. 54-64) five ways by which plants can change their species: first by improvement or deterioration of seed (a large number of examples had been given in I, 10, p. 191); secondly by cutting down (felled oaks shoot up again as aspens); thirdly when oak boughs are planted as cuttings and grow up as vines (this is said only to happen in 'Alvernia');[4] fourthly when a tree grows rotten and a different growth springs from it (as in the case of mistletoe); fifthly by grafting. A further example may be cited from VI, 22, pp. 482-92, where he discusses the three 'forms' of plants as, first, 'complexional', that is, dependent on the predominance of heat or cold or moisture or dryness;[5] then 'celestial', dependent upon astrology and the signs of the zodiac; and thirdly

---

[1] *De Plantis*, VI, 29 § 172.   [2] *Ibid.* VI, 31 § 206.   [3] *Ibid.* III, 7 §§ 58-9.
[4] Both this locality and the source of the belief seem undiscoverable.
[5] As with Avicenna and contemporary medicine generally the four 'tempers' are of prime importance to him.

'animal', the quality or hidden life of the plant, which is conditioned by its temper and sign and is apparently recognizable by its taste.

It has seemed useful to give a tolerably full account of St Albert's competence and limitations as a naturalist, partly because no critical study of this side of his work seems to have been published[1] and partly, as has been indicated, because of the significance of the failure to appreciate him. It is manifest that, in spite of his great reputation for learning and sanctity and the influence of his pupil St Thomas, his strenuous attempt to lift the study of nature out of the atmosphere of fable and falsehood was wholly unsuccessful. The tales which he had disproved were repeated as if no warning had ever been uttered; the allegories, which he had set in contrast with the facts, continued to be proclaimed as actual; his plea for first-hand evidence was wholly ignored, and the details of habit and structure which he observed and recorded and which to us seem so obviously fascinating aroused no interest and won no following. He was as helpless as his ill-used contemporary, Roger Bacon, to break through the medieval indifference to the realities of the natural world or to initiate for mankind any scientific movement. Indeed it is very noticeable that it is only in the last few years, since about 1905, that his co-religionists have paid any attention to his position as a scientist. The English version by T. A. Dixon of J. Sighart's biography, published in 1876, omits all reference to his science, includes a number of legendary miracles, and is plainly hagiology not history—just the sort of book against which he so vigorously protested. And the more recent work by S. M. Albert, published at Oxford in 1948, though less unhistorical reveals how recent and uncritical is the appreciation of his work.

If the Platonists like St Bonaventure could not escape the antithesis between natural and supernatural, the Aristotelian Dominicans made no attempt to do more than diminish its sharpness. In this they were only partly successful. St Thomas Aquinas, pupil and friend of St Albert, while sharing his deep

---

[1] H. Wilms, *op. cit.* pp. 26-43, following Stadler, gives a well-illustrated eulogy of his observations, but omits his mistakes and modernizes his explanations.

conviction that reason and faith cannot be inconsistent, yet could not free himself from the basic conviction that they deal with radically different spheres. He lays it down that *impossibile est quod de eodem sit fides et scientia;*[1] that philosophy relies upon proofs which are exclusively rational while theology depends always upon authority; and that any rational proof which contradicts a tenet of faith can only be a mere sophism.[2] It was within this framework of the total separation of nature from revelation that he had to work out his attempt to harmonize the content of the two spheres. His success in producing a logical system which is at once independent of theology and yet wholly congruous with its demands cannot blind us to the fact that this result is inescapably due to his own highly ingenious accommodation of the evidence: reason is so used and its propositions are so formulated that conflict is successfully avoided. But the basic duality remains. Authority stated and faith affirmed that the world was created in six days, just as for Roman Catholics today it is insisted on the same grounds that the Mother of Jesus was herself miraculously conceived; and against such decisions all argument must be rejected as presumptuous blasphemy. If St Thomas could not escape such a position it is not surprising that lesser men received it as axiomatic.

That neither Franciscans nor Dominicans succeeded in establishing a serious regard for the study of nature within the Church, during the century in which medieval Christendom rose to its splendid zenith, made inevitable the upheavals and revolts of Renaissance and Reformation. It is indeed interesting to note that, whereas François Picavet says of Roger Bacon: 'If the Church had followed the road along which he wished to guide her there would have been no room for a Renaissance often hostile to Christianity, nor for a Reformation wholly separated from Catholicism, nor for an open struggle and total rupture between theology, philosophy and science,'[3] Hermann Stadler says of St Albert: 'If the development of the natural sciences had proceeded

---

[1] Q. disp. de Veritate, XIV, art. 9.

[2] The position of scholasticism on this issue deserves fuller examination; the present account is based upon E. Gilson, Le Thomisme (English trans. by E. Bullough, 1929).

[3] In R. Bacon: Commemoration Essays, p. 87.

along the lines laid down by him, the wrong road taken for three centuries might have been spared them.'[1] It is useless though fascinating so to speculate. The fact is that the traditional separation between natural and supernatural was so universally accepted that no developments whether by man of genius or by man of sainthood were strong enough to shake its dominance. Albert for his part made no attempt to do so, and was content to treat the natural world as a domain outside the direct control of theology: like many another he found it possible to hold his religion and his science in separate compartments.

St Thomas, whose thought was clearer and more profound, was less easily satisfied. Yet he too, despite all his efforts to insist that both nature and revelation proceed from God, to establish the principle of analogy and to show that there was positive value in a natural philosophy, was compelled to admit that such a philosophy could not affect, though it must ultimately conform to, the conclusions of faith. The result could only be that his emphasis upon it led precisely to the conceptualism of the next two centuries when men less able to accept his axiom of the essential harmony of nature and revelation asserted the autonomy of reason and the consequent contradiction between it and religion. His attitude towards revelation must indeed, in Professor Emmet's words, 'mean that there can be no real communication on ultimate questions between the theologians and the historians, philosophers and scientists who are pursuing their own methods of inquiry unless these latter are prepared to deny that they are in any way concerned with metaphysical questions';[2] and this would inevitably be to reduce religion to superstition or to banish it into the realm of the unknowable. It is highly significant that the sequels to the great attempt of St Thomas should have been, on the one hand, the work of Duns Scotus and William Ockham, opening the way to pure theological scepticism by the admission that all doctrine lay beyond the possibility of human proof, and, on the other, the mysticism of Jean Gerson and still more that of Eckhart,

---

[1] Cf. his *Albertus Magnus als Naturforscher*, p. 9, quoted by H. Wilms, *Albert the Great* p. 46.   [2] *The Nature of Metaphysical Thinking*, p. 130.

Tauler and Suso, which being founded upon the complete other-worldliness of 'Dionysius the Areopagite' equated religious experience with the Via Negativa and the 'Cloud of Unknowing'.

The effect of the failure of this brilliant century to achieve a satisfying synthesis of science, philosophy and theology is evident not only in the religious but in the scientific interests of the next hundred and fifty years. During this period it is difficult to find any outstanding figures who carried on either the *Summa Theologiae* or the *De Animalibus*. Observation and experiment cease to be applied to the problems of biology or even medicine, and any form of natural theology is regarded as useless and suspect. The result is that only in the relatively trivial field of elementary physics[1] was there much sign of serious interest.

Of this contraction of the field, William Ockham was the symbol and the originator. His independent and logical mind, abandoning all ultimate problems as insoluble by human reason and being singularly skilful in reducing any issue to its simplest elements, fastened upon the Aristotelian doctrine of motion and subjected it to a devastating analysis and criticism. How far in so doing he was influenced by his Franciscan forbears, Grosseteste and Roger Bacon, is not easy to determine; if he lacked their sense of the profoundly religious character of such researches, he shared their strong interest in the facts, the measurements and the experiments by which knowledge could be gained. Formulating his famous 'razor' *entia non sunt multiplicanda praeter necessitatem* and consequently denying the reality of universals, he claimed that science deals only with concrete individuals which, when perceived and compared, give rise to an abstract universal in the thinking mind; and therefore like his predecessors he paid great attention to the modes of perception, to optics and the inductive method.

Though he himself taught both in Oxford and Paris it was in the latter that his work in physics was continued. One of his pupils, Jean Buridan, became rector of the university there in 1328 and

---

[1] It is notable that G. Sarton, *Introd. to Hist. of Science*, III, pts. 1 and 2, does not assign much importance to this field or much originality to the workers in it at this period.

again in 1340. Following Ockham in his criticism of Aristotelian dynamics he rejected the doctrine of movers or intelligences[1] and produced an interpretation of impetus which anticipated the later concept of inertia and promoted discussion of the problem of gravity. He seems to have been among the first to apply the data derived from the observation of small bodies in motion to the interpretation of celestial movement and the problems of astronomy; and in this connexion to have argued in favour of the daily rotation of the earth.[2] In this and in others of his conclusions it is not easy to disentangle his results from those of his younger contemporary, Nicole Oresme, who was working in Paris at the same time and on the same field.

Oresme, whom Sarton describes as 'one of the greatest mathematicians, mechanicians and economists of the Middle Ages',[3] put forward views of motion and of the rotation of the earth very similar to those of Buridan and of his colleague, Albert of Saxony. But he went far beyond them in his criticism of astrology and his attempts to get rid of magic and other marvels. Though he died a bishop, his work both in physics and economics gives little evidence of philosophical or theological interests: it is that of a scientist deeply concerned with problems affecting practical affairs and human welfare. In this respect and in his use and development of the French language he exerted a larger influence than any of his contemporaries.

But it is not easy to discover that that influence had any direct effect upon the origin or the development of the modern scientific movement. Although the work of Copernicus was in some respects anticipated by the teachers at Paris two centuries earlier, and though no doubt some small remembrance of their teaching persisted, the period of moral and intellectual decline which was the prelude to the Renaissance shows abundant evidence of the abandonment and very little of the continuation of the great medieval life and thought. Religion hardened into scepticism and tradition;

---

[1] Cf. H. Butterfield, *The Origins of Modern Science*, pp. 7-12.
[2] Sarton, *op. cit.* III, 1, p. 544 quotes his *De Coelo et Mundo* II, 1. 22 as evidence of this.
[3] *Op. cit.* III, 2, p. 1486.

the papacy lost all claim to spiritual leadership; the inquisition or, where it was not dominant, the strife between orthodox and reformers destroyed freedom and creative advance; the Church for a century or more deserved Professor A. Wolf's condemnation of it as 'the chief obstacle in the path of science'.[1] The fate of Wyclif and the Lollards in England, and of Hus and his followers in Bohemia, testified not only to the obscurantism but to the moral degradation of Christendom.

It is in fact tolerably clear that the medieval outlook with its strong sense of authority and exclusiveness within the gild and of the autonomy of each calling, having failed to attain the sort of synthesis for which Bacon and, to a less degree, Albert had laboured, had proved unable to develop any coherent and continuous scientific movement. In religion, nominalism had led to scepticism and a blind conformity; and this was so impregnably protected by the vested interests of its beneficiaries as to need no defence by intellectual or spiritual weapons. From the scandals of the Great Schism until 'the juxtaposition of the worst of the pontiffs, Alexander VI, and the weakest of the emperors, Frederic III'[2] at the end of the fifteenth century nothing sufficed to shock the world into revolt against a system so intimately bound up with the whole structure of society. The Conciliar movement failed, and with it the hope of reform. The decline of religion infected the universities. Knowledge, which as we have seen had ceased to cover large portions of the field which the early Franciscans and Dominicans had claimed for it, became either formal and lifeless or technical and practical. There was steady improvement in certain of the arts, in engineering and in craftsmanship, lenses and spectacles, the rudder and navigation, gunpowder and artillery, blast-furnaces and metal-working, mining and ventilation, clock-making and machinery; in these and other directions there were inventions of high practical and scientific importance. But medicine, although the school of Salerno had

---

[1] *History of Science, Technology and Philosophy in the Sixteenth and Seventeenth Centuries,* p. 8; he adds 'during the Middle Ages'—a demonstrable exaggeration.

[2] C. Oman, *The Sixteenth Century,* p. 30.

been succeeded by those of Montpellier and Bologna, made no progress;[1] theology, philosophy and literature were in decay and waiting for rebirth. Even in mechanical devices, where the elaborate inventions of Leonardo da Vinci in regard to puppets, fountains and automatic operators show a high degree of technical skill, there is little evidence of any real understanding of the problems of impetus, momentum and the transmission of force or of the mathematical and physical questions to which Buridan and Oresme had drawn attention. Until the rediscovery of the Graeco-Roman civilization and the influx of Greek scholars had awakened Italy to the glories of its classical inheritance, there was nothing to check the spread of moral and intellectual corruption; and when the rediscovery was made its effect at first was to make ancient paganism seem far superior to contemporary Christendom. During the half-century before the Reformation, popes and universities professedly Christian aped the licentiousness and out-did the superstitions of heathen Rome; and the Renaissance of arts and sciences found in the humanism of a Leonardo or an Erasmus its highest expression.

When Lynn Thorndike[2] asks whether this humanism retarded science or diverted attention from it, the answer may well be that science had by the fifteenth century lost so much of its scope and quality and become so restricted to technical and specialized crafts that it required the scholarship and learning of the humanists to give it a fresh inspiration and a wider range of interest. It was the work of the humanists, spread abroad by the invention of printing, that confronted the degenerate tradition of contemporary Christendom with the plain superiority of the classical and biblical literature and thus stimulated not only the reformation in religion but the revival of mathematical, astronomical, biological and medical studies. In these in spite of the praise often bestowed upon Nicholas of Cusa, as a forerunner of Copernicus, and upon

[1] For a useful account of medieval medicine, cf. D. Guthrie, *A History of Medicine*, pp. 102-30.

[2] In his chapter, 'Later Mediaeval Science', in *Science and Thought in the Fifteenth Century*, pp 12 ff., he seems to attach too much value to P. Duhem, against whose exaggerations Sarton gives a needed warning, *op. cit.* III, pp. 146 n. and 1432.

Peurbach and Müller,[1] the mathematicians, there seems to have been almost no progress until the beginning of the sixteenth century; and what there was came not from the scientists but from the scholars. It is very significant that, for example, in botany the first 'modern' herbalists, William Turner and his contemporaries, ascribe the beginnings of botanical science to men of letters, Ermolao Barbaro[2] the Venetian, Niccolo da Lonigo[3] of Ferrara and Filippo Beroaldo[4] whose commentaries upon Pliny started the long-sustained business of identifying the plants named by him and other classical authors.

This matter of exact nomenclature and identification is one of the plainest differences between the naturalists of the Middle Ages and those of the sixteenth and seventeenth centuries. For St Albert it is unimportant to give a precise definition to any species that he may name.[5] On many occasions, as for example with the 'boumgans'[6] or the Oriole 'which the Germans call widewali' [modern Dutch, *Wielewaal*],[7] he gives the contemporary equivalent of the name derived from Pliny or the tradition; but neither he nor any of his contemporaries except Roger Bacon is seriously concerned with accuracy in this respect. With his later successors, Turner or Gesner, or indeed the men of the seventeenth century, Morison or Ray, elaborate proof of the real identity of the plant called 'laus tibi'[8] or of Pontic Wormwood had become central to their interest. Their task is plainly stated by Julius Caesar Scaliger in the preface to his edition[9] of the *De Plantis* (falsely attributed to Aristotle). They must at all costs discover the modern equivalent of the species hallowed by the tradition as ingredients in a

---

[1] For criticism of Müller cf. Thorndike, *op. cit.* pp. 133–50.

[2] Friend of Linacre in Rome; his edition of Pliny was published in 1492.

[3] Also a friend of Linacre; his *De Erroribus Plinii* was published in 1492.

[4] His edition of Pliny was published at Parma, 1476.

[5] Even among his birds many are unidentifiable; Stadler who supplies identifications is often palpably wrong.

[6] *De Animal.* p. 1446 and above p. 67.   [7] *Ibid.* p. 1505.

[8] Cf. Turner, *Libellus*, p. B iii and my *English Naturalists*, p. 63.

[9] Published in Paris, 1556. Scaliger notes as difficulties (1) that plants differ in different places and seasons; (2) that writers use names without descriptions; (3) that descriptions are careless; (4) that classifications are faulty; (5) that herbalists resent all correction of their traditions.

medicine or predestined to a use and must fix its identity by accurate description and classification; they spent a vast amount of time and ingenuity upon the task. Hence came not only an intense precision as to the particularity of each typical specimen, but a discipline in the accurate interpretation of ancient records and in the detailed comparison of the living object with its supposed definition. This discipline enabled nomenclature to be reasonably standardized, but mere description would hardly have sufficed unless it had been accompanied by the admirable engravings and woodcuts which fixed the identification of most European plants, fishes and birds by the middle of the sixteenth century. Fuchs's herbal, Salviani's fishes and Gesner's animals and birds made it possible for any intelligent student to name what he saw in these departments with some confidence, and so to proceed to the comparisons and records necessary for classification. Such taxonomy, the proper naming and arrangement of flora and fauna, was a most important part of early science, not only as encouraging exact observation and discrimination but as providing the necessary material for further and more important research.

V

GESNER AND THE AGE OF TRANSITION

In the natural emphasis upon astronomical and cosmological studies and the speculative thought to which they gave rise, it has been customary to identify the progress of science with an apostolic succession stretching from Copernicus, Tycho Brahe, Kepler and Bruno[1] to Galileo and from them by way of Descartes and the mathematicians to Isaac Newton. To this 'Great Church' attempts have been made to attach men like Gilbert and even Boyle as well as more obvious candidates like Paracelsus and Huygens.

That such a scheme looks attractive when drawn out in coloured chalks on a blackboard is perhaps sufficient evidence of its over-simplification. Its popularity is of course due to the subsequent development of the scientific movement—to the triumph of mechanical methods and techniques in the eighteenth century which produced the industrial age and to the restriction of the New Philosophy, at that same time, to the mathematical and quantitative field. To read the origins of science in terms so limited is as unhistorical as to interpret the history of the earliest Church as if its only concern was the preparation for the Nicene creed. In the sixteenth and seventeenth centuries it is obvious that the scientific revolution owed more to the botanists and zoologists and to the doctors and explorers than to the astronomers.

An alternative scheme, which in these Marxist days has many advocates, would fasten upon economic developments as the chief

[1] Giordano Bruno, as Mrs D. W. Singer's delightful book on him (New York, 1950) demonstrates, is 'in no sense a man of science': his martyrdom for proclaiming the infinity of the universe and the plurality of worlds has won for him a place in the succession.

stimulus to the sciences. That the stored experience of the medieval craftsmen and its application to problems of mining, irrigation and manufacture, when employed in connexion with the exploration and opening up of the Americas, gave an immense impetus to the study and manipulation of natural resources is plainly a factor of great importance in the story of the making of the modern world. The pulling together of the isolated and proprietary skills of the medieval gilds and the consequent and very speedy expansion of technical science are events of great significance for civilization. But to assign to this the intellectual achievements of the New Philosophy is only possible to the sort of mentality that can explain Newton's *Principia* in terms of his employment at the Mint.[1] There is no very obvious economic value in the Copernican hypothesis nor did its author derive any encouragement from the desire to promote navigation. The revolution that produced the modern world and the important and characteristic element in it that we call the scientific movement are due neither to the astronomers nor to the technicians but to something much more universal and many-sided.

It would be easy to describe this revolution in generalities—to speak of the influence of the clerks who first in Italy rediscovered the splendid achievements of the Graeco-Roman classics, and set themselves to recall men from the fables and fancies of the bestiaries to the sanities and science of Aristotle's *Historia Animalium* or Theophrastus's records of plants; to point out the accuracy of observation displayed by artists like Leonardo and Albrecht Dürer and their influence in promoting the anatomical pictures in Vesalius's *Fabrica*[2] and the illustrations of Brunfels's herbal; to indicate the importance of the printing press in enabling the rapid publication of the new studies; and to draw attention to the exploration and discovery going on in every field of human interest from religion to geography.

But it will be more revealing to examine somewhat more

[1] Cf. above, p. 9 n., and B. Hessen, in *Science at the Cross Roads*.
[2] The artist of Vesalius's earlier *Tabulae* was a Belgian pupil of Titian, Jan Stephan van Calcar; and he has usually been credited also with the plates in the *Fabrica*. This is disputed by C. Singer and C. Rabin, *A Prelude to Modern Science* (Cambridge, 1946), pp. iii, x, xi.

closely the actual circumstances of the group of pioneers who were mainly responsible for the astonishing progress of biological studies in the second quarter of the sixteenth century—the group which included the German fathers of botany and had its finest product in Conrad Gesner of Zürich, who more than any other man is in his own person the symbol and instrument of the transition from the medieval to the modern attitude towards nature.

It is a curious and striking fact that the three first herbals which deserve to be called botanical should all have appeared in the same area and within a dozen years, and that their authors should all have been ardent followers of the Reformation.[1] Otto Brunfels, who was born at Mainz, entered a monastery, then left it and taught for nine years at Strassburg where he published his *Herbarum Vivae Eicones* in 1530; Jerome Bock, also destined for the cloister, became Lutheran minister at Hornback and published his *New Kreütter Büch* also at Strassburg in 1539; and Leonhart Fuchs educated at Erfurt and Ingolstadt, converted to Lutheranism and practising medicine at Tübingen, published his *De Historia Stirpium* in 1542 at Basel where Erasmus had completed his New Testament and spent the last twenty years of his life. These three men like their younger contemporary, our own William Turner,[2] had seen and studied the contrast in religion between the ancient lore of the New Testament and the current tradition of the medieval Church: they had found the same contrast in botany between the plain descriptions of plants and their uses in Theophrastus and Dioscorides and the mythical and legendary tales and unrecognizable illustrations of the *Ortus Sanitatis*; and they had set themselves to compare the various species familiar to them with those described by the classics. The difficulty of the task (which they did not know enough of plant distribution fully to recognize) did not daunt them, although the flora of the eastern Mediterranean and of the upper Rhine are not very similar. They were content to debate at

---

[1] As has often been demonstrated, e.g. by A. de Candolle, *Histoire des Sciences et des Savants*, and by R. K. Merton, 'Science in Seventeenth-Century England', *Osiris* IV, pp. 490-5, Protestants greatly outnumber Catholics in scientific societies and achievements both absolutely and still more in proportion to population.

[2] For Turner cf. my *English Naturalists*, pp. 48-137.

length the precise classical representative of the famous simple called 'Poly Mountain' or the modern equivalent of the equally famous 'Abrotanum Romanum'. And if the value of their results was not great, it was at least recompensed by the fact that they all included illustrations of the plants which they strove to identify and for these pictures were able to obtain the help of artists and engravers of quite splendid ability.

It is indeed the coincidence of these authors with such remarkable artists that is the secret of their permanent worth. Mrs Arber is certainly right in claiming that Brunfels's book should more properly be associated with the name of Hans Weiditz.[1] The trio, Albrecht Meyer who drew the plants, Heinrich Füllmaurer who copied them on wood and Veit Rudolf Speckle 'the best engraver in Strassburg',[2] gave Fuchs's book an outstanding excellence. When Bock's work went into a second edition with drawings added by David Kandel also of Strassburg it gained greatly in value.[3] No one having access to such illustrations could fail to identify the species depicted in them far more easily then from dried speciments; and the printed book could be multiplied and transported far more quickly than herbaria.[4]

The fourth of these German fathers, Valerius Cordus, who graduated at Marburg and taught at Wittenberg, brings us into direct touch with Gesner; for Cordus, who died suddenly in Rome in 1544, left behind him the script of his *Historia Stirpium* which Gesner edited at Rihel's request, and which was published at Strassburg in 1561. Of this, many of the pictures were those already used in Bock's book; but Gesner 'added many rare ones

[1] His original drawings in colour have in many cases been preserved in Felix Platter's herbarium and now published in facsimile; cf. A. Arber, *Herbals*, p. 206. He worked at Augsburg and later at Strassburg, was a Lutheran and published portraits of the Reformers in 1523.

[2] So Fuchs in Preface. In spite of W. Blunt, *The Art of Botanical Illustration*, pp. 49-54, Arber's verdict that Fuchs's illustrations are 'the high-watermark' will probably stand.

[3] Gesner was asked by Rihel the publisher to produce a further edition with more pictures and was collecting them; cf. C. Gesner to Fuchs, Oct. 1556, in *Epistulae Medicinales*, III, p. 119.

[4] Books containing dried plants seem to have been first made by Luca Ghini of Bologna. He taught John Falconer and William Turner to make them in 1540. Peter Turner, William's son, sent a 'herbarium' of English plants to Jean Bauhin in 1575.

from his own store and from those sent to him by Johann Kentmann of Dresden'[1] one of his medical friends.

It is no accident that all this output of scientific work should have come from a comparatively restricted area. For in this area, as R. H. Murray has pointed out, Erasmus exercised more influence than Luther.[2] The temper of Alsace and German-speaking Switzerland was liberal and generous; its religious leaders had a breadth of vision and a quality of culture different alike from the typical Lutherans and the strict Calvinists. Luther had no sort of sympathy with science and could dismiss Copernicus with a reference to Joshua; to him humanism was merely pagan; under his influence there was no room for science or natural philosophy. But Erasmus keeping in close touch from his home in Basel with the scholars and reformers of his neighbourhood helped to give to them the sort of character which he himself shared with Sir Thomas More and for which a love of plants and animals was an essential part of religion. Zürich was peculiarly well placed to be the home of a great naturalist. Ulrich Zwingli, one of Erasmus's disciples and devoted admirers, was a scholar with a real knowledge, not only of classical and scriptural literature, but also of the world of nature,[3] who saw the continuity and wholeness of experience as an essential part of his religion, one from whom his successor Heinrich Bullinger and the band of Swiss reformers at Zürich gained a quality not found at that time anywhere else in Christendom. To this circle Conrad Gesner belonged.

Gesner, who might well be put forward as yet another candidate for the title of 'the first modern man', has been curiously neglected in recent years by the historians of science. This is in part due to the general neglect of the biologists as compared with the astronomers, and partly to the foolish and wholly unjust title applied to him of 'the German Pliny'.[4] In consequence of this he has been written down, by those who can never have read his life or any of his

---

[1] Cf. Preface by Gesner to *Hist. Stirp.* and his letter to Kentmann, March 1555 in *Ep. Med.* IV, 5.   [2] *Erasmus and Luther*, p. 141.

[3] Cf. especially his *De Providentia Dei* in *Opera* IV, p. 92; cf. also S. Simpson, *Life of U. Zwingli*, pp. 23-5.

[4] Given to him by Cuvier, who should have known better, and elaborated by Nordenskiöld, *History of Biology*, p. 94.

books, as a mere compiler, heaping up an uncriticized mass of folklore and extracts roughly classified under the common names of animals, birds, fishes or reptiles in alphabetical order but constituting nothing more than a 'pandect' or compendium of traditional knowledge; whereas in fact he had not only an immense learning derived from books and from his voluminous correspondence,[1] but had himself seen, handled and watched a very large number of species.

To give an instance, in the third volume of the *Historia*, published at Zürich in 1555 and devoted to birds, six different Tits are clearly distinguished, including both Cole and Marsh; Fieldfare, Redwing (each noted as a winter visitor), Missel Thrush and Song Thrush are separated; Glossy Ibis, Black Stork, Spoonbill, Wood Ibis (*Comatibis eremita*), Curlew, Stone-Curlew, Avocet, Cormorant, three Grebes (*Podiceps cristatus, ruficollis,* and *nigricollis*), Bean Goose, and a number of different Ducks are described at first hand and with details of locality and habits; and many are the result of his very large circle of friends: Blackcock from Giles Tschudi of Glarus, the pupil of Zwingli; Stilt sent by Jacques d'Aléchamps, the botanist of Lyons; Nutcracker from a friend at Chur; Roller 'captured in the year 1561'; Waxwing from a painter at Strassburg presumably during the great invasion in 1552 which he records; Golden Plover, picture sent by G. Rondelet of Montpellier—'it has no back toe';—Purple Gallinule, 'Johann Culmann sent it to me from Montpellier by the kindness of G. Rondelet'; and Lämmergeier sent from the Rhaetian Alps. Here is a note on the Cuckoo that proves his worth: 'The Cuckoo does not make a nest but lays in the nests of others especially of hedgesparrows and ground-larks. . . . It lays one egg and does not itself incubate it. . . . When the alien chick has been hatched it is said to eject the others so that they perish' (*Hist. Animal.* III, p. 348). If we add that more than 130 of the species described are illustrated with recognizable and often excellent pictures,[2] the value of the

---

[1] In the Preface to *Historia Animalium*, I, he lists fifty-two scholars who have helped him by letters or discussion.

[2] The only artist named is Lucas Schau of Strassburg 'a very careful painter and fowler', who supplied twelve pictures of various Sandpipers.

book is obvious. And birds were only one, and by no means the chief, of his subjects.

Indeed the amazing fact about Gesner is the range and scale of his work. Born in Zürich in 1516 of poor parents and one of a large family, he lost his father, fighting alongside of Zwingli in the battle of Zug, when he was only fifteen. Already a pupil of Thomas Platter, Theodore Buchmann (Bibliander), Oswald Geiss-hüssler (Myconius), and Peter von Frauenfeld (Dasypodius), he was housed for three years by J. J. Amman and went first to Strassburg where he studied Hebrew, and then to Bourges and Paris. Returning to Strassburg in December 1534, he lived for a time with Martin Bucer, but in 1536 went back to Zürich and married. Encouraged by his uncle Johann Frick who had already interested him in plants, he devoted himself to Greek and published his first book, a Greek-Latin dictionary. In the same year, 1537, he was studying medicine at Basel, but later moved to a school at Lausanne where he taught Greek for three years, continued his medical training and wrote a variety of books. In 1540 he paid a short visit to Montpellier and returned thence to Zürich where he received a visit from William Turner. He took his M.D. at Basel in 1541, but settled down in Zürich to his medical practice and to his scientific studies, making his home there for the rest of his life. In the summer of 1544 he spent a month at Venice studying the fishes and other marine creatures brought into its markets and obtaining some fifty pictures for his book. In 1545 he published his *Bibliotheca Universalis*, and in 1548 the first volume of the *Historia Animalium*. In 1551 he travelled down the Rhine. In 1552 he was visited by Girolamo Cardano, then on his way to Scotland. In 1555 he was made professor at Zürich and explored Mount Pilatus. In 1559 he visited the Emperor Ferdinand at Augsburg and made friends with three of his doctors, Johann Crato von Kraftheim, Adolf Occo and Achilles Pirmin Gasser, with all of whom he kept up thereafter a regular correspondence. In 1561 he went on a botanizing expedition with Jean Bauhin[1] to

[1] There are many references to the plants then found in J. Bauhin, *Hist. Plant. Universalis*, cf. especially, II, pp. 349, 352, 376, 926; III, pp. 20 (*Arnica montana*), 854 (*Androsace chamaeiasme*).

the Rhaetian Alps, Bormio, the Val Tellina and Montario,[1] nearly down to Venice. In 1562 he printed the list of the books that he had already published, some sixty-seven in all, and the names of eighteen others still being written. In 1563 he began to press on vigorously with the collection of coloured pictures painted from life for his History of Plants. In 1565 he published his book on fossils with its picture of the fish from Eisleben.[2] In December of that year, when there was a severe outbreak of plague, he caught the disease and died of it in his Museum, just after Thomas Penny had come to him from England, and while he and Caspar Wolf were working at the material for the books on insects and on plants.

Gesner's early years reflect the typical activities of a scholar of the Renaissance. A dictionary, a *bibliotheca* giving particulars of every known author in Latin, Greek and Hebrew, a number of editions and commentaries of little known medical and literary classics, these and a teacher's duties would seem to be his career. Alongside of this he had strong theological and religious interests: from boyhood he had been intimate with the Swiss reformers Bucer, Bullinger, Conrad and Samuel Pellican, Benoit Marti, Johann Wirt and Theodore Zwinger; at one time his life's work must have seemed to be the ministry. Then he developed his medical interests, visited several great schools of medicine, and began his long series of medical letters which have been published in two volumes. With this he combined the production of his pandects, the thousands of pages in which he collected all the available information on animals, reptiles, birds, fishes and amphibians, classified it, criticized it, added to it his own evidence and records, and the pictures which he had spared no effort to collect or to have painted. Here was his real life's work, the laying of a sound foundation for zoological studies. He proposed as we have seen to follow it with a history of plants on the same scale when he had finished the insects.

It might seem that a life so full and for many years so penurious would have made of him a shrivelled recluse, a bookworm, a

---

[1] The reputed seat of the Scaliger family.
[2] *Palaeoniscus freieslebeni* from the Permian Copper Slate; cf. *De Rer. Fossil. Fig.*, p. 162.

pedant. Hear then what he has to say to his friend Jacques Vogel on the love of mountains: 'I have determined, as long as God gives me life, to ascend one or more mountains every year when the plants are at their best—partly to study them, partly for exercise of body and joy of mind. . . . I say then that he is no lover of nature who does not esteem high mountains very worthy of profound contemplation. It is no wonder that men have made them the homes of the gods, of Pan and the nymphs. . . . I have a passionate desire to visit them.'[1] Such sentiments are familiar enough to us; but in Gesner's time and for a century later 'horrid' was the least derogatory epithet bestowed on them; and the religious found it hard to explain how a benevolent deity could have created anything so wasteful, so terrifying, so hideous.

But Gesner is not merely in advance of his time in his love of the Alps. We can get a clear appreciation of his critical alertness and freedom from traditional mythology in his famous letter to our own John Caius, dated 29 August 1561 and written just after his return from the Val Tellina. Caius was then President of the Royal College of Physicians, and Master of his College in Cambridge. He had edited the works of Galen,[2] but had also produced the first clinical account of the sweating sickness.[3] He may stand for an enlightened but fairly typical representative of that time of transition. As a friend of Gesner he was in the habit of sending to him his own drawings of the animals and birds that came into the London markets or menagerie, among them one which he insisted upon calling a Horse-deer. It is in fact a young female elk plainly recognizable from the picture; and Caius admits in his accompanying letter that the Norwegian sailors called it an elk but adds 'in this they are obviously mistaken; for the real elk has legs that cannot bend'—he is referring of course to the famous passage in Caesar's Gallic War[4] in which the story told by others[5] about the

---

[1] Preface to *Libellus de Lacte*, 1541, printed with French translation in *Josias Simler et les Origines de l'Alpinisme* (Grenoble, 1904), by W. A. B. Coolidge.

[2] For his treatment of a doctor charged with imputing error to Galen, cf. my *English Naturalists*, p. 140.

[3] Almost certainly influenza; cf. R. H. Major, *Classic Descriptions of Disease*, p. 211.

[4] *B.G.* VI, 27.   [5] E.g. Aristotle, *H.A.* II, i, 498.

elephant and how it sleeps by leaning against a tree is transferred to the elk. Caius like the vast majority of his contemporaries gave to Caesar what they gave to Galen—a more than biblical inerrancy.[1] To this Gesner replies[2] that Pliny says of the 'machlis' from Scandinavia what Caesar says of the elk and others of the elephant; 'but my dear Caius no one doubts today that both elk and elephant bend at the knees like every other quadruped. Pliny based his report on hearsay, and false hearsay at that.' It is refreshing to find a scholar of the Renaissance ready to refute the classical authorities on the strength of factual observations and analogies.

The fact is that Gesner had begun to do what most scholars did not venture upon until a century after his time—to break away from the authorities and study nature in the field for himself. Caspar Wolf, in the *Hyposchesis* or promise concerning Gesner's *Historia Plantarum* which he sent to the Emperor's doctor, Johann Crato von Kraftheim, in March 1566, has recorded that Gesner had been collecting pictures for it for twenty years; that he had got some 1500; and that 150 of these he had painted with his own hand, 'pictures perfected and elaborated with art and industry ... drawn to scale, reduced by a regular ratio; parts of them, flower or seed or fruit or leaf, enlarged and in some cases opened up'. These were the gatherings of his exploration of the lakes and his ascents of the mountains,[3] his expedition to Mount Pilatus in 1555 of which he published a record,[4] his month's journey to Bormio, Val Tellina, and the south-eastern mountains in 1561, his discovery of *Swertia perennis* on the Bockmattli pass in 1564, and of the expeditions of his friends, Johann Schmid (Fabricius), pastor of Chur, who made an ascent of Calanda, five miles to the north-west and sent him pictures of plants from it,[5] and Benoit Marti

[1] Lest we sneer at Caius we may note that Leonardo da Vinci in his Bestiary tells the same tale of the elk; cf. E. McCurdy, *Notebooks of Leonardo da Vinci*, II, p. 480.

[2] *Ep. Med.* pp. 133b–136b, one of his longest letters.

[3] In 1563 he wrote to A. P. Gasser: 'For the pictures I collect living plants from meadows, fields, paths, vineyards, gardens, hills, mountains, woods, streams, rivers, marshes, lakes, shores and every other locality. I have swum these very days in our lake to get plants.' *Ep. Med.* p. 276.   [4] *Descriptio Montis Fracti iuxta Lucernam* (Zürich, 1555).

[5] Cf. Gesner's letter to him, *Ep. Med.* I, iii, p. 19; 'I cannot praise the skill of your painter and prefer that in future you send me plants fresh if possible, or dried in a book: my painters can make dried specimens look more alive than yours can fresh ones.'

(Aretius), who discovered plants on Niesen and the Stockhorn.[1] It is a calamity that though a few of these pictures were published in 1759-60 by C. C. Schmiedel[2] and though part of the collection was recently discovered at Erlangen[3] they were in effect lost to science at the time when they would have been invaluable.

In considering this group of Strassburg scientists the first obvious feature that they have in common is their religion. All four of them, and at least one of their artists, like our own William Turner, are enthusiastic disciples of the Reformation. It would plainly be untrue to say that the biological sciences grew only on Protestant soil: to do so would be to ignore the great contribution made by the universities of northern Italy, especially Padua, and of Montpellier. But the strongholds of Catholicism, Spain,[4] Rome and Paris, did in fact produce hardly any outstanding scientists in the sixteenth century; and until the rise of the Society of Jesus, orthodox circles were in the main unfriendly.

The reason for this is worth consideration. It is plainly too easy to ascribe it solely to the contrast between the natural and the supernatural, or to the power of tradition and legendary lore. Examination of the evidence suggests a deeper cause. The reformers based their position upon that 'comparison between the old learning and the new' as Turner called it, which Urbanus Regius had expounded and which led them as it had led the scholars of the Renaissance to the enthusiastic advocacy of the literature of the classical period. They attacked Catholic tradition on the ground of its contrast with the New Testament just as their colleagues in medicine or botany attacked the *Ortus Sanitatis* in the name of Dioscorides and Pliny. But there is more in it than this. Catholicism had been a religion of authority: only the ecclesiastics were entitled to expound its teaching or to understand

---

[1] Published by Gesner at the end of his edition of Val. Cordus's *Historia Stirpium*.

[2] C. Wolf, Gesner's executor, sold them to J. Camerarius. They were found, according to A. Haller, *Epist.* II, p. 236, in the Volckamer museum at Nuremberg and thence came into the possession of C. J. Trew for whom Schmiedel had some published.

[3] Cf. A. Arber, *Herbals*, pp. 111-13.

[4] Only Amatus Lusitanicus, a Jew from Spain, dealt with European plants; Turner called him 'Mattioli's ape'; and of Mattioli both Turner and Gesner had a low opinion. Cf. *Ep. Med.* I, p. 76.

its mysteries; it was for the layman to hear and obey. When Luther raised the standard of revolt, it was upon the right of every Christian to study the open Bible that he based his policy. The 'Way' was not a secret path but an open road on which 'wayfaring men, though fools, would not err'. Sound knowledge was not the perquisite of a class, it was available for all; the reign of prescription and privilege was over; the common man had the right to learn and to study for himself.

Nor was the challenge thus delivered confined to the Scriptures or to religion. Medieval gilds, whether merchant or craft gilds, each had their own secrets; each, like the executioner's trade in *Saint Joan*, was a skilled mystery; members of the gild were pledged to practise its particular and strictly defined trade and maintain its special prerogatives; and apprenticeship was in fact a closely guarded initiation into a privileged society. This hierarchical ordering of the separate callings and professions is one chief reason for the failure of the Middle Ages to produce a combined scientific movement or indeed to apply the discoveries of one field of work to the problems of another.[1] For it was the chief business of each 'mystery' to prevent any encroachment upon its territory and to repel all attempts to learn or pass on to others its secret processes. It was not until the success of Luther that a similar readiness to challenge the secretiveness and to divulge the professional techniques of other callings manifested itself, and then only in regions already familiar with the reformers' claim to unseal the sources of knowledge.

A clear example of this revolt against professional secrecy can be seen in the preface of William Turner's first *Herbal*. He thinks it necessary to apologize at some length for the issue of his book in the vernacular; and he does so with his customary vigour. After explaining the incompleteness of his work he says: 'Others will thinke it unwysely done, and agaynst the honor of my art that I professe, and agaynst the common profit, to set out so much knowledge of Physick in Englyshe: for now (say they) every man ... nay every old wyfe will presume not without the mordre of

---

[1] Cf. above, pp. 59, 76.

many, to practise Physick.' He replies with a fine defence of the freedom of knowledge, beginning with a claim that, as it is, many practitioners cannot in fact read Pliny in the original or Dioscorides in a Latin translation and consequently cannot identify the herbs used in their drugs any more accurately than the old wives or grocers who sell them. An English herbal will teach the doctors; and if laymen read it the danger of misuse is no greater now than when Galen wrote in Greek for a Greek-speaking world. 'If Dioscorides and Galen were no hynderers from the study of lyberall sciences then am I no hynderer wryting unto the English my countremen an Englysh Herball.' Turner would evidently have agreed with the unkind suggestion recently made that the medical profession can only expect to be treated as genuinely scientific when its members cease to write their prescriptions in bad Latin and an illegible script.

Gesner, though throughout his life an ardent supporter of the Reformation and a close friend of Bullinger and other leaders, was saved from narrowness or bitterness alike by the generosity and friendliness of his own character and by the liberal atmosphere of his upbringing. Zwingli under whose ascendancy in Zürich he spent his boyhood is justly described by A. F. Pollard as 'a combination of the humanist, the theologian and the radical, the most modern in mind of all the reformers'.[1] Bullinger, who succeeded him, was at once more orthodox and more pacific, and did his uttermost not only to maintain the union of protestants but to befriend the exiles and visitors who came to see him from Britain and all the west of Europe; and Bullinger as his tributes to Gesner immediately after his death demonstrate[2] regarded him with admiration and deep affection. Moreover, Basel with which he was intimately connected was at this time a great centre of religious, artistic, literary and cultural activity, eminent for its university and for its publishing houses, for its hospitality to strangers and for the famous men associated with it. There

---

[1] *Cambridge Modern History*, II, p. 208.

[2] Cf. Bullinger's letters to Johann Schmid of Chur and to his own son in J. Hanhart, *Lebensbeschreibung C. Gesners*, pp. 281–3.

Erasmus had published his Greek New Testament and made his home for the last twenty years of his life. There John Calvin found refuge and published his *Institutio*; but when, seventeen years later, he burned Servetus, Basel showed itself akin to Erasmus rather than to him. It is typical of Gesner that the strongest protest against this cruelty came from his intimate friend[1] Nicolaus Zurkinden, the chief secretary of Berne, and the most effective public defence of tolerance came from the professor of Greek in Basel University.

The tolerance of Gesner's own temper, indeed the rare sweetness and generosity of his disposition, is testified to by the tributes of his correspondents and manifested repeatedly in his letters. The Emperor had said of him in 1559, 'Gesnerus est tota probitas';[2] and every one of his contemporaries pays homage to his integrity and piety, his modesty and friendliness, his monumental learning, his energy and versatility, his patience and courage. Our own countrymen, John Caius, the Catholic, and William Turner, the Protestant, alike speak of him with reverence.

That he deserved such praise is evident from his attitude towards the most queer-tempered of the botanists of the time, Pierandrea Mattioli, the Italian. In 1557 the Prussian botanist, Melchior Wieland, then studying at Padua had written to him[3] a long denunciation of Mattioli and a violent criticism of his work. To this Gesner had replied, admitting that the book had in it many faults, urging in excuse that it was a first edition and that the errors would be corrected later, advising Wieland to send Mattioli a list of emendations and begging him if he must criticize to castigate the mistakes but not the author—advice badly needed in those days but, unfortunately, disregarded. Writing in 1563 to his friend, Dr Johann Kentmann of Dresden, and commenting upon a picture in Mattioli's book in which he had combined the root of one plant with the leaves of another, he admits that this and others of the pictures are deceptive; but he adds 'This is for your

---

[1] Cf. Gesner's letter to him, *Ep. Med.* pp. 130-1.
[2] Cf. J. Hanhart, *op. cit.* p. 185.
[3] These letters are printed in Wieland (Guilandinus), *De Stirpibus* (Padua, 1558).

private ear: I take no pleasure in stirring up a hornet's nest publicly'.[1]

To mention his letters is to indicate the second great circumstance which promoted the development of a scientific movement. In medieval times the exclusiveness of the gilds was not counteracted by the activities and correspondence either of skilled amateurs or of independent professionals. The learned world cared little for technology except in medicine, and the investigators of nature, alchemists, astrologers and herbalists, derived their emoluments from their reputation for esoteric lore. There were available no organs of publicity; and students of such subjects lived lonely lives and were not encouraged to put their secrets upon paper. We who appreciate the enormous importance of our journals, conferences and associations can realize how completely their absence inhibited the possibility of any orderly progress in science. That the work of Albert the Great, for all his learning and prestige, left almost no influence upon man's knowledge of nature or that Roger Bacon's brilliant experimenting led to nothing but suppression and embitterment ceases to be surprising when we understand the isolation of their efforts.

It was one of the important achievements of the Renaissance that it restored to the learned world the habit of letter-writing in the mode of Cicero and of the younger Pliny, letter-writing upon subjects of technical and professional interest and in a form suitable for publication. Originating in Italy the practice spread with the New Learning. Latin, the universal language of the learned, was the appropriate medium—on paper the problem of pronunciation which has usually made the Englishman unintelligible did not arise—and the problem of postage though difficult could be overcome by the agency of merchant adventurers. Big financial houses like the Fuggers, big printers like Fröben or Froschauer were sending regular mail-bags from market to market and from land to land; and private correspondence was readily accepted by them for transmission. It was not always easy: Gesner, for example, in maintaining his contact with his friend

---

[1] *Ep. Med.* ap. J. Hanhart, *op. cit.* p. 329.

and helper, Johann Kentmann of Dresden, sent sometimes by Froschauer's agent to the market at Frankfurt, and at others to his friend Jerome Herold, the Leipzig doctor, then living at Nuremberg; and Kentmann replied either by the same routes or through another doctor, Laurence Hiel of Jena. Losses were not infrequent, and delays were inevitable. But, as Gesner's case abundantly proves, even his distant correspondents, Parkhurst or Caius in England, Johann Brettschneider (Placotomus) at Danzig, Cosmos Holtzach at Schaffhausen, or Taddeo Duno at Locarno received and sent letters with confidence and regularity.

The sheer volume of this correspondence for a man so busy with literary work and medicine is sufficiently amazing. The fraction of it published by Caspar Wolf after his death constitutes a massive volume and even so is limited to a short term of years and a portion only of his friends. There is nothing earlier than 1550 and the majority date from the last five years of his life; nor is there anything in it to Bullinger, nor to his English friends except the one long letter to Caius, nor to Rondelet or D'Aléchamps or any of his French friends in Montpellier or Lyons or Paris, nor to Herold of Leipzig to whom he dedicated his edition of Valerius Cordus, nor to Andreas Schadeovius of Cracow to whom he dedicated his book on fossils, nor to Petrus Coudenberg, the apothecary of Antwerp,[1] nor to Joachim Camerarius,[2] nor to De l'Ecluse who wrote to him in 1565 describing his Spanish journey.[3] Yet of the letters actually published,[4] and dated between January 1564 and December 1565, there are no less than 119, all different and addressed to nineteen different correspondents, some of them several printed pages in length. In addition to these it was his custom to compose at intervals a 'scheda' or circular, duplicated by his secretary and enclosed with the personal documents. The influence of such letters, covering as they do a very wide range of

---

[1] Cf. Gesner, *De Rer. Fossil. Fig.* (Zürich, 1565), pp. 133, 163b, 169.

[2] Cf. Gesner to Crato, 17 April 1564, *Ep. Med.* p. 20.

[3] Cf. Gesner to B. Marti, 24 Nov. 1565, *Ep. Med.* p. 121b.

[4] In three books: C. Bauhin, *Gesneri Epistolae* (Basel, 1591); C. Wolf, *Ep. Med.* I–III (Zürich, 1577); J. Hanhart, *Ep. Med.* IV (Winterthur, 1824); and in two articles by G. Rath in *Gesnerus* vii and viii. For list cf. Note IV below, pp. 206–8.

interest and dealing frankly in advice and criticism, must have been very great. It made available to 'his friends in France, Italy, England, Germany and Poland' masses of knowledge which until then would have been jealously guarded, and encouraged a full exchange both of experiences and of material. It laid down lines for study and research which without breaking contact with the past challenged any slavish obedience to its authority and pointed away from the tradition to the observation of the actual facts and to an experimental verification of their evidence. Those who claim, and rightly claim, that the scientific movement as a New Philosophy owed its origin to Francis Bacon and the seventeenth century will be constrained to admit that, in his sense of the unity of all knowledge, of the need for co-operative effort and the accurate sifting of all available data, Conrad Gesner anticipated and by his heroic labours enabled the later developments.

That these developments had begun before the turn of the century is clear. Gesner's colleague and pupil, Jean Bauhin, and his brother Gaspard were, according to John Ray, by far the greatest of his own predecessors in botany. Gesner's English friend, Thomas Penny, who visited him just before his death, carried on his work on insects and, if his partner and executor Thomas Mouffet had been less unworthy, would have given to us a book as good as any of the volumes of the *Historia Animalium*.[1] His rival, the Italian Ulisse Aldrovandi, who in the years 1599-1603[2] produced his own pandects, copied largely both text and pictures from Gesner, although he never quoted him by name or acknowledged his debt.[3] These and the other volumes[4] that derive from him show that indeed Gesner inaugurated an era. Before Copernicus had been appreciated enough to be condemned, biological studies had already reached a high level of achievement.

[1] The *Theatrum Insectorum* was prepared by Mouffet for publication in 1589, a year after Penny's death; the manuscript is in the British Museum, Sloane 4014. Neither then nor in 1604 did Mouffet have it published. The script was bought by Sir Theodore de Mayerne and published in 1634.

[2] The volumes on birds and insects; the others appeared posthumously between 1612 and 1648.

[3] He alludes to him usually with sneers as 'ornithologus'.

[4] E.g. E. Topsell, *Of Foure-footed Beastes* (London, 1607), *Of Serpents* (1608).

In order to appreciate the truth of this contention it is only necessary to look at the list of men of the sixteenth century and compare those eminent in anatomy and medicine, botany and zoology, and even geology, with those who can be reckoned as chemists or physicists, astronomers and mathematicians. In addition to those associated with Gesner, there are Jean Fernel, now, thanks to Sir Charles Sherrington, given his meed of honour,[1] Girolamo Cardano of Milan, another great doctor and scholar, and Julius Caesar Scaliger,[2] poet, critic, doctor and botanist; Andreas Vesalius, the famous anatomist, Ambroise Paré,[3] the greatest of surgeons at Paris, Felix Platter, president of the medical faculty at Basel, and a multitude of other medical pioneers; Rembert Dodoens, Charles de l'Ecluse, Mathias de l'Obel, and, on a different level, our own John Gerard, and James Cargill of Aberdeen, the first Scottish botanist; Pierre Belon, traveller and student of birds, Guillaume Rondelet of the medical school at Montpellier and Hippolyto Salviani, the papal physician, all three of whom wrote large books on fishes;[4] George Bauer (Agricola), the German doctor, who wrote on metals and mining, and Bernard Palissy, the potter, who was one of the first scientific students of fossils and geology. But the men who applied a similar scrutiny to the traditional astronomy, physics and chemistry are few: Mikolaj Kopernik[5] on his tower in Frauenburg sifting the cosmology of Ptolemy and the lore of the astrologers and building up the cautious hypothesis which was to give his name to an era when, a century later, the value of the *De Revolutionibus Orbium* was at last acclaimed; Tycho Brahe,[6] the Dane, the patient observer of comets and stars, who abandoned the Ptolemaic cycles

---

[1] Cf. *The Endeavour of Jean Fernel* (Cambridge, 1946).

[2] He collected and painted plants claiming to have been a pupil of Dürer, and edited Theophrastus, *Hist. Plant.*; cf. V. Hall, 'Life of J. C. Scaliger' in *Transactions of Amer. Phil. Soc.* XL, pt. 2, p. 141.

[3] Cf. S. Paget, *Ambroise Paré and his Times*; F. R. Packard, *Life and Times of Ambroise Paré* (New York, 1926).

[4] Of similar date is C. Zancavola's Italian version of Paolo Giovio, *De' Pesci Romani* (Venice, 1560); Giovio's book in Latin (Rome, 1524) is interesting chiefly because of its period.

[5] Cf. *Nicholas Copernicus 1473-1543* by J. Rudnicki (London, 1943).

[6] For whom cf. J. L. E. Dreyer, *Tycho Brahe* (Edinburgh, 1890).

but never called himself a Copernican; Giordano Bruno, speculative philosopher, heretic and martyr, but hardly either scholar or scientist; Theophrastus Bombastes von Hohenheim, usually called Paracelsus,[1] born near Zürich and working from 1525 till 1529 in the University at Basel, a competent doctor whose use of opium and mercury and metallic remedies was associated with astrology, alchemy and demonology; and a century later Johann Baptista van Helmont, highly praised by Dr Partington.[2] Such a list makes it abundantly clear that the modern scientific movement began in the biological fields.

[1] Cf. *Life of Paracelsus* by E. Hartmann (London, 1896).
[2] Cf. his *Short History of Chemistry*, pp. 44-54, and A. E. Bell, *Christian Huygens and the development of Science in the Seventeenth Century* (London, 1947).

VI

CUDWORTH AND THE AGE OF GENIUS

IF it is evident that for the expansion of science in the sixteenth century the work of Gesner was for his contemporaries vastly more influential than that of Copernicus, the history of the first half of the next century underlines the same truth, that the scientific movement cannot at this period be properly explained in terms of its astronomers and mathematicians. The modern world owes its origin not to the Renaissance and Reformation nor yet to Copernicus and Galileo, but to the 'New Philosophy' as the scientists of the seventeenth century called it, of which Francis Bacon was the principal exponent and whose central purpose was nothing less than to provide a frame of reference, consistent in theory and attested by experiment, for the whole range of physical phenomena if not for all knowledge.

Hitherto it is broadly true to say that anatomists, astronomers, herbalists and alchemists had been concerned with the use of observation in order to test the differences and correct the mistakes of the medieval and classical traditions. Their labours had prepared the way for the formulation of the inductive method in the *Novum Organum*, for the great plan of mapping out and exploring the whole field of nature which is the theme of the *Parasceve* and its accompanying *Catalogus* and for the resounding insistence upon progress which is the recurring refrain alike in the *De Sapientia Veterum* and *The New Atlantis*. But for Bacon, as his greatest editor J. Spedding long ago affirmed, the second of these tasks was fundamental and indispensable. Induction and experiment were valuable instruments: they were to be employed in order to elaborate an accurate and all-embracing account of the whole realm of nature. Without this objective there could be no co-ordinated scientific movement; all would still be fragmentary and disordered, incapable of giving guidance and proportion to humanity or any appreciation of the wholeness and coherence of the universe.

How vastly important was such a survey and correlation will be clear as we ponder upon the failure of the technical achievements of medieval agriculture, architecture, milling, mechanics and manufacture to promote any general advance in technology or science. Obviously the Devonshire farmers who debated the merits of the black and of the large oats, or the builders of the octagon at Ely Cathedral, or the vitriol-makers at Brightlingsea had special and empirically tested knowledge which might well have led to far-reaching changes in our way of living; but in fact their skill remained local and restricted, yielding no insight into principles and no application to other cognate fields. Bacon seems to have been one of the first to realize the dependence of one branch of work upon another and the possibility of establishing analogies and of linking up discoveries in one subject with problems in another. If, as is arguable, it was precisely this failure to integrate the various known techniques and so to build up a coherent system of scientific theory and practice that explains the relative stagnation of medieval industry, we may well feel that this insistence by Bacon upon a catalogue of natural history and of inventions marks the beginning of a new epoch.

That he was himself conscious of the practical benefits for mankind to be derived from the co-ordination and expansion of knowledge is clear from his constant emphasis upon 'fruit'. Macaulay in his famous essay,[1] F. M. Cornford in an important paper,[2] and Professor B. Farrington in his recent book[3] are fully justified in emphasizing this element in the whole Baconian scheme: it played an important part in commending the new studies and gaining influential patronage for the new scientific

[1] He compares Bacon with Plato at much length to prove Bacon's insistence upon utility.
[2] 'Greek Natural Philosophy and Modern Science' in *The Unwritten Philosophy*, pp. 81–94.
[3] *Francis Bacon, Philosopher of Industrial Science.*

societies; and as we shall see the mechanistic developments fostered by it achieved such remarkable successes as to dwarf for a whole epoch the other and larger fields of inquiry. But as a matter of history it is not fair to assign to Bacon or to the New Philosophy a primarily utilitarian motive or a practical end. With them, as with us all, the advantage of fuller knowledge was not nicely adjusted between educational and material gains, nor was its pursuit yet divided into 'pure' and applied, academic and technical fields.

Certainly Bacon insisted that a first necessity for progress is the composition of a complete, classified and described compendium of the whole field of human activity. With the exception of religion which he regards as revealed and therefore to be accepted without the attestation of inquiry or experiment, all possible knowledge must be co-ordinated into 'a single systematic treatise, a Natural History such as may supply an orderly foundation for philosophy and include material reliable, abundant and well arranged for the task of interpretation'.[1] This natural history will at once give a sense of proportion and perspective to man's outlook and will disclose successive ranges of endeavour so that a new sense of purpose and direction will guide our efforts and inspire our energies. In consequence a great co-operative movement for the control of our environment will become possible. 'We need fear no lion in the path nor set any limit to our journey.'[2]

Thus Bacon, like his contemporaries François Rabelais, who had fled from the Franciscans of Fontenay-le-Comte owing to his devotion to humanism, and the Dominican Campanella, who wrote the *Apologia pro Galileo*, took up the concept of history as a real progress which St Paul and Seneca, Clement of Alexandria and Augustine of Hippo had alike affirmed, but which both the medievals and the men of the Renaissance had hardly dared to maintain. If we criticize his lack of scientific knowledge, we must remember that he said 'I am but a trumpeter not a combatant' and give him full credit both for his challenge and for his vision of the greatness of the adventure to which he summons us.[3]

---

[1] Preface to *Parasceve*.   [2] Cf. *Redargutio, ad fin.*
[3] For this cf. I. Masson, *Three Centuries of Chemistry*, pp. 17-22.

That he absurdly underestimated the difficulties of the general survey which he demands is obvious from his allocation of time for its fulfilment. That he was wholly right in emphasizing its importance and in devoting himself to preliminary sketches and then to further expositions of it can be proved from the effects of his work. For it was precisely this sense of the magnitude and integrity of the task that inspired men like Samuel Hartlib[1] and his friend Comenius to fulfil Bacon's vision of 'Solomon's House' in *New Atlantis* by their plan for a Pansophic College, and to follow his repeated exhortations to go forward by their lifelong efforts to arouse and rally and unite all who could be persuaded to undertake the adventure. How widely such a plan appealed can be seen not only from the schemes put forward by Edward Bolton[2] and later by Abraham Cowley[3] and John Evelyn,[4] and actually realized in the 'Invisible College', but from the interest in similar societies all over Europe. The discussion of such schemes and the general approval extended in one form or another to them did much to give solidarity and status to scientific studies and to encourage and unite those who had hitherto been either like the apothecaries or anatomists, mainly professional in their outlook, or like Gilbert and Agricola, lonely pioneers in less familiar fields. If for our purpose we examine the movement in Britain, it must be remembered that similar pansophic plans were familiar in other countries and notably in Italy, France and Holland.

The scheme in this country did not prove easy of realization. Even Comenius's visit to England in 1641-2 had little influence except upon the small group, Joachim Hubner, John Dury, John Peel, Theodore Haak and Hartlib, whom he met in London. Two of them, Hartlib and Dury, formed the nucleus of the Invisible College which Hartlib called Antilia and of which John Worthington said: 'The design did pretend to such high things

---

[1] Hartlib was devoted to Bacon's works which he had read in 1628 before he came to England. [2] Cf. R. F. Young, *Comenius in England*, p. 4.
[3] Cf. *Works*, ed. Hurd, I, p. 219. Of this Hartlib said that it had no effect on the group that met at Gresham's College (cf. *Diary and Correspondence of Worthington*, p. 366) while Sprat, *History of the Royal Society*, p. 59, declared that it greatly hastened the formation of the Royal Society. [4] In a letter to Boyle (cf. Boyle, *Works*, V, p. 397).

and stupendous effects that I could never much build upon it.'[1] Another, Haak, was indeed largely responsible for the foundation of the Royal Society, but this could hardly have been successful without the support brought to it by John Wilkins who not only attached to it the group which had gathered round him in Oxford,[2] but enrolled as members men like Henry More, and (later) Walter Needham, Francis Willughby and John Ray whom he had known during his brief residence in Cambridge.

The composition and proceedings of the Royal Society are in themselves sufficient to demonstrate beyond doubt that the history of the scientific movement cannot be told in terms of astronomers and mathematicians. It is easy to exaggerate, as Sprat[3] and many moderns have done, the element of practical utility which was one of its professed and primary objects. But certainly the desire for agricultural, military, medical and social advancement lay behind very many of its activities and experiments and its most active members would all have refused to separate science from technology or the pursuit of truth from that of utility. Nevertheless nothing is more striking in its early *Proceedings* or in its list of members than the very wide range of interests represented; and the same is true of the inquiries set on foot by the Council and of the correspondence carried on by its Secretary. Not only did it try to cover the whole field of natural knowledge, but it welcomed projects like Wilkins's proposal for a Universal language which went far outside what is usually regarded as the sphere of science. And many of its investigations (those, for example, which led to the abandonment of belief in witchcraft or in spontaneous generation or in the transmutation of species) were for human progress not less significant than those which culminated in the law of gravitation. The belief in an orderly cosmos, a reign of law and a reliable frame of reference, such as had been Bacon's ideal, was in

---

[1] *Miscellanies*, p. 230 (letter to Hartlib, 29 Nov. 1660).

[2] For the disentangling of the relationship between the Invisible College and the Oxford group, and their respective connexions with the Royal Society, cf. R. H. Syfret, 'The Origins of the R.S.' in *Notes and Records of the R.S.* v, no. 2, pp. 75–137.

[3] *History of the R. S.* published in 1667 for the purpose of proving the value of the new philosophy to human welfare.

fact the aim and in no small measure the achievement of the first great creative epoch of the Royal Society.[1]

The extent of its success was indeed remarkable. In 1662 Britain, though it had been regarded by Comenius as a fruitful field for his sowing, was in fact still scientifically backward. There had been no Englishman comparable with Kepler or Galileo or Van Helmont, Gesner or Aldrovandi, De l'Ecluse or the Bauhins. Apart from William Gilbert's work on magnetism, William Harvey's on the circulation of the blood and possibly Thomas Penny's on insects, there had been nothing of first-rate importance. Indeed the development such as it was owed much to immigrants from the continent, to the great botanist De l'Obel who made his home in England after the death of William the Silent, to Samuel Hartlib and Theodore Haak, and to Henry Oldenburg, the devoted secretary of the Royal Society. But, although thus backward at the start, within less than a generation Britain had gained a position in the front of scientific progress in almost every department from astronomy to economics and had produced pioneers in them all, so that it seemed natural for the great Italian physiologist Marcello Malpighi to send his book on the development of the embryo in the egg to London for publication, for the great Dutch microscopist Leeuwenhoek to submit to the Royal Society his discovery of spermatozoa, and for Christian Huygens to select it in preference to the Académie as the recipient of his unfinished work during his illness in 1670.[2]

This pre-eminence could never have been attained had there not appeared a galaxy of men of genius in England who turned with relief from the conflicts of the sects, the place-hunting of the politicians and the profligacy of the court to the exploration of nature and the development of experimental science: John Ray who, first in company with and then in memory of his friend and

---

[1] Thus Sprat (in spite of the emphasis on utility necessitated by his propagandist intention) defines its aim as 'to make faithful records of all the works of Nature or Art which can come within their reach: . . . to restore the Truths which have lain neglected: to push on those which are already known to more various uses, and to make the way more passable to what remains unrevealed'. Cf. R. H. Syfret in *Notes and Records of the R. S.* VII, no. 2, p. 213.

[2] Cf. Francis Vernon's letter to Oldenburg in A. E. Bell, *Life of Huygens*, pp. 65-6.

patron Francis Willughby, strove to produce a complete *systema naturae*[1] and started a new era in botany and zoology; Robert Boyle and his assistant, Robert Hooke (the first professional scientist in Britain), who laid the foundations of modern chemistry and opened up a field for experiments in a wide variety of scientific researches; George Ent, Walter Needham and Edward Tyson whose dissections of different vertebrates initiated the subject of comparative anatomy; Robert Morison of Aberdeen, Paris and Oxford, the Royal Botanist; Nehemiah Grew, the pioneer of vegetable physiology; Francis Glisson, Thomas Willis, Richard Lower, John Mayow, Thomas Sydenham and Hans Sloane, the doctors who were among the chief founders of modern medicine; the astronomers, William Gregory, Edmund Halley, John Flamsteed and his assistant, Abraham Sharp; Edward Lhwyd and John Woodward, the geologists; and above all Isaac Newton. These constitute a group of scientists unequalled in any age or country. And along with them were a multitude of others less distinguished but yet adding greatly to the general interest in science and creating for the men of genius a movement which had a profound historical significance.

It is of importance to recall some of these lest their contributions be forgotten. There was, for example, Joshua Childrey, whose *Britannia Baconica* was the first survey, county by county, of the geographical and faunal characteristics of England and who provided much material for the poet Drayton's *Polyolbion* and still more for the relevant sections of Christopher Merret's *Pinax*. There were the botanists, John Goodyer, Thomas Johnson, John Parkinson and later Leonard Plukenet; and the founders of collections, the two Tradescants and William Courten. The Tradescants, father and son, in their garden in Lambeth introduced many American plants to British horticulture and their museum, including the famous Dodo, passed to Elias Ashmole and so to the University of Oxford. William Courten or Charleton, who lived later, filled his rooms in the Middle Temple with 'a repository of

---

[1] He published books on mammals, reptiles, birds, fishes and (posthumously) insects and also the three great folios of the *Historia Plantarum* and the various British floras.

rare and select objects of natural history and art'[1] which was acquired by Hans Sloane and so formed part of the earliest British Museum. There was Sir Thomas Browne who not only collected and wrote of the birds and fishes of Norfolk, but took up Bacon's plea for a catalogue of errors and superstitions in his *Pseudodoxia epidemica* and achieved literary immortality by his interpretation of the religious significance of the new sciences in his *Religio Medici*. And there was Samuel Pepys whose fame at the Admiralty and as a diarist must not make us forget the years of his presidency over the Royal Society or the value of his support to it in the darkest period of its youth. Along with them there was, by the latter half of the century, a large number of others. Many were in London, like Martin Lister the great conchologist, Tancred Robinson, Ray's close friend and correspondent, Richard Waller a good entomologist and Secretary[2] of the Royal Society, Henry Compton Bishop of London, planter of the arboretum at Fulham, or, at a different social level, Samuel Doody and James Petiver: others were scattered over the country; Thomas Lawson the quaker schoolmaster in Westmorland; Ralph Johnson vicar of Brignall, the explorer of Teesdale; Samuel Langley of Tamworth; John Aubrey the historian of Wiltshire; Robert Plot of Oxford and Staffordshire; John Morton of Northamptonshire; William Vernon the entomologist of Cambridge; Walter Moyle the ornithologist of Cornwall; Samuel Dale, Ray's neighbour in Essex; and throughout the period John Evelyn at Sayes Court. It is not surprising that the common interests which drew them together exercised a powerful influence on public opinion.

But the appearance of such a brilliant generation would not have sufficed alone. That their influence changed the whole outlook of western man so rapidly, and that in Britain especially it met with hardly any opposition is due to the fact that the general climate of intellectual and religious life at the time was highly favourable to it. For more than half a century in England there was among Christians a degree of friendliness often amounting to

---

[1] So Ray, *Hist. Plantarum*, II, p. 1800.

[2] Elected 30 Nov. 1687; author of a paper on glow-worms, *Phil. Trans.* XIII, p. 841.

an enthusiastic welcome for the New Philosophy which contrasts sharply with the attitude of Catholics and Protestants alike on the continent of Europe. The remarkable group known as the Cambridge Platonists gave it a secure position in the university; and outside it churchmen like Jeremy Taylor and John Tillotson and nonconformists like William Penn and Richard Baxter had in common a sincere conviction that the works of the Lord were rightly sought out by His people. This is a fact that deserves fuller attention than it has as yet received and should be examined in some detail.[1]

Francis Bacon himself, as is well known, adopted the traditional position that religion and philosophy must not be 'commixed together'[2] since the latter follows the light of nature whereas 'the other is grounded only upon the Word and Oracle of God'.[3] He makes the divorce between them absolute by such phrases as 'out of the contemplation of nature to induce any verity or persuasion concerning the points of faith is in my judgment not safe'[4] and 'I do much condemn that interpretation of the scripture which is only after the manner as men use to interpret a profane book'.[5] Moreover, with an almost modern emphasis he warns inquirers against teleological interpretations, such as 'the hairs of the eyelid are for a fence about the sight',[6] on the ground that these discourage the search for physical causes and so prejudice further discoveries. He is in fact, as F. H. Anderson[7] has lately shown, a thoroughgoing naturalist who sets aside religion and scripture with a rather hollow show of reverence. Whatever his own beliefs, he plainly advocated the strict segregation of the New Philosophy from the old religion; but, though his references to the subject often seem almost contemptuous, he was careful to avoid occasions of conflict.

It is this refusal of Bacon to give a religious basis to his

[1] R. K. Merton, 'Science in Seventeenth Century England' in *Osiris* IV, pp. 360–632, shows conclusively how much it was helped by puritanism; but he ignores the very special prominence in this respect of the Cambridge Platonists and obviously does not know English religion of the period very well.

[2] *Advancement of Learning*, II, 6, I. [3] *Ibid.* II. 25, 3.

[4] *Ibid.* II. 6, I. [5] *Ibid.* II. 25, 17. [6] *Ibid.* II. 7, 7.

[7] *The Philosophy of F. Bacon* (Chicago, 1948).

philosophy rather than his emphasis upon the utility of scientific pursuits,[1] that accounts for the hesitations of the Cambridge Platonists about him. Worthington,[2] for example in his twenty-first letter to Hartlib, argues that it is the truths which 'tend to vindicate the attributions of God and salve the phenomena of Providence' that are 'indeed the true Instauratio Magna'. Henry More, though Hartlib urges him to the study of Bacon, replies with an evident lack of enthusiasm for his writings;[3] Culverwel, who speaks more frequently and more respectfully of him, does not show many signs of his influence;[4] and Cudworth in his *Intellectual System*[5] specifically attacks Bacon's rejection of teleology and of final causes as 'the very spirit of Atheism'. Such criticism is consistent with Harvey's poor opinion of Bacon as a scientist and with the general attitude of the university towards him;[6] for Cambridge was influenced rather by his insistent pleas for observation and experiment than by his specific writings and proposals. This must not be taken to suggest that the Cambridge Platonists did not share his interest in nature or identify themselves with the activities of their scientific contemporaries. In fact they threw themselves eagerly into the sort of pursuits which Joseph Mead,[7] the great tutor at Christ's, who may well be reckoned a principal source of their convictions, had encouraged and imparted to his friend John Alsop and perhaps to More. But such interest was by this time becoming almost universal: the seeing eye of the carvers of the roof bosses at Southwell or the Lady chapel at Ely had now

---

[1] This is not the opinion of E. Cassirer, *Die platonische Renaissance in England* (Leipzig, 1932): he argues that it is Bacon's advocacy of natural studies as a means of gaining power over nature which the Cambridge school specially disliked.

[2] *Misc.* p. 305.

[3] Letters in the possession of Lord Delamere lent to me by Prof. G. H. Turnbull. This is Ep. IX of 27 Aug. 1649.

[4] Cf. *The Light of Nature* (ed. J. Brown, 1851), pp. 83, 208, 210, 259.

[5] In ch. V (vol. II, p. 608, ed. Mosheim).

[6] I cannot agree with J. Tulloch, *Rational Theol.* II, pp. 19-21, that, though the Cambridge Platonists were wholly out of sympathy with Bacon, yet Barrow, Ray and Newton studied him closely; Barrow alone shows signs of reverence for him.

[7] 'An accurate philosopher, a skilful mathematician, an excellent anatomist', so Worthington; and also 'a curious florist, an accurate herbalist, thoroughly versed in the Book of Nature', *Life*, p. viii. It is a pity that none of those who have written on Cudworth —or indeed on Milton—has paid attention to him.

been recognized as a proper part of education by the nobility and gentry; and to ascribe its prevalence to Bacon or any other is to exaggerate his importance.

The Cambridge Platonists were in fact more influenced by Descartes than by Bacon. Henry More, urged to it both by Alsop (who met Descartes) and by Hartlib, had written his first letter to Descartes in 1648 expressing enthusiasm for his philosophy and, at this time, full agreement with its principles. He and very many others found in the French thinker precisely what they had missed in Bacon, a systematic attempt to form a consistent and at the same time a theistic interpretation of the universe. Here was a system which in its stress upon observation and experiment, in the wide range of its interests, in the skill of its synthesis, in its acknowledgment of religion seemed to satisfy all their requirements. Being accustomed to the dualism of mind and matter they were not dismayed by his contrast between *res cogitans* and *res extensa*, or by the materialism of his physical philosophy. It was only when they discovered that the logical outcome of such mechanism was to treat all subhuman life as purely automatic[1] and so to deny any sort of intelligence or feeling to animals that they rebelled. More himself[2] and Cudworth after him anticipate the arguments which Ray afterwards used with greater effect[3] and insist that the contention, that 'a saddled horse has no more sense than its harness',[4] is in flat contradiction to the evidence; and having attacked the Cartesian scheme at this point they go on to recognize that in fact its acknowledgment of God solely in relation to the spirit in mankind, if perhaps consistent with its interpretation of the rest of the universe, yet leaves the basic relationship between extension and spirit unexplained and inexplicable. It is indeed interesting to note that they fastened upon the characteristic weaknesses of both the great men: for Bacon was a lawyer who knew and insisted upon the importance of exact evidence, but knew also by

[1] Descartes in this contention was accepting Catholic doctrine that 'animals have no souls' and also vindicating the right to vivisect them.

[2] In his letter to V.C. appended to 2nd ed. of *Enchiridion Ethicum*, he states his reasons for admiring Descartes; in the preface to *Ench. Metaphys.* he criticizes and condemns him.

[3] Cf. his *Synopsis Quadrupedum*, pp. 1-13, and *Wisdom of God*, pp. 42-4.

[4] More, *Opera Omnia* (1679), I, p. 137.

experience how easily such evidence might be distorted by interpretation; and Descartes was a systematist for whom facts were
indeed important but primarily as supporting his hypothesis and
who, if data and dogmas were in conflict, might easily let his
presuppositions dictate his results. It was fortunate for British
science that it kept a clear sense of the necessity both for accuracy
of observation and for coherence of interpretation.

That it did so was due partly, as we have seen, to the breadth
and inclusiveness which Bacon and the Invisible College had given
to it, but partly, and in large measure, to the quality and influence
of the Cambridge Platonists. Their help was to some extent direct
and immediate. Benjamin Whichcote profoundly affected John
Ray and his contemporaries by the long succession of his Sunday
lectures.[1] Henry More, whose book *The Antidote against Atheism*
combines a very fine statement of Christian philosophy with a full
and congruous interpretation of natural phenomena, was an early
member of the Royal Society. John Worthington took a strong
and active interest in the development of natural history. Ralph
Cudworth,[2] by his profound and ingenious doctrine of a 'Plastic
Nature' as well as by the massive erudition of the rest of the *True
Intellectual System*, gave a plain lead to those who felt that neither
Bacon nor Descartes had provided an exposition of the New
Philosophy which did justice to all the requirements. No one can
study Ray's immensely influential book *The Wisdom of God in the
Works of Creation*—the book which more than any other deter-
mined the character of the interpretation of nature till Darwin's
time—without seeing how much he and the whole scientific
movement owed to the wise, liberal and reverent teaching of the
Cambridge school and to the climate of opinion which it created
in the middle and latter part of the seventeenth century.

[1] 'Every Lord's day in the afternoon for almost twenty years together he preached in
Trinity Church . . . and contributed more to the forming of the students to a sober sense
of religion than any man in that age.' J. Tillotson, *Funeral Sermon*, p. 24.

[2] Master of Christ's College 1654-88, father of Damaris (Lady Masham) the friend of
John Locke (cf. F. A. Keynes, *Byways of Cambridge History*, pp. 118-26). Locke in his
Journal, 18 Feb. 1681-2, acknowledges Cudworth's *Intellectual System* as a source of his
Essay. Forty letters from Lady Masham to Locke, signed Philoclea, are preserved in the
Lovelace Collection: cf. W. von Leyden, in *Sophia* (1949), pp. 74-5.

This indirect influence of their work can hardly be overstated. If none of them was immediately concerned with the development of scientific studies they all encouraged an attitude towards nature radically different from that which had prevailed in Christendom since the death of Origen. Like the Christian Platonists of Alexandria, John Smith can affirm that 'every art and science must start from certain precognita, and theology involves in its very nature the supposition of a power within us answering to and apprehensive of a Power above us';[1] Henry More can write

> Hence the soul's nature we may plainly see
> A beam it is of th' Intellectual Sun,
> A ray indeed of that Eternity.[2]

Whichcote's favourite words had expressed the same belief: 'The spirit of man is the candle of the Lord, lighted by God and lighting man to God.'[3] N. Culverwel could frame upon them a reasoned theory of knowledge. Hence nature and the natural order are to them not only God's creation but the foundation of true religion both moral and philosophical; there is nothing incongruous, indeed nothing contradictory between nature and grace. Whichcote like Browne can speak of two lights, two books, that of Creation and that of Scripture, and bid us use them both.[4] Under such influence Ray could plead that 'to contemplate the works of God is part of the business of a Sabbath-day',[5] that is, is a matter of particular religious obligation.

While all the Cambridge Platonists are agreed in this estimate of nature and though More and Worthington followed it up by special interest in field studies, it is in Cudworth's *The True Intellectual System of the Universe* that the subject is treated in detail

---

[1] Discourse I, 'Of the true way of attaining to Divine Knowledge'.

[2] 'Life of the Soul', II, 22. For More's basic insistence upon the unity of reality as against the dualism of Descartes and the materialism of Hobbes, cf. F. I. Mackinnon, *Philosophical Writings of H. More*, pp. xviii–xxv.

[3] 'Sermon on the Exercise and Progress of a Christian', *Works*, I, 370. Prov. xx. 27 is, of course, the text of Culverwel's *Discourse of the Light of Nature*.

[4] Cf. e.g. *Aphorisms*, 109 and *Religio Medici*.

[5] *Wisdom of God*, 1st ed. p. 124; this, although not published till 1691, would seem to be part of the discourses delivered in Cambridge in 1659 when he was in touch with Whichcote, More and Worthington.

and at length; it is no exaggeration to say that the candour and profundity of his handling of it have seldom been surpassed.[1] That his book is long and overloaded, ill-arranged and incomplete; that its author can never resist following every side-issue and elaborating an array of detailed argument at every stage of his inquiries; and that very much of his discussion has only an academic interest —these defects must not blind us to the frankness with which he faces real problems and the honesty which forbids him to be content with partial or conventional answers to them. Striking testimony to his lasting worth comes from studying his book in Mosheim's edition,[2] and comparing Cudworth's text with his learned editor's comments and dissertations; for to do so is to realize that for a modern reader the text often speaks of matters of permanent importance in language which is still appropriate and significant, while the comment always reflects an outlook and presuppositions which no one today could share. Of Cudworth, Professor Passmore writes: 'His was the first major attempt in England to reconcile the new science with the older philosophical tradition.' It was this, but in its main contribution to thought it was much more.[3]

Cudworth more clearly than any of his contemporaries realized that, if nature was in some sense a coherent and intelligible system, then it could not be explained in terms either of the random movements of matter in space such as Hobbes supposed[4] or of arbitrary and incalculable acts of God and other supernatural and demonic agents.[5] It must be an orderly whole, manifesting not

[1] In view of Professor J. A. Passmore's valuable *Ralph Cudworth. An Interpretation*, it is unnecessary for me to vindicate Cudworth against the criticisms of Leslie Stephen, E. A. Burtt and others; he was much more than a classicist and a reactionary, he was indeed, alike in his relationship to Descartes and the Royal Society and in his criticism of Hobbes, a man fully familiar with the best thought of his time.

[2] Published originally in Latin in 1733 but translated and published in England by Harrison in 1845.

[3] J. H. Muirhead, *The Platonic Tradition in Anglo-Saxon Philosophy* (London, 1931), p. 35, calls him 'the real founder of British Idealism', expounds his position very sympathetically and specially praises the modern note struck by his doctrine of a plastic principle.

[4] That Hobbes is Cudworth's chief target is argued by F. J. Powicke, *The Cambridge Platonists*, pp. 120-6.

[5] Cudworth is wholly free from More's belief in witchcraft and spiritualism.

only a reign of law but a continuous and rational meaning. The *True Intellectual System*, to which he devoted the results of a lifetime of thought and study, should have dealt with this theme. But unfortunately only the first part, dealing with the examination and refutation of the various forms of atheism, was published;[1] and we can only discover his own constructive teaching from those passages in which after criticizing his opponents he passes from the negative to the positive in order to dispose more adequately of their errors. Fortunately he is so discursive a writer that such passages often lengthen out into full-scale presentations of his position.

This position has plainly some similarity in its broad outline to that expressed by William Gilbert of Colchester in his work on magnetism.[2] From his study of the loadstone Gilbert had been faced with a problem of movement that could not be reduced to contiguous push and pull: the iron flew to the magnet from a distance; and the attraction seemed 'animate', analogous rather to the organic energy of a living creature than to the thrust of dead stuff.[3] Regarding the earth itself as a great magnet he assigned to it a great soul[4] capable of exerting an influence or 'effluvium' at a distance on the moon and other astronomical objects.

Henry More, Cudworth's colleague, developed a fuller theory of a 'world soul'. After his first attachment to Descartes, More had come to insist that the phenomena of the world cannot be explained merely mechanically but involve the presence and action in them of a diffused but incorporeal spirit.[5] This is not only present, as Descartes held, in the conarion and diffused throughout the body, but is 'a spirit of nature' or *anima mundi* permeating the

---

[1] Of the MSS. listed by T. Birch in his life of Cudworth prefixed to the second edition of the *True Intellectual System*, that described as 'A discourse of the Creation of the World' would seem to be very relevant to our subject. Unfortunately Prof. Passmore who has made a detailed and valuable examination of the MSS. concludes that this has disappeared completely; cf. his appendix, p. 113.

[2] *De magnete magneticisque corporibus et de magno magnete tellure physiologia nova*, 1600.

[3] From such phenomena and the problem of the transmission of motion arose the question whether space was a 'vacuum' or a 'plenum'.

[4] As an argument for this he emphasizes the spontaneous generation of plants from soil without sowing of seeds. Cf. *De magn.* (trans. P. F. Mottelay), p. 310.

[5] Cf. his letter of 1665 to Boyle in Boyle's *Works*, VI, p. 513.

entire world, regulating the heavenly bodies, uniform in its operation, rational and purposive.[1] Obviously this belief which is an
essential part of More's philosophy has definite links with Cudworth; and it is possible that here as in the matter of his book on
ethics More's greater facility and speed of writing may have
prevented Cudworth from a fuller expansion of this theme. But
in the passages of the *True Intellectual System* that deal with it
there is hardly any trace of direct relationship with More's work.
Passmore is probably right in supposing that Cudworth deliberately
avoided emphasizing points on which he did not agree with his
colleague.[2]

The most important of Cudworth's digressions is the long
section, xxvii, inserted into Chapter III, dealing with his theory of
'plastic nature'. In this, having now criticized the materialism of
the four types of atheistic hypothesis, he faces what he feels to be a
real dilemma. If the universe cannot be explained as due merely to
the movement of matter 'without the guidance and direction of
any mind or understanding', are we driven to conclude that 'God
himself doth all immediately and as it were with his own hands
form the body of every gnat and fly?' He has already stated very
frankly the objection to this, quoting the atheists' objection, 'the
supposed Deity and Maker of the world was either willing to
abolish all evils but not able; or he was able but not willing; or
thirdly he was neither willing nor able; or else lastly he was both
able and willing. This latter is the only thing that answers fully
to the notion of a God'.[3] Accepting this he recognizes the difficulty
of reconciling it with 'that slow and gradual process that is in the
generation of things' and with 'those ἁμαρτήματα (as Aristotle
calls them), those errors and bungles which are committed when
the matter is inept and contumacious'.[4] If God is an omnipotent
agent he 'could despatch His work in a moment' and 'would
always do it infallibly and irresistibly'.

It is not clear to what extent, if Cudworth had completed his

---

[1] Chiefly discussed in his *Immortality of the Soul*, III, chs. 12 and 13.

[2] Passmore, *op. cit. passim*, discusses this matter at some length but without any more
definite result.   [3] *True Intellectual System*, I, p. 129.   [4] *Ibid.* p. 223.

task, he would have explained that omnipotence in the sense here defined represents an inadequate and sub-Christian concept of Deity.[1] With his strong insistence upon moral conditions and his fine sense of the value of human freedom and reason he might well have seen that the exercise of arbitrary power in creation is inconsistent with the purpose of bringing free and moral beings into existence and so he might have found a way to reconcile the facts of gradualness and of error with belief in an immediately active God.[2] But in the present book he does not pursue this aspect of the subject; instead, at this point, he introduces his contention that 'there is a plastic nature under God which as an inferior and subordinate instrument doth drudgingly execute that part of his providence which consists in the regular and orderly motion of matter' but nature 'cannot act electively nor with discretion'.[3] If so, then this plastic nature might 'extend farther to the regular disposal of that matter in the formation of plants and animals and other things in order to that apt coherent frame and harmony of the whole universe'.[4] This in his usual manner he proceeds to vindicate by full reference to 'the best philosophers in all ages'.

After an exposition of Aristotelian, Stoic and Platonic teaching he returns to his own interpretation and says: 'We shall here endeavour to do these two things concerning it, first, to set down a right representation of it and then to show how extremely the notion of it hath been mistaken.'[5] Quoting Aristotle's analogy from shipbuilding[6] he first defines plastic nature as 'art itself acting immediately on the matter as an inward principle', and then goes on to show how superior it is to our human art: 'Nature is art as it were incorporated and embodied in matter which doth not act upon it from without but from within vitally and magically' (and here he quotes Plotinus, *Ennead*, III, 8); 'nature acts immediately

---

[1] His strong criticism of the Calvinists in his *Treatise concerning Eternal and Immutable Morality* clearly points in this direction; but he would have resisted the idea that God's purpose could involve the occurrence of evil.

[2] Muirhead, *op. cit.* p. 35, insists that Cudworth always regards 'the divine principle in the world as the action not of an arbitrary will acting on it from without but of an immanent will to good whether conceived as beauty, justice or truth'.

[3] P. 224. [4] P. 226. [5] P. 235. [6] *Physica*, II, 8.

upon the matter as an inward and living soul or law in it.' Unlike human art, 'nature is never to seek what to do, nor at a stand . . . but is always readily prompted, nor does it ever repent afterwards . . . but it goes on in one constant unrepenting tenor from generation to generation because it is the stamp or impress of that infallibly omniscient art of the divine understanding, which is the very law and rule of what is simply the best in every thing.' Next he argues that nature is not 'the divine art, as this is in itself, pure and abstract, but concrete and embodied only, . . . not the divine art archetypal but only ectypal, a living stamp or signature of the divine wisdom'.[1] In this regard he again insists that nature 'is such a thing as doth not know but only do, . . . nor can it act electively or with discretion', and that its activity resembles that of a habit or natural instinct like that of 'the bees in framing their combs and hexagonial cells, the spiders in spinning their webs'.[2]

In thus attempting to define plastic nature Cudworth realizes that he is controverting the Cartesian formula of extension and thought and argues that this would have been more adequate if it had been extension and life. Plainly the sort of cogitation which he ascribes to nature and to living plants and animals is not the thought which Descartes ascribes only to man; nevertheless it is obviously not a mere 'local motion' but a 'vital energy' akin rather to thought than to extension. This vital principle he then goes on to ascribe to individual animals in the form of a plastic power peculiar to each, which constitutes the element that distinguishes it from a merely mechanical structure and enables its growth and functioning. But he is careful to put this forward tentatively and to affirm that it may well be merely a special manifestation of the 'one plastic nature of the universe'.[3]

In the main his thought is expressed in terms of quotations from Plotinus, though Aristotle and other ancients, and on two

---

[1] Pp. 237-8; for an interesting treatment of this part of Cudworth's argument, cf. A. Arber, *Natural Philosophy of Plant Form*, pp. 202-5.

[2] P. 243.

[3] P. 271. A good but brief account of Cudworth's doctrine by which 'the laws of the machine become the vital expression of the indwelling plastic principle' is in J. A. Stewart's article on the Cambridge Platonists in *Encyclopaedia of Religion and Ethics*, pp. 170-2.

occasions Harvey, are also quoted. But in spite of these borrow-ings it seems clear that he is not merely reviving the familiar belief in an *anima mundi*, still less multiplying entities in the way imputed to him by Tulloch.[1] Behind his long and rather involved speculations is a conviction that the universe cannot be described in less than organic terms, that the dualism of matter and spirit which he adopts against the materialists is itself unsatisfactory,[2] and that the order and coherence of the whole demands an integrative explanation. His attempts to define constantly suggest some acquaintance with the subconscious levels of human per-sonality; he is groping after an explanation of the phenomena of racial character, of routine behaviour and conditioned chains of conduct—though his knowledge is plainly fragmentary and un-analysed. It would be an exaggeration to interpret his thought in terms of Bergson's *élan vital* or of Smuts's Holistic principle; but the purport of his endeavour is manifestly along similar lines: if he had finished his proposed treatise, we might have been afforded a fuller exposition of a thesis which in any case deserves serious consideration. We have dealt with it at some length, not because Cudworth is a thinker of the first rank or the author of a com-pletely coherent philosophy but because from his continuous emphasis upon an organic interpretation of nature and from his many and suggestive foreshadowings of future ideas we can dismiss the belief that science has always and necessarily been mechanistic. In fact, as Professor Passmore has shown, his influence on the course of thought was considerable.

To the scientific world his work was introduced by the bio-logical writings of his younger contemporary, the eminent naturalist John Ray. Unlike most of the early botanists and zoologists, Ray had a first-rate training in classical literature and thought and an acquaintance with the ablest philosophers of his time. At Cambridge where he was *socius studiorum* to Isaac

---

[1] *Rational Theology*, II, pp. 272-3. A better account is by J. A. Stewart.

[2] It is notable that both his contemporary, Pierre Bayle, and apparently Passmore charge him with bridging 'the gulf between mind and nature on which theology has ordinarily insisted' (Passmore, *R. Cudworth*, pp. 27-8). His 'plastic nature' is plainly an attempt to escape a sharp dualism.

Barrow and a pupil of Duport, the great tutor of Trinity, he sat under Benjamin Whichcote during his remarkable ministry at Holy Trinity church, lectured upon Henry More's *Antidote against Atheism*, was intimate with John Worthington and through him was known to Samuel Hartlib, and evidently studied fully and carefully Cudworth's theory of plastic nature. In his last years, when after the finish of his immense work in botany he returned to the wider and more speculative interests of his younger days, he produced two books in which Cudworth's work is expounded, endorsed and applied. In 1691 the first edition of his *Wisdom of God in the Works of Creation* contained an explicit approval of his doctrine of plastic nature. Answering Boyle's theory,[1] that creation consisted in the imparting of motion to the mass of atoms and that once this had been done the whole subsequent course of the universe was determined, he insists that mass and motion cannot explain or produce sensation, intelligence and conscious purpose, that creation is not an act done once for all but a continuous process, and that the integration of the organism and its changing and purposive development can only be explained in terms of its whole constitution and of a sensitive and plastic element.[2] He summarizes the arguments in Cudworth's *True Intellectual System* and adduces a number of illustrative and supplementary points from the growth of plants and the behaviour of animals to prove that any explanation which treats them as mere antomata or machines is false to the facts. In the book as a whole the teleological argument is never so crudely stated as in Cicero or Paley. Ray has Cudworth's awareness of the imperfections and delays of the process and looks to the individual autonomy of the several organisms as a possible source of its complications.[3] He was indeed uniquely qualified by his training, by the very wide range of his studies and interests and by his long years of investigation and reflexion so that he 'saw life steadily and saw it whole', and it is this sense of the wholeness and consistency of the natural

[1] He refers to *Free Enquiry into the Vulgar Notion of Nature*, pp. 77-8 and 124-5.
[2] *Wisdom of God*, pp. 32-4.
[3] He inclines to assume both a 'vegetative soul' in each individual and a 'plastic nature' or animating principle in the whole; cf. *Wisdom of God*, pp. 35-7.

order and its congruity with a reasonable Christian philosophy that gave his work its influence and constitutes its principal merit. He shared the general outlook and broad culture of the Cambridge Platonists but, far more than any of them, knew and had researched into the whole field of natural knowledge. In the increasing bulk of evidence in his successive editions of the *Wisdom of God*[1] he opened up most of the problems of form and function which a century and a half later became the chief concern of biological science; and underlying all the accumulated data is the clear conviction that neither the traditional doctrine of Christendom with its emphasis upon a single creative act in the beginning, upon spasmodic interventions on later occasions, and upon the relative brevity and simplicity of the whole story, nor the mechanistic ideas of Descartes, Gassendi, and Willis which endeavour to explain the higher in terms of the lower and in so doing ignore not only the noblest and most characteristic values of the whole but the evidence of the natural order itself, can give an adequate account of the universe as the New Philosophy discloses it.

Two years later in 1693, when he published his *Synopsis Quadrupedum*, the introductory sections contained a fuller and more precise account of the principal points of his position. The first section discussing the definition of an animal is chiefly directed against the belief that it is an automaton without consciousness or any sort of intelligence. Here in addition to resuming his previous arguments he brings forward a mass of evidence largely from Johannes Faber, the anatomist and botanist of Bamberg, who was living in Rome and had written on the animals of New Spain.[2] Quoting his stories of the dogs employed by blind men and supplementing it by evidence of his own, he sums up in a sentence from Colbert, 'No one can sincerely assign to a machine such skill as we recognize in horses, dogs, monkeys, elephants and almost all animals'.[3] While maintaining the traditional distinction

---

[1] Four in his own lifetime and eighteen reprints; cf. G. Keynes, *J. Ray: a Bibliography*, pp 91-106.

[2] *De Animalibus apud Mexicum* (Rome, 1651) as a comment upon F. Hernandez, *Nova Historia*.

[3] *Syn. Quad.* p. 11; cf. my *John Ray*, pp. 347-5.

between *anima* and *ratio* he indicates that the difference between animals and man is less large than the Cartesians suppose.

In the second section he deals with three problems affecting the generation of animals. His complete rejection of the ancient and universal belief in spontaneous generation, the first problem, is one of the greatest achievements of seventeenth century science. Based both upon Scripture and the Classics this doctrine had been a principle obstacle to advance both in botany and in zoology. So long as it was believed that the London Rocket (*Sisymbrium irio*) had been generated, after the Great Fire, by wood ash, or that insects were produced from leaves, lice from sweat and frogs from clouds, any serious study of metamorphosis or of heredity was out of the question. Ray had always been sceptical of the evidence, and had long ago applauded Francesco Redi's experiments against it. Now he marshals all the arguments, summarizes the views of Redi, Malpighi, Swammerdam, Lister and Leeuwenhoek, and deals specifically with the vexed issues of the frogs in clouds and the toads in stones, of lice and other animalcules, and of the parasitic ichneumons in caterpillars. In the history of science this result should rank with the abandonment of the geocentric astronomy as an event of primary significance.

On the other two problems, that of preformation or epigenesis and that of ovarians and spermatists, he has long and interesting summaries of the contemporary arguments but is less ready to reach a conclusion. Though he makes his own position tolerably clear he ends on a note very characteristic of his modesty and insight: 'If I am to be quite honest there are many points on these subjects still open to doubt; questions can be raised which I confess that I am not competent to solve or to disentangle; this is not because they have not got definite natural explanations but because I am ignorant of them.'[1]

That one so widely experienced and so judicious as Ray should have been able to follow up the general position of the Cambridge Platonists and publish his results, in spite of the religious and political upheavals of the time and of the manifest decline of the

[1] *Syn. Quad.* p. 46.

Royal Society, is sufficient proof that the combination of genius and opportunity to which science in Britain owed its golden age had had a far-reaching effect. During his last twenty years of unequalled productivity when he was not only garnering the fruits of his life's work but, in his pioneering study of lepidopterous insects,[1] breaking fresh ground with all his old flair, he initiated a new era in biological studies, an era which the relapse and neglect in the next century could not do more than delay.

Nor was Ray alone in following up the lines suggested by Cudworth. Nehemiah Grew, the eminent compiler of the Catalogue of the Museum of the Royal Society and of very important treatises on plant physiology, deals in the second book of his *Cosmologia Sacra* with a vital principle in the vegetative life, the sense-perceptions and the intellect, and represents it as being responsible for the unconscious functions of the body. This contention though obviously similar in some respects to Cudworth's Plastic Nature is probably not deliberately derived from it; for Grew in his preface claims to have drawn his ideas not from other men's books but from the contemplation of nature. 'Nature', he writes, 'hath been in a manner my only book.' But he was a Cambridge man and up while Cudworth was still in residence; and it is natural that ideas so familiar to Ray would have been in the air.

The work of Grew laid the foundation for the serious study of the structure, growth and nature of plants; that of Stephen Hales who[2] went up to Corpus Christi, Cambridge, in 1696 and beginning as a field botanist went on to the physiology of vegetables and animals and carried out experiments on sap and blood-pressure in his parish of Teddington, explored the character of the subject and disclosed the impossibility of satisfactory progress until chemistry and physics had been developed. In criticizing the mechanism of the subsequent period in science it is very necessary to realize that Ray and his generation had carried biological studies to the point at which it was inevitable to call a halt until chemistry could be

---

[1] He collected and described the larvae and imagines of some 300 species insisting (unlike his followers and Linnaeus) that the whole metamorphosis of each must be studied.
[2] Cf. A. E. Clark-Kennedy, *Stephen Hales*, pp. 15-20.

freed from the last remains of magic, astrology and alchemy; and the ancient classification of the four elements earth, water, air, fire could be rejected and replaced. In the seventeenth century the inquiries of Richard Lower and John Mayow on the phenomena of respiration[1] showed that as yet the basic knowledge essential to such a subject was wholly lacking; and Ray who wrote a book on the matter decided not to have it published. Hales was speedily drawn[2] by his investigations of animal functioning to a study of gases and to the discovery of the two oxides of carbon;[3] but his work, valuable as it was, could not be effectively pursued. If biology was not to remain superficial, it must await the development of researches into the true nature of matter. It is surprising that without these foundations so great a progress had been made.

How much Britain owed to Cudworth and his colleagues at this crucial period in the development of science becomes clearer if we compare the position here with that in almost all the countries of the continent. There the ruinous effects of the Thirty Years' War had not only set back civilization in Central Europe by nearly a century but had produced a state of recurrent strife and chronic insecurity which made any serious intellectual efforts difficult. If there was no room for tolerance in secular affairs there was less still in religion; for Catholics and Protestants alike were involved in bitter and almost continuous controversies. The Roman Church had burnt Bruno in 1600 and Marco Antonio de Dominis after his death in prison in 1624, and had forced Galileo to abjure his published view in 1633; the Holy Office threatened the life and liberty of any venturesome investigator; and the fear of it not only exerted an evident influence upon the actions and upon the thought of Descartes,[4] but inhibited original speculation and free inquiry

[1] For an account of these, cf. M. Foster, *Lectures on the History of Physiology*, pp. 181-99.

[2] He began with the experiments on 'the Analysis of the Air' in ch. 6 of *Vegetable Staticks*, pp. 155-317.

[3] Since he had no agreed nomenclature and no knowledge of the chemical elements involved, Hales's definitions 'fixed air', 'vital air', 'elastick air', etc. are none too clear.

[4] A. B. Gibson, *The Philosophy of Descartes*, pp. 42-73, defends him against charges of 'prudence' and insincerity; I cannot think that the defence is wholly successful. H. More, in General Preface to *Collection of several Phil. Writings*, p. 11, had charged Descartes with distorting his true views through fear, and attacked the harm done by persecution to the Commonwealth of Learning.

in Italy, Spain and France; 'nothing', as Milton declared in *Areopagitica*, 'had been written there now these many years but flattery and fustian'. The cities and universities which had been the seed-plots of the Renaissance lost their pre-eminence, and even in the France of Le Roi Soleil, when science became fashionable, neither Montpellier nor Paris made any progress in discovery worthy of their early promise until the second half of the eighteenth century.[1] The countries of the Reformation, more severely devastated by war, were with the exceptions of Holland and Scandinavia in even worse case. Luther had despised science, quarrelled with Erasmus and abandoned all ideas of toleration; his followers by their exaggerated emphasis on 'faith alone' and the consequent antithesis between nature and grace, the depreciation of human endeavour and the division of sphere between State and Church tended to reduce religion to pietism and to regard all natural philosophy as mere worldliness.

Calvin had burnt Servetus, set up a theocracy and, by the strictness of his religious discipline, discouraged activities which did not make directly for the edification of the saints; his stress upon election and the extremes to which this led his followers did not favour scientific studies or any deep concern with the world of nature. In the seventeenth century the torch of the new learning was passed from Italy, France and Germany to Holland and England, where alone there was eagerness for the race and the ability to carry it forward. Even with them the first fine achievements were not long sustained, and the narrowing of the field of endeavour produced a grievous restriction and distortion of the whole scientific movement. At the close of the seventeenth century the prospect in both countries was brilliant. Thirty years later many of the most promising lines of advance had been abandoned and effort was almost confined to the fields of physics and chemistry. Very characteristic of the whole change is the report on the Royal Society sent by Walter Moyle, the Cornish

[1] Cf. the excellent chapter in H. Butterfield's *The Origins of Modern Science*, pp. 143-58. Whereas in England science remained religious and progressed rapidly, in France it became popular, sceptical and in the main superficial. But see below, the account of the biologists of Paris in Ch. VIII and of the chemists and physicists in Ch. VII.

naturalist, to his friend, the botanist Dr William Sherard, lately returned from Smyrna in 1719, 'I find that there is no room in Gresham College for Natural History: Mathematics have engrossed all; and one would think the Gentlemen of that Society had forgot that the chief end of their Institution was the advancement of natural knowledge'.[1] How complete was the transformation can be seen from almost every 'history' of science in which the whole succession of biologists from Gesner to Ray is virtually ignored.

[1] *Works* (ed. Sergeant), I, p. 422.

VII

NEWTON AND THE AGE OF THE MACHINE

To describe the New Philosophy of the seventeenth century without primary and immediate reference to Galileo, Descartes and Newton may well cause surprise; it is in some sense to play *Hamlet* without the Prince of Denmark. But if we are not to isolate the scientific movement of the last three centuries from the rest of man's dealing with nature or to confine the scope of science to quantitative techniques, it is appropriate to consider the progress of that great period in mathematics, physics and cosmology against the background of its wider achievements. This is the more excusable because, as we have noted, most histories of science concentrate upon these relatively recent developments and the mechanistic and practical sequels to them and, if they go back beyond Francis Bacon, only deal with a few of the astronomers and alchemists, the physicians and engineers who preceded him. To repeat in full detail the story of the researches and inventions of the Newtonian age[1] would be to traverse familiar ground; to scrutinize and revise the verdicts upon them—a task that in certain cases needs doing—would require not only a fullness of presentation but a range of knowledge beyond my capacity. What we are here concerned with is to record the steps by which certain seemingly abstract discoveries in regard to the problem of movement and the relationship of the earth to the sun not only had a revolutionary effect on man's outlook, but with the aid of the instruments devised to further the study initiated a development

[1] My colleague Prof. H. Butterfield has given a recent, clear and sufficient account of it in his book *The Origins of Modern Science*. Cf. also Sir William Dampier, *The History of Science*; H. T. Pledge, *Science since 1500*; and A. Wolf, *A History of Science, Technology and Philosophy in the Sixteenth and Seventeenth Centuries*.

of vast practical, intellectual and social significance; and then to show how this development won pre-eminence over all other scientific activities so that the term 'science' has become almost equivalent to mathematical, physical, chemical and technological research and its application to industry; and finally to indicate how by the beginning of the nineteenth century its offspring modern industrialism had transformed the life, conditioned the progress and infected the thought of mankind.

It is not true to say that modern science in the narrower sense began with Copernicus, for forerunners can be found as far back as Grosseteste[1] and Roger Bacon. But the hypothesis published in his *De Revolutionibus* in 1543, though not, as he stated it, the result of great scientific research and in any case placed on the Index in 1616 and taking a long time to gain acceptance,[2] certainly stimulated astronomical study and made him the founder of a great succession. Tycho Brahe the observer and Kepler the mathematician did not in themselves add anything of revolutionary importance;[3] but Galileo Galilei, quite apart from his treatment by the Inquisition, was a man of outstanding ability, one of the greatest experimentalists and inventors, and a thinker both original and important. His invention of much-improved telescopes, by which he was able in 1610 to discover the four moons of Jupiter and the strange excrescences of Saturn,[4] of a tubular microscope and, at the end of his life, of the pendulum-clock, set an example for scientific invention. His *Il Saggiatori* (1624) defined the primary and the secondary qualities of an object—shape, position, movement inseparable from it, and taste, smell, colour, sound conditional upon a percipient—and encouraged the belief that the quantitative attributes were of a higher degree of reality than the qualitative. His final *Dialogues* (1636) dealt with problems of

[1] Cf. Dr A. C. Crombie in *Bulletin of the Brit. Soc. for the History of Science*, I, p. 86.

[2] In 1669 when Cosimo de' Medici visited Cambridge he was entertained by a discourse denouncing the Copernican doctrine; cf. Cooper, *Annals*, III, p. 536.

[3] Kepler's *Mysterium Cosmographicum* (1597) and his *Harmonices Mundi* (1619) are merely numerical curiosities; and his whole outlook is as much astrological as astronomical. But he believed in exact measurements and had much influence on Descartes.

[4] These were not discovered to be rings until Huygens saw them in 1655 and Cassini divided them in 1671.

dynamics, the mechanics of motion, of falling bodies and of projectiles. But it was the *Dialogues on the Copernican and Ptolemaic Astronomies* which brought him in 1633 into collision first with the Jesuits and then with Pope Urban VIII and finally before the Inquisition, when he was compelled under threat of torture to abjure and condemn the Copernican doctrine as 'error and heresy'.[1] There is a certain irony in the fact that they persecuted him for the truth that he advocated, but not for promoting quantity above quality, the machine above the man.[2]

That the picture of the world of nature as a self-contained mechanical system, capable of being interpreted mathematically in terms of the motion of matter in space and time, owed its first preliminary outline to Galileo, and that his suppression for a different reason did not destroy his work or influence in this field, is sufficient reason for regarding him as an epoch-making figure. That he was as influential as E. A. Burtt and others suggest, may, however, be fairly questioned. If his philosophy ignored the human and religious world of value and purpose so completely as they represent, it could hardly have won its way—as the example of Thomas Hobbes of Malmesbury demonstrates[3]—had it not been popularized by Marin Mersenne and followed by the dualism of René Descartes, the mathematical and practical ability of Christian Huygens and the piety and brilliance of Isaac Newton. Indeed the attempt to treat the scientific movement of the seventeenth century as synonymous with a mechanistic interpretation of the universe can only be made if, as in Burtt's case, a small selection of workers are studied and these are expounded in a very one-sided fashion.[4] The fact is, as Dr Trevelyan has stated,[5] that practically the whole thinking world at that time was in its general

[1] Cf. the long abjuration translated in J. J. Fahie, *Galileo, his Life and Work*, pp. 319-21.

[2] This point is strongly pressed by E. A. Burtt, *The Metaphysical Foundations of Modern Science*, pp. 73-80. F. Sherwood Taylor, *Galileo and the Freedom of Thought*, p. 171, argues that Copernicus's doctrine was never a heresy because it had only been condemned by the Congregation of the Index, not *ex cathedra* by the Pope.

[3] He was one of those who compensate for physical timidity by intellectual violence; but his materialism aroused at the time more opposition than his arrogance.

[4] Much of his language, e.g. his account of Newton's metaphysics (especially pp. 236-7), is grotesquely exaggerated; it reads back into Newton a crude form of nineteenth-century materialism. [5] *England under the Stuarts*, p. 60.

concepts genuinely Christian. It did not see the inconsistency between a 'corpuscular' or mechanical view of inanimate nature and a firm belief in divine purpose and human responsibility. Boyle and Newton like Galileo and Descartes would have argued that mechanism and teleology were by no means antagonistic, that indeed a machine was the product and instrument of purpose and itself always subordinate to and expressive of its controller. They did not foresee and would not have accepted the conclusions which a subsequent age drew from their ideas; and these ideas were not given by them in any complete or coherent form.

Of Descartes we have already indicated two chief lines of thought, his definite dualism of matter and mind, *res extensa* and *res cogitans*, and his locating the human manifestation of mind in man's *conarion* or pineal gland. In doing so he did not intend to confine the *res cogitans* to humanity, but maintained the existence of a realm of intelligent beings and a genuine belief in God. By refusing intelligence to animals[1] he got into conflict with More and most naturalists, though the Roman Church had always denied, as it does still, that they possess souls. Here as elsewhere he was careful to avoid the sort of precision which had brought trouble upon Galileo; but there is hardly sufficient evidence to justify us in identifying his caution with conscious insincerity.[2] That he regarded his vision of 1619 as a genuine call, and its contents as in no way inconsistent with its divine origin may be accepted as his authentic conviction.[3] His influence in Western Europe was stronger than that of the astronomers or Galileo largely because he had escaped collision with the Church; but, as we have seen, More, Cudworth and the Platonists in England, like the Jansenists in France, were increasingly critical as they came to realize the extent to which his views divorced mechanism from teleology. Indeed in Britain he never received a following

---

[1] He affirmed in the *Discourse on Method*, (1637) pt. v, that as they lacked speech and reason they were radically different from men, and were automata formed by God as machines are made by us; cf. above, p. 109.   [2] Cf. above, p. 122, note 4.

[3] J. Maritain, *The Dream of Descartes*, pp. 9-23 is interesting but hardly satisfactory: he acknowledges its decisive importance but cannot bring himself to accept its religious character.

comparable with that attaching itself to him in France.[1] It was not until the high religious seriousness of the seventeenth century had passed into the scepticism and worldliness of the eighteenth that Descartes became the figure-head of science.

But on the practical and mathematical side of his work he had a larger and more immediate influence. All over Europe economic conditions were becoming important. The increase of activity in mining and metallurgical work and in certain manufactures is a factor in the development of science that cannot be ignored. In England for example coal (sea-coal, as it was called in London because it came by ship from the north) had amounted to over a million tons a year before 1700, of which 653,000 tons were shipped from Tyne and Wear.[2] Tin almost wholly from the stanneries of Cornwall rose to more than three million pounds a year at the same period.[3] Glass, alum and copperas showed a similarly large increase; and iron, though the Sussex smelting works were beginning to decline, was widely and successfully mined. It is an exaggeration to describe this expansion as an industrial movement or to compare it with the changes which mills, mines and factories made possible a century later. But it undoubtedly represented a new and important element in the life of the country.[4] With such interests constantly producing problems for the scientists, a technological and mechanistic emphasis was inevitable. Descartes the engineer and mathematician was the man for the age.

His eminence and influence upon the future are less due to the intrinsic merits of his system—which indeed are not of a very high order—than to its timeliness. It is easy to exaggerate, as many recent writers have done, the utilitarian value of the New Philosophy; and in presenting their case to their contemporaries, to the statesmen and princes whose support made their experiments

[1] Cf. H. Butterfield, *Origins*, pp. 141-58. England, in spite of Huygens and Leibniz, followed Newton not Descartes.

[2] Cf. E. Lipson, *Economic History of England*, II, p. 114.

[3] Cf. R. K. Merton, in *Osiris*, IV, p. 500.

[4] It is significant that Ray, the naturalist, wrote full accounts of various metallurgica works in the supplement to his *Collection of English Words*, 1673, such as silver at Machynlleth, tin in Cornwall, iron in Sussex, copperas at Brightlingsea, and alum at Whitby.

possible, apologists like Sprat, or Francis Bacon before him naturally emphasized it out of proportion to other arguments. But while the evidence is plainly insufficient to prove Dr Hessen's case that science owes its development to economic and technical considerations, it is nevertheless obvious that these are of great importance and that in the main they favoured mechanistic rather than organic and biological studies. Gardening and agriculture, medicine and surgery had had large influence in the earliest days: Luca Ghini and the German herbalists, Fabricius and Vesalius, are proof enough of that. But in the seventeenth century the needs of mining, navigation, warfare, textiles and other industrial developments began to press their claims upon scientists; and institutions like the Royal Society were very sensitive to their requests.[1] In its early years it was confronted with problems ranging from the improvement of engines for striking whales[2] to the construction of a double-hulled ship[3] along with more detailed researches into the velocity and course of bullets (repeating Galileo's work upon parabolas), and into the construction and operation of siphons and pumps for draining mines. Boyle's air-pump, Hooke's watch-springs and microscopes, Newton's reflector, Savery's steam-engine, Morland's calculating machine all contributed to its success.

It was in fact the co-operation in the Royal Society during its early years of the three sorts of men indispensable for scientific progress that made possible its remarkable achievements. There were first the thinkers, often but not always mathematicians, the philosophers as Boyle called them, those, as he said of himself, who were driven by 'an unsatisfied appetite of knowledge' and possessed of sufficient intellectual power to meet its needs. Without the thinker science can never deserve its name. Then there are the practical men like William Petty or Sir Robert Moray whose concern is with public service and the solving of contemporary and remunerative problems, and who directed the thinker towards concrete issues, appreciated the factual consequences of his theories

---

[1] R. K. Merton, *loc. cit.* has a valuable appendix (pp. 598-620) giving an abstract of the amount of research devoted to socio-economic needs by the Royal Society as recorded in the four volumes of Thomas Birch's *History of the Royal Society*.

[2] Birch, *History of the Royal Society*, I, p. 327.　　　　[3] *Ibid.* I, p. 131.

and developed the results of his inventions. Finally there are those for whom science has primarily an aesthetic, almost a religious, appeal, men like Robert Hooke or Thomas Sydenham or John Ray for whom the study of nature has a fascination distinct from intellectual interest or practical utility. Plainly these three qualities are not mutually exclusive. Men like John Wilkins and Christopher Wren and, for that matter, Hooke and Boyle possessed all three; and no great scientist is wholly lacking in the first and third. But it was the fortune of the Royal Society to combine them to a unique degree. It was saved by the intellectual brilliance of its leaders from overmuch concern with gadgets and profit-making, by the sagacity of its men of affairs from overmuch abstract speculation, by the enthusiasm of its naturalists from narrowness of outlook and consequent boredom or factiousness.

Eminently representative of the new type of scientist both in the astonishing range of his interests and in his combination of theoretical and practical capacity is Robert Hooke. The son of a parson at Freshwater, a weakly but 'very sprightly' child he spent his first thirteen years making little mechanical toys,[1] then went to Dr Busby at Westminster, thence as chorister and servitor to Christ Church in 1653 and so to Boyle and his career. His work on the airpump and its vacuum chamber, on contrivances for flying, on a longitude clock, on the spring movement for watches and the circular pendulum might suggest that he was merely an inventor and mechanic. But already by 1665 he had devised a compound microscope, and published his *Micrographia*. He was one of the earliest to maintain that fossil shells, bones and plants were organic remains. He devised a lecture 'on the manner of rowing of ancient galleys' based upon Trajan's column and the mechanics of one-oar propulsion. He designed and actually had built a hospital in Hoxton and prepared plans for the rebuilding of London after the Great Fire.[2] He lectured on optics and light—

[1] Cf. R. Waller's *Life* prefixed to *Posthumous Works*, p. ii.

[2] Some of the work ascribed to Sir Christopher Wren may in fact be Hooke's; cf. e.g. 'Dr Busby's church' at Willen, Bucks., which is certainly his. He collaborated in the Monument and in some of the City churches. I owe this information to Mr H. M. Colvin, St John's College, Oxford.

and incidentally upon memory and the storing of visual images, —and upon gravitation, so far as to create a claim that Newton had borrowed from him. As curator for the Royal Society, it was his duty to produce three or four new experiments weekly at their meetings; and he did so for at least twenty years and indeed to some extent until his death in 1703. And his character was as remarkable and to the student of human nature as intriguing as his activities. Too devoted to his work to refuse the patronage and exploitation of the virtuosi, too awkward in manner and quaint in appearance to escape their ridicule, too sensitive not to resent it and become embittered, he never received and perhaps never deserved the credit for any great achievement, and yet more than any other he was the midwife who brought to its birth the new age of experiment and discovery, and fulfilled what Bacon had dreamed and Descartes propounded.

Within the Royal Society a similar attitude towards the Cartesian dualism is shown by the two eminent English scientists, Robert Boyle and Isaac Newton, both of whom were ardent advocates of the 'corpuscular' or mechanistic view of the physical universe and not less ardently religious as students of the Scriptures and champions of a theistic philosophy. It is indeed a mistake to regard either of them as a profound or consistent thinker; neither of them is comparable in this respect with Cudworth. They did not see clearly the contrast between the old world-view and the new, nor realize the difficulties that were to arise in reconciling them; and they both accepted belief in God as axiomatic. Boyle, in spite of his heredity, kept through life the charm and innocency of a child, always alert to ask questions and make experiments and frame hypotheses, always struggling against ill-health, saved from self-pity or dilettantism by his devotion to God, to his friends and to his work. Men like Ray, honest and free from sycophancy, felt for him a reverence not given to any other contemporary; and his quality earned him an influence and an affection beyond his peers —and perhaps beyond his strict intellectual and scientific deserts. Yet it was a great achievement to have released physical studies from their preoccupation with astrology and the philosopher's stone; to have worked out the problem of the vacuum and the grounds of Boyle's law;[1] to have explored so many reactions in the field of chemistry and laid down the principles of the *Sceptical Chymist*;[2] to have produced and befriended Robert Hooke, and to have treated Hobbes with courtesy.[3] As Dr Sarton has pointed out,[4] Boyle's greatest service was in clearing the ground. He did not propound any consistent philosophy himself, though he inclined towards the corpuscularian or atomic ideas[5] of Pierre Gassendi: but he did challenge the traditional doctrine of the four elements, earth, water, air and fire, and riddle with criticism Paracelsus's theory of the three hypostatic principles, salt, sulphur and mercury. This made possible a genuine chemistry, free from the prejudices and the absurdities which until his day made alchemy the sanctuary of imposture. But the greatness of his achievement is not in its specialization but in its range and integrity; he was a great Christian equally concerned with the translation and circulation of the Scriptures, with the medical and philanthropic activities of Sydenham, and with the strange phenomena of phosphorus:[6] his character was the principal and worthy cause of his renown.[7]

Isaac Newton, for whom Ray's friend, Isaac Barrow, resigned his chair of mathematics at Cambridge in 1669, was in general outlook very similar to Boyle. In religion he was less orthodox but equally sincere; in devotion to the Scriptures and especially in the interpretation of the Book of Revelation he rivalled Henry More; in chemistry though an adept and a zealous practioner he was free from the extravagancies of the alchemists; in his *Principia* (1687), he formulated the law of gravitation, brought order into

---

[1] *New Experiments Physico-Mechanicall touching the Spring of the Air* (1660).

[2] A dialogue between a corpuscularian, an Aristotelian, an alchemist and an inquisitive guest, published in 1661. [3] Cf. L. T. More, *Life and Works of Boyle*, p. 97.

[4] Cf. his article on 'Boyle and Bayle' in *Chymia*, III, pp. 155-68.

[5] He asserted that these did not seem able to explain all natural phenomena; cf. *Works* (ed. Birch), II, p. 47 etc. [6] Cf. his *The Aerial Noctiluca* (1680).

[7] It is necessary to protest against the attempt of L. T. More to fit Boyle into a 'place in that dynasty of intellectual giants which began with Copernicus and included also Kepler, Galileo, Descartes and Newton' (*op. cit.* p. 288). This attempt colours and distorts More's portrait: in interests, abilities, activities and achievements Boyle has little in common with any of those named except the last.

the confusion of cosmic speculation and gave a triumphant impetus to mathematical research and to the materialistic concept of the physical universe; in his *Opticks* (1704)[1] he recounted his experimental study of the spectrum and of chromatic aberration in lenses, formulated an explanation of the rainbow and by his theory of colours made another great contribution to human knowledge. Newton himself was constant in affirming the presence, energy and control of God as the ground and cause of all that is. But his followers enthusiastic over the completeness of his demonstration—the first great integrative principle to be formulated by the New Philosophy—naturally regarded it as a vindication of a mechanistic outlook: and this was accentuated in the next century by the lack of worthy representatives of the biological sciences or of religion. In consequence Newton's own breadth of view and his interests other than mathematical were neglected, and he was made responsible for the conviction that the physical universe was a vast machine which men could understand, explain, manipulate and ultimately control. This belief, with its consequent enhancement of economic and industrial values at the expense of aesthetic and moral, persisted until, with Charles Darwin, man himself was deposed from the position of controller and graded as part of the machine; and by that time mechanism was so securely established that it took two generations for the absurdity of this final step to be recognized.

Out of this mechanistic period in biological science the real start in chemistry was made. Boyle had left the subject unformulated. He had broken away from alchemy but had by no means replaced it by any definite and intelligible successor. A modern chemist reading the experiments of the seventeenth century will be able in most cases to recognize them and give them their appropriate descriptions;[2] but the world to which they belong is not his. He only begins to feel at home in chemical literature when

[1] This, though published last, dealt with subjects on which he had done his first important work at least as early as 1665; cf. Dr A. R. Hall, 'Sir I. Newton's Notebook' in *Cambridge Historical Journal*, IX, pp. 245-6.

[2] Cf. the fascinating and valuable studies by Professor John Read, *Prelude to Chemistry* (London, 1939).

he comes to the chemists of the eighteenth century. These men drew their principal inspiration not from alchemy or even from Boyle but from the group of doctors and physiologists, of whom Hermann Boerhaave was the outstanding figure and who were led to chemistry by their desire to explore the working of the human mechanism.[1] Starting from problems of respiration and digestion they investigated the nature of the air, began to isolate, describe and name different gases, examined the chemical changes effected in the digestive organs and by the circulation of the blood[2] and tried to give a coherent account of the functioning of the whole organism. This was promoted by the work of Friedrich Hoffmann and his colleague, Georg Ernst Stahl, both of Jena and afterwards Halle, whose famous theory of phlogiston, erroneous though in fact it proved to be, yet gave a working hypothesis which promoted the integration and solution of a wide range of problems.

Starting largely from this biological concern, chemistry soon became the chief interest of scientists and by the middle of the century was producing remarkable results. It was natural that there should be a transfer of study from the organic to the inorganic field, that demands for results should come from the medical, social, industrial and technical worlds and that progress should be greatly accelerated by the improvement in instruments and equipment. Hales's work had been done with makeshift apparatus incapable of registering exact measurements or giving consistent results: to contrast his laboratory with that of Joseph Black or Joseph Priestley is to realize how the provision of reagents, of balances and of the microscope had made rapid progress possible. Black's work like that of Hales was based upon physiological studies, as his inaugural lecture on acidity of the stomach and the action of magnesia clearly proves; his main researches on quicklime and the alkalis led to the rediscovery of Hales's 'fixed air', carbon dioxide, and his lectures at Edinburgh

---

[1] Cf. Sir E. Thorpe's *History of Chemistry*, I, p. 67, for a tribute to him as author of 'the most complete and luminous chemical treatise of the time'.

[2] Cf. Boerhaave, *Elementa Chemiae* (1732), English abridgment (London, 1734), pp. 22-7 etc.

and Glasgow though unpublished had a wide influence, not least upon James Watt. Henry Cavendish in London, Carl Wilhelm Scheele in Sweden and Joseph Priestley at Bowood and in Birmingham were working at the same period on 'the different kinds of air' and hydrogen, oxygen, nitrogen, chlorine and other gases were discovered by them. Now at last the beginnings of accurate analysis and intricate experiment had been made; the influence of alchemy and white magic had been forgotten, and the field could soon be surveyed and parcelled out. Steady advance began to be maintained as the number of workers increased and, forsaking the secrecy of the alchemists, consulted one another about their results. The consequence was that before his execution in 1794 Antoine Laurent Lavoisier had been able to complete the main structure of chemical science and already in 1772 had begun to remove the temporary scaffolding of the phlogiston theory which had by then served its purpose.[1]

Associated with Lavoisier was the remarkable group of scientists who gave splendour to the Académie des Sciences and made Paris the centre of progress during the second half of the eighteenth century: Claude Louis Berthollet and other chemists; Jean de Rond d'Alembert the physicist and philosopher; Joseph Louis Lagrange and Pierre Simon, Marquis de Laplace the astronomers and mathematicians; Jean Etienne Guettard, Nicolas Desmarets and the Abbé J. L. Giraud-Soulavie, the geologists; Bernard and Antoine Laurent de Jussieu the botanists; Jean Baptiste Pierre Antoine de Monet, Chevalier de Lamarck,[2] Etienne Geoffroy Saint-Hilaire and Georges Léopold Chrétien Dagobert Cuvier, the zoologists. Remarkable as was their work in all departments the contribution made in physics and chemistry was unquestionably the most significant. Lavoisier himself, by his researches into combustion, his accurate weighing of materials burnt and his consequent proof of their increase in weight, was able to lay before the Secretary of the Academy in 1777 a statement which effectively disproved

---

[1] Priestley, then almost alone, championed phlogiston until his death in America in 1804.

[2] He was first a botanist and author of *Flore française*, but was appointed a professor of zoology by the National Assembly in 1794.

the existence of phlogiston, established the significance of oxygen and vindicated the law of the conservation of mass. This 'Chemical Revolution' completed by the publication of *La Traité élémentaire de la chimie* in 1789 opened the way to quantitative analysis and to the identification and naming of elements, thus superseding the traditional and often fanciful titles given to their products by the alchemists and their successors, and providing the starting-point for the differentiation, identification and classification of the constituents of the material world.

What Lavoisier did for chemistry, Laplace by his *Mécanique céleste* (1799-1825) strove to do for cosmology. Taking Newton's *Principia* and the law of gravitation as his starting-point he set himself to complete the reduction of all physical phenomena, fluid and solid, to a single mechanical system and his results including the first notice of his nebular hypothesis were set out in more popular form in his *Exposition du système du monde*. With this the Newtonian system received its complete vindication—as was indeed asserted by Laplace's famous reply to the Emperor's inquiry about the Creator, 'Je n'avais pas besoin de cette hypothèse-là'.[1] The nature and working of the universe had been apparently explained without any reference to a Creator or to the supernatural, in the traditional sense of those words. By such work, supplemented in certain respects by that of their biological colleagues which we shall consider later, a scientific *Weltanschauung* appropriate to the industrial age was fashioned and corroborated. To appreciate its immense influence and so to understand the ease with which it challenged and overthrew the traditional religion of Western Europe it is necessary to remind ourselves of the transformation which was taking place in the whole economy and circumstances of human life, and which seemed to supply pragmatic proof of the validity and sufficiency of a mechanistic philosophy.

It would be as big a mistake to suppose that the increase of

[1] The incident is recorded by W. W. Rouse Ball, *History of Mathematics*, p. 388; Sir E. Whittaker (*Mathematical Gazette*, xxxiii, p. 2) challenges the assumption of Laplace's atheism.

scientific knowledge was the direct cause of the industrial revolution as to suppose that economic and industrial needs produced the scientific movement. The fact of course is that the immense enlargement of life in Western Europe in the sixteenth and seventeenth centuries due to the discovery of the New World, the opening up of Asia and Africa, the improvement of communications and of trade, the increase of wealth and the raising of the standards of life, the fuller knowledge of medicine and of sanitation, of agriculture and manufactures were consequences of the same expansion of human energies which produced the intellectual and scientific achievements of the time. As a result a great development both in the number of the population and in its aptitude for technical labour made itself felt before the middle of the eighteenth century, and by 1760 industrial reform was gathering momentum.

To examine in detail the agricultural, technical, commercial and financial history of the time so as to set out the elements which produced industrialism would be merely to summarize the data noted in many specialized studies both of economic history and of particular lines of progress. But a few scientific contributions may be noted.

It might have been expected that botanical and zoological studies would speedily improve the diet of the people and so increase their numbers, yet, when William Turner introduced the growing of lucerne in 1550[1] or the Royal Society in 1663 urged the importance of planting more potatoes, there is little evidence that they effected changes in cropping. Nor can the slight betterment of the breeds of sheep and cattle be regarded as influential. But before the end of the century medical progress, the provision of better drugs, the improvement in the education of doctors, surgeons and apothecaries, certainly contributed much to the health and longevity of the people; and the increased care of children and of the sick tended more slowly in the same direction. At the end of the sixteenth century sympathetic magic and astrology suggested remedies like stallion's dung boiled in beer for jaundice and the doctrine of signatures led to the less noxious

---

[1] Cf. his *Herbal*, II, pp. 51-3.

treatment of phthisis by lungwort tea or flesh wounds by poultices of woundwort; and the prescriptions must often have been deadlier than the diseases. A century later the efforts of the Royal College against charlatans,[1] the accurate identification of vegetable remedies, the clinical observations of the great doctors from John Caius to Thomas Sydenham were having their effect; and even the villages might look, as Ray did at Black Notley, to solid practitioners like Samuel Dale or bright young scientists like Benjamin Allen instead of to the herb-woman and the witch.

Along with the improvement in medicine went a gradual improvement in diet. Early in the eighteenth century Jethro Tull by the invention of the sowing drill, the introduction of hoeing, and the use of turnips and clover in a new system of rotation showed the way for the new agriculture which Lord Townshend, Coke of Norfolk and many others, including King George III, developed during the subsequent period. So too by the middle of the century Robert Bakewell of Dishley had produced his Leicester and New Leicester sheep with their stocky frames and abundant mutton; Coke was shearing his thousands of Southdowns on his reclaimed saltings at Holkham; new breeds of cattle, Shorthorns, Herefords and Devons more than doubled the weight of beeves; and similar experiments were producing fresh strains of pigs and poultry. Though the science of genetics was unknown, the scientific breeding both of plants and animals was advancing rapidly.

This change in the method of agriculture and stock-rearing was accomplished by a revolution in land-tenure which had far-reaching consequences for the whole life and character of mankind. The old system of open fields, in which each member of the community had his unfenced strips and the sheep and cattle roamed freely, was incompatible with the development of intensive cultivation and the segregation of new types of crop and beast. It was neighbourly, but wasteful and ineffective. The case for fenced and privately owned fields, for larger farms and great estates was unanswerable. Enclosure proceeded apace after 1760

[1] Described by C. Goodall, *Historical Account of the College's Proceedings against Empiricks.* London, 1684.)

and the whole appearance of the country was changed from open stretches of arable and pasture and great tracts of moor and woodland into the tidy pattern of hedgerows and shaws, stone walls and ditches of modern England. This meant the disappearance of the small yeoman farmers and cottagers who for centuries had been the backbone of the nation. Needing ready money for the hedging and developing of their land, undersold by the factories in the home industries of their households, unable to obtain the new sheep and oxen that the markets demanded, they were forced to sell, and either to sink to the level of the agricultural labourer or to give up the countryside for the town. So the great mass of the dispossessed who formed the urban proletariat of the next century was produced and rendered defenceless.

For the whole revolution was haphazard and uncontrolled. Huge hives of industry were assembled without forethought or planning, indeed with hardly more intelligence than animates a swarm of bees. Blind competition and the enthusiasm to speed up production and make money directed the location, management, recruiting and conditions of labour; and if a measure of mutual consideration usually influenced the masters, any such protection or co-operation was denied by law to the men. It is difficult for us who look back upon the process of industrialization to believe that the advocates of *laissez-faire*, who rejected all attempts to raise wages, restrict hours of labour or save women and children from exploitation, were often like William Wilberforce, men genuinely Christian and in other respects splendidly altruistic. But in fact the change, notable as it must have been, came so naturally and so rapidly that the authorities accepted and welcomed it, the more observant were bewildered and hesitant and the few voices raised in protest did not succeed in penetrating to the true significance of what was happening or in obtaining the attention of their contemporaries. There was indeed such manifest benefit for the country and for mankind from the new agriculture, the new industries, the new communications, the new trade and commerce that the thrill of it swept men into its advocacy with the power and passion of a crusade.

But the Spectre, like a hoar frost and a Mildew, rose over Albion,
Saying, 'I am God, O Sons of Men! I am your Rational Power!
Am I not Bacon and Newton and Locke who teach Humility to Man?'[1]

With the general rise in the population and the change in its
way of life came a marked advance in technical skill and equipment. The harnessing of the water-power of the Pennine streams
gave to Yorkshire and Lancashire their first mills and factories for
cotton and woollen goods; and various inventions Arkwright's
frame for spinning cotton, Hargreaves's jenny for working spindles
mechanically and Crompton's mule for muslins and fine yarn in
the decade 1769-79 combined to facilitate the production of
textiles. Chemical bleaching followed Scheele's discovery of
chlorine in 1774; and colour printing became easy when Bell
invented the revolving cylinder in 1783. Villages and small towns,
the first fruits of industrialism, sprang up all over the northern
counties and drew to them the rural labourers, dispossessed by
enclosures and the changes of agriculture. The discovery of the
use of coal for smelting iron fixed the location and speeded the
growth of heavy industry and transferred the foundries from
Sussex to the Midlands. At the same time Cornish tin was in great
demand; and the county was the scene of a highly skilled and
vigorous industrialism. When Thomas Newcomen took over and
improved Savery's steam-engine of 1698, and when fifty years
later James Watt[2] perfected his invention, almost the first employment of their 'engine to raise water by fire' (their steam-pump)
was in the stanneries of the west. So too in the potteries, when in
1750 Ralph Wood set up his works at Burslem, a group of other
potters followed his lead and Staffordshire became the centre of
the industry which Josiah Wedgwood at Etruria brought to
world-wide fame and from which he created in 1785 the General
Chamber of Manufacturers of Great Britain.

[1] Blake, *Jerusalem*, ch. 54, ll. 15-17. Blake like Charles Williams and other moderns
illustrates the use of extravagantly supernatural imagery in reaction from an over-
mechanistic science. For a translation of the Spectre into prose, cf. J. L. and B. Hammond,
The Village Labourer, 1760-1832.

[2] Newcomen was a smith and iron-worker; Watt was a real scientist who has some claim
to have anticipated Cavendish in the discovery of the composite nature of water in 1783.

By this development of production in the north, midlands and west Britain ceased to be a country with one huge metropolis and a small-town population and became urbanized, large masses of its people dwelling round the various centres of industry and others gathered at the sea-ports and chief markets. In consequence, means of communication both internal and overseas became vitally important. The roads which John Ogilby had first mapped in 1675 and which for Samuel Pepys and even for William Paley had been scenes of disaster remained impassable except for packhorses until in 1784 mail coaches were introduced and the Turnpike Trust took up its proper task and revolutionized road-construction. Meanwhile water-ways were cheaper, safer and more rapid: rivers were dredged and canalized, locks were built, and inland towns became ports; and in 1761 the first of the network of canals was dug and opened to barges. For overseas trade and the coastwise traffic which served London with its fuel and heavy goods, the shipbuilding centres were kept busy; seas were charted and lighthouses built; and all round the coasts, wherever any harbour facilities were possible, ports for the receipt of cargoes and the repair of shipping sprang up or were expanded. Moreover, a succession of wars gave us Newfoundland, Nova Scotia and Gibraltar; Canada, the West Indies, the Punjab and Bengal; Malta, Cape Colony and Ceylon; and these meant an immense extension of distant markets which naval supremacy kept open for our merchantmen. In consequence a period of exploration[1] similar in character and result to that of the Elizabethan age but now on a world-wide scale was in preparation.

By the end of the eighteenth century though steam-power had hardly begun to play an effective part in production or distribution the resources of the country had been vastly developed, mobilized and made accessible; and the stage was set for the transformation scene that was to follow. Stimulated as it had been by the long struggle with Napoleon and surviving its issue with less damage and greater reputation than any other country, Britain could take full advantage of the succession of discoveries

[1] Cf. below, pp. 165-6.

and inventions which placed steam, gas, electricity, and all the miracles of the past hundred years at the service of mankind. It would be out of place here to comment upon the method or to estimate the effects of the changes: they have been described in all their aspects and from every possible viewpoint; and the evidence of them is plain for all to see and appreciate. But as a visible sign of their extent it is of interest to take Morden's admirable county maps printed in 1696 in Edmund Gibson's edition of *Camden's Britannia* and to compare them with those of 1816 in Thomas Dix's edition of John Carey's *Complete Atlas of English Counties* and so with the similar areas in a gazetteer of 1860 and the ordinance survey of today.[1]

For our present purpose we are concerned less with the physical, social and cultural changes than with the consequences for religion and theology. The old adage 'God made the country; man made the town' may be met by the reminder that the Bible begins with a garden and ends with a city. But, whatever the truth of it, a population cut off from contact with the rhythm of nature, the slow processes of agriculture, and the small communities of village life is in danger of becoming artificial, hectic and mob-minded. Like Antaeus in the old Greek legend, the children of earth need to keep their feet on the ground, and for their recreation the soil is better than the pavement. Natural religion is not exterminated in urban areas—witness the passion of the slums for caged birds and plants in pots, for the canary and the aspidistra. Indeed too many of our best field naturalists are city folk for there to be any question of eliminating the appreciation and wonder that nature arouses in us. But, if not destroyed, such religion is starved of its sacraments and frustrated in its activities; and for most men there is real loss of the depth that comes from solitariness, the sensitiveness that responds to beauty, and the generosity that belongs to good neighbours.

Such generalizations do not get us very far—are indeed little more than truisms. What is more relevant is that with the

---

[1] Full details for a single county can be found e.g. in *A Descriptive List of the Maps of Lancashire* by H. Whitaker (Chetham Society, 1938).

development of the mechanical in life and thought there came at first a deistic and then a virtually atheistic outlook. Already in John Locke, the Oxford contemporary of the younger Cambridge Platonists and the friend of Cudworth's daughter Lady Masham, there is a concept of faith in purely intellectual terms and an insistence that since all knowledge is based upon experience and ultimately upon sensation the field of knowledge is small, speculation is to be discouraged and tolerance to be advocated. Locke remained substantially orthodox; but Lord Herbert of Cherbury and, still more, Matthew Tindal had insisted upon the supremacy of reason and identified reason with argumentation,[1] and John Toland, more openly hostile, had by his famous pamphlet, *Christianity not miraculous*, emphasized the contrast between natural law and orthodoxy, and reduced religion to an obedience to natural law. Even William Paley at the end of the eighteenth century, though in *The Evidences of Christianity* he argued for the veracity of the Apostles in their account of the miracles and resurrection, yet in his *Natural Theology* and indeed in his whole attitude to religion presented it in terms of the utility of conformity with the divine purpose and interpreted that purpose solely on Cicero's ancient analogy of watch and watchmaker. In spite of Bishop Butler's efforts to give a wider meaning to the whole controversy, it is this analogy, and the mechanical concept of the universe presupposed by it, that is put forward by Cleanthes and demolished by Philo in David Hume's *Dialogues concerning Natural Religion*; and Hume's scepticism was dominant in British thought until the growing influence of Immanuel Kant challenged it in the middle of the nineteenth century.

---

[1] 'The Holy Ghost can't deal with men as rational creatures but by proposing arguments to convince their understandings.' Tindal, *Christianity as Old as the Creation*, ch. XII.

VIII

LINNAEUS AND THE COMING OF SYSTEM

IT is one of the strange vagaries of history that after the amazing achievements of the seventeenth century there should have followed the dullness and disappointment of the eighteenth. Both in the more abstract sciences, mathematics, physics and astronomy, and in the concrete, geology, botany, zoology, physiology and medicine, the century following Francis Bacon had seen immense development. But in addition there had been almost equal progress in archaeology and linguistics, in geography and history. The creation of libraries and museums, the exploration of east and west, the initiation of new lines of research had accompanied the advance in scientific and historical studies. It had been a wonderful period, a worthy fulfilment of that wholeness for which Francis Bacon had pleaded and Ralph Cudworth had philosophized. Why did its brilliance suffer so sudden and complete an eclipse?

That the end of an epoch came in this country by the second decade of the eighteenth century can hardly be questioned. With the solitary exception of Stephen Hales there was no one in Britain to carry on at the same level the great work of Ray, Willughby, Lister and Grew. Halley and Flamsteed, the astronomers, Lhwyd and Woodward, the geologists, Tyson in anatomy, Mayow in physiology, Sydenham in medicine left no successors. Indeed, to survey the list of Fellows or to read the *Transactions of the Royal Society* in the last years of Newton's presidency is to wonder what sort of meetings so mediocre a gathering could have produced. It would be unkind but not wholly unfair to say that it deserved the treatment which Sir John Hill[1] afterwards bestowed

[1] *A Review of the Works of the Royal Society* (London, 1751), dedicated to Martin Folkes, its President, and justified e.g. by C. R. Weld, *History of the R.S.* 1, p. 428 etc.

upon it. What is true of science is true also of other fields of study. Somehow a blight had fallen upon most forms of intellectual growth. When Dr D. C. Douglas declares that 'medieval scholarship in England underwent during the eighteenth century not a development but a reaction',[1] he records a verdict appropriate to almost every department of learning.

So far as Britain is concerned there were local circumstances which would in any case have threatened a general collapse of morale. The later Stuarts had combined a strong emotional appeal with a total lack of moral worth or political wisdom. The profligacy and opportunism of the court spread corruption; the vindictiveness of the anti-puritan legislation drove the best elements of the districts which had supplied the highest percentage of genius overseas to Holland and America; the non-juring schism deprived the State Church of its few outstanding leaders; the scandals associated with the names of Titus Oates or of Judge Jeffreys indicate the instability of the time; the revolution gave a temporary relief but did not prevent the decline in public standards, in the intellectual life of the universities and in the maintenance of scientific, literary, philosophical and religious interests. When Bishop Butler wrote his famous complaint in 1736, 'It is come, I know not how, to be taken for granted by many persons that Christianity is not so much as a subject for inquiry but is now at length discovered to be fictitious',[2] he was addressing not the authors of the enlightenment in France and Germany but his own fellow-countrymen.

But such local conditions, though explaining the completeness of the collapse here, only intensify the dullness and depression characteristic of the first half of the eighteenth century over most of Europe. It was a period in which creative work and particularly the scientific movement of the previous century came almost to a standstill. When we have made full allowance for all secondary causes—such as we have outlined in the case of Britain—it is clear that the real position is due to the particular situation that had

---

[1] *English Scholars*, p. 355; the same point is made and illustrated by Stuart Piggott in his *William Stukeley*, cf. pp. 180-5. [2] Preface to *The Analogy*

arisen within science itself and which we have already noted. Progress in the previous century had been most conspicuous in the biological field: immense developments had taken place in botany, both in the definition and classification of species and in the beginning of physiological studies; and in zoology, though less had been done, similar ground had been covered. But it was increasingly evident that the lack of any adequate knowledge of chemistry and physics was making future progress difficult. Anyone who studies, for example, the attempts of seventeenth-century physiologists to explain respiration in terms of a fiery element in the chest, or to investigate nutrition and digestion, or to appreciate the relationship of a plant to the soil will realize that biological studies had almost reached a point at which they must mark time till sound foundations had been provided for further advance.

How badly such a foundation was needed may be seen if we consider that hitherto the most successful attempts at physiology had been those which approached the subject from its mechanical aspect, as if its problems belonged to the engineer or the mathematician.[1] Thus Borelli, the follower of Galileo, had striven to apply to the movements of muscles or the pulsation of the heart such methods for assessing weight and measurement as were appropriate to astronomy. Like his older contemporary Descartes, he regarded the body, whether of man or animal, as merely a machine whose actions are the automatic response to an external stimulus: animals have no soul and therefore no right to be treated as living creatures; to subject them to experiment and vivisection is as proper as to take to pieces a bicycle. It was only necessary to admit that for the operation of this machine man alone among creatures possessed a particular organ, the pineal gland, whereby his soul made contact with and directed his body, to be regarded as orthodox and therefore safe from the Inquisition. Such an interpretation was, as we have seen, violently rejected by Henry More

[1] Cf. C. D. Broad, 'The New Philosophy: Bruno to Descartes' in *Camb. Historical Journal*, VIII, p. 54: 'At certain periods in the development of human knowledge it may be profitable and even essential for generations of scientists to act on a theory which is philosophically quite ridiculous.'

and John Ray; but it persisted on the continent[1] and gave rise to the experiments of the schools of Paris, and of the great Italian Spallanzani and to a concentration upon the mechanics of animal behaviour which in the days before the chemical aspect of organic metabolism was understood, reduced living creatures to puppets to be pulled and pushed by strings, and the study of them to intricate calculations of the weight in pounds of the pressures involved.[2]

While the growing-point of the scientific movement thus shifted from biology to chemistry the great biological tradition established in Paris carried on the study of plant and animal life. After Tournefort, botany was not very flourishing. But the anatomist of the Jardin du Roi, Claude Perrault, had been succeeded by Duverney and Gouye who kept this side of the Academy's work going,[3] and they had with them the polymath and pioneer of insect study, René Antoine Ferchault de Réaumur. A man of large means, wide interests and great abilities, he took up the researches of Willughby and Swammerdam and, in the six volumes of his *Mémoires pour servir à l'histoire des insectes*, gave a monumental record of their anatomy, metamorphoses and habits. Considering the state in which he found the subject owing to the tragic incompleteness of Ray's book,[4] the extent and sagacity of his observations created a new epoch in it. Entomology was also studied by other isolated workers, Charles de Geer, the Swede, Pierre Lyonet of the Hague, and the Englishmen, Eleazar Albin and Moses Harris; but for at least a century, indeed until Fabre, Réaumur stood in a class by himself.

But the chief glory of Paris and indeed of biology in the eighteenth century was Georges Louis Leclerc de Buffon. Born in the same year as Linnaeus but very unlike him in character and circumstances and forming a radically different concept of the

[1] In Britain David Hartley, author of *Observations on Man* (1750) and the first to use 'psychology' in its modern sense, stands almost alone.

[2] H. Butterfield, *The Origins of Modern Science*, p. 109, quotes Borelli as calculating that every heart-beat involved an expenditure of 135,000 pounds weight!

[3] For a full description of the members and their work, cf. F. J. Cole, *History of Comparative Anatomy*, pp. 393–442.

[4] His *Historia Insectorum* was published posthumously from his rough notes and descriptions without editing or even arrangement.

scope and quality of science, he strove to carry on the Baconian tradition and to interpret coherently the whole field of natural knowledge. For this task he was in most respects admirably qualified. Well born, well-to-do, gifted with an alert mind and an energetic temperament, living in a cultured society and constantly conversing with experts in every field of learning, he had spent a year in scientific circles in England with his friend Lord Kingston[1] and throughout life had every opportunity for satisfying his ambition. His love of pleasure might have filled too much of his time; his range of interests might have made him a dabbler or a dilettante; his mastery of language might have produced mere glibness and superficiality. None of these criticisms can fairly be levelled at him; for in addition to his care for the Jardin du Roi he produced a massive volume of work in which a continuous effort after completeness was successfully maintained. The *Histoire naturelle* is the most important attempt yet made to collect, describe and assay all the available knowledge of nature. In spite of its huge bulk it is still only a fragment; but in its fullness of detail, its fertility of ideas, and in general its soundness of judgment it served to summarize the work of the first phase of natural science and (though to a lesser degree) to initiate the second.

Yet when this is said, something must be added. There certainly is in Buffon a lack of that profound concern with the importance of his subject, that conviction of the worth of truth, that basic sincerity of outlook which should characterize the great scientist. In the last resort his work is to him an interesting pastime, and a satisfying objective. But, if it comes to a conflict between his comforts and his studies, or even between convention and conviction, the former always comes first. In his dealings with Voltaire[2] on the one side and the Catholic authorities on the other his essential weakness is disclosed.

---

[1] As a result he published French translations of Newton's *Fluxions* and Hales's *Vegetable Staticks*.

[2] He properly ridiculed the absurd notion that fossil shells found inland in Italy or France are those brought by pilgrims at the time of the Crusades; cf. *Hist. nat.* (Eng. trans. 1812) I, p. 222. Discovering, however, that the source for this was a letter by Voltaire, he added a long footnote of obsequious apology; cf. *Hist. nat.* (Eng. trans.) I, pp. 223-4.

His dealings with the theologians are of special importance not only as illustrating his character but as indicating the extent to which research was restricted by their influence. The first volume of the *Histoire naturelle* deals with his theory of the earth. It contains chapters criticizing the views of Whiston, Burnet and Woodward, an important and intelligent discussion of fossil shells, and a full treatment of physical geography. He plainly recognizes that the earth's surface has seen very many and long-continuing changes, and that these have not ceased. While not attacking the stories of the Creation or the Flood, he is not prepared to employ them as the sole source of our knowledge or the sufficient explanation of all the phenomena. But his book would not strike a modern reader as heterodox, or as offensive—not nearly so offensive as the gynaecological details in his volume on man. Nevertheless, two years after its publication, he received an official letter from the Sorbonne warning him that it contained fourteen propositions which were censurable as 'contrary to the faith of the Church'. Upon a demand for recantation, he published as a prelude to his fourth volume an apology beginning with a statement to the effect that he had no intention to contradict the Scriptures, that he believed most firmly all their statements as to the Creation, both as to its sequence and its events, and that he withdrew everything that he had written respecting the formation of the earth and in general all that might not agree with the teaching of Moses, 'since he had presented his hypothesis about the formation of the planets as a mere supposition'.[1]

The incident has a special interest in view of the subject of the complaint. It was natural and proper for the Paris faculty to take exception to the writings of Julien de la Mettrie: his *Histoire naturelle de l'âme* was a direct attack upon religion; and the Dutch with whom he took refuge found his flippant materialism equally offensive. But Buffon was not in fact a materialist or even a Cartesian—in days when biology was largely mechanistic, he

---

[1] The letter of the deputies and syndic of the faculty of theology dated 15 Jan. 1751, Buffon's reply dated 12 March and their acknowledgment of 4 May are printed in *Hist. nat.* IV, pp. v–xvi (Paris, 1753).

might well have won the approval of the religious. It is significant, and regrettable, that the theologians should have been as sensitive in regard to the Creation stories as they were to a flat denial of the spiritual nature of man; it is interesting that the long conflict between Genesis and geology should have been begun not by Protestants but by Catholics.

As regards the biological sciences and apart from the French progress in anatomy and physiology, the chief concern of the century was with collecting and classifying. In England Ray and Willughby gave place to James Petiver[1] and Charles Owen;[2] Elizabeth Blackwell and Moses Harris set the fashion for sumptuous picture-books; the amassing of libraries, sculpture-galleries and cabinets of curiosities became the occupation of the virtuosi; the universities produced no one of any merit at all in the sciences and hardly anyone to be remembered in any field of scholarship; and London which in the previous century had rivalled the universities was now equally destitute. Society, in places, was cultured and charming, a pleasant leisurely world for young men who could set out on the grand tour with a proper equipment of lacqueys and money and return with the marbles of Italy and the curios of the Indies. But its scientific representative was Sir Hans Sloane, the great 'toy-man', who had succeeded Newton in the chair of the Royal Society and was gathering the hoarded and miscellaneous treasures which have since become the British Museum, an Irish-man still genial and generous, but one in whom the collector's passion had long obscured all serious scientific interest.[3] We owe a debt to such men: they stored up material for future use, and it was perhaps inevitable that progress in botanical and zoological research should be delayed. But it remains true that between Ray's *Wisdom of God in the Works of Creation* and Paley's *Natural Philosophy* there was 'not a development, but a reaction'. The vital

[1] Cf. my *John Ray*, p. 233.

[2] Presbyterian minister of Warrington, author of *An Essay towards a Natural History of Serpents* (London, 1742), an entertaining but valueless compilation.

[3] Sloane had once produced a flora of Jamaica and even discovered a new *Salicornia* at Gravesend; but even in 1710 it needed all Tancred Robinson's energy to extract from him the script of Ray's *Historia Insectorum* which had else disappeared unpublished into his treasure-chests.

questions raised and studied in the seventeenth century are ignored in favour of trivalities during the eighteenth.

That this is an inevitable conclusion becomes plain if we turn from the small folk of Britain to the accredited representative of eighteenth-century biology. Carl von Linné, Carolus Linnaeus, has received so large a meed of honour both in his own day and subsequently,[1] has become so generally regarded as the chief founder of botanical and zoological studies, and has left behind so rich a legacy both of learning and of legend that it is important to understand his precise place in the development of science. This, as he himself understood it, he has made abundantly plain. When his disciples printed the motto *Deus creavit, Linnaeus disposuit*, under his portrait,[2] we may question their taste but cannot mistake their claim. For him classification, the arrangement and naming of species, is science and he is the great classifier. That is a true verdict.

As such it is easy to underestimate the scale and value of his work. The binary nomenclature whereby every species is known by a generic name, which it shares with its cognates, and a specific, usually a descriptive adjective or (if a noun) its Latin name or the name of a classical personage—*Linnaea borealis*, *Felis leo* or *Papilio machaon*—had been foreshadowed both in botany and zoology by several of his predecessors;[3] and as known species became more numerous and the alternative to the system was the use of longer and more elaborate descriptions, its convenience was evident. But full credit must be given to Linnaeus for adopting it as a universal principle, and for the skill and fertility of invention with which he applied it. In his day when the simple definition of a species as that which proceeded at the creation from the hand of God was generally accepted, and when there was no need for elaborate rules of priority and no cleavage between botanists and

---

[1] Cf. for example the extravagant estimates of his greatness in E. Nordenskiöld, *History of Biology*, pp. 202-18, 222, 235 etc.; K. Hagberg, *Carl Linnaeus* (Eng. trans. London, 1952) though equally eulogistic is much more revealing of his astonishing defects.

[2] Cf. frontispiece of D. H. Stoever, *Leben des Ritters C. von Linné* (1792) and its English translation by Joseph Trapp.

[3] Notably by C. Bauhin, preface to *Phytopinax*.

zoologists in their elaborations of his system, the result had an immense value in giving clarity and simplicity to nomenclature. The present chaos and the perpetual changes which make the study of synonyms a life's work must not be laid to his account. When he produced the tenth edition of his *Systema* and when this and the year of its publication, 1758, were accepted as a fixed starting-point,[1] a good beginning had unquestionably been made. If science or even natural history meant nothing more than identification Linnaeus would well deserve his title of *princeps*.

For indeed his efforts to collect or obtain material from as much of the world as possible were strenuous and incessant. Though in 1732 he had toured Lapland and in 1741, 1746 and 1749 the rest of Sweden, he did not, as compared with Ray and several others, himself do much field work. But he encouraged his pupils to travel very widely; he sought for specimens whether by gift or loan or purchase from a vast circle of correspondents;[2] he promoted the formation of museums and fostered the collector's passion wherever he could; and he devoted his time without stint to the business of scrutinizing, naming and cataloguing the resultant specimens. No single person before him had amassed any comparable series of pressed plants, preserved insects, fishes and reptiles, bird skins and eggs, and the skins and bones of mammals; and he had seen and named far more than he possessed.

Handicapped always by his ignorance of languages—his Latin was not good and he knew nothing else except Swedish—and harassed in his youth by poverty and in later life by domestic worries and ill-health, he yet maintained touch with a very wide circle of correspondents, drew to him at Uppsala a large number of pupils, and achieved an immense reputation with all the learned societies of the world. Material was thus available for him as it had not been for any earlier naturalist,[3] and in sorting, describing and

[1] Botanists date their starting-point five years earlier from the first edition of his *Species Plantarum*.

[2] He asked for and received specimens without hesitation, but made little return. 'It is a general complaint that Dr Linnaeus receives all and returns nothing' wrote to him his friend Peter Collinson (J. E. Smith, *A Selection from the Correspondence of Linnaeus*, I, p. 18).

[3] Cf. the list of collections contributed to his herbarium, 'the largest ever seen', in his Diary (Pulteney, *General View of the Writings of Linnaeus*, pp. 574-5).

naming it he showed a remarkable accuracy and skill. His particular abilities lay precisely in this direction. He had no concern with philosophy or with ultimate questions: the very word 'philosophy'[1] on his lips meant little more than the compilation of an appropriate vocabulary. He had little interest in anatomy or physiology except so far as to recognize that differences of structure might be important for identification. He hardly shared Ray's desire to see the living plants and birds in their natural environments, or his flair for observing peculiarities of habit and behaviour. For nomenclature, however, he had a real passion and to add new items to his lists was the quest of his life.[2] Regarding the naming of plants and animals as Adam's chief prerogative and occupation in Paradise, he found a sacred calling and a source of boundless pride in his own similar task.[3] His skill in noting, and his clearness in defining, differences gave his work a high and permanent value. In a very real sense he initiated a new epoch in botany and zoology by discriminating and naming so wide a range of species.

Of his systems of classification the defects are due to his peculiar interests. He was not profoundly concerned with questions of structure or habit—he was indeed less competent in these respects than many of his predecessors. But he had a passion for orderly arrangement and, rejecting a 'natural system' as impossible, he fastened upon characters which were simple and distinctive, in botany the number and arrangement of the stamens and pistil. The idea of concentrating upon a special organ was in fact as old as Andrea Cesalpino and had been used by Colonna.[4] Linnaeus followed S. Vaillant[5] in selecting the sex organs; and if a single character was to be chosen, this selection was probably the best possible—though it yielded a number of quite fantastic results. Linnaeus himself briefly investigated the sex organs but took no

---

[1] As e.g. in the title of his book *Philosophia Botanica*, published in 1751.

[2] Cf. his dictum, 'A person is a better botanist in proportion as he knows more species', *Linnaeus and Jussieu*, p. 54 (Parker, 1844).

[3] Cf. K. Hagberg, *op. cit.* pp. 198-9 for Linnaeus as the second Adam.

[4] For an account of early classification cf. A. Arber, *Herbals*, pp. 163-84.

[5] *Sermo de Structura Florum* (Leiden, 1718).

steps to consider the importance of their position: indeed he was ignorant of plant-physiology even when he became interested in breeding and hybridization. He admitted that his arrangement was 'artificial' but defended it as enabling an easy classification of new species and as preparing for the time when a more 'natural' system could be formulated. To that system he hardly contributed a single idea or discovery;[1] for the result of the doubts, which his hybridizing raised as to the dogma of the immutability of species, was only the suggestion in his Diary[2] that in the genera only one species had originally been created and that this, accidentally impregnated by others of different genera, gave rise to further cross-bred species. Fortunately Bernard Laurent de Jussieu of Lyons and Paris and his nephew Antoine, and (later) Joseph Gartner of Tübingen and afterwards of Petrograd, the pupil of Haller, Augustin Pyrame de Candolle of Geneva and Montpellier, and Robert Brown and John Lindley in London resisted his dominance and formulated a series of more 'natural' systems.

As regards the animal kingdom his choice of determinative characters was still less satisfactory. His six classes, Quadrupeds, Birds, Amphibians, Fishes, Insects, Worms, were based upon superficial, not as with Ray on anatomical, characters, and the two last are miserably insufficient to replace Ray's four. He was in fact uninterested in the invertebrates with the exception of the highly coloured lepidoptera—partly because they did not in general produce good specimens for the museum. But even in the classes with which he was more familiar it is true to say with Alfred Newton that 'for the most part he followed Ray and where he departed from his model he seldom improved upon it'.[3] If at the end of his career he at last included the Whales among the

---

[1] Nordenskiöld's claim (*op. cit.* p. 214) that he founded groups 'palms, grasses, Liliaceae, Umbellata still regarded as entirely natural' ignores the fact that these families and many others had been known and named a century before and that their names were in common use. The similar claim (p. 215) that 'phenological, ecological and geographical zoology and botany has its origin in him' is equally unjust to his predecessors.

[2] Pulteney, *op. cit.* p. 556; and cf. the account in *Genera Plantarum* (6th ed.) quoted by J. von Sachs, *History of Botany*, p. 105. The chapter on this subject in Hagberg, *op. cit.* pp. 196-205 shows vividly how complete was his bewilderment.

[3] A. Newton, *Dictionary of Birds*, Introd. p. 8.

Mammals, he also transferred the Cartilaginous fishes, under a misapprehension of the nature of gills, to the Amphibia.

But, as with plants so still more with animals of which his knowledge was much smaller, there is plain proof that the living creature was not his primary interest. A single example will suffice. He had laid it down that Swallows did not migrate but spent the winter under water in ponds. His faithful correspondent Collinson pointed out that most of the learned world disagreed with him, that if so their anatomy should be searched to discover how they could breathe for months under water and that experiments such as he suggested should be carried out. Collinson was a pertinacious man, and for five years[1] urged Linnaeus to explain and vindicate his statement. He was wholly unsuccessful: Linnaeus had spoken; the case was settled.[2]

Unfortunately his appetite for fame which in later life became almost overweening[3] made him contemptuous of any other form of biological science. Thus his strictures upon Ray,[4] from whose work he borrowed largely but with scanty acknowledgment, reveal both his conviction that the fundamentals of botany were nomenclature and classification;[5] and his failure to realize that classification must be based upon truly structural characteristics. Anyone who was not content merely to describe and name, anyone who treated taxonomy as a matter rather of convenience than of profound importance was dismissed by him as no true scientist. As he acquired an almost legendary reputation and until the

[1] J. E. Smith, op. cit. I, pp. 54-76.

[2] For similar examples cf. his insistence that spermatozoa were not 'animalcules', that in hybrids the temperament came from the female the physique from the male parent, or more generally, his adherence to the Aristotelian doctrine of the four elements.

[3] The later pages of his Diary contain a series of extravagant boasts: 'No person ever had a more solid knowledge of the three kingdoms of nature', 'No person ever proved himself a greater botanist or zoologist', 'No person ever became so celebrated all over the world', 'No person ever discovered so many animals', etc. (cf. Pulteney, op. cit. p. 565 and K. Hagberg, op. cit. pp. 208-9). The process by which the simple naïve youth of the Lapland journey grew into this arrogant and acquisitive old man can be traced in his letters, e.g. the series to Haller or, reading between the lines, in K. Hagberg's Life.

[4] Cf. his letter to Haller: 'Ray ... What was he? Undoubtedly an indefatigable man in collecting, describing, etc. but in the knowledge of generic principles less than nothing, and altogether deficient in the examination of flowers' (J. E. Smith, op. cit. II, p. 281).

[5] As he explicitly stated in Philosophia Botanica, p. 97.

present day has been treated with a reverence out of proportion to his merits, his influence upon the development of biology has been by no means as beneficial as is commonly assumed. He is in fact responsible for that exaggerated attachment to collecting and catalogue-making which has distracted attention from the problems of form and function, of behaviour and of ecology, and been responsible for the destruction of much of our wild life in order to fill the cabinets of the well-to-do.[1] Collecting is an important preliminary, an adolescent phase, in the development of biology and biologists; if made an end in itself, it produces arrested development and subsequent distortion.

His self-satisfaction would have been less unpleasant, and perhaps less imposing, if it had not been accompanied by a naïve and voluble pietism. His religion was sincere but entirely simple,[2] expressing itself at first in a genuine cosmic emotion but hardening into the belief that his own success and reputation were signal proofs of the divine favour and that therefore to question his authority was something of a blasphemy. Although he was deeply impressed by the problems presented by the ruthlessness of the natural order, he nevertheless assigned that order immediately to God without question or argument. As his own business was to name and arrange, those problems did not in fact intrude themselves. The 'enlightenment', the breakdown of Christian conformity, the anxiety which troubled so many of his contemporaries, these meant nothing to him.

We have said that in a sense it was inevitable for biological studies to mark time until physics and chemistry had been properly developed. But this must not conceal the damage that resulted.[3] Linnaeus led botany and zoology to abandon their concern with vital issues and with the larger problems of biological, philosophical and religious significance; and the result was to hand over the intellectual development of the scientific movement to the mathematicians and mechanists. In the seventeenth century Cartesian influence was counteracted by thinkers and workers who

[1] He persuaded the Swedish king and queen to set a fashion for collecting.
[2] Cf. Nordenskiöld, *op. cit.* pp. 206-7.
[3] For a concrete example cf. Note v, below, pp. 208-9.

knew more biology than Descartes and had a larger and more integrated philosophy. In the eighteenth, when theology degenerated into pietism and obscurantism and biology became mere collection and identification, there was little effective opposition to a purely materialist outlook.

Nevertheless though Linnaeus's dominance, and the excitement of exploring, collecting and naming, obscured the more important tasks of biological science, it would be unfair to describe the eighteenth century as wholly a time of reaction. Hermann Boerhaave, the greatest of all doctors,[1] was not without his followers; and though many of them went to chemistry one of the most remarkable men of the period, Albrecht von Haller of Berne and Göttingen, found in botany his favourite pursuit,[2] was also a competent geologist and rose to high distinction in human physiology.

We have already referred to his long correspondence with Linnaeus; and few series of letters between men of similar interests display a wider difference of outlook or a more subtle psychological situation. Haller was a man of wide and liberal culture, a remarkable linguist, a poet and writer, a man of letters and a man of affairs. In science he was primarily a doctor, interested in the functioning and structure of the organism, regarding nomenclature as secondary, and only sure that, if it was necessary to classify, this must be done on natural lines so as to indicate genuine affinities. Linnaeus exasperated him almost beyond endurance by his insensitiveness to the living plant and his insistence upon obedience to his own highly artificial regulations.[3] Like most real scientists Haller thought names a necessary nuisance and objected strongly to their being arbitrarily changed: but he realized the convenience of his friend's system and accepted his advice in the hope of being able to influence him towards a deeper appreciation of his task.

[1] To his Christian character Haller testifies, cf. *Letters to his daughter*, p. 64.

[2] His *Historia Stirpium Helveticarum*, the final product of his Alpine exploring, contains engravings of orchids and other plants of singular excellence.

[3] In the preface to the first volume of his *Epistolae ab eruditis viris ad Hallerum* (Berne, 1773) Haller refers to the charge that he was jealous of Linnaeus, admits that he had been constantly attacked by him and says that he is printing Linnaeus's letters to him in full in order to demonstrate that the charge is without foundation.

His eight volumes *Elementa Physiologiae Corporis Humani*, published in 1757, together with the series of bibliographical records on diseases and on medical and surgical practice and on botany, represent his real life's work. By them he laid the foundations for a scientific physiology, and gave a lead to those who tried to study it in terms not of separate pieces of mechanism but of the whole life of the organism. These great series of books, produced after he had given up his chair at Göttingen and was devoting himself to public service in his native city, mark, as Sir Michael Foster put it, 'the dividing line between modern physiology and all that went before'.[1] It was from his work that the revival of biological science was to begin.

His most important detailed researches were those devoted to the sensitiveness of the tissues and to the distinction which he was the first to draw between the 'sensibility' of nerves and the 'irritability' of muscles. Demonstrating that the latter quality was not directly dependent upon contact with the brain and ascribing it therefore to the constitution of the physical substance itself, he found himself charged by Julien de la Mettrie, the clever and cynical author of *L'Homme Machine*, with being the source of his radical materialism. The dismay of the profoundly religious, and serious, Haller at the suggestion that he could be giving support to infidelity was only relieved by de la Mettrie's death three years later—when he discovered that no one else had taken the charge as more than a gibe. But the incident plainly influenced him to transfer his activities from academic medicine to religious, philanthropic and political service. His three political romances[2] and his series of letters to his daughter expounding the Christian religion[3] are proof of the extent to which he feared the course upon which scientific civilization seemed to be embarking. The letters especially are an impressive tribute to his quality in their frank acknowledgment of difficulties, in their insistence upon evidence and the need for study and for experience, and in their humility and sincerity.

[1] So W. C. Dampier, *A History of Science*, p. 187.

[2] *Usong*, 1771; *Alfred*, 1773; *Fabius et Cato*, 1774; expounding respectively benevolent despotism, constitutional monarchy, and aristocracy.

[3] Written in German; an English translation was published in London in 1780.

They are the work of one who has thought deeply and suffered much.

If Buffon and Haller were right in protesting against the concentration upon collecting and classification, yet the exploration so ardently encouraged by Linnaeus had great value in opening up knowledge of the world and preparing material for the biologists of the future. The travels of P. S. Pallas throughout the Russian empire, of Captain Cook in the southern seas, of De Saussure in the Alps and of many other pioneers gathered results which gave their impetus to the great savants of Paris[1] who in the latter half of the century led the world, and gave the Académie des Sciences an indisputable pre-eminence.

Outside France there were individuals of genius, notably the great physiologist Lazaro Spallanzani. Like Copernicus and Stensen before him and Gregor Mendel a century later, he was a high dignitary of the Roman Catholic church: but this did not prevent him from devoting himself to patient experiments both with animals and plants, and, later in life, to travels for the study of volcanoes. His account of his success in the first experiment in the artificial insemination of a mammal is proof of the ardour of his enthusiasm and the accuracy of his work.[2]

Spallanzani is a lonely figure. In Italy, and indeed almost everywhere, biological science remained principally associated with charming trivialities like the writings of Thomas Pennant[3] and the picture books of Thomas Bewick. There was a time coming when the youngest of the sciences, geology, fully emancipated from obsession with the novity of the earth and the universality of the deluge, would bring a new sense of continuity and development to biological studies and the stimulus of a battle with tradition to their students. But though James Hutton had published his epoch-making essay the influence of Werner and his school obstructed progress; and the impulse of geology was for the

[1] See above, p. 136.

[2] Cf. *Dissertations relative to Natural History* (Eng. trans. 1789), II, pp. 248-51. His work was largely used by W. Paley in his *Natural Theology*.

[3] Yet in his *Tour in Scotland and Voyage in the Hebrides* (London, 1790) he included pictures by M. Griffiths of some interesting plants, *Loiseleuria procumbens* on Cruachan and Ben More, *Eriocaulon septangulare* and *Cornus suecica* 'about Loch Broom'.

future. At the turn of the century the growing-points were still in mathematics, physics and chemistry and the applied sciences dependent upon them. And how immense was their influence!

While the century seemed to close upon a scene dominated by mechanism and the industrial era which was its product, yet there were a few who kept alive the interest in living creatures, and the study of their ways. It would be absurd to place Gilbert White of Selborne among the scientists or to give him a very high position among field naturalists. Yet his letters, attaining a popularity never elsewhere equalled by any book of natural history,[1] not only testified to and revived the love of plants and birds but turned the attention of his readers from questions of identification and classifying to the larger and more important problems of form and function, of behaviour and way of life. He described his little monograph on the House Martin (*Martula urbica*)[2] as 'an humble attempt to promote a more minute enquiry into natural history, into the life and conversation of animals';[3] and in this gentle protest on behalf of the study of the living organism and by the mass of charming illustrations by which he emphasized it he joined his voice to that of Haller and the others against the treatment of the science of life as if it was merely the collecting and examination of the dead. As a spiritual influence his work will rank high among the writings of eighteenth-century Anglicanism; for in spite of its much lower scientific value it recaptures that sense of the worth and cohesion and wholeness of the natural order which the great men of the seventeenth century had revealed. It is important that the century of reason and industrialism should close with the fascinating letters of Gilbert White, the equally admirable pictures of Thomas Bewick and James Sowerby, and the botanical studies of William Curtis responsible for the *Flora Londinensis* and the *Botanical Magazine*;[4] of William Sole, the

---

[1] White's *Selborne* is still being reissued and must now have reached more than its hundredth edition.

[2] Letter XVI to Daines Barrington dated from Selborne 20 Nov. 1773.

[3] Letter XVII to the same.

[4] For an account of Curtis, cf. W. H. Curtis, *William Curtis, 1746-1799* (Winchester, 1941).

Bath apothecary and authority on the Mints; of William Withering the Birmingham doctor who in addition to his *Arrangement of British Plants* gave to medicine the first discovery of digitalin; and many others. Public opinion, tested by the popularity of such work, had not yet become machine-minded or machine-made. Indeed, thanks to their persistent influence and to the multitude of their disciples, there was never a time, in Britain at least, when the concept of science was wholly formulated in mechanistic terms. Hence among us the divorce between science and religion, between natural and supernatural, between an empirical democracy and a conservative Churchmanship never became absolute. We alone among the white peoples were free to combine socialism with Christianity and a belief in the natural worth of man with a belief in his need for redemption.

Yet before the century ended, a very different work, also by a parson, a work preliminary to and in large measure procreative of the fiercest of controversies had in fact appeared from an unlikely quarter and in scarcely recognizable form: Thomas Robert Malthus, fellow of Jesus College, Cambridge, student of economics, had published his *Essay on Population*. It would be an exaggeration to say that out of this tiny seed grew the two great upas trees of Marxism and Nazism; but it is nevertheless true that Malthus's doctrine that the population always increased to a point beyond the subsistence level was the chief source of the Ricardian economics and the iron law of wages which were the starting-point of Marx's *Das Kapital*: and it is also true that the consequent doctrine of the struggle for existence supplied to Charles Darwin and to Alfred Russell Wallace the basic principle of their theory of natural selection, which developed by way of Galton and Weismann into the doctrine of Nordic racialism. That the innocent clergyman, who died a house-master at Haileybury, should have thus made history is sufficiently surprising; but its strangeness is typical of the haphazard events through which the student of nineteenth-century progress has to make his rather breathless way.

In fact, the century of analysis and particularity, taxonomy and dissection, necessary as it may have been for the progress of science

162

but increasingly dominated as it was by the categories of physics and chemistry and by inanimate and mechanistic analogies, went far towards destroying all consciousness of the wholeness of nature and of the integrative life of the organism. Split up into systems respiratory, digestive, reproductive and the like, man became a thing of shreds and patches to be taken to pieces like the wheels and screws and spring of a watch, cleaned up and put together in better shape for keeping time. Cudworth's sense of the continuity and creativity of nature was being replaced by the concept of progress by random and unco-ordinated variation sifted by cut-throat competition in a world of robots.

IX

DARWIN AND THE CENTURY OF CONFLICT

THE nineteenth century was heralded by revolutions and begun in strife; and the conflict between science and religion overlaps in some respects the struggle between industrial democracy and the traditional and still largely feudal order. Although the French Republic, regarding the Academy of Sciences as a royalist institution, had sent its greatest ornament, Lavoisier, to the guillotine its leaders were none the less active in encouraging applied science and technology. Tom Paine speaking for France and America had, by his two books, *The Rights of Man* (his reply to Burke) and *The Age of Reason* (his attack upon orthodoxy), convinced the English-speaking world of the peril of innovation in science, politics or religion. His influence was that of a bogy-man; and obscurantism was the obvious safeguard. So, while physics and chemistry were advancing with amazing speed and the application of their results to industry was transforming man's way of life, the representatives of Christianity neither realized the character nor foresaw the effects of the changes which they were encouraging. Only the poets, Blake the prophet, Shelley the rebel, and Southey the tory, aligned themselves with Godwin and the philosophic radicals to protest against the ravishing of the countryside and the oppression of the poor. So far as the Churches were concerned there was a generation of *laissez-faire* almost as completely stagnant as that which gave a similar régime to the State. It is typical of the general attitude of the governing class that three years after Waterloo they should have passed 'Young's Act', whereby the Church of England was given a million pounds for building churches as the best insurance against the spread of democratic ideas. The work of John Wesley, though he had tried to give his preachers a background of natural knowledge, now produced in the main an other-worldly emphasis and an indifference to social and political exploitation. Apart from the Evangelical protest against the slave trade and a few heroic efforts at reform by Nonconformists there was little to indicate the controversies that were to come.

Nevertheless in this period of *laissez-faire* the exploration of the southern hemisphere and the settlement of Australia were having an effect upon botanical and zoological studies not unlike that which two centuries before had followed the opening-up of the Americas. The discovery of the Marsupials, so different from and yet in their various families so closely parallel to the Mammalia of the Old World, and the discovery, in 1799 by Shaw, of the egg-laying Platypus aroused enthusiasm for problems of comparative anatomy, phylogeny and geographical distribution; botanists though their novelties were less sensational were similarly confronted with a mass of fresh and interesting material much more easily transported and acclimatized;[1] if there was nothing to rival tobacco and potatoes, there were the blue gums and wattles and tree-ferns and a multitude of brilliant shrubs and flowers to test the gardeners of western Europe. With the unique bird life and the fossil and geological riches of New Zealand added to the tale, the data plainly called for a new study of the earth and its inhabitants.

Nor was exploration confined to any one part of the world's surface. The travels of Alexander Mackenzie in Canada, of Lewis and W. Clark in the Middle West, of A. von Humboldt in South America; of M. Flinders, G. Bass, C. Sturt, Sir Thomas Mitchell and others in the development of Australia; of Mungo Park and later of Livingstone, Speke, Stanley and the rest in Africa; of the Russians, from Muraviev to Prjevalsky, and of John Wood and his successors in Central Asia; all these were followed by important scientific discoveries. The great mountain ranges and river valleys, the deserts and the oceans, the arctic and antarctic regions all yielded new and important material. Both at home and abroad

---

[1] Joseph Banks who accompanied Cook on his first voyage in 1770 brought back a wonderful collection.

and among people of all sorts and conditions[1] an interest in natural history became widespread.

With the opening up of new lands and the exploration of the whole surface of the globe there was also an intense development in physics and chemistry—a development so rapid and so important practically that science began to be identified with these two fields of study. The foundation of the Royal Institution in 1799, at which Humphry Davy and Michael Faraday lectured and researched, of the British Association in 1830, with which John Dalton did much of his last work in chemistry and to which Justus von Liebig in 1840 gave his very important report on the relation of organic chemistry to agriculture,[2] and of the Science and Art Department after the holding of the Great Exhibition in 1851 provided Britain not only with centres for the conferences and training of scientists but with instruments of publicity for the education of the country. The result was an astonishing increase of knowledge both in pure science and in technology.

In physics L. H. M. Carnot in 1803 had extended Lagrange's conception of conservation to potential energy; Augustin Jean Fresnel in 1823 showed that it applied also to light; J. R. Mayer of Heilbronn in 1842 worked it out in relation to physiology; and in the same year James Prescot Joule of Manchester established the equivalence of energy, potential energy and heat, thus enabling H. L. F. von Helmholtz's statement in 1847 that the conservation of energy was a universal principle and that its transformation now supplied the chief problems of the physicist. In 1850 Michael Faraday in his Bakerian lecture declared that 'all the forces of nature are mutually dependent', a unification which has perhaps not yet been fully effected[3] in spite of the achievements of James Clerk Maxwell, William Thomson, afterwards Lord Kelvin, and very many others.

It is probably true to regard Clerk Maxwell as the outstanding representative of this phase of scientific development. Combining

---

[1] For the very important activities of working men in these subjects, cf. Note VI, below, pp. 209-10.

[2] This was based on the analysis of plants and soils carried out by him with de Saussure and Boussingault. It paved the way for chemical manuring and J. B. Lawes's work at Rothamsted.   [3] Cf. Sir E. Whittaker, *From Euclid to Eddington*, p. 131.

to a unique degree imaginative originality and logical lucidity, wide culture and intense concentration, he established the dynamical theory of gases (Maxwell's law) and the electro-magnetic theory of light between 1860 and 1865 during his professorship at King's College, London, and when in 1871 he went back to Cambridge as first Cavendish professor he not only planned and organized the new laboratory but in his own papers predicted and initiated the subsequent progress of physics. His prophecy of electromagnetic waves was fulfilled by Heinrich Hertz's discovery of them in 1887. His inaugural lecture at Cambridge foreshadowed the quantum theory and the indeterminacy principle. His successors after his early death in 1879 recognized that his *Treatise on Electricity and Magnetism* was not only the climax of the whole process of establishing the identity of the luminiferous and magnetic media but the starting-point for much of the work which is associated with the names of Einstein and Planck. He was a man of profoundly Christian character, a disciple of F. D. Maurice and a lecturer at Maurice's Working Men's College.[1]

From this work of Clerk Maxwell and Hertz came the development of broadcasting. Wireless telephony was achieved by Joseph Thomson and Ernest Rutherford in Cambridge as early as 1896,[2] but it was only with the perfecting of thermionic valves and Marconi's use of an antenna or aerial to catch and transmit the waves that commercial development and all the subsequent expansion became practicable.

A new development opening up the whole subject of radioactivity and so giving rise to knowledge of atomic structure and to the achievement of nuclear fission was made possible in 1895 by Wilhelm Konrad Röntgen's almost accidental discovery of X-rays. These rays emitted by electric discharges passing through vacuum tubes caused the fogging of photographic plates in light-proof holders and threw shadows of the human skeleton on to a

[1] 'The modernity of Maxwell's science and the antiquity of his sociology and religion appear incongruous.' J. G. Crowther, *British Scientists of the Nineteenth Century*, II, p. 350. Comment on such a remark is superfluous.

[2] When it was proposed to develop this commercially, Thomson was advised that it was not likely to be successful; cf. Lord Rayleigh, *Life of J. J. Thomson*, pp. 62-3.

fluorescent screen. Their value for surgery was obvious; but scientifically their chief importance lay in the consequent discovery first by Henri Becquerel in 1896 of radiations in uranium and then in 1900 by Pierre and Marie Curie in the radium isolated from pitchblende. At the same time Joseph Thomson during the work on cathode rays, to which he returned in 1896, was led by the close of the century to the formulation of his theory of electrons, to belief in the electronic structure of matter, and to his popular title, 'the man who split the atom'.[1] To attempt any account of the manifold consequences of these discoveries or of the men and women responsible for their development would need far more space and capability than can be given to it here. From the practical problems of the atomic bomb to the philosophical revolutions of relativity and quantum mechanics, the new physics has transformed the life and thought of mankind.

In the special field of electricity, progress had been even more rapid. Before the beginning of the century Luigi Galvani, the physician of Bologna, from the twitching of a frog's leg had revived an interest in the subject; and in 1800 his fellow-countryman, Alessandro Volta of Pavia, had developed his pile and reported it to Sir Joseph Banks. Very shortly afterwards William Hyde Wollaston, one of a family of 'natural philosophers' and afterwards Secretary of the Royal Society, established the identity of galvanic and frictional electricity and also the effect of a current passing through liquid solutions in producing decomposition, the basic principle of electro-plating. In 1819 Oersted of Copenhagen had discovered the action of a current upon the magnetic needle, which gave the basis for the electric telegraph of Cooke and Wheatstone and for the development of it in America by Samuel Morse. In 1830-2 Faraday worked out the facts of electromagnetic induction and the idea of the dynamo, though the generation by this means of electricity on a commercial scale did not take place for nearly half a century, when Thomas A. Edison, John Hopkinson and the Siemens brothers produced cheaper and effective current. So too with lighting, Davy had proved in 1809,

[1] Cf. A. Wood, *The Cavendish Laboratory*, pp. 31-5 and Rayleigh, *op. cit.* pp. 76-96.

:en years after William Murdoch had used coal gas for illumina-
:ion, that electric light could be produced by passing a current
across a gap between copper rods. But it was not till 1880 that
[ablochkoff candles, the first 'arc lights', were employed on rail-
roads and docks and large buildings; and the electric lamp with a
carbon filament was hardly able to compete with the incandescent
gas-mantle until tungsten or other metals replaced carbon in 1906.
The use of electricity for transport came later, the first electric
railway being shown at the Berlin Exhibition of 1879; but horse
trams were well established and not widely replaced until the end
of the century. Similarly though Gottlieb Daimler had invented
the petrol engine in 1884 motor transport did not become common
until after 1900.

For chemistry, Lavoisier's work had opened a new era, and
progress was rapid and continuous. His idea of chemical elements
was developed by John Dalton, the quaker schoolmaster of Kendal,
who became Professor of Mathematics and Natural Philosophy at
New College, Manchester, and who in 1803 published his first
account of atomic weights. Wollaston's somewhat similar theory
of equivalents, and the development of the subject by Amadeo
Avogadro and Ampère did not suffice to establish the atomic
theory till half a century later. Much work showing remarkable
analytical skill was done on atomic weights by Jöns Jakob Berzelius
in Stockholm, and his invention of the alphabetical chemical
symbols (still in use) made him the great organizer, the Linnaeus,
of this branch of science. Unfortunately for him his system did
not win the universal approval which had greeted the Linnaean,
and in his last years his temper, never very conciliatory, was
bitterly exercised in controversy in its defence. His work was
carried on by Louis Joseph Gay-Lussac the explorer of the
cyanogen compounds, and by Justus von Liebig and Friedrich
Wöhler who opened up the unexplored field of organic chemistry,
and led the way for the researches which in the latter half of the
century produced the mauve and other aniline dyes of William
Henry Perkin and the synthetic indigo of Adolf von Baeyer.

What is in some respects the most remarkable scientific advance of the century arose from the study of fermentation. In 1838 Cagniard de Latour had discovered that yeast is composed of minute living cells. In 1854 when Louis Pasteur became a professor at Lille, he investigated a commercial problem, the undesirable production of lactic acid in the fermentation of beet sugar; and in doing so discovered the presence and effects of bacilli. This led on to similar discoveries in connexion with diseases, microbes being found in silkworm disease in 1868 and in anthrax in 1877, to the foundation of the Pasteur Institute in 1888, and to the application of antiseptic treatment by Joseph (afterwards Lord) Lister in surgery. The researches of Heinrich Hermann Koch into the tuberculosis bacillus and the exploration of the complicated life histories of the micro-organisms that cause disease, which culminated in the discovery of the part played by the *Anopheles* mosquito as the carrier of malaria by Sir Ronald Ross, are outstanding events in the campaign which has opened up so much of the earth for human habitation and so greatly enlarged the span of human life. From the study of fermentation came also the discovery of enzymes, organic catalysts whose importance for physiology and medicine gave an impetus to the view that 'the physics of colloids and the chemistry of the proteids' could supply explanations for all the phenomena of organic life.[1] As a result of such achievements, a challenge to religion by scientific materialism became inevitable.

Yet the actual course of events was very different from what might have been expected. The development of a mechanistic philosophy, involving the restriction of the field of science to the categories of weight and measurement and the extension of it to include the organic and the human, was obviously the most serious challenge to religion. But the actual conflict broke out in the fields of geology and biology, where trouble might have arisen long ago but now seemed hardly likely. It is indeed a clear indication of the lethargy of the eighteenth century that in these fields there had not then been a clash over Genesis; for Ray, who had been one of the first to assert that fossils were the remains of

---

[1] Cf. Sir W. C. Dampier, *History of Science*, p. 281.

living organisms and that their position could only be explained by large changes in the surface of the globe, had hinted that these facts were hard to reconcile with the traditional account of Creation[1] or with the general belief in the 'novity' of the earth.[2] But it was not until the *Theory of the Earth* in 1785 had been published by James Hutton, developed by his friend John Playfair, carried to a successful conclusion by Sir James Hall and his Edinburgh colleagues, and accepted as against the Wernerians that the true classification of geological epochs could be attempted; and only when the study of the sequence of organic fossils initiated by Giraud-Soulavie in his account of the stratification of the French limestones[3] had been taken up by Lamarck and Cuvier and when William Smith had issued his complete *Geological Map of England and Wales with Part of Scotland*[4] in 1815, did the full story of the ordered changes in the earth's structure become plainly known. The world-wide interest aroused by this knowledge, the consequent exploration for fossils,[5] the production of text-books and the obvious evidence for the antiquity of the earth and the evolution of life throughout the ages made the naïve beliefs of Linnaeus and the historicity of the Creation stories in Genesis difficult for honest men to maintain.

For already in his inaugural address on the Invertebrates[6] in 1800, Lamarck had begun to proclaim the progressive development of living creatures and to describe those series of fossil shells from the tertiary deposits round Paris which gave plain evidence of the relationship of species one to another and of their successive appearance. His *Philosophie Zoologique* published in 1809 set out the theory of evolution which he derived from this evidence and from his conviction of the immense periods of time covered by

---

[1] It was argued that God could not have allowed any of the species created by Him to perish; yet Ray knew that many fossil plants and ammonites were wholly unlike living species.

[2] Catholics, Protestants and unbelievers all accepted a date about 4000 B.C. as the time of Creation. [3] Cf. his *Histoire naturelle de la France méridionale*, I, pt. 2, ch. VIII.

[4] For his remarkable history, cf. *Memoirs of W. Smith, LL.D.* by his nephew J. Phillips, afterwards Reader in Geology at Oxford.

[5] The term previously applied to anything dug out of the earth was now confined to organic remains—the 'formed stones' of early geology.

[6] The seven volumes did not appear until 1815-22.

the changes in the earth's surface,[1] and interpreted it in terms of
these changing circumstances and the conscious effort of the
organism to adapt itself more fully to its environment. This
pouvoir de la vie or holistic and organizing power of the living
plant or animal he credited not only with a chief effect upon the
development of one type from another but also with an influence
upon the physical and chemical structure of the earth. In both
these directions his arguments brought him into conflict with the
general beliefs of his time, and are legitimately open to criticism.
But in spite of some mistakes his work is based upon a far wider
and closer study of botany, zoology and geology than his modern
critics are willing to allow and deserves praise not only as the
first coherent doctrine of evolution but for its recognition, in a
mechanistic age, of the importance of the living organism.

That in spite of the influence of Rousseau and the doctrine of
perfectibility,[2] it attracted little contemporary attention is due to
the charm and influence of his younger colleague Cuvier, the great
anatomist and palaeontologist, whose skill in reconstructing and
interpreting the remains of extinct vertebrates revealed the extent
and strangeness of the prehistoric fauna, and whose doctrine that
the earth had suffered periodic catastrophes of such violence as to
transform its surface and destroy its inhabitants was combined
with a definite denial of evolution. This 'cataclysmism' was
regarded with more favour than Lamarck's views; for if it was
not easy to reconcile with the six days of Creation it agreed well
with the story of the Deluge, and with the belief in specific
creative acts rather than a continuing and 'natural' process. As
regards the age of the earth and the succession of different types of
living creatures upon it there is no great difference between him
and Lamarck: both of them have moved a very long way from
Milton and the traditional cosmogony.

Though by this time men no longer believed that creation had

---

[1] Cf. his *Hydrogéologie* (Paris, 1802), pp. 88-9.

[2] The suggestion that Lamarck and other advocates of evolution were largely influenced
by the idea of progress and perfectibility is developed by Dr S. Lilley, 'Social Aspects of
the History of Science' in *Archives Intern. d'Histoire des Sciences*, XXVIII, pp. 376-443. His
evidence is not very convincing.

taken place in six days and less than six thousand years ago, though Immanuel Kant, both in his *Anthropology* and in his *Critique of Judgment* had introduced the idea of historical development into astronomical and biological studies, even suggesting that man had changed and that apes might in time attain human form,[1] and though, as Erasmus Darwin's poem shows, evolution was a not unfamiliar idea, yet for the majority of educated Englishmen Archdeacon Paley's *Natural Theology* was the standard text-book and his familiar teleological argument of the watchmaker and his watch was the favourite illustration of the nature, purpose and method of the Creator.[2] To replace this by an acknowledgment of creation as a slow and age-long process conditioned to some extent at least by the creature's own power of adaptation seemed an infringement upon the divine supremacy and a further concession to the dominant and materialistic naturalism of the time. Belief in the sole authority of a God operating from without and at His own inscrutable pleasure seemed to be at stake; and, in an age bewildered by change, scared by revolution and shaken by war, authority must at almost any cost be maintained.

That there was widespread anxiety as to the effect of recent scientific developments upon the traditional faith of Christendom may be judged by the provision of the Bridgewater Treatises in 1829. The eighth Earl of Bridgewater bequeathed to the President of the Royal Society a large sum of money on condition that he selected scholars capable of covering the whole field of science and of proving that its findings were in conformity with and corroborative of the Christian tradition. In fulfilling this bequest the President (Davies Gilbert) consulted the Archbishop of Canterbury (William Howley) and the Bishop of London (C. J. Blomfield) and with their help chose the authors for the series.[3] It is customary to ridicule the results: they are naturally uneven in merit; but a dispassionate study of them indicates that

[1] Cf. An article by F. A. Paneth on 'T. Wright and I. Kant' in *Durham Univ. Journal* (1941), pp. 118-19.

[2] Paley mentioned but rejected the argument for evolution by use from the humps of the Camel and the pouch of the Pelican, cf. *Natural Theology* (ed. 1837), pp. 286-90.

[3] For details see Note VII below, pp. 210-11.

they were fully representative both in the level of their learning and in the diversity of their religious ideas of the best thought of the time. A team which included Thomas Chalmers of Edinburgh, William Whewell, afterwards the great Master of Trinity,[1] William Buckland, the geologist, and William Kirby, the doyen of entomologists, could not be easily improved. Chalmers wrote the first volume and set the tone for the rest: he developed an argument from design, somewhat less simple than that put forward by Ray and Paley, supporting it by a wide range of arguments, and presenting it with generosity and dignity. Buckland's volumes were the most controversial; for he threw over the traditional cosmogony and dating of the Creation, declared that the Bible did not contain 'historical information respecting all the operations of the Creator', and insisted upon the vast length and continuous change of the earth's development, and the impossibility of reconciling this precisely with the account in Genesis.[2] Kirby's was the most orthodox—an elaborate attack upon Lamarck followed by acceptance of the Miltonic picture of the Creation and of the literal historicity of the Flood.

But the bewilderment was too general and too genuine for the treatises to remove it; indeed the differences in interpretation between the various authors were too evident to escape notice. If among a team specially chosen by responsible leaders of science and religion there was no agreement as to the problem of creation, there was an even wider divergence among scientists in general. It is interesting to compare the views of four typical naturalists of the middle of the century, all of them men of high principle and real concern for religion, Philip Henry Gosse, Charles Darwin, Thomas Henry Huxley and Charles Kingsley—interesting both as illustrative of the prevailing confusion and as typical of very many others down to our own time.

[1] His findings concerning the appropriateness of the physical world to the life of man were highly praised by L. Henderson, *The Fitness of the Environment* (New York, 1913).

[2] A considerable literature of books and pamphlets attacked him, e.g. *A Letter to Prof. Buckland* by Dean W. Cockburn (1837); *Afterthoughts* by S. Best (1837); *Remarks* by Eretzsepher (1837); *Reflections on Geology* by J. Mellor Brown (1838); *A Vindication of Genesis* by F. de Johnsone (1838); *Scriptural Geology* by G. Young (1838). He was defended e.g. in *Scripture and Geology* by J. Pye Smith.

Gosse is well known to us by the books in which his son alternately commended[1] and condemned[2] him. In his own day he was the great authority on marine biology, the man who opened up the museum of the high-water mark and the aquaria of the rock pools to our great-aunts, and set them pressing seaweeds and painting shells. At a time when the invertebrates were still little known to the microscope, Gosse did a notable work; and in geology as well as botany and zoology he was competent enough to know the difficulty of reconciling Genesis with the evidence. To maintain his own rigid belief in the verbal infallibility of the Scriptures and yet to be loyal to his scientific knowledge was a necessity, but a strain. It is obvious from his son's records how earnestly he wrestled with his dilemma. In 1857 he found a solution and published at his own expense and in a large edition his 'attempt to untie the geological knot', the book called *Omphalos*.[3] In it he defined 'the cause of nature as a circle' and the Creation as 'the sudden bursting into a circle', explained the stratification of the earth, the fossils and the vestigial organs in ourselves as evidence of a 'prochronic' phase in which the earth existed uncreate in the mind of God, and argued that on the days of Creation this prochronic world came into objective existence. He was honest enough to begin his book with a number of similar speculations which he felt bound to reject: he was confident that his own solution was the truth. It is a sufficient comment to say that similar myths have been invented for the same purpose since Gosse's time—and that Kingsley felt bound to confess that he had never doubted that Creation was an act at a particular time until he read *Omphalos* which 'tends to prove this, that if we accept the fact of absolute Creation God becomes a deceiver'.[4]

If Gosse was able to invent a means of holding each of the contradictions and in effect blinding himself to what he did not want to see, Darwin did almost exactly the same thing on the

[1] *Life of P. H. Gosse* (1890).

[2] *Father and Son*, published anonymously in 1907.

[3] I.e. navel; so called because his problem narrowed itself to the simple question, 'Was Adam, though never born of a woman, created with a navel?'

[4] *Life of P. H. Gosse*, pp. 280-1.

other side. He was a man of fine integrity, at one time contemplating ordination and always scrupulously honest. But few confessions are so poignant as the passages in his autobiography which describe the effect upon his life of the intense concentration of all his powers upon the one subject: how his love of music, his sense of the wonder of nature, his consciousness of God had all been atrophied, so that he is bound to say 'It is an accursed evil to a man to become so absorbed in any subject as I am in mine'.[1] Nor is his confession misplaced. Anyone who reads his letters cannot but see how frequently he fails to understand objections raised against his theory, for example, by Asa Gray or J. A. Lowell, and how confused and incoherent are his attempts to reply. He has in fact often reached the point at which he can only see the evidence that tells in his own favour.[2]

These two represent the simple cases of those who, when confronted with a plain clash between old and new, refuse to allow either of them to be modified and choose according to their preference. More interesting are the two other representatives.

Huxley, Darwin's champion,[3] was a man of strong though not fully trained mind and of equally strong ethical principles, one of those who in an age of transition can neither live with religion nor live without it. He could not blind himself to the contrast between the findings of scientific research and the traditional cosmogony; he saw that to reject religion would be to weaken if not to destroy the sanctions of morality: his science drew him to materialism; his conscience refused to let him rest in it; his mind insisted that morality could not be expected of a beast or a machine. The tension often expressed itself in outbreaks of vituperation or of self-pity; and the effort to resolve it led only to the inconsistencies of his Romanes lecture and the futilities of his conflict with Gladstone.

Kingsley, though much less distinguished as a scientist than the other three, was a man of wider interests and more general

[1] *Life of C. Darwin*, II, p. 139.   [2] For further details see below, pp. 182-4.
[3] Cf. H. F. Osborn, *Impressions of Great Naturalists*, p. 91, 'He wrote upon the subject for thirty years and yet he never contributed a single original or novel idea to it.' Outside his own field he was a journalist rather than a scholar.

education. As novelist and historian, reformer and preacher, he had learnt a broad and coherent philosophy from his friend F. D. Maurice, the greatest Christian prophet of the century, and from him drew also the conviction that Christianity, if it be true, must be expressed not only in a righteous social order but in terms consistent with the whole cosmic process. He was not himself fully capable of formulating a restatement of the tradition; but he knew enough of the issues raised by scientists to be confident that such a reconciliation was possible. So he could welcome Darwin's work with genuine enthusiasm—'they find' he wrote[1] 'that now they have got rid of an interfering God—a master-magician as I call it—they have to choose between the absolute empire of accident and a living, immanent, ever-working God'—and could devote himself to his task of proclaiming the truth and universal relevance of Christianity, and incidentally to the foundation of the Natural History Society at Chester, the forerunner of a myriad others, and to the writing of his charming books, *Glaucus, The Water-Babies* and *Madam How and Lady Why*.[2]

Four such typical examples of the confusion of the time illustrate adequately the effect of the failure to appreciate or co-ordinate the immense changes in life and thought achieved by the application of scientific research to the transformation of the human scene. Behind the bewilderment was the hysterical fear which besets a prosperous society when it feels its way of living to be threatened and finds itself bankrupt of the spiritual and moral resources needed to restore courage and a cool judgment. No one paid much attention to Engels and the communist manifesto or would have accepted its new dogma of the class struggle and the inevitability of the triumph of the proletariat; but no one was unaffected by the upheavals and revolutions of 1848, and ignorance of their significance was fostered by and in turn fostered an anxiety easily startled into panic. The sense of insecurity so evident in the first century of the Roman empire was paralleled by the very similar

---

[1] *Life of Charles Kingsley. Letters and Memories* (ed. by his wife), II, p. 171.

[2] It is fashionable and (in view of his wife's eulogy) easy to sneer at Kingsley, cf. *Canon Charles Kingsley* by Una C. Pope-Hennessy, but in this aspect of his work, as indeed in his Christian socialism, he was a great and good influence.

mentality of the Victorian age—immense and unthreatened prosperity producing its nemesis, a haunting awareness of man's helplessness and mortality.

Into such an age Darwin's great book came with a singular and explosive appropriateness. Its influence can only be explained by the fact that it exactly matched its moment. It was not, strictly speaking, new: evolution was in the air and Darwin, like Alfred Russell Wallace, merely applied to its interpretation the familiar principles of Malthus's *Essay on Population*. It was not well written; its author never had any gift for popular exposition or any training in literary art. It was loaded with immense masses of detail, some of it merely cumulative in its effect. It put forward an argument which its author knew would be unpopular and which the spokesmen of science were likely to dismiss as the work of a meddlesome amateur. Yet it, like Newton's *Principia* and perhaps no other scientific publication, marked an epoch: Newton made it clear that the universe was a realm of law and amenable to interpretation in terms of mathematics and physics; Darwin explained the whole evolution of life in terms of the simple principle of natural selection and in a way which seemed to rule out all moral and teleological elements and any idea of man's special status or of God's loving care. Each of them produced their work when its subject had been receiving long but confused attention; each of them provided a clue which suddenly made the whole subject plain.

Darwin's work, though he himself added other possibilities and reservations, depended in its main contention upon three elementary facts: that all living organisms show a slight variability, that these variations are inheritable, and that in the fierce struggle for survival a favourable variation will give an advantage and increase the likelihood of reproduction. All three were incontestable: every family photograph proved the two former—young John differed from but took after his father—the whole economic system, the free competition so universally belauded as essential to England's greatness, demonstrated the third. Nature was after all ordered on familiar principles. Even the conclusion which Darwin drew from his three points, that the accumulation of small and successful variations would in time give rise to new species—a point which he could not prove and which in fact has not yet been conclusively demonstrated—was so plausible in view of the experience of stock-breeders and pigeon-fanciers as to win easy acceptance: the rocks supplied sufficient missing links to support belief that, given time, even the largest differences could be thus explained.

Moreover, in spite of the opposition of orthodox science and religion, the theory was eminently congenial to the broad characteristics of the contemporary outlook. Life *was* a struggle: every business-man knew it and if he was honest admitted that a certain ruthlessness in securing the safe margin between success and failure was inevitable. Every little helped: thrift, utility-value, the commercial significance of the trivial, this was the philosophy for a nation of shopkeepers. The weak to the wall; sentimentalism was all very well; 'Nature, red in tooth and claw' was a nasty fact, but it was no use crying over it; a great nation could not afford to be squeamish; and if the survival of the fittest was a law of nature . . .! So the arguments ran. They had long been familiar. Francis Place, Lord Shaftesbury, Charles Kingsley and every critic of *laissez-faire* had been confronted with them whenever he had tried to raise wages, or restrict child labour, or advocate co-operation. Small wonder that the assurance that such arguments could now be drawn from the essential principle of the whole evolutionary process sent a glow of self-righteous satisfaction through the veins of the prosperous. God, if the word had any longer a meaning, was after all on the side of the mighty. The *Magnificat* though still sung was definitely out of date.

So stated, the case would seem to have been rightly attacked by the leaders of religion. Unfortunately they were in no position to argue it; for in fact they had condemned Place as an atheist, boycotted Shaftesbury as a crank, and persecuted Kingsley as a revolutionary precisely because of their protest against the struggle for existence and the rights of the wealthy. Samuel Wilberforce when he attacked the *Origin* at Oxford in 1860 did so first as the mouthpiece of Richard Owen and the professional scientists, then in defence of the days of Creation and Genesis, and finally to disclaim the possibility of man's descent from a monkey—in other words on behalf of biblical infallibility and human pride; and it was on these grounds that the subsequent battle was fought. The Churches, already alarmed by the geology of Dean Buckland and very soon to be shocked by the higher criticism of Bishop Colenso and the liberalism of *Essays and Reviews*, sprang to the defence of Moses, and before *The Descent of Man* rekindled the strife the supposed threat to man's special status and spiritual heritage had already been felt and resented. When in 1864 an unholy alliance between Dr Pusey the tractarian and Lord Shaftesbury the evangelical issued the Oxford Declaration, eleven thousand clergy joined them in denouncing those who denied that the whole Bible was the Word of God and that the wicked were punished everlastingly.[1]

It was unquestionably a misfortune that in presenting the theory of natural selection Huxley should have laid the sole stress upon the struggle for existence. His description of the world of animate nature as a gladiatorial show and his indictment of the cosmic process in his Romanes lecture of 1893[2] caught the imagination of sensitive Victorians so that Wordsworth's 'vernal wood' became the slaughter-house of Tennyson's *Locksley Hall*, and 'Nature, red in tooth and claw with ravine' shrieked against the Christian concept of God. Unfortunately Huxley was a typical example of what the field naturalists called a 'two-pair-back-garret' naturalist, a man of museums and laboratories, an anatomist, physiologist, taxonomist who took little interest in the living bird or beast in its native setting.[3] Darwin, who was a good naturalist and observer,[4] never concealed his view that a far wider meaning attached to natural selection; that habit, use and disuse, courtship

---

[1] Cf. *Life of E. B. Pusey*, IV, pp. 54-68.   [2] 'Evolution and Ethics' in *Collected Essays*, IX.

[3] Even when he became interested in gentians in the Alps in 1887, it was their morphology that attracted him; cf. L. Huxley's *Life and Letters*, II, pp. 32-3. For his contempt for field work, cf. *ibid.* p. 422.

[4] An attractive account of his field work at Edinburgh, 1825-7, is given by J. H. Ashworth in *Proceedings of R.S.E.* LV, p. 10.

preferences and other elements in the day-to-day life of organisms played their part. In this the field-workers supported him—as they still do—by insisting that the charnel-house picture was false, that the actual business of killing and being killed was not a primary factor and that a true appreciation of animal life would lay little stress on pain or terror and much upon sensitiveness to environment, spontaneity of reaction, social adjustments to mates and offspring and, at the higher levels of life, on the emergence of a rudimentary appreciation of value. Natural selection today has a very different meaning from that which Huxley gave it; but at the time the mechanistic tendencies of science had created a wide breach between laboratory work and field studies—an indication of the extent to which biology was becoming false to its name.[1]

Nevertheless, as Huxley himself admitted,[2] the opposition from Christians was by no means universal. Gilbert White had had many successors among the clergy; a goodly number of them, men like J. G. Wood,[3] C. A. Johns,[4] F. O. Morris,[5] J. C. Atkinson,[6] T. A. Preston,[7] W. W. Newbould, if not great scientists, did valuable work in producing popular hand-books, encouraging field work, fostering local talent and presiding over natural history societies. There was never such a cleavage in Britain as occurred on the Continent either between religion and science or between field studies and the laboratory. It was in fact to Continental Darwinians, Ernst Haeckel and August Weismann, that the hardening of the master's work into a rigid and mechanistic system was mainly due. Haeckel, whose chief contribution was

[1] Cf. for example the lament of R. Bowdler-Sharpe in the Preface to his *Handbook to Birds of Britain*, IV, pp. ix-xi (Lloyd's Nat. Hist. Ser. London, 1897): it was not his fault that he worked in the British Museum and had no opportunity for the shore-shooting of his youth.

[2] In a letter of 2 June 1863 to C. H. Middleton; cf. my *Science, Religion and the Future*, pp. 46-7.

[3] Author of *The Illustrated Natural History* (1853, 3 vols. 1862-3), *Homes without Hands* (1865), etc.

[4] Author of *Flowers of the Field* (2 vols. 1853; 33rd ed. 1911), *British Birds in their Haunts* (1862), etc.

[5] Author of *A History of British Birds* (6 vols. 1851-7), *A History of British Butterflies* (1853; 10th ed. 1908), etc.

[6] Author of *Sketches in Natural History* (1861), etc.

[7] Author of *Flora of Marlborough* (1863) and *Flowering Plants of Wilts.* (1888).

the doctrine of recapitulation (that every creature climbs its family tree or reproduces the structures of its ancestors in its pre-natal growth), was a vigorous critic of religion and gave his exposition a strongly materialistic bias. Weismann, author of the doctrine of the total segregation of the germ-plasm, provided by it a disproof of the inheritance of acquired characteristics and advocated so strict a determinism as to deny any possible effect of environment or behaviour upon the physical future of the race. Each, as we now see, overstated his case; but each promoted a more intransigent and aggressive presentation of a mechanistic universe.

That evolution has been one of the great integrative ideas in the study of the order of nature and that its originator will always stand out as an example of patient research and the hero of a remarkable achievement cannot be questioned. Some of the subsidiary evidence brought forward in support of his theory has been abandoned: his own hypothesis of sexual selection never won general acceptance; H. W. Bates's doctrine of mimicry, though supported by much remarkable evidence and linked up with cases of adaptation almost equally astonishing, is only partial in its application, and even when supplemented by the speculative hypothesis of warning colours does not fit more than a selection of the facts. Until more work has been done upon the chemistry of colour, the causes and interpretation of pattern, the direct influence of the environment and many similar problems which occur to the experienced field naturalist, such theories cannot be accepted as more than provisional. Nor is it yet as clear as many biologists suppose that natural selection[1] itself is more than a contributory cause of the appearance of novelties, a sifting-process which eliminates the less viable mutants rather than a means for improving and fixing stocks. Darwin's claim that natural selection operating upon small and random variations can produce species mutually sterile can be supported by some definite evidence and is accepted as the only demonstrable hypothesis by many zoologists. Botanists on the whole find it less convincing. Many

[1] As has already been indicated 'natural selection' has a much wider significance than the 'struggle for existence'.

of us though accepting its importance cannot agree that it is adequate to all the facts or proven by sufficient examples. It does not provide a convincing explanation of the appearance of wholly new forms of life in which the change of a number of elements in the structure of the organism must have taken place simultaneously. Nor does it fit the facts, so far as they are known, of the appearance of such novelties; for the evidence goes to show that they arrive suddenly as mutations.[1]

That evolution has manifestly taken place and is still proceeding is a fact as securely established as any in the whole range of scientific knowledge. It will, however, be generally granted that its explanation is not so simple and uniform as Darwin and his followers supposed, and that we are still far from a complete interpretation of all the evidence. We shall consider at length on a later occasion the effect of this on the doctrine of Creation and the concept of God. But there is one point in this connexion, the effect of Darwin's work upon teleology, which has had such influence upon the general outlook of scientists as to require mention here.

It is evident from almost all pre-Darwinian biology that there was strong and general acceptance of the belief in the divinely ordered adaptation of every form of life to its environment and of the teleological argument derived from this belief. Ray's *Wisdom of God*, Paley's *Natural Theology*, the Bridgewater Treatises and so down to the popular text-books, all alike contained examples of the evidence for design. It had become the most familiar of the arguments for the existence of God. In its simple form this argument was shattered by Darwin's evidence that these marvels of adjustment were due not to the special artistry of the Creator but to the automatic influence of natural selection. As Huxley wrote:[2] 'The teleology which supposes that the eye was made with the precise structure it exhibits for the purpose of enabling the animal to see has undoubtedly received its death-blow.' But he hastened to add that 'the teleological and the

---

[1] For a brief illustration from Lepidoptera cf. Note VIII below, pp. 211-12.
[2] *Life of C. Darwin*, II, p. 201.

mechanical views of nature are not necessarily mutually exclusive
. . . the teleologist can always defy him to prove that the machine
was not intended to evolve the phenomena of the universe'.[1]
Asa Gray had similarly congratulated Darwin on having re-
established teleology and to this Darwin had replied that he was
'in an utterly hopeless muddle. I cannot think that the world as we
see it is the result of chance, and yet I cannot look at each separate
thing as the result of design.'[2] But in fact teleology was so generally
understood in terms of the watchmaker and the watch that most
people regarded Darwin as having destroyed it. This conclusion
was accepted by scientists, and in resisting attempts to reaffirm
an element of design they have set up a sort of phobia or taboo:
any mention of teleology in their company has until lately
produced a violent reaction—a reaction which, it must be noted,
has generated more heat than light.[3]

It was not until the turn of the century that the study of heredity
still further mechanized biological thought. When in 1901 William
Bateson rediscovered the records by the Abbot Gregor Mendel[4]
of his work on Sweet Peas and himself formulated, expanded and
illustrated the Mendelian law, the new science of genetics came
into prominence. In the next ten years experiments were carried
out in the case of a large number of plants and animals; and the
principle of the differentiation of characters in the gametes and the
rules governing their behaviour in crosses of the first and of the
subsequent generations[5] were found to be generally valid. When
Bateson in his Inaugural Lecture in 1908 intimated not only that
the law was universally true but that it ought to be applied in our
treatment of intelligence and morality, it seemed that a predestination more strict than Calvinism was being fastened upon mankind.

Hardly less influential in the fostering of mechanistic methods

[1] He quoted Paley, *Natural Theology*, II, ch. 23 as stating his teleology in exactly this way.
[2] *Life of C. Darwin*, II, pp. 353-4.
[3] That a remarkable change is now taking place is evident from the work of E. S.
Russell, W. E. Agar and many others; see below, pp. 196 ff.
[4] Originally published in 1865 but entirely forgotten.
[5] In the simplest possible case black paired with white gives in first generation all
heterozygous grey; these greys if paired give one black, two grey, one white. Cf. below,
p. 192.

upon biology were the investigations of physiologists and bio-
chemists into the endocrine secretions and their effects upon
human metabolism. Under the leadership of F. G. (later Sir
Gowland) Hopkins great progress was made in the analysis and
interpretation of the chemistry of vital processes and in research
into glandular defects and hypertrophies, into diet and the newly
discovered vitamins. The value of this work for medicine, for the
maintenance of health and the treatment of disease has been
revolutionary: to it probably more than to any other cause since
Lister's development of antisepsis are due the improvement in
physical well-being, the lowering of infantile mortality and the
lengthening of the expectation of life. But for a time at least it
strengthened the belief that Descartes was right about animals and
that man was only a complicated automaton whom it might soon
be possible to produce in a laboratory. Materialism in its crude
form was a popular philosophy in Europe and America at the
opening of the present century, and even those who would have
repudiated it found that it powerfully affected their thinking.
That it was possible to combine a purely quantitative science of
physical nature, even if this covered all the functioning of
humanity, with a purely spiritual and religious experience and
belief was freely maintained; but inevitably such dualism was
especially difficult for the Christians who took the basic tenet of
their faith seriously. Physics and chemistry which had taken the
centre of the stage at the beginning of the century seemed to have
sole possession of it by the end. The machine, the symbol and
instrument of man's power, had now constrained him to fashion
his picture of himself after its image. Science had dethroned the
emblematic lion in the seventeenth century; it seemed ready to
replace him by the behaviourist lion in the twentieth.

X

THE NEW SITUATION

THE closing years of the nineteenth century, as we have seen, foreshadowed the culmination of the mechanistic era of scientific thought. Darwin's work, narrowed by Weismann and his followers into a rigidly determinist system, seemed to provide a sufficient and satisfying solution to the problems of the method of organic evolution; advances in organic chemistry, if they did not supply the basis for a materialistic interpretation of the origin and nature of life, at least demonstrated the possibility of such an interpretation as Behaviourism was to advocate; physicists were engaged upon the investigations into radioactivity and atomic structure which had already yielded far-reaching results; and the application of scientific research to industry was producing the internal combustion engine with its adaptations, the motor car and the aeroplane. It seemed plain that the triumphant achievements of scientific techniques justified mankind in assuming that in a few more decades when the mathematicians had completed the solution of the last remaining equations, when the basic character of the physical universe had been disclosed, and when living protein had been synthetically produced under laboratory conditions, his descendants if not he himself would be able not only 'To grasp this sorry Scheme of Things entire', but, when analysis revealed the means to reconstruction, to take it to pieces bit by bit 'and then Re-mould it nearer to the Heart's Desire'. The universe for all its magnitude and mystery was in fact a 'closed system': it had shown itself amenable to exact measurement and objective study; in the sciences humanity possessed a measuring-rod to assay, and, potentially at least, the instruments to reform, his whole environment.

It was a dream not altogether incompatible with belief in other and non-material aspects of experience and fields of activity. Even Sir Thomas Browne had spoken of man as 'the great Amphibium' and a naïve dualism of matter and spirit, body and mind, has been generally accepted. Even if new areas were constantly being brought under scientific survey, the gaps still remained wide enough for religion to be fitted comfortably into them. Provided scientists maintained their own self-imposed restrictions, confined their work to the quantitative and the phenomenal, and did not press the anti-religious corollaries of their hypotheses; and provided religion exercised a similar restraint, gave up its attempts to dictate conclusions and to institute heresy hunts, and accepted as its sufficient domain the realm of the eternal values, a frontier might be established and peace be preserved. 'The things which are seen are temporal, but the things which are not seen are eternal': the suggested frontier had good apostolic authorization.

So a succession of scientists proclaimed to the British Association that science and religion had nothing in common, that Descartes had long ago exempted the human soul and all that it involved from the scope of his inquiry, and that his successors had no intention of infringing the independence of the spiritual authorities. They were met by a grateful assurance that this was fully understood on the other side of the frontier, that the autonomy of intellectual investigations was of course an essential condition of progress, and that religion was not in fact concerned with researches into the nature of the physical world. As for the borderland, the ancient beliefs about creation and indeed about redemption could be tacitly and tactfully handled by both parties; the relationship of brain and mind could wait till more evidence was available; the particular controversies over miracle or immortality were undoubtedly difficult, although there too patience and a policy of silence would prevent open collision. So, in Britain, a gentleman's agreement was reached and, during the next decade, somewhat precariously observed. Whether the result was a testimony to the common sense or to the muddlement or to the insincerity of the British temperament depended and still depends upon the prejudices of the judge rather than upon the character of the defendant. There was a modicum of truth in all three verdicts. Because of an obscure conviction that all the facts were not on the table, we did not face the facts; we maintained an illogical compromise in keeping with the pragmatism of our outlook; we adopted our national hero's strategy of applying the telescope to the blind eye and then speaking the truth. It postponed a clash; but the generations educated under the conspiracy of silence cannot be expected to be grateful.

It is unnecessary to comment at length upon the dilemma in which honest students found themselves. If Christian, they could not easily accept the position that an incarnational religion, or indeed any faith not wholly other-worldly, could remain uninterested in studies which were transforming man's concept of the natural order; nor could they try to give an intelligible statement of their beliefs without discovering that the whole trend of recent science in all fields was towards an uncompromising determinism which left no room for religious experience or moral responsibility. The liberal scholars who kept alive the great tradition of British theology found themselves constrained in the interest of reason and sincerity to ask questions about the character, limitations and significance of the physical world which science could only answer in a manner incompatible with theism and destructive of much that was cherished by the orthodox in Christendom and enshrined in its creeds. Inevitably they found themselves in the unenviable position of maintaining their honesty at the expense of being accused of heresy by their colleagues or of besmirching it in their own eyes by accepting tenets contrary both in general and in particular to the best knowledge of the time. An agnostic humanism or an authoritarian supernaturalism seemed the obvious answer to their dilemma.

Before we go on to consider the causes which have revolutionized the scientific outlook and changed the whole position, a word of gratitude is due to those who, on each side of the frontier, kept in touch with one another and refused to accept the alternative.

There were very many, and in all lands, who insisted upon maintaining a reasonable faith and in challenging both the omni-competence of scientific materialism and the inerrancy of religious authorities. Their influence was an invaluable encouragement, and in many cases their work has still an unappreciated worth and deserves fresh attention from those who are now in a position to carry it forward. We in England owe a debt to F. J. A. Hort[1] and William Sanday, to James Ward, Hastings Rashdall and J. F. Bethune-Baker which has never yet been properly acknowledged; Scotland with its stronger tradition of partnership between Church and State gave us Henry Drummond, J. Arthur Thompson, the Cairds, J. Y. Simpson and many more. Such men may not have succeeded in solving the problem; at least they kept us mindful of its existence and testified to the belief that it was not insoluble.

But at the very time when 'Science announced nonentity, and Art admired decay' work was in process which would transform the whole situation. It was fitting that, since it was the abstractions of mathematics that had prepared the way for the mechanistic age and the explanation of life in terms of physics and chemistry, out of mathematics should come the discovery which brought the age and its claims to an end. Albrecht Einstein was beginning at the turn of the century to develop the researches which in 1905 led to the formulation of his first theory of Relativity; and though it was not at once realized how far-reaching would be the con-sequences not only for our concept of nature but for our whole philosophy, the significance of the challenge to the doctrine of a closed universe, to the objectivity of scientific knowledge and to the confidence and claims of scientists could not be long un-recognized. The naïve but universal assumption, that weight and measurement were categories of absolute validity and that in consequence what was amenable to them could be known and controlled with an exactitude nowhere else obtainable, was in

---

[1] Probably the greatest scholar of the great Cambridge trio, he published first-rate work on plants before his twentieth year. In 1857 he discovered a new Bramble, *Rubus imbricatus*, in the Wye Valley; he examined in the Natural Sciences Tripos in the same year in which he delivered his Hulsean lectures.

face of Einstein's conclusions no longer acceptable. Newtonian physics were still adequate for practical purposes; they could no longer supply a precise measuring-rod or ultimately accurate results. Instead of a universe easily visualized, mapped and depicted in three dimensions, we had a mysterious space-time continuum, multi-dimensional, only relatively measurable, and definable if at all in a series of equations which none but the mathematical expert could understand. Instead of a complex but exactly measurable mechanism we had a repudiation of the basic orthodoxy of contemporary science—*eine Kritik der Mechanik als Grundlage der Physik*.[1]

It is not within the competence of one who is no mathematician to describe or estimate the progressive steps which followed upon Einstein's first publication of his theory. He had demonstrated the insufficiency of Newtonian physics and the necessity of the time-factor in mensuration. This of itself might only have meant the substitution of the complex for the simple and have left us with a seemingly complete and omnicompetent system.[2] But further investigations into the nature of radiation by Max Planck supplemented by Einstein's own work initiated the quantum theory. These were supplemented by Niels Bohr and others, who made it plain that certain phenomena of inescapable importance, inexplicable on the wave theory of light advocated by Hooke and Huygens, which since the days of Thomas Young had been generally accepted, could only be explained in terms of quantum activity, a theory which recalled Newton's belief in 'light-particles' and Laplace's corpuscular doctrine; and that physicists facing the whole evidence must be content to employ two distinct hypotheses which were each valid for its own data but were mutually irreconcilable. The problem has been debated with the closest attention for nearly a generation, and there does not

---

[1] Autobiographical Notes, p. 20 in *Albert Einstein: Philosopher-Scientist*; cf. H. Reichenbach, *Atom and Cosmos*, p. 28, 'Modern physics dethrones that world of concepts with which earlier epochs believed that they could compass all of nature's happenings'.

[2] It is, however, of interest to note that E. W. Hobson, the mathematician, in *The Domain of Natural Science* (1923), described the breakdown of the doctrine of the closed universe, though he was sceptical as to Einstein's work.

yet appear to be a full solution of the contrast.[1] Indeed when Heisenberg, perhaps the most brilliant of all younger physicists was lecturing in Cambridge in 1948 he insisted that at present the four hypotheses associated with the names of Newton, Riemann, Einstein and Planck must all be accepted as appropriate to different groups of phenomena. The old doctrine of a 'closed universe' objectively measurable and shortly to be comprehended by mankind has passed into limbo.

These changes in physics involved a challenge to the basic assumption that natural phenomena were rigidly and universally conditioned, that a determinate system of cause and effect was uniformly manifested, and that this could be expressed in terms of 'laws of nature' always and everywhere valid. Heisenberg drew attention in 1927 to the evidence that it is impossible to know at exactly the same moment both the location and the momentum of a given particle, and deduced from this the necessary recognition of a principle of uncertainty. And though so startling a claim was inevitably criticized, the progress of research has established, both for electrons and for photons, the basis on which he put it forward, and the principle has had a revolutionary influence upon the whole idea of scientific law. Whereas it had been a chief accomplishment of the science of the seventeenth and eighteenth centuries to replace the old idea of random happenings by the concept of a clear, consistent and universal law of nature (and the immense value of this concept had been abundantly demonstrated), it now appeared that in atomic physics there was an element of the unpredictable and that such indeterminacy is not due to our inability but is inherent in the nature of things. This inevitably suggested that the term law was no more than a useful metaphor and that our observations yielded evidence not of rigid exactitude but of statistical averages, not of a uniform and invariable system but of a norm not inconsistent with a measure of indeterminacy, slight indeed in its range but universal in its scope. That indeter-

[1] It appears that mathematicians are now doing work along lines of the theory of information which involves a more complete departure from the Newtonian physics than Einstein or even Planck and Bohr have yet contemplated.

minacy is now being interpreted by some scientists in terms of creativity indicates at least the direction in which research and thought seem to be moving.

Here was a revolution which though based upon immensely difficult mathematical researches had an immediate significance for workers in other fields of science. Indeed a somewhat analogous change in the concept of law had already been projected in the field of genetics. Mendel had formulated a law of heredity which laid it down that the offspring of a first filial generation cross[1] would, as to 25%, resemble each of its grandparents while as to the remaining 50% would be 'heterozygote' or similar to its parents. This numerical formula, tested over a wide range of complicated examples, had seemed to give a universal result so clear as to justify W. Bateson's insistence upon the absolute rigidity of inheritance, the determinism of all organic life and the consequent immorality of punishing criminals for defects of character for which they had no responsibility.[2] But in fact when large numbers of cases were investigated as by G. Udny Yule in his statistical research into wheat[3] it was found that the expected proportion was not exactly verified, but that a small, but incalculable, 'margin of error' was invariably present. This conclusion has been repeatedly confirmed and is now generally accepted, so that we have in genetics a position not unlike that in physics—Mendel's law, like Newton's, being sufficiently exact for practical purposes but not being strictly and universally valid. It is proper to add that variability in the organic realm had been generally recognized and was of course the basis of Darwin's hypothesis, whereas in the inorganic it had been generally denied.

A change of a rather different kind involving not only the character but the scope of scientific studies was taking place slowly but definitely at the same period. It had been assumed, as we have seen, ever since the triumph of Newton at the end of the seventeenth

[1] The familiar limerick 'There was a young lady called Starkie' quoted by Miss Dorothy Sayers in *The Mind of the Maker*, p. 4, as illustrating Mendel's law is in fact contradictory of its basic principle.

[2] Cf. his Inaugural Lecture in Cambridge, *William Bateson, Naturalist*, pp. 327-8.

[3] Cf. *Journal of Genetics*, XIII, pp. 255-331.

century, that quantitative categories and laboratory technique were the criteria of science and that what was not amenable to these lay outside its field. During the two subsequent centuries this self-imposed limitation became more and more rigid: science was concerned with the ponderable, religion with the imponderable; science with the general, history with the particular; science with fact, everything else with fancy. Such antitheses were proclaimed as axiomatic. They are indeed still widely accepted.

The difficulties which this identification of science with physico-chemical investigation produced are sufficiently evident. It meant that the characteristic attributes of the living organism, its psychic, mental and personal qualities, must either be dismissed as outside the sphere of scientific investigation or explained in materialistic categories as somehow the by-product of bodily processes. As it was evident that emotional and intellectual experiences were closely associated with the physical condition it was not easy to take the former course—though the history of the long-debated theme of maternal impression shows how anxious scientists have been to evade the issue. As it was equally clear that a thorough-going materialism led to the impossible result that men were merely robots and could be treated as such, the attempt to keep within the frontiers of science and yet to deal adequately with the physiology of the living man was a forlorn hope. Yet, so long as medicine or indeed even biology was regarded as scientific, the problem was inescapable.

The matter became acute when psychology began to present its claim to be a science, and still more so when it invaded the medical profession and demonstrated its importance in medical practice. James Ward's *Psychological Principles* might be dismissed as philosophy rather than science; William James's *Varieties of Religious Experience* was too interesting and informal to be accepted as truly scientific; but with the coming of Sigmund Freud and psycho-analysis and especially when the first world war produced shell-shock and a multitude of cases which traditional medicine could not cure but which yielded almost miraculously to psychiatric treatment, it was impossible to keep the barriers firm. Psychology

o   193

won its way into the medical schools, into the universities, into the science faculties and, less desirably, on to the bookstalls; and the isolation of the sciences from other departments of human study and interest was at an end.

For a time (in Britain at least) psychology was admitted into the more austerely scientific circles only so far as it confined itself to physiological observations and experiments and to research into behaviour patterns and anthropology. Introspective methods were out of place in a laboratory and psychiatry belonged rather to the hospital than to the university. There are still some scientists who maintain that Dr J. B. Watson's ingenious but self-contradictory behaviourism which reduces all thought to movements of the larynx is the only psychology that can be regarded as scientific— even though its author admits that these movements are imperceptible and therefore by his own definition non-existent. Hesitation in accepting psychology when presented in such forms was indeed intelligible.

For in its early stages the analytical methods applied by the various schools seemed both arbitrary and incomplete. Indeed they consisted in little more than fastening upon some, preferably obscure, element in man's natural equipment—whether an infantilism like the Oedipus complex, or a nervous reaction like the conditioned reflex, or a social neurosis like the will to power—and employing this as the clue to the interpretation of the whole character. That they served a valuable purpose in disclosing the extent of the unconscious and repressed elements of personality, in revealing the influence of a man's origin and upbringing upon his psychic as upon his physical structure, in exploring the source and significance of many perversions and abnormalities, and in enlarging the sphere of therapeutics was quickly evident. But the publicity given to them, the claims made on their behalf and the charlatanry in which the subject became for a time involved justified the scientific world in maintaining an attitude of reserve. It seems probable that psychology will not win full recognition until it has found its Darwin and been adequately interpreted by a thorough investigation of the origin, evolution and development of behaviour.[1] At present the lack of such study is obviously a serious defect and a frequent source of error.[2]

It is indeed probable that the chief effect of the remarkable outbreak of psychological and psychiatric analysis, apart from its unwholesome influence upon the post-war generation, has been to emphasize the inadequacy of analysis and to expose the fallacies so often attaching to it. Certainly the subsequent progress of psychology has consisted in an increasing attention to the wholeness of the organism and a recognition that its analysable elements are themselves transformed when they are combined in a developed personality. Here as elsewhere the whole is larger than the sum total of its parts. We have only to observe the influence of psychology upon biology to see how significant this consequence has been. For biologists who were at one time disposed to limit their field to the physics and chemistry, the description and taxonomy of dead organisms, are now insisting that the living plant or animal must be studied not only physiologically but ecologically and sociologically, that is as a living whole and in relation to its proper environment. New techniques are in consequence being developed and the old distinction between 'laboratory' and 'field' studies is becoming an anachronism. As the revolt against mechanism extends, organic and holistic concepts will become familiar; at present (and inevitably in view of their long dominance) our thinking is still too much conditioned by analytical methods and materialistic imagery.

The breakdown of materialism and of the Cartesian dualism is likely to be accentuated as the transition from the inanimate to the animate becomes more clearly understood. Until a century ago it was easy to separate the two and indeed to posit a unique creative act as responsible for the appearance of life on the earth. The discovery of micro-organisms, the increasing knowledge of molecular structure and the inferred existence of non-filterable

---

[1] Though much detailed observation of particular species has been recorded and is being undertaken, no satisfactory survey of comparative psychology has yet appeared.

[2] It is, for example, plain that Freud's insistence upon the primacy of sex is hard to reconcile with the fact that relatedness and reproduction long precede the appearance of sex-organs and sex-differentiation.

viruses had suggested a generation ago that the ancient distinction was no longer absolute and the synthetic production of living matter no longer an impossible fantasy. With the construction of the electronic microscope and the consequent discovery and sight of viruses as rod-like objects of which it is not yet possible to state whether they should be classified as animate or inanimate the gap has been narrowed if not bridged. 'Continuity of process and the emergence of real differences', as Pringle-Pattison long ago defined it,[1] would seem to be characteristic of the whole sequence of evolution from the atoms to the saints; and the whole must fall within the proper field of scientific inquiry.

This extension of the field of the sciences is of course only a return to the intention of Francis Bacon and the founders of the modern world in the seventeenth century. The 'New Philosophy' aimed deliberately at claiming all knowledge, except perhaps religion, for its province; and the best of its representatives, Boyle and Ray and Newton, Huygens and Malpighi and Leibniz, were convinced that they must take the whole creation into account. It was no doubt inevitable that the necessary concentration upon physics and chemistry and the immense achievements that it accomplished should have led to a narrowing of the field of research, and that the interference of politicians and churchmen should have driven scientists in self-defence to make of this limitation a fortified frontier. But this period of rigid isolation is manifestly passing: the need today is not so much for mechanistic advance as for a fuller understanding of life and personality, of behaviour and community, of ethics and of religion; and those who argued twenty-five years ago[2] that science, if it was to fulfil its proper service to mankind, must claim the *totum scibile* for its province must be surprised at the speed with which their prediction is being fulfilled.

Yet even then it was plain that the changes which we have noted had been accompanied by a development in philosophy characterized by its emphasis upon evolution and wholeness, teleology and the concept of organism. Three series of Gifford lectures,

---

[1] *The Idea of God*, p. 103.   [2] Cf. e.g. my *The Creator Spirit*, pp. 112-15.

S. Alexander's *Space, Time and Deity*, C. Lloyd Morgan's *Emergent Evolution* and *Life, Mind and Spirit* and A. N. Whitehead's *Process and Reality*, and the very remarkable volume, *Holism and Evolution*, by J. C. Smuts represent in the main a similar outlook and emphasize the breakdown of the old mechanistic and compartmentalized concept of science. The appearance shortly afterwards of J. Oman's *The Natural and the Supernatural* and W. Temple's *Nature, Man and God* showed a similar movement of a more specifically Christian type. By the year 1934 it looked as if the divorce between science and religion would shortly be annulled.

For in religion also there had been movement. The 'conspiracy of silence' based upon the claim that the eternal verities of the Christian religion could not be affected by scientific researches, whatever their results, had been broken—not, alas, by the orthodox but by the attacks of self-styled heretics. The result had been its repudiation by Christians awakened to the recognition that the segregation of religion from science was wholly incompatible with any real belief in an Incarnation. If 'the Word was made flesh' was a true saying, then what was known about the flesh and indeed about the natural order could not be irrelevant to Christendom. The critical studies of the Scriptures and the consequent rejection of their infallibility had made it clear that the traditional doctrines of the Creation and the Fall and the theology based upon them must be revised in the light of new knowledge and that the traditional arguments from miracles and from prophecy must be re-examined. Indeed it was evident that, if religion was not to become the sectional interest of a dwindling minority, its significance for the interpretation of the universe, its bearing upon all human thought and action, its value in illuminating present problems and judging present evils, in guiding and inspiring, redeeming and uniting mankind must be affirmed, demonstrated and made effective. The efforts that were made after the great Edinburgh Conference of 1910 to draw together all Christian denominations for the study of the faith and order, and likewise of the life and work, of the Church, interrupted as they were by war and hindered by lack of resolute leadership, yet gave signal proof of a new and vigorous awakening. During the twenties and in spite of post-war difficulties real progress was made in the expansion and consolidation of the 'younger' Churches in Asia and Africa, in the formulation of a Christian critique of the economic, political and social activities of mankind, and in the development of mutual understanding and theological agreement between the separated denominations. It was evident that much more searching and constructive work was needed, especially in the fields of biblical exegesis and of doctrinal and philosophical restatement, if Christianity were to be commended to modern man and made applicable to his needs and knowledge. But the war had shattered his complacency and revealed his disease, and he was becoming ready to accept a healer. Too often the Churches seemed to him to deserve the ancient rebuke, ' 'Tis not the good physician's part To chant incantations over a wound that craves the knife.'[1]

That we have examined this situation almost entirely from the British standpoint is largely but not solely due to the fact that we share it and have experienced it 'from the inside'. It is probably true that in Britain, thanks to its history since and even before the Reformation, there has been a closer connexion between Church and State in the public life and a fuller combination of worship and service in the Christian society than can be found in any Continental country. We have escaped the antagonism between socialism and churchmanship characteristic of Belgium, France, Spain and Italy, the duality of Church and State characteristic of Lutheranism, and to a lesser degree also the conflicts between Protestant and Catholic theologies and between fundamentalist and liberal views of inspiration and authority. Science and religion have dwelt together in our ancient universities, and a genuine toleration and respect for academic freedom are a still valued inheritance. Typical of our position are our great tradition of Church music and hymnody in worship and the Christian activities and social service of our Quakers and pietists. If we have not succeeded in keeping our duty to God and to man inseparable we have at least refused both in national and in ecclesiastical life to see them set in contrast.

[1] Sophocles, *Ajax*, 581-2.

It would be much easier to illustrate the course of events which we have been describing from American than from Continental examples: for in the United States the contribution to the New Reformation has been impressive in itself and full of promise for the future. Ever since the days of John Winthrop who corresponded with Hartlib about matters of education and science, of Jonathan Edwards whose close contact with scientists and thinkers deserves to be better known and of Bishop William White whose liberal theology has lately been described[1] there has been a succession of preachers and scholars who have combined a generous and profound devotion with a fine intellectual and moral integrity. It is one of the misfortunes of the Englishman that he knows so little of the development of a reasonable theology in a land where the dead hand of traditional creeds and ceremonies and the memory of ancient controversies do not restrict and embitter and where it is possible to pull down and rebuild with a speed and on a scale unthinkable in the Old World. The example and the works of men like Philips Brooks of Boston, Francis Greenwood Peabody and Josiah Royce of Harvard, Walter Rauschenbusch of New York and Rochester, Shailer Matthews of Chicago, William Porcher Du Bose and Bishop Francis McConnell, and among scientists (to name a few at random) Asa Gray, Henry Fairfield Osborn and Robert Andrews Millikan should be known and studied. We should learn from them how the crisis of the past century could have been handled here and be encouraged to hope that the 'new model' for which the Church waits may be given to us from the Christendom of the western hemisphere. And that this contribution was not limited to scholars and thinkers is plain from the world-wide influence of the Student Christian Federation which owes its origin and achievements to J. R. Mott, R. F. Wilder and their colleagues, and from the splendid adventures of American evangelism especially in China and Japan but indeed all over the non-Christian lands.[2]

But during the period between the wars with which we are

[1] *The Common Sense Theology of Bishop White* by S. A. Temple Jr. (New York, 1946).
[2] For this cf. the last two volumes of K. S. Latourette, *Expansion of Christianity*.

immediately concerned it is not unfair to say that American vigour and success gave to their philosophy and theology a preponderantly humanistic bias. In spite of the wise warnings of Dr Ernest Hocking and later the prophetic violence of Dr Reinhold Niebuhr the liberalism of the Churches tended to accept an exaggerated scepticism with regard to Scripture and Christian origins and an equally exaggerated reliance upon human excellence, psychiatric techniques and sociological experiments. There was in much popular religion neither a Redeemer nor a need for redemption: freedom, democracy, progress, the American way of life, Christianity and the Kingdom of God became interchangeable terms. Such a verdict is certainly untrue if applied to the leading centres of Church life; it is not unjust as describing the general outlook and optimism of the Churches as a whole. Indeed the extent to which American liberals had lost interest in the historical sources of the faith, in its credal and doctrinal presentation and in the metaphysical and transcendental elements in theology came as a surprise and shock to English liberals and represented something wholly unfamiliar in Christian circles in this country.

It is important to emphasize this because of its bearing upon the reaction which obstructed the progress of the New Reformation during the thirties. This reaction to a traditional and professedly more orthodox theology is an important element in the present situation; but to discuss it adequately would demand greater detail than its relation to the subject of these lectures would strictly warrant.[1]

That a measure of reaction should have taken place can hardly be matter for surprise in view of the immensity of the task and the real danger that, in discharging it, essential Christian convictions arising out of profound and verifiable experience would be ignored. To interpret man's most intimate and personal characteristic, his total reaction to his environment, his awareness of the fascination and terror of the Universe and of his own solitariness in it, in terms appropriate to the scale and quality of his new

---

[1] Cf. for a brief and mainly historical account Note IX below, pp. 212-15. It takes a place in the second series of these lectures.

knowledge and to the vast changes which this knowledge had effected was in itself a superhuman undertaking; and it had to be fulfilled when the traditional standards and relationships of the past which had previously served as an authoritative criterion were now themselves no longer generally accepted. In the intellectual sphere the basis of epistemology had been shaken by the impact of new psychological insights, and philosophy was preoccupied with semantics. In the moral sphere the contrast between the lawyer's maxim 'Hard cases make bad law' and the Christian belief that 'every case is a hard case' had given rise to a confusion which threatened to reduce all ethics to relativism. In international affairs an increasing nationalism conflicted with the fact that by the transformation of time and space the world was now one neighbourhood;[1] and totalitarianism in its appropriate efficiency seemed to be crushing all the individuals' hard-won liberties. In each of the three chief human relationships which St Paul said were integrated in Christ ('neither Jew nor Greek, . . . neither bond nor free, . . . neither male nor female'),[2] a situation had arisen as a result of centuries of slow development which had suddenly become inescapably critical. Small wonder that Christians clung convulsively to 'old paths in perilous times'.

Perhaps inevitably the scope of theological restatement tended to confine itself to a re-examination and re-affirmation of the chief types of previous orthodoxy. If Dr Karl Barth had gone back to an extreme Calvinism for the main lines of his teaching, a similar return to orthodox Lutheranism was evident in the theologians of Scandinavia, Aulen, Nygren and, to a less extent, Nathan Söderblom. Catholic scholars like Jacques Maritain and Etienne Gilson were giving contemporary reference to neo-scholasticism. Nicolas Berdyaev gave to western Europe a rich and timely reminder of the Christian Platonists of Alexandria.[3] It might be argued with good reason that such revivals of the ideas of the third or thirteenth or sixteenth centuries were hardly relevant to the scale and

---

[1] In 1852 my father went to New Zealand by sailing-ship in six months: in 1950 I made the same journey by plane in six days. [2] Gal. iii. 28.
[3] He admits to a special affinity with Origen; cf. *Dream and Reality*, p. 165.

character of the changes demanded in the twentieth. But such work, faithful, scholarly and, in its setting at least, modern, was in itself a testimony to the pressure of the situation and a preparation for a more adequate response to it. The magnitude of what was needed could be seen the more clearly by the failure of such notable attempts to revivify the past. It was perhaps inevitable that they should attract many of those who might otherwise have carried on the larger and more thoroughgoing restatement. In the 1930's, in spite of the Ecumenical Conferences at Oxford and Edinburgh, Christians failed to realize or to maintain the intellectual adventure which the previous decade had foreshadowed.

Thus, in spite of the signs of an increasing readiness for co-operation on the part of scientists, of an emancipation of philosophy from the logical positivism which had confined it to the critical scrutiny of meaning, of a stabilizing of the scope and character of psychology and a readiness to explore psychic and extra-sensory phenomena, and of a strong desire to counteract the tendency to specialization and to advocate larger interchange between the several fields of study, the general prospect looked almost ironically depressing. Just when a synthesis was becoming possible, Christians who were surely committed to the integration of experience and of life seemed to be retiring into their own ivory towers, cells and catacombs. Twenty years before they had been eager for partnership; now when it was being offered they were rejecting it. The old antitheses were reaffirmed; the old dualisms revivified. It only needed the atomic bomb upon Hiroshima to underline the irony of the situation.

Those who had known such pioneers of atomic research as Sir Joseph Thomson, Lord Rutherford and Sir Arthur Eddington and had realized the faith which had sustained and the dreams which had beglamoured their work, can share something of the shock caused when the greatest achievement of human research, the result of a generation of intense intellectual and scientific effort, was announced to the world in the name of the two Christian democracies by the annihilation of a city. If this were the result of their science, if mankind could only use a source of energy, which

might eliminate drudgery and transform the whole physical
environment, for his own pugnacity, if religion and ethics, statesmanship and sanity were unable to prevent racial suicide, then a
desperate situation demanded desperate remedies: something must
surely be done to reinstate a measure of moral control. The atomic
scientists of America and Britain were not slow to repeat the
protests they had made before the destruction of Hiroshima;
attempts to mobilize opinion for the formulation of sanctions and
standards of conduct were made in many quarters; co-operation
with theologians, philosophers and men of letters was invited;
the sense of urgency created an opportunity to fulfil the efforts of
the twenties. Unfortunately the Churches were no longer ready to
respond. Commissions were set up, but no effort was made to get
scientists to join them; reports were issued which expressed
nothing but bewilderment: on an issue on which Abraham had
had no hesitation[1] Christendom seemed to have nothing to say.
All of us who profess and call ourselves Christians stand together
under that condemnation.

[1] Cf. his plea for Sodom, Gen. xviii. 23-33.

NOTES

I. THE BELIEF IN THE TRANSMUTATION OF SPECIES

The belief in the transmutation of species both in animals and in plants goes back to Aristotle and Theophrastus. Thus at the end of the *Historia Animalium* (IX, 49) there is a list of birds which change; the Robin into the Redstart the former being the summer and the latter the winter species; the Ortolan and the Blackcap where the change takes place in autumn and has been seen when incomplete; the Nightingale whose song and colour are wholly altered at the end of summer; and the Hoopoe which, according to Aeschylus,[1] in the spring becomes the Cuckoo or Hawk. Theophrastus (*De Plantis*, II, 4, 4) quotes and apparently accepts such changes, Hoopoe and Hawk, Water-snake and Viper, and quotes the metamorphoses of insects as supplying an analogy. He cites a number of cases in plants: 'sisymbrium' into Mint and Wheat into Darnel; this latter degeneration he discusses more fully in VIII, 7, 1 and 3 and appends to his account a list of other weeds which infest particular crops. Pliny (*Naturalis Historia*, XVIII, 76 and XIX, 176) repeats the same records and adds the change through old age of Marjoram into Thyme.

These admitted transmutations in the great authorities are accepted by almost all the medieval writers. We mention St Albert in Chapter IV. A few other examples may be added.

The pseudo-Aristotelian *De Plantis*,[2] I, 17, gives a variant of Theophrastus: Calamint into Mint, 'Terugena' (?) into 'Sesebra' (sisymbrium), Wheat and Flax into other species. Julius Caesar Scaliger, in his *De Plantis*, Bk. I (ed. Geneva, 1566, p. 80), quotes Theophrastus but adds, as a thing that he has himself seen, the growth of *Alliaria* from Parsley seed, and, the strangest of all such changes, the story 'falsely told of the Phoenix but veraciously of the Bernacle Goose'.

---

[1] He quotes fourteen lines from a lost play (Nauck, fr. 297).

[2] The story of this book, Alfred's Latin version, and Nicolaus of Damascus's claim to be the author, are obscure. I quote from the edition by E. H. F. Meyer. In the Greek text the passage is 821a, 7 (Teubner ed. p. 22).

That the scholars of the Renaissance should have accepted so authoritative a belief as readily as they did the similar belief in spontaneous generation is not surprising: the infallibility of Aristotle[1] was as unquestioned as that of the Bible. Nevertheless it comes as a surprise to find that even our own William Turner, a shrewd observer and an excellent botanist, accepted transmutation as a commonplace event. That rye in a bad season 'doth go out of kinde' into cornflower,[2] that in poor soil corn after one year turns into rye, and the same rye in its second year turns into 'Darnell and suche other naughty wedes',[3] and that ants change into flies, cabbage caterpillars into butterflies, and serpents into dragons[4]—these are unquestioned facts to him.

II. THE 'PESSIMISM' OF THE GREEKS

It is worth adding a note to protest against the prevalent emphasis upon the pessimism of Classical Greece. Since J. B. Bury in his very tendentious volume, *The Idea of Progress*, drew attention to the Stoic doctrine of cycles of time repeating themselves, and combined this with stress upon the assertions of degeneracy (familiar in Horace and perhaps assignable to Plato) and of Moira, the fixed conditions under which human life exists, there has been a chorus of lamentation over the hopelessness and resignation of Hellenic culture. Dr Reinhold Niebuhr makes this a cardinal point in his denunciation of this world and its ways.

As one who was brought up in the rigour of the Classical discipline and came from it to natural history and Christianity I cannot but wonder if such people have ever seen the Parthenon or, for that matter, a vase of the best period; or read Pericles' funeral oration and the *Oedipus Coloneus*; or been entranced by the Hermes of Praxiteles and the Demeter of Ceos; or spent an hour in recapturing the perennial youth and shameless gaiety of that brief and brilliant springtime. Pessimism! Do such critics not realize that when a normal man bemoans the cruelty of fate and the degeneracy of the age it is safe to assume that he is young and happy? Do they not see that one who lived in Athens with Aeschylus or Socrates might well pray for a repetition of the experience—even though a dweller in Birmingham or New York

---

[1] Even as late as 1681 Nehemiah Grew in the preface to his catalogue *Musaeum Reg. Soc.* comments upon those who insist on quoting Aristotle to prove that a man has ten toes.
[2] *Herbal*, I, p. 189.　　　　　　　　　　　　[3] *Herbal*, II, p. 129.
[4] *Hunting of the Romyshe Wolfe*, p. B. 1; for these cf. my *English Naturalists*, pp. 131-2.

would find such a prospect depressing? Have they never appreciated the loveliness of earth and the lust of the eye and the pride of life?

Heaven lies about us in our infancy.

There were times when the Greeks behaved like dirty and very naughty children, times when they were pathetically immature and inefficient. But to interpret them, as Bury does, by quotations from Horace is as absurd as it would be to illustrate Shelley by citing W. S. Gilbert.

There is, and no one will deny it, a sense of boredom and disillusionment in the very best of Roman literature: it is never quite spontaneous and often, too often, pretentious and vulgar. But that is not the fault of the Greeks; nor is it true of them. Byron's picture of the isles of Greece, extravagant as it is, is nearer the truth than Bury's—or Niebuhr's.

III. BASIL'S USE OF PSEN

Basil identifies Psen (ψήν) with the pollen-dust of the male palm. But Herodotus (*Hist.* I, 193) describes how the Babylonians impregnate the female date-palm by the Psen or Gall-fly which bores into the fruit. Theophrastus (*Hist. Plant.* II, 8, 4) tells how the male flowers of the date are shaken over the female so as to release the male dust which prevents the fruit from falling off; in this passage he says nothing of Psen. But he has described the caprification of figs by the Psen or gall-fly in the previous paragraph. Basil may have taken his misinterpretation of Psen from a confused reading of Theophrastus. It is interesting that Pseudo-Aristotle (*De Plantis*, I, 6, 7) uses Psen as pollen; but the Greek version of this treatise is notoriously a Renaissance production so the mistake in it may be due to Basil.

IV. GESNER'S PUBLISHED LETTERS OF 1564 AND 1565

1 Jan.	*to* Adolf Occo, doctor at Augsburg	8 Jan.	*to* Achilles Pirmin Gasser, doctor and man of letters, Augsburg, editor of Peter Peregrinus's book on the magnet, published 1558
6 Jan.	*to* Jean Bauhin, then doctor at Lyons		
7 Jan.	*to* J. Bauhin		
8 Jan.	*to* Johann Crato von Kraftheim, physician to the emperor at Augsburg	21 Jan.	*to* A. Gasser

? Jan.	*to*	Johann Culmann, physician to Duke of Wurtemburg	21 July	*to*	Johann Schmid, pastor at Chur
22 Jan.	*to*	A. Occo	22 July	*to*	T. Zwinger
5 Feb.	*to*	J. Crato	24 July	*to*	J. Crato
11 Feb.	*to*	J. Bauhin	5 Aug.	*to*	Joachim Camerarius of Nuremberg
12 Feb.	*to*	A. Gasser	23 Aug.	*to*	Felix Platter, Medical School, Basel
15 Feb.	*to*	Theodore Zwinger, Medical School, Basel	27 Aug.	*to*	J. Kentmann
15 Feb.	*to*	J. Bauhin	29 Aug.	*to*	A. Gasser
16 Feb.	*to*	Johann Kentmann, doctor at Dresden	30 Aug.	*to*	J. Camerarius
			16 Sept.	*to*	A. Gasser
20 Feb.	*to*	A. Gasser	24 Sept.	*to*	C. Holtzach
22 Feb.	*to*	J. Crato	2 Oct.	*to*	Wilhelm Stuck, of Zürich at Tübingen
5 Mar.	*to*	J. Crato	5 Oct.	*to*	A. Occo
19 Mar.	*to*	A. Gasser	20 Oct.	*to*	A. Gasser
24 Mar.	*to*	J. Bauhin	5 Nov.	*to*	J. Bauhin
26 Mar.	*to*	J. Crato	6 Nov.	*to*	A. Gasser
? Mar.	*to*	Johann Funck	? Nov.	*to*	F. Platter
5 April	*to*	J. Bauhin	15 Nov.	*to*	J. Funck
7 April	*to*	T. Zwinger	19 Nov.	*to*	J. Funck
14 April	*to*	Cosmos Holtzach, doctor at Schaffhausen	4 Dec.	*to*	A. Occo
			12 Dec.	*to*	A. Occo
			13 Dec.	*to*	T. Zwinger
17 April	*to*	J. Crato	17 Dec.	*to*	A. Gasser
24 April	*to*	T. Zwinger	? Dec.	*to*	J. Funck
28 April	*to*	A. Gasser	? Dec.	*to*	J. Bauhin
Whitsunday	*to*	J. Crato	20 Dec.	*to*	F. Platter
Whitmonday	*to*	J. Funck	5 Jan.	*to*	Conrad Forer, doctor and pastor at Winterthur
19 June	*to*	A. Occo			
24 June	*to*	A. Gasser	7 Jan.	*to*	A. Occo
? June	*to*	J. Kentmann	15 Jan.	*to*	A. Gasser
30 June	*to*	J. Bauhin	? Jan.	*to*	A. Occo
10 July	*to*	J. Crato	21 Jan.	*to*	J. Funck
14 July	*to*	T. Zwinger	25 Jan.	*to*	J. Culmann
			26 Jan.	*to*	Benoit Marti, professor at Berne

27 Jan.	*to* Jerome Herold of Nuremberg	9 Aug.	*to* T. Zwinger
		22 Aug.	*to* B. Marti
27 Jan.	*to* J. Camerarius	27 Aug.	*to* J. Camerarius
27 Jan.	*to* J. Kentmann	27 Aug.	*to* J. Herold
28 Jan.	*to* F. Platter	27 Aug.	*to* A. Occo
Feb.	*to* A. Gasser	? Aug.	*to* J. Kentmann
4 Feb.	*to* A. Occo	28 Aug.	*to* T. Zwinger
? Feb.	*to* B. Marti	29 Aug.	*to* W. Stuck
18 Feb.	*to* A. Occo	29 Aug.	*to* Anton Raphael
23 Feb.	*to* T. Zwinger	31 Aug.	*to* C. Forer
25 Feb.	*to* A. Gasser	31 Aug.	*to* J. Bauhin
25 Feb.	*to* J. Bauhin	2 Sept.	*to* A. Occo
3 Mar.	*to* B. Marti	22 Sept.	*to* J. Camerarius
16 Mar.	*to* J. Bauhin	26 Sept.	*to* A. Occo
23 Mar.	*to* J. Kentmann	28 Sept.	*to* A. Occo
31 Mar.	*to* A. Gasser	6 Oct.	*to* J. Bauhin
3 April	*to* A. Occo	11 Oct.	*to* J. Bauhin
4 April	*to* J. Herold	25 Oct.	*to* A. Gasser
8 April	*to* T. Zwinger	29 Oct.	*to* J. Bauhin
18 April	*to* A. Occo	5 Nov.	*to* A. Occo
19 April	*to* A. Gasser	18 Nov.	*to* A. Occo
5 May	*to* A. Occo	24 Nov.	*to* B. Marti
5 May	*to* F. Platter	26 Nov.	*to* T. Zwinger
16 June	*to* A. Occo	27 Nov.	*to* Johann Wirt, professor at Basel
24 June	*to* T. Zwinger		
8 July	*to* A. Occo	30 Nov.	*to* T. Zwinger
9 July	*to* J. Bauhin	3 Dec.	*to* A. Gasser
19 July	*to* A. Gasser		

V. AN EXAMPLE OF THE INFLUENCE OF LINNAEUS

An example which I am permitted to quote by the kindness of my friend Dr Hamshaw Thomas will illustrate the harm done by the Linnaean influence.

Richard Bradley, admitted a fellow of the Royal Society in 1712 and given the title of Professor of Botany at Cambridge in 1724, published a number of books and articles[1] recording his researches into

[1] The chief are 'Microscopical Observations on the vegetation of moldiness' (*Phil, Trans.* 1716, pp. 490-2), the first record of fungal spores; *History of Succulent Plants,* 1716-27; *New Improvements of Planting and Gardening,* 1717; *A Philosophical Account of the Works of Nature,* 1721; and *A general treatise of Husbandry and Gardening,* 1722.

the pollination and hybridization of plants and into the spread of what we now know to be virus diseases among them. His experiments with tulips, auriculas and carnations gave clear evidence of the whole process of fertilization; and in 1721 Philip Miller head of the Chelsea Physic Garden wrote to him reporting that in consequence of the evidence in his *New Improvements* experiments had been carried out at Chelsea which demonstrated the part played by bees in pollination. Plainly Bradley was a real scientist with a good knowledge of research, of the use of the microscope, and of the importance of physiological investigation. Yet to his successors and the Linnaean age such a man was 'no botanist' but 'an adventurer who hoodwinked the University';[1] and the sort of studies which he advocated in spite of their great economic and horticultural value disappeared from Cambridge until the latter part of the nineteenth century. Of the two Martyns, father and son, who held the chair of botany after Bradley's death in 1732 successively for ninety-three years, the father John did no lecturing after 1735 and in 1762 handed over the professorship to the son Thomas who did little more than reiterate Ray's Catalogues and arrange them in Linnaean order.

VI. BRITISH WORKING-MEN NATURALISTS

In addition to the scientists, amateur and professional, there was the wonderful galaxy of working-men naturalists, many of the most notable of whom came from Scotland; in spite of grievous handicaps through lack of education, books, leisure, resources and friends, they contributed greatly to the knowledge of our flora and fauna, investigated little-known orders of invertebrates and insects and produced in the second half of the century a splendid following. There was George Don, the botanist of Edinburgh, whose discoveries of new and rare plants in Scotland were recorded by his second son, David, in a paper to the Wernerian Society in 1820; there was Charles Peach the coast-guard in Norfolk, Cornwall and then in Scotland who did valuable work in marine biology before he turned to geology; his friend Robert Dick, the baker of Thurso, who discovered the Holy Grass there in

---

[1] So Winstanley, *Unreformed Cambridge*, p. 162, basing his verdict upon G. C. Gorham, *Memoirs of John and Thomas Martyn*, pp. 31-3. This is weak evidence, mere unsubstantiated gossip, reproducing the paragraph on Bradley in the appendix to J. Martyn's *Dissertations on the Aeneid*.

1834, and then became an expert on the fossils of the old red sandstone; Hugh Miller, the stone-mason of Cromarty, author of a book on the same subject and many other popular works; Thomas Edwards, the shoemaker, whose exploration of the coasts of Banff and Aberdeen is that of a pioneer in the study of behaviour as well as the work of a man of heroic patience;[1] Alfred French, the baker of Banbury, who became an attendant in the botanical department of the British Museum and did much field work in Oxfordshire; and there were his colleagues at Kew who, being employed as gardeners, were sent out to explore and bring home the flowering plants of Australia or South America or the Himalaya or the Barrier Reef.[2]

VII. ON THE BRIDGEWATER TREATISES

The Earl (the Rt. Hon. and Rev. Francis Henry) who died in 1829 left £8000 for a selected person or persons to publish one thousand copies of a work *On the Power, Wisdom and Goodness of God as manifested in the Creation; illustrating such work by all reasonable arguments, as for instance the variety and formation of God's creatures in the animal, vegetable and mineral kingdoms; the effect of digestion and thereby of conversion; the construction of the hand of man and an infinite variety of other arguments; as also by discoveries ancient and modern, in arts, sciences and the whole extent of literature.*

The team selected and their treatises were the following:

Thomas Chalmers, D.D., Professor of Divinity, Edinburgh.

The Adaptation of External Nature to the Moral and Intellectual Constitution of Man.

John Kidd, M.D., F.R.S.

On the Adaptation of External Nature to the Physical Conditions of Man.

William Whewell, M.A., F.R.S.

Astronomy and General Physics Considered with Reference to Natural Theology.

Sir Charles Bell, F.R.S.

The Hand: its Mechanism and Vital Endowments as Evincing Design.

Peter Mark Roget, M.D., F.R.S.

Animal and Vegetable Physiology (2 vols.).

---

[1] He is the subject of S. Smiles's *Life of a Scotch Naturalist* (London, 1876).

[2] For a charming account cf. A. W. Anderson, *The Coming of the Flowers* (London, 1950).

William Buckland, D.D., F.R.S., Professor of Geology, Oxford.
  Geology and Mineralogy considered with Reference to Natural Theology
  (2 vols.).
William Kirby, M.A., F.R.S.
  The History, Habits and Instincts of Animals (2 vols.).
William Prout, M.D., F.R.S.
  *Chemistry, Meteorology and the Function of Digestion considered with
  Reference to Natural Theology.*

VIII. ON EVOLUTION IN LEPIDOPTERA

It is impossible to discuss the problems of evolutionary theory without
plunging into a mass of detail, and this would be out of place. But, if
I may choose examples from one field, as a lifelong lepidopterist, I
would urge that consideration be given to such illustrative cases as the
following: *Arenostola brevilinea* Fenn, the new moth first taken in 1864
near Ranworth in the Norfolk Broads, where it is still abundant, an
area thoroughly explored for many years before that date by the local
schoolmaster, who took and sold all the other rare species;[1] *Cryphia*
var. *impar* Warren, the isolated Cambridge race of the coastal moth,
C. muralis Linn. which represents an extreme case of local modification,
but which on rare occasions produces examples identical with the type;
examples of what is misleadingly called 'industrial melanism'[2] in the
Boarmiid family, practically all the British members of which have
produced black mutants, often in areas wholly outside industrial
activity; the larval symbiosis of *Maculinea arion* Linn. with the red ants,
Myrmica laevinodis and *M. scabrinodis*,[3] a habit not easy to explain by
the hypothesis of a casual step-by-step development; or, most difficult
of all, the geometrical perfection of the web of the Diadem Spider
(*Epeira diademata*), which can hardly have been achieved by random
trial and error methods—or (for that matter) by a process analogous
to that of a human architect. The problem of the 'opus perfectum',
the novelty which depends for its viability upon the simultaneity of a
multitude of changes, remains a serious if not a fatal obstacle to the

---

[1] Cf. my account of this in *Entomologist*, Sept. 1908, and *The Creator Spirit*, pp. 131-4.
[2] It is well known that the chief locality for melanic mutants is Delamere Forest which
although in Cheshire is entirely unaffected by industrialism.
[3] Cf. F. W. Frohawk in *Entomologist*, XXXVI (1903) and *Nat. History of British Butterflies*,
II, pp. 138-49.

traditional Darwinian hypothesis.[1] It is disappointing that so many biologists appear to dismiss it, as he did, unexplained.[2]

IX. ON THE RECENT REACTION IN THEOLOGY

On the Continent during the years of tragic suffering and insecurity that followed the first world war, a situation, closely parallel to that confronting Augustine after the sack of Rome in A.D. 410 and during the Vandal invasion of his province, had arisen. It was natural that Christians sensitive to the evil and pain of the times and seeing no clear prospect of recovery should have sought in a restatement of Calvinism the message appropriate to the times. In so doing they were powerfully assisted by the writings of the Danish writer of the previous century, Sören Kierkegaard. His brilliant, poignant and morbid presentation of the Christian judgment upon the Church and upon human society had exerted small influence in his own day; and it is probably true that his own character did little to commend it. But in the period between the wars the climate was eminently congenial. Dr Karl Barth and his colleagues fastened upon him, and their exegesis of St Paul vivified by his literary skill met the need of the time and place with a completeness which surprised them.[3] In its uncompromising emphasis upon the sole authority of the Bible, its denunciation of all human activity whether of science or of statesmanship as irrelevant to religion if not actually idolatrous, its insistence upon the transcendence and 'otherness' of God, the total corruption of man, the absolute antithesis between nature and grace, and the impossibility of any coming of the Kingdom within history, Dr Barth's version of Christianity seemed to forbid any possibility of the Christian social order or the scientifically intelligible theology to which in this country and in America we had been devoting our lives.

How far such an interpretation of Dr Barth's work at that stage in his career is fair to him will be disputed by those who come to him in his later utterances. There is, in such work as his recent lectures on the

[1] This was of course repeatedly urged by critics like Asa Gray in Darwin's own lifetime. He never succeeded in answering it or even appreciating its character. His successors have not been much more successful.

[2] Dr Julian Huxley (*Discovery*, Feb. 1943) replies to it by admitting that tissue 'has the faculty of responding to demands upon it both by excess growth and by changes in the direction of the fibres'. This, as Dr G. Rabel shows (*Nineteenth Century*, June 1945), is pure Lamarckism.

[3] See the preface to the third edition of Barth's *The Epistle to the Romans*.

Creed, breadth as well as depth, and a sense of proportion quite absent in his first writings. Perhaps he has himself developed a fuller appreciation of what is involved in incarnation, and has grasped the significance of the manhood of Jesus and the scope of the operation of the Holy Spirit. Perhaps the change is due to the audience: in the early days he was addressing the liberal protestants of the German-speaking world, those descendants of Ritschl who seemed to him to reduce Christianity to a bare humanism; if so, it was a mistake to apply his polemic to the very different liberalism of this country. That in any case he did a great and wonderful work, that he brought to us all, even if we felt his emphasis to be one-sided and his strictures unfair, a deeper insight into the grandeur of religion, the miracle of God's grace, and the extent of our blindness and rebellion, and that even though we could not accept his denial of natural religion or his attitude to the Word of God, yet he stimulated, even by his negations, a vital interest in aspects of theology which had been neglected to our loss, all this remains an obligation which even his critics must thankfully acknowledge. It is not his fault that some of his followers seized the scourge with which he smote his co-religionists on the Continent and used it to belabour those in this country who were almost as far as he from accepting a humanist position.

It seemed unlikely that in England Dr Barth would have much influence. Calvinism has never been strong among us, and our most revered teachers, from F. D. Maurice to Archbishop W. Temple and from Henry Drummond to Dr Scott Lidgett, had been from their different standpoints champions of a social and doctrinal reformation. Indeed apart from the much loved teacher, Sir Edwyn Hoskyns, and a few of the younger free-churchmen there was almost no one prepared to accept Dr Barth's challenge as appropriate. His exegesis seemed subjective and one-sided and was obscured by the length and rhetoric of his comments; his doctrine was dangerously near heresy and could easily be criticized as gnostic in its Christology and Arian in its attitude to the Creator; his denunciation of human effort dismayed us at a time when the world was rushing down to disaster; his denial of any attainable goal hamstrung hope and fostered defeatism. The belief so widespread on the Continent that, because Pelagius was a Welshman, therefore all Englishmen are Pelagians may find support from our refusal to become Barthians; at least and in the main we carried on with our efforts in 'Life and Work' as much as in 'Faith and Order'.

In America, as also (though for different reasons) in Scotland, the influence of the Barthian school was more notable. Dr Reinhold Niebuhr, acutely sensitive to the ruthlessness of industrialism and the complacency of humanism, devoted his brilliant gifts of eloquence and of generalization to a drastic criticism of the social order and of the individual impotence of civilization. As preacher and writer, teacher and theologian, he carried forward the challenge that Kierkegaard and Barth, Forsyth and Hoskyns had uttered, and interpreted it with such insight and vigour that the English-speaking world could not but listen. To America which had forgotten about sin and come to regard happiness as its birthright and all the world as for sale, his words came with the force of a scourge; to Britain which had been stricken and bled white and was beginning to despair of escaping a second holocaust, his message that peace was a utopian dream, and the less of two evils the only practicable course, brought a measure of consolation. The outbreak of the second world war vindicated his words of doom; the authorities in this country welcomed him as 'a hammer of pacifists';[1] and the theology of crisis was hailed as the neo-orthodoxy. It was perhaps unfortunate that his admirers should have applied without hesitation his denunciation of the humanism of John Dewey to the very different theological liberalism of England; but they were young, the times were evil, and they needed a target at which to direct the arrows that he provided for them. If the result was to convince the scientists, who were beginning to look for moral and intellectual help to Christianity, that the Churches were still living in the sixteenth century, such consequences could not be expected to deter the apologists and historians of the anti-liberal crusade.[2]

Yet in fact this has been the situation that developed in Britain during the period between 1935 and 1945. Theology had hitherto been concerned with the study of 'God and everything else together'[3] and especially with restating the great doctrines; Creation, now regarded not as an act in the past but as a continuing evolution; Incarnation, and its relationship to the creative process and to the indwelling of the Holy Spirit; Redemption, and the light thrown by it upon the whole business of life through death; Community, and the relationship of individual to

[1] A title originally given to G. G. Coulton.
[2] A vivid account of this crusade written by a crusader constitutes the two volumes of Canon R. Lloyd's *History of the Church of England in the Twentieth Century*.
[3] I wish I could remember the source of this pleasant definition.

corporate well-being. To explore this restatement and its relevance to the life and thought of contemporary man had been the task laid upon every thoughtful Christian. Now theology was bidden to restrict itself to a rigidly specialized task, 'the study of Christian existence in history today',[1] and told that concern with anything outside the Bible was 'vanity and vexation of spirit'. The suggestion that scientific or historical researches could have any influence upon such matters as belief in miracles was repudiated as an intrusion into a sphere in which only those inside the Christian fellowship could appraise the evidence. The proposal to treat the disciples of other religions as, at least in some sort, fellow-seekers was condemned as infringing the uniqueness of Christ. The claim that the activity of the Holy Spirit could be traced in the whole development of humanity and was analogous to, if not identical with, the *nisus* observable in the evolutionary process, was rejected on the ground that no adequate exposition of it could be found in the Bible. The progress made since the abandonment of the conspiracy of silence was halted and condemned.

[1] Canon A. Richardson, *Christian Apologetics*, p. 50; this is Barth's definition not of theology but of dogmatics, cf. *Dogmatics in Outline*, pp. 9, 10. Richardson, *Science, History and Faith*, p. 38, gives a wider definition of theology, but in the rest of the book limits it to 'the study of the phenomena presented by the existence of the Christian Church'.

INDEX

Adam and the Fall, 34-5
Adelinus, 67
Aesop, 53
Agar, W. E., 184 n.
Agricola, *see* Bauer, G.
Agriculture and enclosures, 139-40
Albert, St, 61; and nature, 65-71; and nomenclature, 78
Albert, S. M., 71
Albigenses, 58
Albin, E., 148
Aldrovandi, U., 96
Alembert, J. de R. d', 136
Alexander, S., 197
Alexander the Great, 29
Alexander of Hales, 61
Allegorizing and nature, 49
Allen, B., 139
Alsop, J., 108
Amber, a gum, 47
Ambrose, St and nature, 47
Ampère, A. M., 168
Anderson, A. W., 210 n.
Anderson, F. H., 107
Antiochus Epiphanes, 29
Apocalyptic and nature, 30-2
Aratus, 43 n.
Arber, A., 18, 83, 90 n., 154 n.; on Cudworth, 116 n.
Archimedes, 28
Aristotle, 5, 27, 40; his works, 62; his repute, 65 n.; and Cudworth, 115; and transmutation, 204
Ashmole, E., 105
Ashworth, J. H., 180 n.
Astronomers, succession of, 7
Athenagoras, 43
Atkinson, J. C., 181
Atomic energy, 202-3
Aubrey, J., 106
Augustine, St, 49; and nature, 51-2
Augustus, 41
Aulen, G. E. H., 201

Avicenna, 66, 69
Avogadro, A., 169

Babrius, 41, 53
Bacon, F. and New Philosophy, 99-101; his intention fulfilled, 196
Bacon, R. and Nature, 61-4; and nomenclature, 78
Baeyer, A. von, 169
Bakewell, R., 139
Banks, J., 165 n., 168
Barbaro, E., 78
Barnacle Goose, Albert on, 67
Barrow, I., 108 n., 118, 133
Barth, K., 36 n; his Calvinism, 201; and Kierkegaard, 212; his influence, 213
Bartholomew the Englishman, 58; his book, 60
Basel, its tolerance, 93
Basil, St, and nature, 46-7; and palms, 205
Bass, G., 165
Bates, H. W., 182
Bateson, W., 16; and Mendelism, 184, 192
Bauer, G., 97
Bauhin, C., 95 n., 96
Bauhin, J., 83 n., 206-8; and Alpine plants, 86 n.; his greatness, 96
Baxter, R., 107
Becquerel, H., 168
Behaviourism, 186; self-contradictory, 194
Bell, A. E., 98 n., 104 n.
Bell, C., 210
Belon, P., 97
Bentley, R., 11
Berdyaev, N., 201
Bergson, H., 18, 117
Bervaldo, F., 78
Berthollet, C. L., 136
Berzelius, J. J., 169
Best, S., 174 n.
Bethune-Baker, J. F., 189
Bewick, T., 160-1
Bible and nature, 22-39

FOLKTALES OF *France*

 *Folktales*
OF THE WORLD

GENERAL EDITOR : RICHARD M. DORSON

FOLKTALES OF
France

EDITED BY

Geneviève Massignon

TRANSLATED BY JACQUELINE HYLAND

FOREWORD BY

Richard M. Dorson

THE UNIVERSITY OF CHICAGO PRESS

Library of Congress Catalog Card Number 68-14008
SBN 7100 3870 4
The University of Chicago Press, Chicago 60637
Routledge & Kegan Paul, Ltd., London E. C. 4
© 1968 by The University of Chicago
Published 1968
Printed in the United States of America

Foreword

In the age of the sun king, Louis XIV, the fairy tales of peasants incongruously found their way into the glittering court at Versailles. The courtiers and their ladies amused each other with telling and listening to country stories, and one court attendant, Charles Perrault, printed some in 1697 in the first European book of folktales, *Contes de ma Mère l'Oye*. This title appeared on the frontispiece depicting an old woman spinning and telling tales to a little group, but the title page carried the phrase, *Histoires ou contes de temps passé. Avec des moralités*. Perrault had mingled with the Versailles nobility while enjoying an appointment (1663–83) with Jean-Baptiste Colbert, controller general of finances, to assist in superintending the royal buildings. Hearing the tales at court, and having a bent for letters, Perrault set down in verses, in the manner of La Fontaine, "The Silly Wishes," "Griselda," and "Ass's Skin," published in a little magazine by Moetjens in 1694 at The Hague; he reprinted them that year as a book that received unkind notices. Then Perrault attempted prose versions, in Moetjens' miscellany, and they were collected in Paris in a little book destined for fame. The given author of these *Contes de ma Mère l'Oye* was Pierre Darmancour, the son of Perrault, who heard them from his nurse. Presumably the versions of the boy stimulated his father, recalling the recitations at Versailles, to write out the eight tales since become immortal: "Sleeping Beauty," "Red Riding Hood," "Bluebeard," "Puss in Boots," "The Fairies," "Cinderella," "Riquet of the Tuft," and "Hop o' my Thumb."

The *Contes de ma Mère l'Oye* proved to be a landmark in literary history and the history of folklore. Direct communication between the intellectuals and the folk would have to wait until

the Grimms' collection of German Märchen in 1812, but still
France could lay claim in 1697 to the first sampling of traditional
tales. Perrault's styling is evident in occasional moral asides and
personal witticisms, in some created characters, like his fairy god-
mothers, in the removal of ugly incidents, and in the too perfect
story line, but on the whole the manner is simple and plain and
peasant-like. Only one of the Mother Goose tales, "Riquet of the
Tuft," owed little to tradition, but the others have taken their
place as household classics and are known to flourish in chimney-
corner circles among many peoples. Perrault added little rhymed
"Moralités" at the end of each conte. After Little Red Riding
Hood is devoured by the wolf in the clothes of her grandmother,
the point at which Perrault ends his version, he adduces the
moral that genteel young ladies should beware of all sorts of
strangers; a quiet-voiced Wolf may be the most dangerous.[1]

Perrault's *Contes* ushered in a long century of literary imita-
tions, powdered and perfumed and prolix. An embroidered rendi-
tion of *Beauty and the Beast* in 1742 ran to 362 pages. Usually
they were written by ladies of the boudoir, and preserved in an
endless series under the title *Le Cabinet des fées*. For the student
of folklore these contrivances by Mme d'Aulnoy, Mme l'Héritier,
and other estimable ladies hold little interest except to illustrate
how the literary genre of the fairy-tale novelette grew and departed from Perrault's simple contes. The salon fashion of recit-
ing tales aloud shifted to reading them in the cabinet. Well into
the nineteenth century, the concern with folk tradition remained
in France a sterile scholastic exercise, as in Baron Charles A.
Walckenaer's *Lettres sur les contes de fées attribuées à Perrault
et sur l'origine des contes de fées* (1825) and Alfred Maury's
Les Fées du moyen âge (1843). In spite of the exemplary collections of the brothers Grimm and their emulators throughout
Europe, fieldwork lagged among the French. When Lang wrote
about "The Folk-Lore of France" in 1878, he observed that the
folktales of France had not yet been collected with "method
and system." [2] Then between the Franco-Prussian War of 1870

---

[1] Andrew Lang's introductory essays to *Perrault's Popular Tales* (Oxford, 1888), pp. vii–cxv, give valuable biographical and critical details.
[2] Lang in the *Folk-Lore Record*, I (1878), 113.

and the outbreak of the First World War, the French folklore movement suddenly flowered, with the quickening of interest in philology, archaeology, and ethnography. These were the years of the founding of journals and societies, of the cultivation of the cultural sciences, of the quest for Celtic, Romanic, medieval, and peasant contributions to the French soul. In particular three giants emerged as French savants of folklore, all born in the 1840's. The careers of Emmanuel Cosquin (1841–1921), Henri Gaidoz (1842–1932), and Paul Sébillot (1846–1918) would intertwine in curious ways.

The line of influence from the Grimms to Cosquin is direct and clear. In 1862 Cosquin, then a youthful law student, is writing the brothers Grimm in admiration of their stories and notes in the *Kinder- und Hausmärchen.* He expresses joy at discovering in his natal Barrois one of their Märchen told in French country dialect. In the house of his great-uncle he had found a true old housemaid, serving in the family for fifty years, who corresponded to the Grimms' "Viehmannin," their tailor's wife, as a fountain of peasant fictions.[3] Cosquin would do for France what the Grimms had done for Germany. Enlisting his sisters to aid him, he gathered the folktales of Lorraine from the village of Montiers-sur-Saulx in the Barrois region, publishing them piecemeal in the journal *Romania* from 1876 to 1881. Such eminent folktale scholars as Gaston Paris in France, Reinhold Köhler in Germany, and W. R. S. Ralston in England praised Cosquin's articles and urged his assembling them in book form. In 1886 he brought out *Contes populaires de Lorraine,* a book that marked the coming of age of French folklore. If stimulated by the Grimms' *Kinder- und Hausmärchen,* and comparable to it as a pioneer scholarly collection of national folktales, the *Contes populaires de Lorraine* still possessed its own strong individuality, and in a sense even rejected the Grimms. For Cosquin analyzed his eighty-four tales three-quarters of a century after the Grimms issued their first volume, and he stirred to new concepts, apparent in the subtitle: "Compared with the

[3] Nicole Odette Stein-Moreau, "Les frères Grimm, conteurs, et la France au dix-neuvième siècle," in *Brüder Grimm Gedenken 1963* (Marburg, 1963), pp. 553–54.

Folktales of Other Provinces of France and of Foreign Countries
and Preceded by an Essay on the Origin and Diffusion of
European Popular Tales." The opening essay firmly stated his
position. Cosquin was an Indianist and a diffusionist. So his
work offered not only a scientific collection of French contes
and impressive comparative notes but a strongly argued theory
of origin and transmission as well.

Cosquin began by saying that Perrault had not dared publish
humble contes under his own name, as beneath the dignity of
an Academician. In 1887 he would not need to feel this false
shame, but he would face another danger, that of being seduced
by vapory speculations why tales in far distant places resembled
each other. With this preamble Cosquin attacked the theory,
on the one hand, of the Grimms, Max Müller, and J. G. von
Hahn, who saw Aryan myths and beliefs preserved in contes,
and, on the other hand, the anthropological school led by Andrew
Lang, who beheld survivals of savage ideas in popular fictions.
In their place Cosquin advanced the argument of Theodor
Benfey, the German Orientalist who in his 1859 edition of the
Panchatantra presented with powerful evidence the case for India
as the original homeland of European Märchen. Actually Cosquin
could point back to a French predecessor, Auguste Loiseleur-
Deslongchamps, who in 1838 had written *Essai sur les fables
indiennes et sur leur introduction en Europe,* but it was Benfey
who aroused folktale scholars.

With his essay Cosquin announced himself as a polemicist
and not a mere collector, and he plunged into the debate between
the evolutionists and the diffusionists. He pointed out that American Indian tales differed considerably from those of Europe
while European contes showed a strong family likeness to the
popular fictions of India. English civil servants and their families
in India were now putting into print orally collected tales, supplementing the great literary collections of the *Panchatantra* and
the *Katha Sarit Sagara,* and in his notes Cosquin indicated the
Indic similarities to the contes of Lorraine. His treatment of "Le
Loup blanc" (No. 63), the Cupid and Psyche story, illustrates
his method. The three pages of the story text are followed by
sixteen pages of "Remarques." Here he considered the question

of whether the conte of Lorraine and its relatives from Norway, Germany, and Italy derived from the Latin example of Apuleius and Greco-Roman mythology? Cosquin rejects the idea that a myth of Cupid ever existed and turns triumphantly to a folktale published in 1833 from the lips of a Benares washerwoman, telling, as in the fable of Psyche, of a monster wedded to the King's daughter who shed his skin to become a handsome young man. Cosquin concludes that "Le Loup blanc," its European counterparts, and Psyche herself derive from a common Indian source.

Such was the tenor of his argument, running squarely into the survivalist thesis of Lang, who read in Cupid and Psyche the remains of savage belief in transformation. Cosquin dealt with Lang's critical reviews of *Contes populaires de Lorraine* in a paper, "L'Origine des contes populaires européens et les théories de M. Lang", presented to the Congress of Popular Traditions held in Paris in 1889, and followed it up with "Quelques observations sur les 'incidents commun aux contes européens et aux contes orientaux'" at the International Folk-Lore Congress of 1891 in London.[4] He averred that where Lang's method was anthropological, his own was historical. Lang had cited resemblances between Zulu and European tales as proofs of the similar stages of culture and human invention through which widely scattered peoples all passed, and hence as evidence against borrowing. But, countered Cosquin, did not these resemblances prove borrowing? Surely the contes of India could have reached Egypt, Abyssinia, and Morocco with the extension of Islam and been carried by the Berbers from the Arabs to west and central Africa. Lang asked if the ideas of folktales found in India do not appear in other countries. This was not the point, responded Cosquin, but rather, did the ideas in the tales, such as speaking animals, transformation, and magic objects, contradict the ideas of Indian culture? Since they did not, the assumption could be made that many of the master tales originated in India and found their way in popular storybooks and on the lips of traders and travelers to Europe. Can the theme of a maiden saved from a dragon by a hero, for instance, clothed in local details by

---

[4] Cosquin's papers at the 1889 and 1891 folklore congresses are reprinted in his *Études folkloriques* (Paris, 1922), pp. 50–64, 65–72.

modern Greeks, Nubians, and Armenians, have developed from
the savage idea of a person being periodically sacrificed to a
monster? No, such a specialized theme could only have entered
the heritage of many different peoples by being transmitted
from one to another.

The wave of the future indeed lay with Cosquin, for each new
field collection revealed fresh specimens of familiar plots and
strengthened the case for diffusion. As Lang had discredited
Müller the solar mythologist, so now Cosquin drove Lang the
evolutionist to the wall, compelling him to acknowledge the role
of borrowing to explain the world community of oral narratives.
Yet Cosquin did not long enjoy his triumph.

In 1893 Joseph Bédier crushed Cosquin's hypothesis in his
treatise *Les Fabliaux.* This study of popular literature of the
Middle Ages was dedicated to Gaston Paris, Bédier's own teacher
and celebrated scholar of medieval literature, who himself had
said that fabliaux derived from India. Bédier concentrated not
on the theory of transmission but on the theory of origin advanced by Cosquin as twin parts of his argument. For his test
cases Bédier turned to the humorous verse narratives of the
thirteenth century—the fabliaux—since they were traditional and
were preserved in writing in Europe at a relatively early date.
Did the fabliaux betray debts to India? Meticulously Bédier
marshaled the facts. Only thirteen of the four hundred tales
known in 1300 in French, German, and Latin appear in Oriental
collections (six fabliaux, five exempla, two French contes). In
these few similar cases, the Indian examples seem fragmentary
and the European ones the older. The reason India receives so
much attention from folklorists is that Buddhism by its nature
attracted parables which were written down, while Greek and
Roman authors felt no such religious compulsion to record oral
stories. When a conte does appear among the ancient Greeks,
Cosquin perversely calls it a myth. Yet some contes did indeed
get written down by the Egyptians, as Gaston Maspero's *Les
Contes populaires de l'Égypte ancienne* (1882) had demonstrated
and Cosquin himself had recognized. Bédier concludes by assert-
ing the French provenience of most fabliaux, crediting Picardy
with the lion's share; and he denies the possibility of tracing the

origins of any but purely ethnic folktales. How fruitless is the piling up of variants that breed upon each other and never lead to any source!

The Indianist theory suffered heavily from the hammer blow of Bédier, and folktale scholarship on the whole suffered a setback since the search for origins of any sort seemed discredited. Cosquin continued to write his essays and notes tracing the migration of tales from Orient to Occident and tinkering with the ideas of Benfey, whom he felt gave too much credit to the Mongols in transmitting contes. These essays were gathered together in 1922, four years after his death, in *Études folkloriques* and *Les Contes indiens et l'occident*.

Meanwhile another battle front was forming that would engage the talents and energies of other illustrious French folklorists. In 1877 the first journal exclusively devoted to folklore appeared, under the title *Mélusine,* named for the swan-maiden of a cherished fairy tale, with the subtitle "Miscellany of Popular Literature, Traditions and Usages." Henri Gaidoz and Eugène Rolland were the founders and co-editors. *Mélusine* was printed in a folio format, numbered according to the two columns on each page, and at first the contents consisted of small collections, notes, observations, "facetiae," "variétés," notices, and engravings. Volume one offered an opening piece "On the Study of Popular Poetry in France" by Gaston Paris, an appraisal by Gaidoz of Mannhardt's work on Indo-European mythology of the fields and woods, and an exchange between Loys Brueyre and Cosquin. Loys Brueyre, while admiring Cosquin's texts and comments on the tales of Lorraine, protested against his citing a Japanese tale from a literary source to strengthen his thesis of the migration of tales from Asia to Europe. Literary sources could well be influenced from outside the country, as with the *Arabian Nights,* which actually came from India. Loys Brueyre had a point, since the tale of the Good and Evil Hunchbacks which he cited is today identified as a well-known European tale type (Type 503, *The Gifts of the Little People*). But Loys Brueyre's illustration of the *Arabian Nights* coming from India simply played into Cosquin's hand.[5]

[5] *Mélusine,* I (1878), cols. 235–39, 276–79.

The second volume did not appear until 1884–85, and its Foreword specifically spoke of "folk-lore" as the object of study in the journal, to achieve for France what folklore societies in England and Spain and folklore periodicals in Italy and Portugal had accomplished. Gaidoz and Rolland announced plans to enlarge their domain. In the first volume they had shown France to Frenchmen; now they would show humanity to itself, and they invited their readers to join in making *Mélusine* the central organization of universal folklore. Yet Gaidoz and Rolland soon faced Parisian rivals in the *Revue des tradition populaires,* founded in 1886 by Paul Sébillot for the publishing of current field reports, and *La Tradition,* initiated in 1887 by Emile Blémont to maintain old traditions and regional values. Sébillot's journal served as the organ for the newly founded Société des Traditions Populaires, printing its program on the opening pages, and stating how France after a long sleep was now vying with its neighbors in the investigation of oral literature and popular arts. Supernatural legends, sayings, folksongs, proverbs, charms, riddles, games, customs, linguistics, imagery, chapbooks—all would come under the umbrella of the new science. Besides these journals, two extensive series of folklore collections were launched in the 1880's, *Contes et chansons populaires* (1881–1930, Éditions Leroux, 44 volumes) and *Les Littératures de toutes les nations* (1883–1903, Éditions Maisonneuve, 47 volumes). And the first international folklore congress was held in Paris July 29 to August 2, 1889.

So well established had the study of popular traditions become in France that it could even nurture a bitter factionalism, based not on conflicting theories but on claims to priority and preeminence and scholarly integrity in the development of the subject. The two dominant figures of Gaidoz and Sébillot, with their respective journals and coteries, presided over the opposing camps.

Henri Gaidoz was the academic scholar, trained in Romance philology and Celtic studies, and a founder of the *Revue celtique* (1870). Neither the field collector nor the producer of general books, he specialized in the erudite monographic essay, frequently reprinted as a separate brochure, on such varied Romanic

subjects as Gargantua in Celtic mythology, Latin inscriptions in
Ireland, the religion of the Gauls, Rumanians in Hungary, and
rabies and St. Hubert. Some of his papers dealt purely with
folklore matters: a comparison of Cuchulainn, Beowulf, and
Hercules; the study of popular traditions in France and abroad;
and the change of sex in Celtic folktales. He published these
pieces of varying length in numerous journals, proceedings, and
encyclopedias, while filling his own *Mélusine* with caustic reviews and commentaries deflating meretricious folklorists.

Paul Sébillot, by contrast, was the independent artist of the
seaside and the country who became a prodigious collector and
assembler of French folklore. His beloved province of Haute-
Bretagne, the French-speaking section, as opposed to the Breton
speakers of western Brittany, provided his first hunting ground,
and he published in separate volumes its folktales, oral literature,
traditions and superstitions, popular customs, and local legends.
His talent as a marine painter led him to collect the lore of
fishermen and the legends, beliefs, and superstitions of the sea.
From fishing to other occupations was a logical step, and
Sébillot pioneered in exploring legends and curiosities of trades.
His success as a collector of regional and occupational traditions
gave him national authority, and he broadened his scope from
regional folktales of the moor and the strand, the earth and the
sea, to folktales of all the French provinces and ultimately to his
major four-volume encyclopedic inventory *Le Folk-Lore de
France* (1904–7). Here he systematically grouped peasant beliefs
and legends about the heavens and the earth, the ocean and the
rivers, animals and plants, prehistoric remains, historical monuments, and traditional history. His short survey *Le Folk-Lore*
(1913) condensed these materials of oral literature and traditional ethnography. In addition he wrote poems, stories, and
plays based on Breton folk themes.

Such were the two dissimilar figures who moved into the
center of French folklore activities. Where Gaidoz tracked Gargantua into ancient Gaulish religion, Sébillot pursued him in
the spoken traditions of the people. Yet the two joined forces
for a brief period. They planned a series on the marvelous and
legendary history of France, published parts of a bibliography

on the traditions and popular literature of France, and collaborated on one book, *Blason populaire de la France* (1884). This ingenious work has given its title to a folklore genre in English, the *blason populaire* that wittily gibes, in rhyme or saying or cryptic phrase, at a nationality, a region, a city, or a village.

The honeymoon ended with a devastating review by Gaidoz in the third volume of *Mélusine* of Sébillot's *Coutumes populaires de la Haute-Bretagne* (1886).[6] Here the precise library scholar goes to work with his scalpel on the mass traditions, assembled in seemingly orderly fashion by the prolific collector, dealing with the life cycle, household affairs, occupations, and recreations of north Breton peasants. First there are the omissions. Why not discuss costumes and popular jewelry as well as furniture, inns as well as houses, aphorisms inscribed on the façade of houses or at the bottom of chimneys? If Sébillot is reserving the customs of fishermen for another book, why does he leave out the customs of hunters? If he gives formulas for greeting, why does he neglect oaths? On these and other matters Sébillot would have profited from reading recent articles in *Mélusine*.

Further, Gaidoz chides Sébillot because he, along with other provincial writers, neglects to do the necessary historical research on the background of the customs he observes. Folklore to be more than an amusement or curiosity, and to become a proper scientific study, depends on history to explain genesis and on comparison to explain psychology. Sébillot's carelessness is evident in his loose manner of citation, his stringing together notes without proper synthesis, and his repetitions from his own previous publications, particularly *Traditions et superstitions de la Haute-Bretagne,* sometimes without acknowledgment! Thus he repeats himself on well worship and saints' offerings to fatten pigs. He even repeats passages in the present work, for instance on January 25 as a lucky natal day. Will he use the same items in subsequent inflated volumes of his inflated list of publications? Like theater revues in which dancers enter by one wing and leave by another, then reenter again, the books of Monsieur

[6] *Mélusine,* III (1886–87), cols. 220–22.

Sébillot give a pleasing illusion of an army of facts—but they are always the same.

After this review, Gaidoz and Sébillot ceased to collaborate. Sébillot continued rapidly to turn out his repetitive books, and Gaidoz his learned articles, and each edited his own journal. Then in the years preceding the First World War, the latent hostility between them flared forth in a *cause celèbre* illuminating in comic relief the whole French folklore movement. This was the affair of the Dinner of Mother Goose.

It began innocently enough with an obituary in 1909 of Loys Brueyre by Paul Sébillot in the latter's journal, *Revue des traditions populaires.*[7] Sébillot praised civil servant Brueyre's accomplishments in comparative folklore,[8] and incidentally mentioned that when "le Dîner de ma Mère l'Oye" was instituted in 1882 as a means of bringing together French folklorists, Brueyre and he had signed the invitations; at the one hundredth dinner Brueyre had given a highly applauded speech.[9] This innocent aside triggered off a violent if delayed reaction by Henri Gaidoz, "Eugène Rolland et son oeuvre littéraire," appearing in 1912 in *Mélusine.*[10] In this lengthy essay on the career of his lifelong colleague, Gaidoz dwelt on the Dinner of Mother Goose and credited Rolland with its conception. In the 1883 volume of the *Almanach des traditions populaires,* which Rolland had edited from 1882 to 1884, Sébillot himself told how Rolland had planned a monthly dinner to assemble the steadily growing group of French savants interested in oral literature. In order to give the dinner a French title, rather than the English "folklore," the name *Dîner de ma Mère L'Oye* was chosen, with the subtitle, "Réunion des folkloristes." The first meeting was held February 14, 1882, under the presidency of Gaston Paris, the famed

[7] *Revue des traditions populaires,* XXIII (1908), 459–60.

[8] Loys Brueyre's article, "Littérature orale et traditionnelle, éléments de folklore," in the *Revue de la société des études historiques,"* LXII (1896), 10–35, presented the first general theory of comparative French folklore, including the Creole.

[9] Loys Brueyre's speech is printed in *Revue des traditions populaires,* X (1895), 132.

[10] *Mélusine,* XI (1912), cols. 417–40.

author of, among many notable works, *Le Trésor du roi Rhamp-sinitus* (1874), suggesting that folktales originated in ancient civilizations.

Gaidoz could not recall the author of the poetic title for the banquet, but the important point was, he proclaimed, that the namer was only the godfather and Rolland the true father. Yet Sébillot had taken unto himself the mantle of the originator of the dinner, much as Amerigo Vespucci had sought to eclipse Columbus, the true discoverer of America. Gaidoz liked this analogy and repeated it in later ripostes.

From his country residence in la Beauce, at Aunay-sous-Auneau (Eure-et-Loir), Rolland designated Brueyre and Sébillot as his commissioners to make arrangements with the Parisian restaurateur and to send out the invitations. This fact, alleged Gaidoz, had been carefully concealed by Sébillot until the death of Rolland in 1909, when in writing his obituary Sébillot did acknowledge Rolland as one of three discoverers of America.[11] But still this was inexact, a grudging concession to the true and sole founder of the Dîner de ma Mère l'Oye. And Gaidoz again printed, this time in capital letters, the tell-tale phrase from the 1883 publication:

> M. EUGENE ROLLAND SONGEA QU'UN DÎNER MENSUEL . . .
>
> *Signé:* Paul Sébillot

Furthermore, continued Gaidoz, on the occasion of the one hundredth Dinner of Mother Goose, February 28, 1895, Sébillot had the irony to invite Rolland on a printed card in an open envelope with a five-centime stamp. Rolland and Gaidoz had laughed philosophically about this "love letter." Needless to say, neither attended the dinner, which was described at length in the *Revue des traditions populaires*.[12]

Reading about the dinner must have severely agitated the editors of *Mélusine*. It was apparently a joyous and self-gratula-tory occasion for the participants, who complimented each other on the durability of their gatherings now fourteen years old and

---

[11] Sébillot's obituary of Rolland appeared in *Revue des traditions populaires*, XXIV (1909), 250–52.

[12] *Revue des traditions populaires*, X (1895), 129–35.

on the consequent gains for the cause of scientific folklore. According to the printed account, the president, E.-T. Hamy, toasted Sébillot and Brueyre as the founders and preservers of the dinner, in spite of the indifference and hostility of certain other persons. Brueyre toasted his fellow-founder Sébillot as one to whom the science of folklore owed much. Sébillot toasted the foreign visitors present and the foreign folklore societies which had sent their emblems in honor of the occasion (the Chicago Folk-Lore Society sent their ornament, but the American Folklore Society had none). The table was decorated with bouquets of hollyhocks, whose leaves were customarily plucked by country folk to divine their future, and before each banqueteer was placed an earthenware dish with minced pork bearing a likeness of Mother Goose as an old lady and a small loaf of bread shaped like a goose. After the report there were melancholy and happy French folksongs and a sidesplitting folktale of the wolf and the gendarme and poems based on popular themes. It was an evening to remember—by those present and by those absent.

Accompanying Sébillot's account of the dinner was a spirited full-page illustration by Félix Régamey with a flapping goose in the foreground spreading its wings over an open volume of the *Revue des traditions populaires,* surrounded by goslings in the foreground and folktale characters in the background. A caption read, "Centième Dîner de Ma Mère L'Oye."

Eugène Rolland (1846–1909), the hapless pawn in this vehement controversy, was born at Metz and died in Paris after spending forty years doing research in the Bibliothèque Nationale to the neglect of his bookshop. He devoted all his available energies to diverse folklore collections, although the folktale escaped his net. In 1877 he compiled a volume of French riddles, *Devinettes ou énigmes populaires de la France,* to which Gaston Paris contributed a preface and examples; and in 1883 he prepared a book of children's games, *Rimes et jeux de l'enfance,* which Sébillot called one of the best volumes in the *Collection des littératures populaires de toutes les nations* and van Gennep called one of the weakest. But his major efforts were reserved for heroic series: the compilation of French folksongs, *Recueil des chansons populaires de la France* (6 volumes, 1884–90), and the folk dictionaries of French flora and fauna, *Faune populaire de la France* (13 volumes, 1877–1911) and *Flore populaire de la France* (11 volumes, 1896–1913), which brought together patois names, proverbs, charms, and superstitions linked by the peasantry with local animals and plants. In 1877 and again from 1884 to 1887 he collaborated on *Mélusine* with Gaidoz, who now sought to honor his late comrade at Sébillot's expense.

In his biographical sketch of Rolland, Gaidoz intensified his complaints against other folklorists. He stated that Rolland, on returning to Paris in 1884, disinterested himself in the Dinner of Mother Goose since he could now regularly see his confrères in folklore. Sébillot continued the dinner and used it as a springboard for his *Revue des traditions populaires,* founded in 1886. Accordingly Rolland organized a simpler weekly dinner at the Café Voltaire, where Gaidoz frequently joined him to talk of folklore. In April, 1884, Rolland and Gaidoz resumed *Mélusine,* which they had let lapse in 1878. (Sébillot wrote in his obituary of Rolland that he had never heard of it in 1877 and that it reached only twenty subscribers.) The weekly dinners gradually limited themselves to the circle of *Mélusine* contributors and friends, to whom Rolland offered an informal course in folklore. Because of its high standards, continued Gaidoz, *Mélusine* antagonized rival journals which sought to emulate it but printed inferior materials. Gaidoz himself had on an earlier occasion pointed out, as he reminded his readers, that dilettantes in folklore were forming a mutual admiration society. In that earlier article of 1890 Gaidoz had expressed his surprise that Sébillot had lifted a quotation from an old song first quoted by Rolland without acknowledgment in a miscellany edited by Henry Carnoy, and he now repeated his charge.

This outspoken piece of 1890, titled "La Collection internationale de la *tradition,*" and reviewing a new series bearing that title, was indeed not calculated, as Gaidoz recognized, to win friends, but its severe chastisement of popularized and pretentious scholarship still hits the mark.[13] Gaidoz began with an appraisal of a new series of small works on folklore initiated by Émile

[13] *Mélusine,* V (1890), cols. 25–36.

Blémont and Henry Carnoy, the editors of the journal *La Tradition*. This series dealt with books of divination translated from a Turkish manuscript; with music and dance in the traditions of Lithuanians, Germans, and Greeks; and with Japanese musical folk arts. Gaidoz scorned the editors (even though he considered Carnoy one of his disciples) who would reprint an ancient manuscript on books of divination with no indication of its age or provenience. He derided Carnoy for declaring that Edmond Veckenstedt, editor of one of the booklets, was introducing in France his novel theory of interpreting popular traditions that had obtained a wide success in Germany. Bold words, worthy for presenting a Max Müller or an Andrew Lang! But this theory turns out to be a commonplace statement that the science of tradition should investigate the changes in tales and myths effected by the language, customs, and ideas of a culture. And nowhere does Veckenstedt apply the method. As for Veckenstedt's fluvial, verdant, and astral explanations of the origins of the Greek dance, who can fathom them! For all his pretensions, Veckenstedt now reveals himself as belonging to the rejected school of nature mythologists. Why should this old-hat theory be translated from German into French?

The only reason, conjectures Gaidoz, seems to be that Veckenstedt has initiated an international group of mutually admiring folklorists. He had founded in Leipzig a folklore journal, *Zeitschrift für Volkskunde,* serving as the German counterpart to Sébillot's *Revue des traditions populaires* and Blémont and Carnoy's *La Tradition.* The able Breton collector François-Marie Luzel had recently derided eulogistic articles written by folklorists in praise of one another. But now Veckenstedt had come up with a still more ingenious idea—that of international exchanges of folklore. He would print in his journal, in German, articles by editors of folklore journals in different countries, who would then return the favor. Thus pieces by the Frenchman Henry Carnoy, the Belgian Auguste Gittée, and the Italian Giuseppe Pitrè have appeared in the *Zeitschrift für Volkskunde,* and writings by Veckenstedt turned up in the respective journals of those folklorists. New journals with similar aims keep emerging. Here from Italy was the first number (January, 1890) of

Rassegna di letteratura popolare et dialettale, avowedly devoted
to serious criticism of new publications in place of sterile praises,
and yet indulging in just such sterile praise of the *Collection
internationale de la tradition!* Furthermore, a third of the *Rassegna* was occupied with summaries of such journals as *La
Tradition* and *Zeitschrift für Volkskunde.* So did the folklore
journals batten upon each other, filling up their pages with
rubbish which would have been better placed in cheap news-
papers (as *Romania* said of *Revue des traditions populaires* and
Tradition). These long summaries are but the shadow of a
shadow.

Thus the biting Henri Gaidoz, striking home, for the Veckenstedt of his gibes would be publicly exposed in *Mélusine* as a
plagiarist.[14] But there was more to come. Gaidoz now turned
to an impartial commentator, the German philologist Karl Weinhold, professor at the University of Berlin, who had written in
the *Zeitschrift für Völkerpsychologie* (XX, no. 1) on "Was soll
die Volkskunde leisten?" ("What services can the study of folklore perform?"). Weinhold acknowledged the scholarly international status of the subject, made manifest in the 1889 congress
of folklorists held at Paris. Yet the professed science was no more
than a sport, a vogue. The journals rarely contained serious
articles based on methodical research but mostly a frightful accumulation of small broken pebbles or a heap of straw thrown
to the wind. Properly the science of folklore demands familiarity
with history and linguistics, anthropology and psychology, as well
as legal history, political economy, the arts, literature, and natural
sciences.

Gaidoz thoroughly approved this large view of the subject,
except that he would go even farther than Weinhold, who restricted folklore to the study of one people. While it was true
that certain parts of folklore, falling under ethnography, such
as dwellings, costume, and material culture in general, were
fixed in a regional place at an historic time, when it came to
beliefs and oral literature Gaidoz considered folklore a science

[14] For the exposé of Veckenstedt, see E. Sidney Hartland in *Folk-Lore,*
II (1891), 100–107, summarizing the charges made against Veckenstedt
in *Mélusine* in 1890.

as much international as national, as much comparative as historical. Actually the history of popular literature presented a second, later division of folklore, dependent on the first—the history of beliefs and customs.

Is folklore then a science? Gaidoz preferred to call it a new method of research. The method consisted in the study of a religion, a mythology, an institution, a belief, a custom, not in its final and complete crystallization, but from the germ of its origin, following it through all the degrees of its development, taking account of all the influences shaping it, and at the same time determining (but in an experimental manner) the psychological point of departure of this or that cultural item. These researches, which are a branch of "demopsychology," depend especially on direct observation of the people and on documents dealing with popular origins. One must pay the closest scrutiny to the manifestations of the popular soul, whether as survivals in civilized societies or as parallels among less advanced peoples. One must search for the links of the chain scattered among many countries and peoples, just as the naturalist must search for and juxtapose fragments of an extinct species scattered over a vast continent. Such, thought Gaidoz, was the method of folklore study.

But who, he asked, has the erudition and the patience to cover this vast realm? The few savants in France occupied with these studies are swallowed up like trappers in the American Far West. Too many folklorists on the continent discredit their subject in the eyes of the knowing public with vain and arid agitations. The numerous works on folklore, falling thick as autumn leaves, suggested to Gaidoz Voltaire's witticism in *Candide*. "Sir, how many theatrical pieces are there in France?" asked Candide of the abbot, who replied, "Five or six thousand." "That is a good many," said Candide. "How many of them are good?" "Fifteen or sixteen," replied the other. "That is a good many," said Candide.

The severe judgment of Weinhold, perhaps even involving *Mélusine,* should warn all folklorists seeking popularity at the expense of scientific merit. So concluded Gaidoz in his editorial pronouncements of 1890, appraising the state of the field, and sideswiping several of his close competitors in a manner strangely prophetic of the "fakelore" controversy of mid-twentieth century.

Resuming the thread of his biographical essay of 1912 on Rolland, Gaidoz continued his innuendos against Sébillot, whose abilities he did not deny. Rather he made of Sébillot a diligent pupil learning from Rolland, who introduced the Germanic mode of scholarship into France. Before Rolland, amateurs presented folklore materials in florid style, with moral reflections and comparative commentary on superstitions and customs mixed together. Rolland confined himself to facts, and, from 1880 on, others observed and followed his method. Unfortunately, gibed Gaidoz, those who followed were men of letters rather than philologists; hence the great inferiority of French as compared with German folklore studies. In France the amateurs endlessly report local examples of "If the slow worm sees . . ." and "Bees, your master is dead." To correct this amateurism, Rolland undertook in 1884 to revive *Mélusine* with Gaidoz, changing the format of 1877 from an anthology of French traditions and popular literature to a medium for comparative studies. Rolland contributed the idea, copied by rival journals, of cooperative investigations, in which readers could add their notes, documents, and ideas to topics presented in *Mélusine*. And it was Rolland who first investigated meteorology and the folklore of the sea, subjects since vulgarized in France and English-speaking countries. (Again this was an obvious dig at Sébillot, who wrote on traditions of fishermen and beliefs connected with the heavens.) Further, Rolland refused to print in *Mélusine* articles or documents their authors had published elsewhere, a common practice of folklorists seeking to expand their bibliographies, nor did he invite such "repreneurs" to collaborate with him on the new journal.

Gaidoz praised the field method employed by Rolland in gathering data for his *Faune* and *Flore*. Like the Russian nihilists from another point of view, Rolland practiced "going among the people." When he spotted a man of the people adept in his patois, whether a peddler, street merchant, or other vendor, he engaged him for about forty sous an hour to discourse on folklore. Rolland revealed neither his name nor his address, which would have been dangerous, but led his man to a café or a cabaret, where they could order and reorder refreshments, and there, notebook in hand, he interrogated the "son of the earth" on the local names of animals and plants. Rolland would draw from his pocket a botanical album with colored plates that never left his side. "Do you know this plant? What do you call it in your town? What do you do with it?" he would ask. Sometimes his subjects were suspicious, wondering why this bourgeois so interested himself in the village affairs and whether he was from the police. Rolland had a ready response: "I am doing a book for pharmacists; they need to know the names of the plants to gather them in the countryside." If one meeting did not suffice, Roland made a rendezvous for a second. Rolland once told Gaidoz that with money he could collect all the folklore of France right in Paris. Upon the death of Rolland in 1909, Gaidoz acquired his books, manuscripts, and working notes in order to continue and complete the *Faune* and *Flore* as far as possible during his remaining years.

Besides his well-known works, Rolland conceived the idea for publishing a "secret museum" of the folklore too free and raw in character to be issued through ordinary channels. He discussed the idea with Gaston Paris, who approved and suggested the discreet title *Kryptadia (Secret Things)*, and recommended the translation of a certain collection of Russian tales for the first volume. Brueyre collaborated on volume one and Gaidoz on subsequent volumes, which could be considered as the "subterranean overflow" of *Mélusine*.[15] (The *Kryptadia* does indeed represent one of Rolland's most permanent and courageous contributions to folklore researches, making available in print, although necessarily in a highly restricted edition, the obscene texts that flourish orally but are screened from pretty collections of tales and ballads.)

So ended the lengthy obituary essay on Rolland. The gauntlet was now thrown to Sébillot, who responded with equal ampli-

---

[15] Details about *Kryptadia,* initiated in Heilbronn, Germany, in 1883, are given in Gershon Legman, *The Horn Book* (Hyde Park, N.Y., 1964), pp. 477–78, but he does not mention Rolland as an editor.

tude and also in a personal and revealing manner, in the *Revue des traditions populaires* for 1913.[16] Sébillot titled his two-part article, "Notes pour servir à l'histoire du folk-lore en France." He cast it in autobiographical vein to refute immediately Gaidoz's assertion that Sébillot changed from a painter of the scenes of Haute-Bretagne into a folklore collector after reading the first issue of *Mélusine* in 1877. Sébillot had, as he reminded Gaidoz, related in his preface to the *Contes populaires de la Haute-Bretagne* having collected in 1860 about twenty tales, of which half a dozen were printed in that book. Rolland himself had suggested in a letter of 1884 that Sébillot describe in his prefaces how he came to discover folklore, as a contribution to the history of folklore studies in France. In these "Notes" Sébillot retraces the circumstances of his early life that brought him into contact with oral traditions before he became professionally committed to folklore. He had indeed already begun a manuscript auto-biography of *Mémoires,* at the request of his children.

From his earliest recollections, Sébillot had the taste for folk-lore. As a schoolboy he set down in his notebooks songs, riddles, rhymes, and such scraps of tradition sung or recited by peasants and domestics. At the college of Dinan in 1860 he maintained the practice but added other materials—things seen or legends heard. While at college Sébillot chanced on the book *Foyer breton* (*Breton Hearthside*), and was entranced by the drawings of Breton scenes and the accompanying contes, of Sleeping Beauty, the Golden Bough, and Beauty and the Beast, taken from Per-rault, Madame d'Aulnoy, and Madame Leprince de Beaumont. The illustrations of the peasant costumes of Vannes in Souvestre recalled to his mind those he had seen while visiting his father's farms at Merdrignac (Côtes-du-Nord) at the border of Morbi-han. And the contes related by the laborers, artisans, and sailors of Souvestre seemed more real and familiar than ones Sébillot had encountered in other collections. Narrative incidents about the world of the dead recalled to Sébillot incidents he had heard in his childhood, and he decided to search in his native country during his vacations for marvelous or fantastic stories worthy

---

[16] Paul Sébillot, "Notes pour servir à l'histoire du folk-lore en France," *Revue des traditions populaires,* XXVIII (1913), 49–62, 171–82.

of a Gaelic "Hearthside." At the time he did not contemplate publishing them but rather of bolstering his local pride, deflated at all the talk about the picturesqueness and the legends of Basse-Bretagne. Surely the Gaelic country, in particular that of Pen-thièvre, could not be so barren as one supposed.

Now Sébillot charmingly tells of his first tentative probings into local tradition. Back in Matignon he hunted up his old nurse, Vincente, who at first claimed that she had forgotten all the old contes but, prompted by the mention of Jean de Diot and the thief Finn, began to recall them from her service in Saint-Pôtan, one of the most rural regions of the canton of Matignon. There shepherds gathered in the open air to cook apples in hollowed-out bake ovens in the earth, while posing riddles, singing songs, and relating contes about ghosts and drolls but not about fairies. Twenty years later Sébillot published Vin-cente's tales with small changes and other contes from different storytellers whom he also described.

But, beginning in 1867, he turned to marine painting and for a decade neglected contes. In 1870 the pioneer Breton collector, François-Marie Luzel, sent him a copy of his article "Contes bretons," one of a series of field reports finally published in 1879 in the book *Veillées bretonnes*. Luzel employed the literal rather than the embellished style of presenting tales, which thenceforth Sébillot followed. It was Luzel who gave Sébillot the Paris address of Gaidoz early in 1879 and wrote Gaidoz in advance about Sébillot's work with the Gaelic patois and his collecting the traditions of Haute-Bretagne. The same year Sébillot met Rolland at the home of Gaidoz. Common interests stimulated friendship and exchange of ideas among the three. Gaidoz wrote Sébillot in 1881 about their collaborating: "I have in my head several books that we could easily do together. Rolland is strong, like the champion whose name he bears; but I have the idea that we could be supporting pillars for each other, that we could accomplish great things." In January, 1883, Gaidoz proposed the title "France Marvelous and Legendary" for a series of some sixteen volumes they would jointly edit on various aspects of folk tradition—a series that never materialized. In his *Traditions et superstitions de la Haute-Bretagne,* Sébillot adopted in large part

Rolland's classification in his *Faune* of animal names, adding contes to the proverbs and beliefs. But Sébillot had investigated folklore of sailors and the sea before he ever met Rolland.

Thus Sébillot assembled memories and documents, in elaborate detail, about his early career in folklore. He even printed a table of the forty folktales he had collected before meeting Gaidoz and Rolland. Now he turned to the Dinner of Mother Goose.

Sébillot quoted from a letter Loys Brueyre had sent him in 1880 saying, "I went Wednesday to the dinner of the Celticists and we spoke of the Dinner of Mythographers." Rolland attended the meeting of the Celticists and so must have gleaned the idea at that time, and after leaving Paris he pursued it for the self-interested motive of keeping up his contacts. Rolland in his letters to Sébillot asked him to serve as "commissary" for a mythographic dinner, but Sébillot coined "Dîner de ma Mère l'Oye." Digging into his files, he produced letters from folklorists invited to the dinner, like Jean François Bladé, who preferred "Ma Mère l'Oye" to "Réunion des folkloristes."

Sébillot sent the two copies of his journal to Gaidoz, who addressed a letter to his donor, printed in the same volume of *Revue des traditions populaires*. If it required a subtitle, Gaidoz noted, he would call his epistle "Eugène Rolland, founder of the Dîner de ma Mère l'Oye." He reprinted his documents in behalf of Rolland, calculated the expenses of the dinner borne by Sébillot and Loys Brueyre as two francs maximum for stamps, and corrected Sébillot's use of the verb "neglect." "Rolland did not *neglect,* he *disdained* to concern himself with material details which were discharged by an agent, the commissioner of the Dinner, and this commissioner was you—you chosen and instructed by Rolland." [17]

Following Gaidoz's letter, Sébillot printed his own remarks in small type, headed *Simples Notes.* He deplored Gaidoz's extravagant use of italics, capitals, and quotation marks; raised the ante on the cost of stamps for the letters of invitation from five to fifteen and twenty-five centimes and added the cost of printing; and claimed that he was preserving the credit due Loys Brueyre as co-founder of the dinner. "All this luxurious typog-

[17] Gaidoz in *Revue des traditions populaires*, XXVIII (1913), 271–74.

raphy, all these argumentations could do nothing against the fact that it is to me that the Dîner de 'ma Mère l'Oye' owes its name, that Brueyre and I organized the dinner and made of it a reality." [18]

Within a year Europe was devoured by war, and the Dinner of Mother Goose faded into the antiquarian past. Yet the writings it provoked testify today to the passion and dedication of strong personalities at the height of the French folklore movement. This was no tempest in a teapot but a scholarly debate over the origins of folklore organization in France.

French folklore found a new titan in the person of Arnold van Gennep (1873–1957) to carry its banner in the first half of the twentieth century, a lean period for scholarship scarred by the two world wars. As Sébillot had entered folklore from painting and literature, and Gaidoz from Celtic studies, so van Gennep approached folklore as an ethnologist and sociologist. He commenced his field researches with accounts of taboos and totemism in Madagascar in 1904 and myths and legends of Australia in 1906, and his first-hand observations on the operation of traditions in society led to two books of high theoretical importance, *Les Rites de passage* (1909) and *La Formation des légendes* (1910). In the first he considered the groupings of powerful ritual ceremonies around the crucial events of human life—birth, initiation, marriage, death. In the second he dwelt upon the forms of folk narrative, distinguishing legend from conte and myth as a localized, individualized, and believed recitation, not connected, like the myth, with the supernatural world and with magic rite. Rejecting arid discussion on symbolic meanings or places of origin for legends, van Gennep concentrated on their social and psychical function among primitive and semi-civilized peoples. His control of the sources for both savages and peasants gave his comments special authority.

In later years he turned to the folklore of his own country, contributing volumes on Côte d'Or in Bourgogne, on Auvergne and Velay, Flanders and Hainaut, the high Alps and Dauphiné to the series on folklore of the French provinces and the popular

[18] Sébillot in *Revue des traditions populaires*, XXVIII (1913), 275–76.

literature of all nations, maintaining his ethnological, linguistic, and psychological emphasis. He provided a brief but meaty overview of *Le Folklore* in 1924, avowedly to propagandize the field. But his magnum opus occupying his final two decades was the multivolume *Manuel de folklore français contemporain* (1937–58), a sweeping panorama of French life-cycle and seasonal ceremonies with a superb analytic bibliography of general, provincial, calendrical, and topical researches on French folklore. That van Gennep's sympathies lay with Sébillot and against Gaidoz is seen in his caustic critique of Gaidoz as exclusively the literary and Celtic folklorist failing to employ the direct method of observation. *Mélusine* died, he noted drily, after an enormous monograph by Tuchmann on fascination. Van Gennep contrasted the acerbity of Gaidoz with the diplomacy of Sébillot.[19]

Another intimate and involuted relationship bound van Gennep to an equally prolific contemporary, Émile Dominique Nourry (1870–1935), a publisher who doubled as an author of French folklore works under the pseudonym Paul Saintyves. In terms of personalities, van Gennep continued the caustic vein of Gaidoz and Saintyves the moderate tone of Sébillot. Saintyves (as Nourry) published van Gennep's *Les Rites de passage,* and the two collaborated on various scholarly undertakings, such as the *Corpus du folklore préhistorique en France et dans les colonies françaises* (1934), an assessment of legendary traditions attached to artifacts from the Stone Age. They united and disunited on journals. Van Gennep founded the *Revue des études ethnographiques et sociologiques* in 1908, to which Saintyves contributed. In turn Saintyves initiated the *Revue de folklore français* in 1930, with the support of van Gennep, who dropped out two years later when the journal added *et coloniale* to its title. As with Gaidoz and Sébillot, these were two brilliant devotees of folklore with fundamentally different visions. Van Gennep was the ethnologist, sociologist, positivist, and agnostic; Saintyves, the rationalist, philosopher, and Christian moralist.

The emphasis of Saintyves' heavy output was on religious

[19] Arnold van Gennep, *Manuel de folklore français contemporain* (Paris, 1937), III, p. 119, no. 107; p. 122, no. 123.

folklore.[20] He scrutinized the documents of tradition in the manner of a biblical rationalist seeking to explain magic and miracles
by natural phenomena and human conceits. Intellectually he was
moved by Emile Loisy, the modernist philosopher who had written on initiation rites among the Australian aborigines. Loisy
belonged to the school of Ernest Renan, author of a naturalistic
life of Christ. So Saintyves ranged over biblical myths and marvels, popular astrology and lunar folklore, the Christian mythology of saints expressed in folk cults and legends, stories of virgin
mothers and miraculous births. The saints of medieval and
modern times had, he contended, succeeded the gods of the
ancient world in popular belief. In his most influential work,
Les Contes de Perrault (1923), he traced the origins of Perrault's
eight prose and three verse contes to seasonal and initiation
rituals by piecing together scattered evidence. Thus "La Belle
au bois dormant" illustrates a primitive rite celebrating the sleep
of the new year. The affinity of Frazer for Saintyves can readily
be surmised, and the author of *The Golden Bough,* at one time
a resident in Paris, financed the circular promoting Saintyves'
Revue de folklore français. Posterity has judged both ritualists
similarly.

Not Saintyves but van Gennep guided their younger contemporary, Paul Delarue (1889–1956), who carried French folktale scholarship to a new pinnacle. Delarue, like Cosquin and
Sébillot, grew up in the countryside imbibing folklore as part of
his milieu. He was born at Saint-Didier in Nevers to a family of
small peasants, received the Legion of Honor in the First World
War, served as teacher and schoolmaster of a school in the
Morvan near Nevers from 1932 to 1936 and then for three years
at a school in Paris until the Second World War, in which he
took part as a battalion commander. After the war he briefly
directed a school at Ivry, but retired in 1946 and devoted his full
energies until his death to the cause of folktale studies. From
1946 to 1953 he presided over the Commission of Folklore in the
League of Teachers. In 1947 he became vice-president of the

[20] A full bibliography is in P. Saintyves, *Manuel de folklore* (Paris,
1936), pp. 209–15.

Society of French Ethnography, of which van Gennep was president. Through the Centre National de la Recherche Scientifique he guided a young group of French folktale enthusiasts to the degree Master of Research. Meanwhile he was publishing regularly in the new French folklore periodicals, *Nouvelle Revue des arts et traditions populaires, Bulletin folklorique d'Ile-de-France,* and the *Mois d'ethnographique français.*

These activities accompanied Delarue's central enterprise—the systematic cataloguing and tasteful sampling of the whole body of French folktales according to modern methods. In a 1953 article in *Arts et traditions populaires,* he surveyed the state of folktale collecting and classification in France as a prelude to two major undertakings of his own. These were a series of volumes presenting the living folktales of the provinces of France, and an exhaustive tale-type index of the French *contes populaires.*

The systematic ordering of folktales in the twentieth century succeeded the bold theories of origin and meaning in the nineteenth, and to this vast international enterprise Delarue contributed a magnificent national index of French tale types, *Le Conte populaire français.* Volume I, covering Types 300–366 in the Aarne-Thompson index, appeared the year after his death, 1957; volume II, almost double in size, with 732 pages, covering Types 400 to 736, in 1963. Marie-Louise Tenèze, a faithful disciple of Delarue, served as co-author of the second volume and continues the monumental task from her position in the Museum of Popular Arts and Traditions in Paris, where Delarue's files are deposited, with the support of the National Center for Scientific Research. In brief, *Le Conte populaire français* presents a descriptive inventory of the printed and manuscript versions of folktales collected in France and in the French-speaking areas of North America and the West Indies. The tales are identified and numbered according to the system devised by Antti Aarne and Stith Thompson in 1928, and revised in 1961, *The Types of the Folktale,* primarily for the folk narratives of Europe. The French catalogue begins with Tale 300, "The Beast with Seven Heads," rather than with Tale 1, as the Aarne-Thompson index begins with animal tales, much less abundant in France than the popular fictions of magic and wonder (*contes merveilleux*), whose numbers start at 300.

Since the Aarne-Thompson index can give but a bare figure for the number of versions of a given tale type reported in each country, national indexes are needed as supplements in an ingenious interlocking apparatus. For the French catalogue, Delarue planned a sensible and informative scheme. Each tale type is given first its Aarne-Thompson number and title, then the text of a representative French variant, then a breakdown of the main divisions and episodes of the conte, and finally a tabulated list of versions with bibliographical sources and notes on deviations from the main form and a summary statement on studies of the tale and its world-wide distribution. Thus to one of the most popular of all French contes, Type 425, "The Search for the Lost Husband," a development of the Cupid and Psyche story intermixed with "Beauty and the Beast," the catalogue devotes thirty-seven pages (72–109), giving three sample texts, and listing 122 versions, with further references (a–m) to New World appearances. The long analytic bibliography begins with three references of 1697-98 to Madame d'Aulnoy's *Les Contes des fées,* and eventually includes texts from Cosquin, Millien (nos. 20–41), Luzel, Sébillot, van Gennep, and Massignon— almost all the great French collectors.

Besides the catalogue proper, the first volume offers an historical review by Paul Delarue of the collection and study of *contes populaires* in France, an analysis of its characters, supernatural and human, and an extensive, well-classified bibliography. In her informative Introduction to Volume II, Madame Tenèze speaks of the necessity to restrict the analysis of overseas tale variants, in order to make her efforts more realistic. The two volumes, running to more than a thousand pages, have still dealt with only 114 tale types (27 in volume I, 87 in volume II) representing a total of some 1,700 variant texts.

The books of folktales from French provinces were intended to sample the regional narrative traditions. Delarue described his plan for the series as follows:

> For folklorists, the annotated edition will furnish a new
> and abundant documentation on all the questions which

can interest them: comparative, stylistic, systematic study of themes; the portion of the individual contribution, of the collective contribution, and sometimes of the bookish contribution by the intermediary of peddlers, etc. . . . From certain comparisons will spring forth new insights. And this is the place to indicate how very different are the materials gathered together in our various collections, in their presentation externally identical. That of Nivernais and Morvan contains contes more developed and, in some part, worded with a concern for precision which applies more to content than to form, as was customary with the contemporaries of Achille Millien, Luzel, Cosquin, and Sébillot; that of the West (G. Massignon) restores to us faithfully the recorded language of the tellers; that of the Alps (Joisten) is composed from the most characteristic of six hundred stenographic versions, of which the whole furnishes, for a region limited enough, a practically exhaustive inventory of a tradition in the course of decomposing and dying; that of Bas-Languedoc and Gascogne (A. Perbosc and S. Cézerac) gives us the most typical forms of the Occitan country, while the original versions of the collection of the Audoises Pyrénées (Maugard) presents us with the oral literature of the neighboring Catalogne; that of Haute-Bretagne (A. de Félice) offers the repertoire of tellers who are carriers of a tradition still living in a milieu of basketmakers; that of Haut-Languedoc and Lyonnais (V. Smith) informs us of some of the most ancient forms of the contes of Perrault that have been gathered in the course of the great research undertaken in the last century; and the collections of French Canada, where the oral traditions of our western provinces are perpetuated, elaborated, adapted to the physical and human milieu and sometimes penetrated with Irish influence, will bring to us great recorded tales, certain of which are the veritable chefs-d'oeuvre of spoken style, thanks to particularly gifted tellers." [21]

For his series Delarue proposed a number of distinctive features. It would, in the first place, make available to the educated

[21] Translated from Paul Delarue, "Présentation de la collection," in A. Millien and P. Delarue, *Contes du Nivernais et du Morvan* (Paris, 1953), pp. viii–ix.

public the choicest specimens of French popular tales whose discovery, in the words of Gédéon Huet, himself an esteemed authority on the *conte populaire,* constituted one of the most remarkable scientific activities of the nineteenth century.[22] Second, he would restrict the contents of the volumes to authentic versions of tales preserving the simple syntax and direct story line of the *conteur,* without literary embroidery describing the features of the hero or depicting the landscape or moralizing on the events. (Delarue was not, however, modern enough to include scatological incidents, which he suppressed in the text and provided in the notes.) Third, he provided two editions of each volume: a popular edition that would supply with the tales full information on the methods of field collecting or procuring manuscripts and the regional areas explored, and an annotated edition for scholars with commentaries on each tale giving data on its variant forms and points of historical, comparative, and literary interest as well as its place in the international classifications of tale types. Fourth, the volume editors would divide their tales in sections according to specific genres, such as wonder tales, animal tales, jocular tales, and so on, rather than heaping them together indiscriminately. This series has indeed richly fulfilled Delarue's promises.

He himself prepared the first volume, for Nivernais and Morvan, based on the manuscript archives of Achille Millien (1838–1927), one of the greatest French collectors and also a reputed poet and a translator of Russian folktales and folksongs. Millien is known for the folksongs he published, but his precious trove of contes had, for the greatest part, never reached print. The discovery by Delarue of Millien's manuscripts in 1933 in the departmental archives at Nivernais, and Delarue's intimate account of his predecessor's life and work, in itself illustrates the continuities in the history of French folklore scholarship. Born in Beaumont-la-Ferriere and inheriting from his father large estates, Millien devoted himself to the collecting of songs and tales—"the flowers of the earth"—that he had learned about from his own peasant servant who became his wife. Nivernais, snuggled be-

---

[22] Gédéon Huet was the author of *Les Contes populaires* (Paris, 1923), a considered review of problems in folktale studies.

tween the valleys of the Loire and Nievre de Premery, bristled
with the activity of woodcutters, charcoal burners, lumbermen,
wagoners, and dairy farmers, while in the town of Beaumont
lived a mixed population of small gentry, peasants, day laborers,
and artisans working for the manorial lord or the forge master.
In this milieu traditions were faithfully conserved, and Millien
set out systematically to gather them on annual forays, contacting
the mayor, the school principal, and the curé, and asking them
to assemble informants for him at an inn, a farm, a school, or a
parish house. To these places he traveled by ferry, carriage, and
cart. Between 1877 and 1895, he collected more than twenty-seven
hundred melodies and texts of folksongs, more than nine hundred folktales, hundreds of legends, plus proverbs, *blason populaire,* beliefs, customs, folk zoölogy and folk botany in notebooks. He published parts of his materials in the journals spring-
ing up in the 1880's, including both *Mélusine* and *Revue des
traditions populaires,* and in a journal he founded in 1896, *Revue
du Nivernais,* with supplementary numbers presenting parts of
his collection, beginning with the songs. But partial paralysis
in 1909 coupled with financial reverses and the subsequent disappearance of his parasitic friends prevented Millien from the
completion of his task. This remained for Delarue.

   In this unusual liaison of a nineteenth- and a twentieth-cen-
tury master folklorist born in the same region, Delarue visited
localities where Millien had collected and sought to clothe in
flesh and blood some of his six hundred singers and tellers of
half a century before. Millien had merely given their names and
place and date of birth. Now Delarue actually met some of the
old men and women who had heard of or known "Mossieu
Achille," and Delarue thus supplemented the information on
Millien's narrators. "In Morvan, at Glux, to which I bicycled in
1942, I found an old man youthful in spirit, François Berthier,
born in 1864, who had been present at the reunion organized
by Millien in 1887, in an inn of the countryside, and he had kept
a precious memory." The old man recalled that the person who
had furnished Millien the best of his contes was Jeanne Martin,
called Jeannie, born at Glux in 1862. Daughter of a roofer using
oak planks, she was unlettered and was considered simple-
minded. Jeannie had married a man come from the "country of

vines"—that is to say, neighboring Bourgogne; she spent all day tending two nanny goats while spinning at her spindle, and it was from the old shepherds that she acquired the contes which she repeated voluntarily at the evening socials.[23]

At the Colonial Exposition in Paris in 1937, an international congress of folklore was held during which Delarue reported on the manuscripts of Millien. In his first printing of Millien's texts, Delarue, hitherto a botanist classifying water plants, took liberties with the wording, but after coming into contact with van Gennep he learned and adopted scholarly procedures. Subsequently, the first volume in the *Contes merveilleux des provinces de France* brought together the work of two renowned folklorists who never met—Millien and Delarue.

Other volumes in the series lived up to the standard of the first. Ariane de Félice's *Contes de Haute-Bretagne* (1954) revealed a whole unsuspected tradition of storytelling among basket makers in the hamlet of Mayun. These artisans regaled each other with long contes while engaged in their tedious occupation, in order to keep themselves from falling asleep. Their *veillées,* or evening socials, vividly described by Mlle de Félice, were conducted according to ritual procedures; the *conteur,* urged to deliver, would suddenly ejaculate, "Cric," whereupon the audience would be expected to respond, "Crac." One narrator while being recorded uttered, "Cric" to the unprepared circle of museum personnel, and when they did not reply appropriately he desisted and the disk had to be recommenced, with the now alerted audience ready to sound out, "Crac." Mlle de Félice expertly analyzes the repertoires and styles of her basket makers, around whom the collection is grouped. She finds that certain passages in contes are fixed and stereotyped and others, usually involving descriptions of the milieu, are flexible and subject to enlargement.

Geneviève Massignon, inspired by Delarue to become the most active modern field worker in France, contributed in 1954 *Contes de l'Ouest,* dealing with the regions of Grande Brière, Vendée, and Angoumois. Among these conteurs of the West, Mlle Massignon discovered a reliance on numerous little formulas and rhymes, fixed passages in the tale aiding the memory of the teller. In 1963 Mlle Massignon published the results of field trips to

[23] Paul Delarue, in *Contes du Nivernais et du Morvan,* p. 247.

Corsica in *Contes Corses,* presenting 106 texts with full scholarly apparatus. Her first forays into the field had been directed to dialect, as charged by the National Center for Scientific Research, which was engaged in preparing a *New Linguistic and Ethnographic Atlas of the West of France;* but Delarue encouraged her in this work to seek contes, and classified her harvest in his great catalogue. Similarly he suggested that on her vacations in Basse-Bretagne she hunt for *conteurs,* and in consequence Mlle Massignon brought out in 1965 an unusual collection of tales told by flax strippers of the Breton-speaking region of Trégor, *Contes traditionnels des teilleurs de lin du Trégor.* Like the basket makers, the flax strippers told tales at work and recreation, localizing and coloring the contes according to their Celtic temperament and personal horizons. The odious priest and wealthy patron appear as hostile figures, matched in the supernatural world by giants and monstrous animals, but fairies do not appear in Trégor. Besides publishing these collections of contes, Mlle Massignon also distinguished herself for her recording of French folksongs and her study of French dialects in Acadia. During her trip to North America on an *enquête* of 1946–47 she also collected contes from French-speaking farmers in Maine.[24] For her research in Acadia, she was given the gold medal of the French Canadian Academy, the first foreign author to receive this honor.

A gifted and industrious field worker, alert to the new techniques of tale collecting that embrace the teller, the style, the dialect, and the milieu as well as the text, Mlle Massignon was superbly fitted to undertake the present volume, completed shortly before her premature death in 1966 at the age of forty-five. The *Folktales of France* is both her memorial and a testament to the illustrious tradition of French folktale savants.[25]

RICHARD M. DORSON

[24] Geneviève Massignon, *Les Parlers français d'Acadie. Enquête linguistique,* 2 vols. (Paris, 1962); *La chanson populaire française en Acadie* (Paris, 1962).

[25] Daniel Massignon, brother of Geneviève, has furnished valuable assistance in seeing the manuscript through the press. I am deeply indebted to Roger Pinon, visiting professor at the Folklore Institute in the spring of 1967, for suggestions on the sources for this Foreword.

Introduction

The traditional field in mid-twentieth-century France may seem an exhausted territory to many scholars. Nevertheless, it yields happy surprises to collectors if they are capable of infiltrating into rural areas far from modern life. There they can listen to the peasant voice of the craftsman or the mountain dweller still linked by their occupations to the traditional life.

The role of tales and legends, of sayings and folksongs still seems to be of some importance in the traditional thinking of many natives of the French countryside. At least this is certainly true when they think back to the early years of their youth.

A map of the French provinces drawn up in 1893 by Paul Sébillot shows an odd distribution of the twenty-five hundred tales collected at that time.[1] This distribution shows us not only the efforts of certain local folklore experts but also the richness of certain fields. If that map were redrawn now, the same would be true. (In 1956 Paul Delarue estimated that there was a stock of ten thousand French tales.)

It has definitely been established, for instance, that North and South Brittany are privileged to have been chosen areas for tales and legends, and have brought to light collectors such as F. M. Luzel, François Cadic, Paul Sébillot, and Adolphe Orain. But not all the provinces of France or its districts have the good fortune like Montiers-sur-Saulx to have had a master of folklore such as Emmanuel Cosquin. He dug out of this village the material for his famous *Contes populaires de Lorraine* (Paris, 1886) and used it as a background for his remarkable outline of the modern comparative method.

In 1953, when, Paul Delarue was bringing out the series *Contes*

[1] *Revue des traditions populaires,* VIII (December, 1893), 584–85.

merveilleux des provinces de France, he noted with bitterness the regrettable gaps in the documentation of folklore collected from provinces where regional flavor was particularly strong, such as Provence, among others. By the end of the nineteenth century, rural life in other regions had already been submerged by industrialization and with it the framework of the traditional life of yesteryear. Delarue patiently made a census of the manuscripts collected at the end of the last century and the beginning of this one. His predecessor, A. Millien, found twelve hundred variants for the regions of Nivernais and Morvan. Delarue rediscovered the volume of tales entrusted to Emmanuel Cosquin by Victor Smith, the famous folklorist of Forez and Velay, and managed to collect together, with the help of both families, tales in manuscript (or published in places almost impossible to find) in exactly the same way as many folktales were culled by Antonin Perbosc in Gascogne and François Cadic in the Morbihan.

A small group of young collectors, of whom I am one, that Paul Delarue had managed to interest in French folktales, extended their investigations into areas offered to them either because the *Musée des arts et traditions populaires* had diverted them in that direction or because the dialectic investigations of the *Atlas linguistiques et ethnographiques de la France* gave them the opportunity. Perhaps they were simply moved by a personal interest in tradition. Ariane de Félice has already given the public her research on the basket weavers of Grande Brière (*Contes de Haute Bretagne* [Paris, 1954]). Her complementary thesis at the Sorbonne deals with the tales from the Bocage Vendéen, and the material resulting from her search in Berry, Marche, and Combraille has been published in part by G. Hüllen and M. L. Tenèze in the bilingual collection entitled *Begegnung der Völker im Märchen* (1961 and 1964).

Charles Joisten stuck with unusual tenacity to the tales from the French Alps, combing through many a valley, where he picked up hundreds of variants in the past fifteen years. These variants belong to a tradition now coming to its close. He published a first installment in *Contes des Hautes Alpes* (Paris, 1956), devoted to Queyras, known as the last stronghold of the folktale. But this did not prevent him from extending his research to the Pyrenees. As for the abbot Jean Garneret, author of a remarkable monograph on the speech of Lantenne-Vertière (Doubs), which was his parish, he also gathered in this small area the last traces of tradition and handed them over bit by bit to Paul Delarue as he found them.

With the study of dialects as a principal aim, research was undertaken under the aegis of the Centre National de la Recherche Scientifique which led to the establishing of the *Atlas linguistiques et ethnographiques de la France*. However, when rural areas are penetrated by the researcher knowing the regional dialect, this knowledge allows him to gain contact with the country people who retain local tradition. These are the narrators of tales or legends or the singers of songs. Pierre Nauton is director of the *Atlas linguistique et ethnographique du Massif Central* (three volumes have already been published, followed by an extensive *Exposé général*), and has done all the research by himself. He has had the opportunity of picking up many folktales in the past twenty years, nearly all recorded on tape. This is for him the most valuable kind of material in the study of the style and grammar of a dialect. It also provides other folklorists with interesting versions of folktales. Marguerite Gonon, who helped in the making of the *Atlas linguistique et ethnographique du Lyonnais,* has collected tales from an old miller's wife in Forez.

Because I was responsible for the research work for the *Atlas linguistique et ethnographique de l'ouest,* I explored the departments forming the "Pays Nantais," the "Pays de Retz" (Loire-Atlantique), the Haut Poitou and Bas Poitou (Vienne, Deux-Sèvres, and Vendée), the Aunis and the Saintonge (Charente-Maritime), the Angoumois and the Ruffecois (Charente), the Basse-Marche (Vienne and Charente), and the borders of the Limousin (Charente). Wherever I found it possible, I gathered folklore material while doing research on dialects in the various districts. My collection numbers about two thousand songs and three hundred tales and legends, some of which have been published in the magazine *Arts et traditions populaires* (1953) and in my *Contes de l'ouest* (Paris, 1953 and 1954).

For more than ten years I was advised by my teacher, Paul

Delarue, whom I miss very much, to extend my research to a district where I had spent many a holiday, the Côtes du Nord in the Pays de Trégor, which Luzel had admired for its oral literature, calling it "the attic of Basse Bretagne."

A search made in the rural craftsman's world, particularly in the valleys of the Leff and the Trieux where the flax *teilleurs* are to be found, allowed me to pick up thirty-one tales. Another search launched into the peasant circles of Trégor enabled me to collect fifty-nine tales there between 1953 and 1954. More than thirty of these were narrated to me by the same informant.

A little later in Corsica, where I already knew the dialect, I undertook another search among the mountain dwellers of Castagniccia and Niolo. This was more detailed and led me to collect ninety tales. Paul Delarue studied and catalogued them for his *Catalogue des contes français.* His faithful collaborator, Marie Louise Tenèze, carried on the master's work, and it is with her that I checked my second collection of Corsican tales made in 1959 (sixty tales), as I mention in the preface to my *Contes corses.*

The liveliness of the French tale in the twentieth century depends very much on the preservation of traditional rural life. It is true that in certain areas this way of life is fast disappearing as traditional customs must give way to modern progress, but we still find that the mountain people of the Massif Central, the Alps, the Pyrenees, and Corsica have a rich repertory of tales today. It is equally certain that the existence of a language or a dialect very different from regular French has helped to preserve local tradition. This is the case in South Brittany, Corsica, and the Bocage Vendéen; a certain conservatism is evident in their customs and their way of life. In the case of the Bocains of Vendée on their widely scattered farms, or in the case of the basket weavers and eel catchers of Grande Brière (North Brittany), their isolation has helped to keep up the traditional evenings spent with neighbors. Then, too, some crafts produce favorable circumstances for the spreading of tales and songs. They tell stories as they weave their baskets or spin the flax, as they carve their spoons of wood or their clogs, because these are jobs done collectively.

How do our narrators of the twentieth century appear to us? They may be craftsmen spending an evening with the neighbors, shepherds gathered around the fire, or peasant grandmothers looking after the young children. All are holders of a tradition communicated orally by their parents and grandparents and neighbors. In rare instances, traditions may come from people passing through the district and staying only temporarily in the countryside through which they traveled. Such persons might have been basket peddlers or livestock dealers taking their flock to the nearest market. Our folktale narrators are filled with their traditions, which they try to pass on as truthfully as they can to an audience which wants to hear a good story of the old days. It is unusual for one of these narrators to hesitate or go back in the telling to some forgotten episode. Only for some tales would he use rhymed passages to help him remember or to embellish the story for his audience.

The way in which these folk narrators tell their tales differs markedly from one province to another. The dialect, which is the usual medium used, imposes its own forms on the narrator's recital, and even if he tries to tell a tale in French, there still remains something of the dialect. Thus the Corsican tale starts with *Una volta era* (*Une fois, il était*) an inversion of our *il était une fois*. Marguerite Gonon, who collected old tales from Forez, mentions one of the sayings prefacing one of the tales best loved by the French narrators, *"Cric Crac; Cuiller à pot; Marche aujourd'hui, marche demain; A force de marcher; On fait beau-coup de chemin"* (cf. our tale No. 52, The Four Friends).

The rhymes ending a tale also vary according with the region. If Corsica ends with *"Fola foletta, dite a vostra; a mea è detta* (Fable, little fable, tell yours; mine is told) (cf. our No. 69, The Shepherd and the Snake), then in the regions of Languedoc you find them often using this: *"Passa per un pitit crô dé rat; moun counte est acabat"* (I've been through a little mousehole; my tale is finished.) Our tale in Limousin speech, The Gold Ball, offers us a variant. Or else a still shorter rhyme shows how the spell is broken, *"Le coq chanta et le conte fut fini."* So goes a tale from the Massif Central (cf. our No. 50, "Jean and Jeannette").

The tale from Poitou and Angoumois and Ruffecois is adorned with rhymed spells whose tone often varies as the tale progresses. An example of this is the tale of The Goat, the Kids, and the Wolf (No. 36). Now and then the magic words are repeated without alteration but addressed to different speakers:

> N'avez-vous pas vu passer
> Mon Jean et ma Jeannette?
> Mon char et ma charrette
> Avec mes chevaux blancs
> Ferrés d'or et d'argent.

In certain tales the jingle is sung. The tale of The Little Devil of the Forest (here it is No. 63), picked up by Charles Joisten in Savoie, is an example of this quite frequent case in the variants of Type 500. On the other hand, a Pyrenean version of *L'os qui chante* (Type 780) entitled The Laurel Flower (No. 66) brings us jingles with a simple rhyme and not *psalmodiées,* as is commonly found.

The narrator's diction varies, not only with the people or with their gifts, but primarily with the area. The Breton narrator loves abundance of detail, especially in long descriptive tales sometimes inbred with mystery; and this is true of North and South Brittany as well.

On the other hand, the Corsican narrator makes the characters talk to each other, revealing little scenes of local life, and going gaily from one episode to another. Limousin tales are short and concise. The thoughts as well as the elements making up the tale are sometimes concentrated dramatically in very short sentences. The tales of Franche-Comté and Poitou, especially those dealing with animals, are spicy and full of imagery.

The gestures and the accents of the narrators also contribute to the appearance of the tale. A Corsican woman narrator used to take my hand and place it over my heart in order to link me with the parts of her tale which she thought most moving. Another one, who was blind, concentrated on vocal inflections to put over the most violent passions occurring in parts of her tales.

The fantastic creatures that you find in traditional French tales are widely varied. If Brittany calls ogres and ogresses *Sarrazins et Sarrazines,* the central area of France containing Poitou, Marche, Limousin, and Nivernais labels them mysteriously *brou, lebrou, loup-brou, malbrou.* (These beings are presumably variants of the French *loup-garou.*) The southern areas sometimes substitute *le drac* (dragon) or the Devil. Corsica has *maghi,* the wizards whose powers are more varied than those of the ogres. More often than the *fada* (fairy), there appears in this island the little old woman who gives good counsel.

The fairy, usually a friendly character (except when she thinks herself slighted), sometimes gives way to the Holy Virgin as godmother to orphans or protector of the persecuted, and this takes place not in the regions thought of as devout areas, such as Vendée or Brittany, but in the provinces of Centre-Ouest, actually thought of as turning away from the Christian faith.

The liking for tales of wonder is common to North and South Brittany and Corsica, but Brittany, which is reputed to be mystical, does not discard facetious tales either. As for animal tales, they seem to be more appreciated in the middle west and in Franche-Comté and the Massif Central.

Together with authentic folktales, three legends are included in this collection. One is linked with a definite place, The Little Elves of La Chausse-en-l'Air (No. 22), and the other is linked to an event thought to be true (discovery of hidden treasure guarded by a diabolical being): The Black Hen (No. 27). As for The Legend of the Oxen's Pass (No. 67), set in Niolo (Corsica), this is one of those oral tales made to explain the strange shape of a mountain, in this case that of the *Cabu Tafonatu,* or "mountain placed by the Devil."

Those who have the traditional tales handed down to them know just as much about the kingdom of legends as that of fictions; but unlike the tales, whose form is rigid and which are passed on word for word to folk who have excellent memories, legends, being more open to variation, travel farther, and many villagers who do not know how to spin a yarn, have heard and spread scraps of these stories. Few informants told me legends as well developed and perfected as the tales.

In this collection I have grouped the chosen stories into fifteen areas, arranging the tales within each region according to the international classification of the Aarne-Thompson *Type Index*. The notes for each version are aimed at placing it within the framework of French tradition and also explaining any local particularities.

GENEVIÈVE MASSIGNON

Contents

V UPPER POITOU

VI LOWER MARCHE

VII ANGOUMOIS AND RUFFECOIS

Part I
Lower Brittany

· *1* · *Yann the Fearless*

• HE WAS A LITTLE BOY who had lost his mother and father and was being brought up by his uncle, the priest. The little boy had no evil in him, but he was a little tricky to manage, if you like, and his uncle was not succeeding in teaching him any discipline.

Once when the priest had put Yann in the church as a punishment, he forgot that he was there, and the child had to stay there all night long. When he saw dusk approaching, he went into a confessional to get out of the cold.

At about midnight he heard a noise in the church. "Get that out of here!" said a voice.

"What is the matter with you?" replied Yann, who was not afraid.

Said the voice, "When I was a priest, I decided to steal something. I pinched the priest's stole, and I also took a golden goblet, and in order to hide them I put them in the priest's garden."

This was the previous priest of the parish. He was dead, and they had buried him under the flagstones of the church, as they still do sometimes.

The voice went on, "I had sworn on my life that I had not stolen them. I even said I would be happy to be dammed forever if I was not telling the truth. Now I am in hell and know no rest. Do tell the present priest not to pray for me every Sunday, as is the custom, for I suffer more when prayers are said for me."

The next morning the sacristan went into the church to ring the Angelus and found Yann shut in there. Astounded, he went to tell the priest, "There is a robber in the church!"

The priest came along, remembering then where he had left his nephew. "It is my fault," he said. "I shut the boy up in the church yesterday."

Yann told his uncle what the previous parish priest had said, remembering to mention that the things stolen from the church were buried in the priest's garden.

"Let us go and see at once!" said his uncle. They dug and searched in the garden and under the arbor, and they found what they were looking for. The priest kept the golden goblet and gave the stole to the boy. Yann had asked to have it, for the dead man had also said to him, "Keep the stole and you will never be afraid."

One day, when Yann was fifteen or sixteen, he said to himself, "With this stole I am sure of never being afraid. I am going round the world."

On his way he came upon an old house, an ancient castle which was crumbling into ruins, and he asked if he could take shelter there for the night. "Yes," he was told, "if you will sleep in the room up there, but no one dares to go in because no one who does ever comes back."

"I will willingly sleep in that room." So he went in and lay down to rest, but all night long there was noise. It was as if a man were there wailing in great pain. "Why do you wail like that?" said Yann out loud.

"I hid stolen money in this castle. I wanted to give it back, but I died before I could." The dead man also told Yann where the stolen money was. It was in the cellar.

The next morning the landlord went to the room and opened the door. (He had locked Yann in the night before.)

The youth explained what had happened that night and where the dead man had hidden stolen money. The landlord started searching the cellar with Yann. They dug under the castle and brought up a great deal of money. "As you found this money," the landlord said to the youth, "it will be yours. You have freed me at last from this dead man's cries of woe."

"I do not need it," said Yann. He took a little and went off saying, "The rest will be for the poor." So he went on his way.

He reached another house and asked to spend the night there. He was told the same story.

"I have no room to give you except one where noises are heard all night. If you are not afraid, take it!" said the landlord.

"Ah," said Yann, "well, I'll keep an eye open and we'll see."

They gave him something to eat—bread and cider—so that he would stay awake. At midnight as he was warming himself by the fire he heard a noise in the chimney. "Make as much noise as you like! I am not afraid," said Yann. Shortly after he saw a leg fall down the chimney. "Well," said he, "here is a skittle. I will set it up." A moment later he again heard a noise, and there was another leg falling. "Well, well, well, now I have two skittles." Yann placed the two legs upright, one next to the other, and resumed his vigil by the fireplace. As the noise began again, he cried, "Go ahead, make as much noise as you like!" One after the other there fell an arm and a few minutes later another arm, which he set up next to the legs like skittles. Then the body of a man came down the chimney. Yann grabbed the body round the middle and put the legs and arms around the trunk. "Now for the head!" And sure enough a head fell in the fireplace. "Well, well, well! Here is a ball to play skittles with."

Yann sat down again by the fire, eating a piece of bread. Suddenly he turned round and saw to his surprise that the body stood up and was saying as it came back to life, "You are pretty fearless, Yann."

"You are the one who is fearless, as you have stolen my skittles!"

This corpse was a devil who had assumed this form in order to frighten everyone. But Yann calmly went to the table to eat, and said, "Come on and eat with me."

Then another devil arrived, then two, then three. They all went to the side of the table opposite Yann, and pushed the table over on him in order to crush him.

"Cut it out!" Yann said. "I have my grandfather's scarf right here. So you'd better watch out!"

The devils kept on surrounding and threatening him. There was one, a cripple, who was meaner than the others. Yann put the stole around his neck, the devil began to yell, and the others all left.

"Now, before I let you go," Yann said, "you'll have to sign this saying that you won't have any power over anyone in this house for the nine *lignées* (generations)."

But the devil didn't want to sign it at any price. So Yann tightened the stole around his neck, and forced him to sign what he wanted him to.

As he left, the devil shouted at him, "You've gone too far!" and he took a rock from the windowsill and threw it in Yann's face, which turned as black as the chimney, it was so bruised.

"If I ever meet you again, I'll sure make you watch your step!" Yann said in turn.

Once again he had rescued the household with whom he had spent only one night. In acknowledgment, the owner offered him his daughter in marriage.

"No," Yann said, "I don't want to; I'm not going to get married." And once again he left and wandered around aimlessly. One day he heard that large numbers of people were gathering in Paris. In fact, long ago the Devil was promised that he would receive a king's daughter every fifty years; and now it was the turn of the King of France's own daughter to be surrendered to him.

Yann said to himself, "I have to go see the King first." Since traveling wasn't any problem for him, he went to Paris and said to the King, "Everyone is saying that the Devil is demanding your daughter."

"Alas, yes!" the King said.

"Let me stay close by her the night you have to hand her over, and I promise you I'll take care of the Devil. Believe me—if you do as I say, your daughter won't be taken away from you. Have a small vat placed in the middle of the large hall, and have it filled with holy water. You'll send for all the bishops, the archbishops, and even the Pope, and when everyone is gathered around the small vat, you'll have a *balai de cour* (farmyard broom) distributed to each one. When the last one of these important dignitaries enters the large hall, you'll see that he doesn't dare take a broom and go near the vat of holy water."

Yann's suggestions were carried out. Everything was in place on the appointed evening. The Devil appeared at the door of the hall; he immediately saw Yann and recognized him.

"Give me the King's daughter!" he said to him.

"Go get her, if you want her!" Yann answered.

"Throw her over here to me!"

"Come get her over here! If you want her, you'll come in this room to get her."

The Devil finally agreed to cross the threshold. Yann immediately threw the stole around his neck, and shouted to the bishops, the archbishops, and the Pope gathered around the vat:

"Quick! Take your brooms and splash holy water on the Devil. Really give it to him! Don't be afraid."

And they all did as he said. The Devil was caught. Then Yann had him sign an agreement that from then on, for a hundred generations, he wouldn't have any right to any daughter of the King of France, and he added, "Before I release you, and as you blackened my face the last time we met, you're going to make me the most handsome boy there is."

The Devil made him the best-looking boy ever seen in the world. However, as he left, he again grabbed a stone that had fallen out of the palace wall (he had to take something everywhere he went!), but this time he didn't throw it at anyone, and then he disappeared.

When the King's daughter met her rescuer, she fell in love with him, and the King proposed to Yann that he become his son-in-law.

"No," the young man answered, "I won't get married until I've faced another danger; I'm trying to learn what fear is."

Since the Princess very much wanted to marry him, she went and found one of these women who study the stars, to ask her how to frighten Yann.

The fortune teller told her, "You only have to cook a loaf of bread, and when it's done, you dig out the inside and put in a blackbird, leaving it a little air so it won't die. Then you tell this young man to cut into this loaf of bread before leaving the palace, and you'll see: when the blackbird flies out, it'll scare him."

Yann was getting ready to leave the King's palace; the Princess came and said to him, "At least do me the favor of eating some of this bread that I've made for you before you leave."

"That, I won't refuse," he said. And as he cut into the crust, the blackbird suddenly flew out! Yann was so frightened that he fell on his rear.

The King's daughter went over to him and said, "You were scared!"

"Yes," he said.

"Well then, since you now know what fear is, there's nothing to keep us from getting married."

"You're right," said Yann. "I can't ever again take chances, since I've been afraid once in my life."

Remember that he was still wearing his stole in order not to be afraid, but this time he was taken by surprise.

Then Yann consented to marry the King's daughter, and later on he in turn became King.

·2· *Old Fench*

• ONCE UPON A TIME there was a King of France who had a son. One day, in looking through his father's papers, the young man found a portrait of Princess Virginia, daughter of the King of Naples. "She is so beautiful! Oh! I must go and find her. Never before in this world has there been such a beautiful woman!"

The King tried to dissuade his son, as he knew he was not very clever. "You will not manage it," he said. "No one has ever seen her in the flesh!"

"Never mind, I dream only of her and I want her so very much to be mine. Father, let me go and try to find her."

The King of France said, "If you go off, my son, take my old servant, Fench Coz (Old Francis), with you; he has known you since you were a child. Go, and obey him in every way. If you follow this advice you may perhaps reach your goal, but if you do not follow it you are a lost man.

One fine morning the young man left, seated in a coach drawn by two horses. Fench Coz, also in the coach, accompanied his master. After a day's travel on the road, just as night was falling, they went into a wood. In a clearing there was fresh grass, and the horses were tired; they put them to graze after unsaddling them.

Fench Coz said to the son of the King of France, "I am going to climb up a tree and spend the night there. You will stay in the coach to sleep, and the horses will eat grass and rest." The young man followed the old servant's advice, and soon he fell fast asleep in the coach where he had lain down. Fench Coz, on the other hand, had climbed a tree and did not sleep a wink before daybreak.

In the middle of the night he heard three characters come and sit at the foot of the tree and start talking. One was saying to the other, "You see the son of the King of France here, hoping one day to find Princess Virginia, but he shall not have her. I know well that at this moment he is asleep in his coach. I will also tell you how he could find her, but if I did not know that he was asleep, I would not speak of it."

"Do tell us then," said one of the others.

"Well, there is a river to cross, not far from here; there is no bridge, but on the bank there is a cluster of willows, and in the middle of the clump is hidden a little wand. All that is needed is to take this wand, hit the bank three times with it, and a bridge will span the river."

The King's son knew nothing of it, but Fench Coz had heard everything.

Another character went on to say, "I know that there is a castle on the other side of the river where Princess Virginia lives. But her father, the King of Naples, does not want anyone to go near her, so he has also given her a governess who watches over her day and night. One would have to signal the princess, who is in a room which has one small window; but if her father or the castle guards saw one signaling to her, they would watch over her even more strictly."

Fench Coz did not miss a word of this.

The third character added, "If, however, the son of the King of France manages to carry off Princess Virginia, which is altogether impossible, he would have the King of Naples and all his guards at his heels. To delay his pursuers it would be necessary to keep the wand found in the clump of willows and to put it back after having crossed the bridge; then the bridge would disappear, and the King of Naples would be delayed in his chase."

Fench Coz did not miss hearing this either.

Next morning, the son of the King of France said to his old servant, "Did you sleep well?"

"Yes, master."

"Me, too," said the Prince. "I did not wake at all."

"Well, our horses are rested; it is time to take to the road again."

It was not long before the Prince's coach stopped at a river;

it was not very wide, but there was no way of crossing it. "Don't worry, master!" said Fench Coz. "I will get out of the coach and see to it that there is a bridge." The old servant found the wand hidden in the clump of willows, hit the bank of the river three times with it, and at once a bridge spanned the river from one bank to the other.

The coach started to cross, and before the end of the morning it stopped before the castle of the King of Naples. Fench Coz then said to the son of the King of France, "Princess Virginia is shut up in that room up there. She has only one little window through which to communicate with the outside world, but if you succeed in seeing her, signal to her and she will be ready to follow you, for she has had enough of living like a recluse in this castle."

Meanwhile, Princess Virginia was in her room alone with her governess. She said to her, "I know that a prince has arrived at the foot of the castle. He has just signaled to me as I showed my head at the window. Let us go down to the garden at once before anyone finds out!"

As she was allowed to walk in the courtyard with her governess, the guard let her pass. They reached the garden gate where the son of the King of France was waiting for them. He made them hurry into his coach while he and Fench Coz leaped onto the two horses. Then they left at full speed. Soon they reached the bank of the river. "Let's quickly cross the bridge," said Fench Coz to his young master, "because it will soon disappear." And as soon as the coach was over, the old servant leaped off his horse and put the wand back in the middle of the clump of willows. The guards of the King of Naples had just reached the bridge when it disappeared, and they were all drowned.

The Prince went on his way up to the little wood where they had stopped the first night. This time he left the coach for Princess Virginia and her governess to rest in, and he said to his old servant, "It is my turn to climb up this tree and sleep there; and you will sleep in the grass in the clearing."

"No, Master, you will sleep there, and I will climb up into this tree again." The Prince let his old servant have his way.

Soon the three characters who had gathered at the foot of the tree the night before came back to it to pick up their conversation. One took over and said, "We have said that the son of the King of France would not succeed in taking away Princess Virginia, and he is over there in this clearing, sleeping at the foot of his coach; but he has not gone back to France, and he will have a good deal of trouble getting back! If, however, he does get there, he will meet a beggar drowning in a pond. This beggar will call for help from him; as the son of the King of France is kindhearted, he will be ready to save him, but if he tries to save him, it is certain that the Prince will come to us to get warm."

Fench Coz was not sleeping any more than the night before, and he missed none of this.

The second character added, "If he stops himself at once and does not rescue the beggar, he will next meet a thief. This thief will ask him to give up all his belongings—his coach, his horses, his money, and even his clothes—and he will put out the Prince and his companions, as naked as worms, to run over the earth; but the son of the King of France, who is proud, will not accept that, and if he rejects the thief's requests, it is then that he will come to us to get warm."

Fench Coz was still listening. It was the third character's turn to speak. "If the Prince accepts the thief's request, they will all, naked and on foot, arrive at an inn which will have as its sign:

> Food, drink, and clothes for three days are given here
> free of charge.

"And if they are foolish enough to go into the inn—well, then they will all come to us to get warm!" Then the conversation between the three characters came to an end. And now all three of them said, "If anyone repeats what we have just said, he will be turned into a marble statue."

Dawn came. Fench Coz woke everyone up, and they set off again. The old servant knew everything, but he did not breathe a word to anyone. They had not gone very far when they had their first encounter. A poor man in rags was thrashing about in a pond as if about to drown and was yelling, "Help!" The Prince wanted to get down from his horse to rescue him.

"No," said Fench Coz, "you shall not do it." The King's son grew angry. "Not only do you want to do everything your own way, but now you are even turning nasty!"

"Your father, the King, entrusted you to me, and I am telling you to leave this beggar behind and let us be off!" The young man, surprised, obeyed against his better judgment.

A little later on, the coach was stopped by a thief who stood in the way on the road. "If you value your life, you must give me all that you have on you and with you!"

The son of the King of France wanted to go past him in a dignified manner. "No, no," said Fench Coz, "we must give him all we have and he will let us by." The young man was very put out. As for the Princess and the governess, they did not want to give into the thief either. "You see," said Fench Coz, "I let it happen to me!" And he started to take off his clothes. The Prince could not get over it.

"Your father told you to obey me," Fench Coz said, adding, "Do as he says, otherwise you're lost!"

Seeing this, Fench Coz's three fellow travelers copied the servant; and there they were, naked, on foot, walking wearily along in the hope of finding shelter. They reached an inn where they saw written:

> Food, drink, and clothes for three days are given here free of charge.

The son of the King of France exclaimed, "Let's go in here!"

"No," said Fench Coz.

"Yes, yes."

"Oh no, we must go on. Follow me, all three of you, and you will soon be home."

The Prince went on in such an angry state that he wanted to kill his servant. In the end he gave up and obeyed him; and, guided by Fench Coz, they reached the King of France without further ado.

His son was proud to come back to his father's castle with

Princess Virginia, but he was angry with Fench Coz, and he told the King all that the old servant had made him do. And so Fench Coz was, at the Prince's request, thrown into prison.

But the King of France, knowing how simple his son was, came and questioned the old servant in prison. Fench Coz explained to him what he had heard up in his tree that first night, and how he had made the most of it; but when he got to the second night, and started to tell about the meeting with the poor drowning man, that very instant his feet changed to marble and his legs also, up to his knees.

As the King insisted on hearing more, the old servant had to tell him how he had heard their meeting with the thief predicted. Then the servant exclaimed, "As I must talk to get out of this prison, ah, well, I shall suffer because of you." Then and there he turned to marble up to his shoulders. The King still insisted, and when the servant told of the predicted meeting at the inn, where what I have told you is written, he concluded, "If he had gone into that inn and had not obeyed me, he would have turned to marble as I am doing." At these words his mouth closed and his whole head turned to marble. When the King and his son saw only a marble statue instead of Fench Coz, they started to weep; but this did no good. So they had the statue placed in the center of the most beautiful hall in the castle, and every day the King's son washed the marble that had been Fench Coz with tears of remorse.

Later the King of France wished his son's wedding to Princess Virginia to take place; and before the end of the year they had a son. But to their utter despair, the child did nothing but cry day and night; there were always three nurses by him, but no one could calm him.

In the end the King's son tired of this. One day he went in secret to a soothsayer to ask her advice. "I don't believe we shall ever know happiness without Fench Coz, my old servant, who has been changed into marble, and I will do anything in order to free him."

The soothsayer replied, "I know. You have a child who cries day and night. He may always have three nurses at his side, but nothing makes him quiet. Well, I will give you some advice.

If you want to set your old servant free, you must first kill your son and spread your son's blood all over the marble image of Fench Coz. When all the stone is washed with it, your old servant will be a man again, and he will bring your child back to life, and he will laugh and run about."

"Fench Coz always told me the truth," said the King's son, "so I shall resign myself to doing as you say."

He went into the King's castle and said to the three nurses, "Leave me alone with my son; I will look after him while you go to Mass with Princess Virginia." The nurses were quite pleased to leave the child for a while, and they gladly accepted the Prince's suggestion.

While all the ladies of the castle attended Mass, the Prince killed his son, spread the child's blood over the marble, and washed it with the blood. Then Fench Coz, very much alive, rose before him and started to weep; but by bathing the child with his tears, he brought him back to life.

When Princess Virginia returned to the castle with the three nurses, she saw her son there before her, toddling about and laughing. Fench Coz was at the Prince's side, and from that day forth he never left him.

3. *Ugly Yann*

• YANN WAS A BOY who was both very ugly and very poor, hence his surname of Ugly Yann (*Yann Vil*). He had done God a favor, I do not quite know how, and it was because of this that he had received as a reward the power to say, "By the grace of God, may this or that be done." He was so simple, however, that he had never thought of using it.

One day he had gone out to pick up deadwood for his mother, and he made a faggot of it. He came home carrying the wood on his back. Feeling tired, he sat down on the bundle of sticks and had a short rest.

"Ah," he sighed, without having too much faith in his powers, "if only it was the faggot's turn to walk instead of mine! By the grace of God, let this faggot carry me."

To his great surprise he felt himself being lifted and carried along, though he was in fact still sitting on his pile of wood. He was not, however, the only one to be surprised. The King's daughter was at the window of her castle. She was busy watching poor Yann. He was ugly and badly dressed, and to her great surprise she saw him go by carried on the faggot.

"Oh, look at him, that Yann—now his faggot is carrying him along with him sitting on it." Yann was vexed by these words. He decided to use his powers this time to punish the Princess for her teasing.

"By the grace of God, may the King's daughter become pregnant."

And that is what happened. The Princess was amazed and confused. Her father, the King, came to hear of it and asked her many questions to find out who was responsible. The Princess assured him that she had never seen anyone.

"But after all," said the King, "you are the same as anybody else! I want to know who the father is."

In good time the Princess had a little boy. She could say nothing more about how he had come to be.

The King was still just as dissatisfied. He said, "When the child can walk, perhaps there will be a way of recognizing his father."

The King then sent for all his lords and dukes and princes and even the kings of other countries that the Princess might have visited. He had firmly decided to put them to the test. The little boy was beginning to walk. He was given a ball and he was told to put this ball in his father's hat. All the nobles were made to pass in front of the child, but in the end the ball was still in his little hand.

The King did not give up his plan. He ordered that all the poor people, the crippled and the weak, should be brought to him. The same ceremony took place. The poor people filed past the child, but suddenly as it was Yann's turn to go by, the child put his ball into Yann's hat.

The King was dumbfounded, and the Princess was not flattered.

Her father said to her angrily, "Now you can no longer say you do not know your child's father."

"Father, I swear to you that I know as little about it as before."

"How can you expect me to believe you from now on? It is useless for you to protest. You have shamed me in front of everybody, and no one can deny that this ugly Yann has been pointed out by your child's hand. Well, marry this man! I banish you from my court, and I never want to see you again."

The Princess found she had nothing to say. She had to make up her mind to marry this ugly Yann whom she found so wretched and so poor.

So they settled down to live together. One day she thought of asking him how he had made her pregnant, and her husband explained to her that he had been given the power to do anything he wished by the grace of God. He explained that he had only to say, "By the grace of God, let this or that be done."

"Well!" said the Princess, "as you have this power, do ask to become Yann *Vrao* (Handsome Yann)."

Ugly Yann took her advice and at once became as handsome as a prince. He was the best-looking prince on the face of the earth.

And in this way the Princess remained married to Yann.

·4· *The Tailor*

• ONCE UPON A TIME there was a tailor who worked for a farmer by the day. While he was sitting on a bench next to the table where he had placed his piece of fabric, a swarm of flies started buzzing around him. Furious, he pulled off his cap and hit them with it. With one blow he killed a thousand flies!

So once he had reached home he wrote on his cap, "I kill a thousand at one blow!"

And then he went on going to work by the day, cutting clothes now at one place, then at another, but he was careful always to take his cap with him.

People began by looking at him in surprise, then in awe.

"There's a strong man," they said to themselves as they saw him go by.

His reputation for strength reached the ears of a giant who lived with his brothers in a secluded castle, and they came to find the tailor.

"Do come with us! If you can kill a thousand at one blow, you can just as well help us with our jobs."

The tailor did not have to be asked twice. He went to their home, telling himself that he would manage to catch them out somehow.

One day the giant who was boss said to him, "This morning we must fetch water from the fountain. You will come with me." There and then the giant took two barrels to fill.

"Oh, it's not worth carrying all that," said the tailor. "I can bring the fountain here to me."

"Oh, no, no, no!" said the giant. "I do not want that. This fountain is very useful where it is. If you took it home with you, what would we do without water?"

Once again the tailor had won!

Another time they went off into the forest to cut wood. The giant, who was very strong, began to cut down trees one after the other.

"It's your turn now," he said to the tailor.

"No, no, I do not bother to cut down trees. I take the forest with me if I want to!"

"Oh, don't do that!" the giant objected. "Leave the forest where it is; otherwise we shall not have any more wood to cut close by our house."

Not long after, the giant and his brothers were playing au palet. (This is a game rather like bowls but played on the ground with flat stones, the object of which is to find who can get closest to a chosen stone.)

"Well, do you want to play with us?" the giant shouted to the tailor.

But the tailor had sat down on a millstone and he yelled from there, "Look out, because I am going to set all these millstones rolling down the path and send them far, far away from here."

The giant rushed over to him.

"Stop! Don't do that, my friend. My brothers and I need these millstones to play au palet, and if you send them far off, we shall never find them again."

Another time, the giant was walking along with the tailor, thinking as he went that he had really had enough of this man's tricks. "This time," he said to himself, "I shall catch him." He took a stone in his hand.

"You see this stone? Well, I shall reduce it to powder in front of you."

The giant well and truly crushed the stone. There was nothing but a fine powder left in his hand. It was like flour. Then the tailor was so terrified that he wet his pants, and so he put his hand underneath and showed it to the giant.

"Well, you see, I can turn a stone into juice!"

The giant did not know what to do with the tailor.

"We shall never see the end of him," he said to his brothers. "So we must kill him."

One night the giant said to the tailor as he showed him a bed, "You are going to stay and sleep here. Lie down there."

"Yes, yes." But the tailor was more wily than the giant. He soon guessed that they meant him no good, and so he hid under the bed watching to see what might happen.

In the middle of the night the giant came along carrying an iron bar weighing two hundred pounds, and he struck the bed with all his might. "This time," he said to himself, "we have not missed; he must be dead."

The next day he went to see the tailor, to make sure.

"Would you like to come to lunch?" he shouted by way of being polite. But lo and behold, there was the tailor pulling himself up onto his backside in the middle of the bed.

"But how . . . !" said the giant. "But . . . how come! Didn't you hear anything last night? No noise?"

"Oh," said the other, "no, not much, a mere nothing."

The giant could not get over it. "There is no way of getting round this one!" he said.

The tailor did not seem to be worrying very much.

"Listen," said the giant. "Have something to eat and then be off. I do not want you as a friend any more. Go away from here."

You have to face it, you know. The tailor had won every time. Blow by blow, he had beaten the giants.

·5· *The Priest's Pig*

• ONCE UPON A TIME there was a poor family. They were very, very poor. The father had a whole tribe of children to feed, and he could not manage it. One day he said to himself, "What if I went and stole a pig from the priest?"

He had known that the priest had in his pigsty a big fat pig, ready for slaughter. He got hold of it without too much trouble, killed it noiselessly, and cut it into pieces.

The next day, the smallest boy was going off to the fields leading the only cow owned by his family.

He started to hum and sing as he walked along.

> Delicious that meat is, of the pig from the priest.
> T'was my father last night who stole the beast!

The priest happened to be coming along the same path on his way to church. He was quite surprised by these words and shouted, "What are you singing, little boy?" But the child did not want to say any more.

"Sing it again! Repeat what you said a moment ago!"

"Oh, no, I can't say that."

"Well, I am telling you. I want you to say it again, and good and loud!"

"Sir, I was only saying the truth."

"All right, so be it. As it is the truth, you will come to church on Sunday, and you will say it in front of everybody."

"Oh, sir, I shall not be able to go to church like this. I have got only old clothes . . ."

"Well, I will buy you a new suit. Don't fail to come and find me on Sunday before Mass."

And that day the priest gave the little boy some smart new clothes to go to church in. In the middle of Mass he announced to his parishioners who were gathered together, "Listen to this child. You are going to hear the truth." And to the little boy he said, "Here is the pulpit of truth. Climb into it instead of me and say in front of everybody what you were saying on the road the other day."

The small boy was not in the least embarrassed. He climbed into the pulpit and he said very loudly:

> The priest and my mother are lovers,
> And glory be to God, my father knows nothing about it.

The priest was furious. He kept protesting, "This is not true! That wasn't what you were saying."

"Yes, that's it. That's what I said!"

"No, it is not!" said the priest, as he gave him a kick in the backside.

"*Monsieur le recteur,* that's all I can say!"

And everybody started laughing with the small boy.

Part II
Upper Brittany

·6· *The Devil and His Three Daughters*

THE NARRATOR: "Do you remember how the tale about the Devil went? Me, I can't remember it!"

His wife: "Wasn't it about the Devil who had three daughters and about the youngest who used to take food to a lad who was working for her father?"

The narrator: "Lor' yes—lad who ate a bit every six months and drank a gulp every year."

His wife: "That's right. The Devil wanted to poison him! The meal that he was making his daughter take to the lad was poisoned, so she always said to him, 'Don't eat what I bring you. By the magic of my little wand, I will give you something else to eat.'"

The narrator: "That's how it was! But that is not all. The Devil gave this lad a skimmer to empty the pond with. How could you expect him to empty the pond! The Devil had said to him, 'You have from now till this evening to empty this pond. If you can't do it, you are to die.'

'How can I, with a skimmer?'

'You have got to do it or you will be killed.'"

The youngest daughter therefore led him to the edge of the pond. Once the girl had gone, the lad said, "I can't do this job. I am going to lie down and go to sleep."

Every day at noon the Devil sent his daughter to the lad with a meal, as was intended. The girl had said to him—to the lad that is, "Above all, don't touch the pond. I'll come and bring you something to eat."

The young man lay down on the grass hoping this would happen. Well, I would have done the same thing. Think of it— a skimmer, to empty a pond!

Noon came. The youngest daughter appeared with her basket. "You haven't done anything? I'll give you something to eat."

"But the pond has not been emptied."

"I'll see to that at once!"

The girl had a little wand. She struck it three times, saying,

"With the help of my little wand, let the pond dry up!" Lo and behold, the pond was dry in a flash.

But that evening it was the Devil's turn to be surprised. The Devil got to the place, and what did he see? The pond was dry. Did the Devil's mouth ever open wide! He went on looking around, but he could see only the lad. "So it must be he who did the job. Well, you are certainly more clever than I am!"

That lad had already surprised the Devil by not eating or drinking anything that the Devil had had brought to him in a basket by his daughter. "How do you do this?" said the devil. "You always send my daughter back with the basket full."

"Oh Lor', I eat once every six months and I take a gulp every year!"

There was the pond, quite dry. Well, the next day, there's the Devil saying something like this: "There's a copse of perhaps about seven acres. The tops must be made into faggots and the trunks grouped into cords by tonight."

So for the woodcutting the girl led him to the edge of the copse which was to be cut down. "Don't do a thing. I will bring you something to eat." (The meal the Devil had prepared was poison. She would not give it to him. She used to say to him, "You will eat what I give you." Each time she took the lad's meal back with her. The Devil could easily see that he was not eating it.)

With a wooden ax the Devil had given him, how could you expect the poor lad to cut down the copse? "Ah," he said, "if I die tonight, never mind, I'm going to lie down by the copse."

At noon she brought him a meal. The same thing happened. She took her wand and said, "With the help of my little wand, let there be something for him to eat and drink." And there was everything you could possibly want. Nothing was lacking, I can tell you.

The young man said, "What shall I do? Even if I had the tools, how could I cut down the whole of the copse by tonight?"

The Devil's daughter struck three times. "With the help of my little wand, let all this wood be cut, made into faggots, and measured out into cords."

When the Devil saw by evening that his copse had all been

cut down, he was beside himself with rage. "So you cut down the copse?!"

"I chopped it all down."

"Oh, this one is smarter than I am," the Devil said to himself.

Then at night when he went home the lad had other things to do but go to sleep. He had to look after the horses. Ah, good gracious! I remember what the Devil used to say to him.

"If you do not empty the hay from my barn to feed the horses, you are as good as dead!"

So the girl gave him tobacco to smoke so that the Devil would not find him asleep. Otherwise he would have killed him!

When the Devil reached the stables, there was nothing but smoke there. You see, the horses had eaten everything in the hay barn—there wasn't even any food in their mangers!

The Devil's daughter, with the help of her little wand, had emptied all the hay from the barn into the mangers, and the horses had eaten it all. And there was the lad smoking all night so's not to fall asleep!

On the third day, what was it now? Oh, yes, a magpie's nest had to be lifted out from the top of a tree which had no low branches. The Devil said to the lad, "There's a magpie's nest to be lifted out of that tall, tall tree. It's ever so tall, and if you don't get the job done, I'll kill you!"

The girl said to the lad, "This time you have got to kill me. You'll put my bones end to end, and you will make a ladder to climb the tree."

"No, I don't want to kill you. You've done so much for me."

"Well, if you don't want to kill me, then I'll kill myself. Remember carefully, though, how to place my bones. You will put them back when you've got the magpie's nest out. When you are down again, you will put back my bones bit by bit."

Well, there were the girl's bones, end to end, and this made a strong ladder to get to the top of the tree. So the lad lifted out the magpie's nest and then came down again. Then bit by bit he put the girl's bones together again, and she came back to life. "Oh," he said, "a little toe is missing." So there it was. He'd forgotten to put back one of her toes.

Then she said to him, "As you have done all the jobs my

father set you, listen to me. He will get you to marry me or one
of my sisters. He will ask, 'How would you like to choose—by
their heads or by their feet?' If you choose by the feet, you will
be able to recognize me."

When the Devil saw that the lad had lifted out the magpie's
nest, he could not get over it. "You're crafty, you are! Now that
you have done everything I asked of you, I'll give you one of
my daughters to marry."

The Devil led the lad into his daughters' room. They were all
three together in a big bed. It was dark. "Choose one. By the head
or the feet, just as you like!"

The lad said he would like to choose her by the feet. He felt
the feet of each one and found the foot with the missing toe.
"You fiend, you," said the Devil, "that's my best one you're
taking!" He was angry, but the deed was done. "Well, if that's
the one, we'll get you married."

So the boy and the girl stayed with the Devil a couple of days,
but the sisters were a bit jealous, so they left with the best horse
and carriage.

The Devil, when he saw what had happened, went after them.

When the girl saw that her father was going to catch up with
them, she changed the young man into a fountain and changed
herself into a frog (in the fountain).

The Devil went to the fountain. "Well, tell me, fountain,
have you seen a boy and girl going by here?" There was the
frog paddling about in the fountain. "Oh, so it's you who are a
fountain and my daughter a frog," said the Devil. But he could
not catch them. He went home and then started after them
again.

This time the girl turned the boy into a cherry tree and herself into a cherry on the tree. "Well, tell me, cherry tree, have
you seen a girl and boy go by here? So you are a cherry tree and
my daughter is a cherry," said the Devil, but he could do nothing
to them.

The third time that the Devil chased after them, the girl said,
"With the help of my little wand, let a river flow between my
father and me." And that time it was all over. The Devil could
not cross the river, and they were safe.

Now the boy wanted to go back to his part of the country. They left each other, and he went back to his parents. After all, she had said to him: "Go back and see your parents if you like, but don't forget that if you let yourself be kissed by anybody at all, you will forget everything that has happened to you. You will not even know that you are married anymore."

So, what happened? He went home. His mother wanted to kiss him, but he would not let her. An aunt whom he had not seen for a long time arrived, however, and threw her arms round his neck and kissed him. It was all over. He then no longer knew he was married.

One fine day he was with two other boys taking a walk. They met a girl by a Station of the Cross. "Lor', is she pretty!"

"You've never seen her?"

"I don't know her."

The three boys would all three have liked to get to know her better, but all three together were really too much. "Well, do we go over and see her anyway?"

They walked on a bit. "Well, what about going there on our walk?" Then they all got to the house where the girl lived. She gave them a good welcome, all three of them. Eight o'clock went by, nine o'clock, ten o'clock, eleven o'clock! . . . One of them said, "Boys, it's time we were going."

And then as they were about to go, she tapped one of them on the shoulder and said softly, "Don't you want to sleep with me?"

"Yes," he said.

But they went off all the same, all three of them.

A bit farther on, the third one said, "I don't know what's the matter with me. I feel I want to be sick. Go on ahead; I'll catch up with you." And he wheeled round to go back and find the pretty girl.

When he reached her house, she said to him, "Are you glad you have found me?"

"Yes," he said.

"Get undressed then." Then she said, "Oh, there's a bucket of water to fetch from the fountain."

"Well, it's not time we are short of," he said. And off he went, just in his shirt. So he got to the well and shoved the bucket in.

When he pulled it up, there wasn't any water in it. All night it was like that. He went down for water, and the bucket was always empty and there was daybreak coming.

"It really is a disgrace! A man who can't pull up a bucket of water! You don't deserve to spend the night with a woman."

"Oh, well, you will let me warm my feet up by the fire, won't you?"

"No," she said, "I wouldn't dream of it, a man like you."

A little later on, the three boys met once more. "Where did you go last night after you left us?"

"I had a stomachache." He did not tell them what had happened to him.

"You know, she is too good to miss."

The next day one of the other two boys said, "Do we go back tonight?"

"If we feel like it."

So off the three boys went to find her. The girl was pleased, too. Nine o'clock, ten o'clock, eleven o'clock, midnight! . . . "Oh, it's time to go to bed!"

The three boys were about to leave again when the girl tapped one of the other two on the shoulder and said to him, "Don't you want to come tonight?"

"Oh, yes," he said. He left with the other two, and a bit farther on he said, "I've got a stomachache. Go on ahead, and I'll catch up with you."

The first one said to himself, "If you're like me, don't fret."

Well, there was the second lad back with the girl.

"You're happy to sleep with me?"

"Yes."

"You won't have much to do," she said. "You've only got to close the doors before getting into bed."

"Can I undress first?"

"Suit yourself."

He had taken off his shirt, and so went out with his top bare. Whenever he managed to get one door closed, the other opened. He was still trying to close them when morning came.

"You can't even close a door," she said. "You couldn't sleep with a woman if you tried!"

And so there went that varmint.

Now, the third lad was the girl's husband. He didn't recognize her any more, but she recognized him.

The three lads did their day's work. "Oh, she's a lively girl when all's said and done. Let's go and see her again tonight."

The evening drew on. Ten o'clock, eleven o'clock, midnight . . . up to one o'clock in the morning.

"It's time to go to bed. Off with you!"

But this time she tapped on her husband's shoulder. She said to him, "Don't you want to sleep with me?"

"Yes," he said. "I'll take my friends a bit farther on, and then I'll come back."

He hadn't even gone two hundred meters when he said to them, *"Ça ne tourne pas rond là dedans!"* ("There's something fishy about all this.") The two others said to each other, "How did you get caught?"

"I was caught by being made to pull up a bucket all night."

"And I got caught having to close the two doors!"

So, what do you know, the third one went back to find the girl.

"You are quite happy about spending the night with me?"

"Yes."

"You won't have much to do. Just damp down the fire in the fireplace. You know how."

Well, the same thing happened! The more ash he piled on, the more the fire kindled. He spent all night looking after that fire.

The next day she said to him, "You can't even damp down a fire."

"Oh, but even so you let me warm up my feet!"

"Well, well," she said, "you don't recognize me!"

You see he'd been kissed by his aunt, so he didn't know he was married any more, but she did. She knew he was her husband.

There and then he recognized her and never left her ever again.

---

[1] Expression used in connection with a cart wheel turning unevenly.

·7· The Boy Whose Mother Wanted to Throw Him in Boiling Water

• HE WAS a wretched little lad whose mother could not bear him. One day she asked him, "Which would you prefer, to be cooked in boiling water or stabbed to death with a knife?"

The little lad saw he would rather be thrown into boiling water. However, while his mother was putting the water on to heat in a huge kettle, the boy ran away.

He ran and ran along the road to get away, far, far away. In the end he didn't know where he was anymore. At night he took shelter in a kind of grotto, and there he met a fairy. "I don't know where to go," he said. "My mother wanted to throw me into boiling water, so I left home.

"Go and ask at the castle over there whether they need a swineherd on their farm, and if ever you need me again you say, 'Come to me, little old woman, come to me!' and I shall come and help you."

The boy thanked her and then he got himself hired at the farm, where they just happened to need a swineherd. It was the King's farm.

Every day they sent the little lad to the heath. Sometimes he had to run after one pig and sometimes another, so much so that he got quite exhausted looking after them. Then he thought of the old woman's words and he called her, "Come to me, little old woman, come to me!"

"What do you want, little boy?"

"I cannot go on looking after the swine from now on, for I am tired out."

"I'll give you a coach to save you from getting tired running after the swine. Wherever your swine go, your coach will go, too, and all you have to do is remain sitting inside it." And the fairy made him a coach out of a turnip, and it was drawn by four white rats who had been harnessed.

The little lad was very pleased. Wherever his animals wandered, the coach was sure to follow.

The next thing was that he became fed up with always having to look after the swine. "Come to me little, old woman, come to me!"

"What do you want, little boy?"

"I don't want to look after the swine any more. I would rather look after the sheep."

"Well then, go back to the farm. They will put you in charge of the sheep, as you wish; and don't worry. Wherever the sheep go, your coach will go, too."

And off went the little lad to the heathland to look after the sheep. You should have seen how he used his turnip coach with the four white rats harnessed to it, and how fast it went.

But again he grew tired of looking after sheep. "Come to me, little old woman, come to me!" he said.

"What do you want, little boy?"

"I am tired of looking after the sheep. Now I would like to look after the turkeys."

"Well, then, don't worry and go back to the farm. Tomorrow they will put you in charge of the turkeys, and your coach will go wherever the turkeys go." He was lucky, wasn't he? But even then that was not enough for him.

One fine day he said again, "Come to me, little old woman, come to me!"

"What do you want, little boy?"

"I would like new clothes to put on and to walk about in when it is a fine day."

So the old fairy gave him three fine suits. One was colored like the sun, one colored like the moon, and one colored like the stars. The little boy, who had grown up a great deal, was very proud at the thought that he could go about dressed like that in his turnip coach drawn by four white rats.

The first day he put on his sun-colored suit and he climbed into his coach to go for a drive on the heathland. The King's daughter, who was at the window of her room, saw him dressed in his sun-colored suit and found him very pleasing.

The next day the little boy put on his moon-colored suit and again went off driving over the heathland in his coach. The King's daughter, who had been watching out for him since the day before, saw him again and could not believe her eyes, he was so magnificently dressed.

The third day it was time to put on his star-colored suit. It sparkled with gold. From her window the Princess saw the little boy go by. He was a young man now and he went by in his coach dressed in this way. She could not take her eye off him.

A few days later she saw a lovely glowing light on the heathland. She went and found him there, and he asked her to get into his coach.

From then on, it was like that nearly every day. He put on his fine clothes to be seen by her; she went to find his coach; and they went for walks together.

When her father, the King, heard about this he soon grew very angry. "You, my daughter, going with a turkey boy?"

"But I love him, Father, and I wish to marry him."

"Marry him, daughter? No, I will never agree to that."

The King had two other daughters who were already married, but to noblemen, and they were rich in the bargain. He, so help him, did not want a son-in-law of this sort. However, the young girl's two brothers-in-law kept saying jokingly, "Come on, turkey boy, you'll get there in good time!"

Some time later, as the King was getting old, he decided to make those who had claims to the throne draw for it, in order to hand it over to the winner of the contest.

Naturally his two sons-in-law were the first contenders. The test was to last three days in succession. The first to get to the goal with his horse would be the winner. But the young Princess said to the turkey boy: "There is an old mule in the stable. If you tried to mount it, perhaps you might win and then we could get married."

They went to the stable together. The mule was so old that he could no longer make her stand up on her feet to be ridden.

The young girl went on, "I know there is an old sword in the hearth. What if you took it? Perhaps it might come in useful to you." But when they saw the sword, it was too old and too rusty. So the young man said, "Come to me, little old woman, come to me!"

"What do you want, my little son of the King?" answered the fairy.

"A horse, a sword, let me have the lot, and by getting these, let me win the fight!"

The fairy gave him a horse and a sword and said to him, "Off you go, little King's son, by you the battle will be won!"

Three times the young man asked the fairy for the same things, and so the race was run three times on three successive days. All three times the young man won against the King's two sons-in-law. Sometimes he left half an hour after them, sometimes one hour, sometimes two. Each time he overtook them and got there before them.

The third time was the test which would decide who was to get the crown.

To their great disappointment, the two brothers-in-law were beaten, but they went and said to the young man, "If you want to live, you must agree to tell the King that it is we who won the fight, or else we shall kill you."

"I am not afraid of you," said the young man, "but I agree to let it be believed that you are the winners on condition that you give up to me the two orange apples that the first two daughters of the King gave to you when they chose each of you for a husband."

The two brothers-in-law gave up their orange apples to the young man. It was in this way that they sort of sold their wives so as not to seem to have lost the fight.

Shortly after, the King was rejoicing with his sons-in-law, saying, "I am so glad, children, that you won the contest."

Suddenly who should turn up before him but the turkey boy, who said, "Sire, you think that it was your two sons-in-law who won the contest, but ask them to show their orange apples they were given by their wives. They sold them to me."

The King had to find out about this from his sons-in-law. They could not deny it, as they did not have the orange apples anymore. So the turkey boy took from his pocket three orange apples.

"Sire, here are the two orange apples belonging to your eldest daughters. Your sons-in-law gave them up to me because I beat them in the contest. Now they have to give up all claims to the crown resulting from their marriage to your eldest daughters. And here is a third orange apple. Your youngest daughter has given it to me because she wishes me to be her husband."

The King was extremely angry with his sons-in-law, who had behaved as if they had sold their wives. After this he really had to choose the turkey boy as heir to the crown.

Thus the young Princess was able to marry him. Later they had a very fine castle built for them in which they then lived happily together.

.8. *The Seven-Headed Monster*

• ONCE UPON A TIME there was a small boy all crippled and hunched. His brothers could not bear him. In the end his parents said to him, "Go and earn your daily bread elsewhere! You are one too many here, and you can see that your brothers can no longer stomach you. Off with you!"

"No," said the small boy. "I do not want to leave the house until you have had a suit of thirty-six colors and a small white stick made for me."

His parents looked high and low before finding a suit of thirty-six colors. At last they found one, and they gave him the suit and the stick saying, "Off you go now and never come back here."

The poor little boy started walking and walking. On and on he went. He got himself hired at a farm, one of the King's farms, as a cowman.

One day as he was looking after the animals there, he let the little black cow go into a field belonging to the giants who had a castle in that neighborhood. This did not go by unnoticed. Before long the first of the giants appeared before him.

"What are you doing there, you wretch. You let your little black cow graze in my fields. Watch out or I shall punish you in no uncertain manner."

"Oh, you may well be a giant, but I am not afraid of you,"

said the little cowman. Thanks to his suit of thirty-six colors and his little white stick, he was afraid of nothing, for they were the secret of his strength.

The fight started, and when the giant was about to defeat him, the little cowman hit him with his stick and soon finished him off. "Oh," said the giant, feeling he was mortally wounded, "if I die, what will become of my black horse of which I am so fond?"

"Don't worry about your black horse. I'll look after it at the stable."

The next day he again let the little black cow eat the grass in the giant's field. The second giant appeared in a fury. "Wretched cowman, you have again allowed your black cow to steal my grass. Now you'll see how I'll deal with you."

The second giant was even stronger than the first, but the little cowman did the same as the day before. He put on his suit of thirty-six colors and hit the giant with his little white stick and the giant crumbled. Knowing the end was near, he shouted, "And my chestnut horse, of which I am so fond, who will look after it now?"

"Don't worry about your chestnut horse. I shall go into your stable and groom it."

The third day the cowman again let his little black cow graze in the giant's field, and so then appeared the third and strongest of the three giants.

"Oh, you unlucky little devil! You steal my grass every day and you have killed my two brothers, but you will not get me!"

The little cowman put on his suit of thirty-six colors and took his little white stick. Once more he gave a mortal wound, this time to the third giant. "Ah," shouted the last of the giants, "and what will happen to my white horse that I loved so much if I die now?"

"Do not worry about your white horse. I shall go and look after it at the castle stable," said the cowman.

There were no more giants. From then on, the little cowman spent half his time in the fields looking after the cows from the King's farm and the other half in the giant's stable, where he cared for the horses and had fun riding them. They were all three magnificent horses. They were very strong and could go anywhere, but the chestnut horse was stronger than the black horse, and the white horse was even stronger than the chestnut.

One fine day news spread throughout the district that the seven-headed monster, who every year demanded that a young girl be given to him, was soon going to come along and fetch her. Every year all the girls in the district drew lots to find out which one of them would be handed over. That year the King's daughter was the ill-fated one. Her father was most upset, but he could not save her from her fate. He was to lead her into the forest at nightfall in order to hand her over to the monster.

Then the cowman who was working on one of the King's farms appeared before him clothed in his suit of thirty-six colors, his white stick in his hand, and seated on a magnificent black horse. It was the one that belonged to the first giant. "Sire, I believe that I am strong enough to fight the seven-headed monster if you will allow me to accompany your daughter this evening."

The King did not recognize him, of course, and, seeing no other way open, he took this proud knight at his word. He put the Princess behind him on the saddle, and soon they reached the part of the forest where the seven-headed monster was supposed to come and take her. There the young man made the Princess get down, and he led her to a clearing. Then he stayed on his black horse to await the monster.

The monster arrived in a fury. Raising his seven heads in a menacing manner, he faced the young knight, but the latter's horse was so strong that he attacked the monster, and the youth, with his suit of thirty-six colors, feared nothing. He managed that evening, thanks to his white stick, to cut off two of the monster's heads. But that was all for that evening. The monster withdrew foaming at the mouth with rage. The youth took the two heads, cut out their tongues and wrapped them both in a handkerchief given to him by the Princess, who was overcome with gratitude.

The monster had agreed to meet him again the following evening. The youth, after having spent the day looking after the cows, this time took the chestnut horse from the giant's stable and appeared before the King in his suit of thirty-six colors. Once again he put the Princess in the saddle and left for the forest. The monster did not take long in coming to the scene of the fight.

This time was harder than the day before. The more heads the monster lost, the more difficult it became to cut off the remaining ones. But the chestnut horse was stronger than the black horse, and he attacked the monster even more fiercely than before.

At last the youth, with the help of his white stick, managed to knock off two more heads. "Tomorrow at the same time!" shouted the monster, who was even angrier than the day before.

The youth cut out the two tongues again, leaving the two heads on the ground. He brought the tongues to the Princess, who gave him yet another handkerchief in which he wrapped them.

The third day he went back to the farm to look after the cows, and that evening he went and fetched the girl from her father's house to take her to the forest to the monster's meeting place. This time he had taken the third giant's horse, the white one, the strongest of all. He intended to have done with the monster even though it still had three heads.

The monster arrived shortly after the young people and seemed to be particularly threatening during the fight, but the horse closed in on it so much that it could not stand up to the blows of the youth, who again managed to cut off two of its heads.

"Let there be a truce!" cried the monster.

"There shall be no truce," said the youth. "This is your last day to draw breath." Though he was exhausted by the previous fight, he at last managed to cut off its seventh head.

The monster was dead. The youth picked up the three tongues, threw back the last three heads, and came and found the Princess, who gave him yet another handkerchief to wrap the tongues in and threw her arms round him to kiss him. "You have saved my life," she said to him.

"Now I will take you back to your father," he said.

He lifted her into the saddle and led her to the castle. There, as soon as the Princess got down from the white horse, the youth ran off and took his horse back to the giant's stable. As the only remembrance of his victory, he took with him the monster's seven tongues wrapped in the King's daughter's handkerchiefs.

Dressed once more as a cowman, he took up his job at the stable in the evening and went back to looking after the cows in the fields during the day. But nevertheless he could not forget the black horse, or the chestnut horse, or the white horse. Not only did he groom them every day, but he also enjoyed himself riding them, jumping hedges with them, and he became a past master in the art of managing them.

One fine day, without putting on his suit of thirty-six colors, he had the idea of cantering round the King's castle on the black horse, and he also had fun crossing the gardens. He made no pretense of stopping but disappeared by leaping over a fence.

The next day he began all over again with the chestnut horse, and then with the white horse, and soon he would do his tricks every day in the King's courtyard, and nothing could be done to stop him.

The King had fences put up everywhere. These were fences so high that neither the black horse nor the chestnut horse was able to leap over them. But the young man came back with the white horse, and nothing would stop that one. He jumped over the highest fence and came to a halt in the King's courtyard in front of his castle. Quickly everybody surrounded him and made the youth dismount. He was soon recognized as being the cowman from one of the King's farms. But the youth had chosen that day for the Princess to recognize him.

It must be stated that all this time the King had tried in vain to have the man who saved his daughter found. As no one showed up, one of his gardeners had the idea of going to pick up the monster's seven heads which had been left in the forest. He took them to the King, saying, "It is I who killed the monster. Here are the heads."

But the King had his daughter brought to him, and the Princess said that the gardener was not the one who had saved her. From then on, she refused all the advances made to her by the noblemen of the court who hoped to marry her, saying always, "I will only marry the man who saved me."

So then the youth presented himself before the King and said to him, "It is I who killed the seven-headed monster, and as proof here are the seven tongues that I have kept wrapped in the handkerchiefs given to me by the Princess."

The King had the seven heads which the gardener fetched from the forest brought to him in the castle, and everyone could see that the tongues fitted exactly into their places in the seven heads.

Then it was the Princess's turn to be led before the youth, and she recognized him at once as her rescuer.

The King gave his daughter to the cowman to marry, as she liked him better than any of the others, and the wedding feast was to take place. But that afternoon he said to his wife, "I would like to go and see my old parents so that they can join a little in the festivities, as it is going to be my wedding day."

They took a carriage and they stopped at his parents' house. "Stay there and wait for me," her fiancé said to her, "I shall just pop in and say hello." Before going into the house, he slipped on his old clothes and appeared before his parents as a cowman. His father and mother and his brothers were not too happy to see him. Without telling them anything, he put his fingers into the dishes and started picking up bacon and potatoes without a fork, by the handful, as a tramp would do in one's house. His family was revolted to have him back. Oh, how he roared with laughter to find himself at home with his family in this way!

In the end he told them his story. "And as I am getting married to the King's daughter," he said, "I shall go and live in her father's house." He put his suit on again and took his fiancée in to see his parents. Everybody was really happy then. So both of them went off to the King's castle.

·9· *The Beast*

• ONCE UPON A TIME there was a Prince who was making a long journey. He met a fairy on his way. The fairy liked the Prince very much and asked whether she could marry him, but he would not agree to it, and so she changed him into a beast, saying, "You will always remain a beast until a woman agrees to marry you."

The Prince owned a castle, and he stayed on there, living mostly in the gardens. In the house there was always a well-laden table. Those who went into the castle found dinner all ready for them.

Now one day three girls happened to be walking around out there. The youngest, who was tired of squabbling with her two sisters, ran away and found herself opposite this gorgeous dwelling. She went in and saw a meal there all ready made. Seeing no one about, and as night was falling, she ate the dinner and stayed on in the castle.

One day she was strolling in the gardens when she heard sighs coming from a bush. She went nearer, and what did she see?—a beast who spoke to her in the following manner: "Do go on living in the castle, if you wish. All your meals will be served to you. Your housework will be done, and you will have nothing to worry about."

The girl accepted. Every day she strolled in the garden and saw the beast there. But one fine day, what did she hear once more?—the sighs and groans of an ailing beast about to die. She ran to him and said: "Oh my poor little beast. If you do not die, I shall marry you!" Hearing these words, the Prince stood up and took off his beast's skin. He was a handsome youth.

The young girl was so happy. They became engaged, but the Prince did not stay with her for long. "Now I must go and find my old parents," he said to her. "I'll soon be back. I give you my animal skin. Lock it up carefully in a wardrobe and be especially careful that no drop of water falls on it."

And so the Prince left. As for the young girl, she had a visit from her two sisters, who were filled with jealousy when they saw her so happy. As she had told them her story, they decided to destroy the beast's skin. The elder said to her junior, "Listen, go and fetch a basin of water, and we shall throw it on his beast's skin."

No sooner had they done this than the Prince came home. He was greatly dismayed. "What have you done? My skin is lost and I can no longer stay here. As for you, I cannot even take you with me, but you can live here in comfort as before. Your two sisters will stay here as doorjambs, so in that way you will have company after all."

But the young girl was absolutely determined to go with her betrothed, and she decided to follow him by hook or by crook.

As the Prince was getting ready to leave by carriage, he said to her also, "I am going to leave you three things to remember me by: a golden spinning wheel, a golden distaff, and a golden spindle. In that way, when you spin you will still be thinking of me."

The young girl began to cry. As he kissed her, she let three drops of blood from her finger fall onto his shirt saying, "No one except me will be able to get these three drops of blood off your shirt."

After this they parted. The Prince left in a carriage to go and see his old parents, and there he stayed. His father begged him to take a wife, but the youth would not hear of it. By going on and on about it, his father managed to overcome his opposition, and the Prince accepted his father's plan.

Meanwhile, the young girl had started off on foot to follow her betrothed, taking with her as tokens of his esteem her golden spinning wheel, her golden distaff, and her golden spindle. By walking like this she reached his father's farm looking all disheveled, and there she was hired as a turkey maid.

A few days later the Prince's wedding was supposed to take place. The girl knew about it. She had certainly recognized him even if he had not recognized her, and she tried to find a way of making herself known to him.

As she led her turkeys along, she went to find the washerwomen who were bleaching the house linen for the wedding. "Lord in Heaven!" one of the washerwomen was saying, "these spots can't be removed."

"No, I agree. There is no way of getting them out," said another.

The turkey maid stopped in front of them. "If you gave me that shirt, I could perhaps remove them."

One of the washerwomen laughingly started to object. "Do you really think that you who watch the turkeys know more than we do about washing clothes?" Another said, "Dear God! here is the shirt—you certainly can't do worse than we have done!"

I must tell you that the Prince wanted to wear that shirt and no other on his wedding day.

The turkey maid took it, rubbed it once, and then again before the spots disappeared.

When the maids returned the Prince's laundry he was amazed to see his shirt was without spots. "Who managed to take these spots out?" he asked.

"The turkey maid."

"Ah," thought he, "it must be she. I was not able to recognize her in her rags."

However, his wedding to the other girl had been arranged, and the wedding feast took place.

Yet the turkey girl had managed to get in to see the young bride, and she showed her the golden spindle on the evening of the wedding. "Oh, what a beautiful spindle! I have not had anything like it as a present."

"I'll give it to you if you like, on one condition, and that is that you let me go to your husband's bedroom to stay with him all night."

The young woman wanted the golden spindle so much that she agreed, but she, too, had some tricks up her sleeve. She gave the Prince *de l'ean d'endormie* (a sleeping draught) so that he slept all night long and the turkey girl was not able to talk to him. However much she kissed him, he would not wake up.

The next evening the same thing happened. One seeing the golden distaff, the young woman agreed to let the turkey girl go up to husband's room, but she had again given him a sleeping draught so that he did not wake until the following morning.

However, the castle maids had heard the sighs and the words the turkey girl let slip during the two nights she spent at the foot of the Prince's bed. They went and found the Prince and said to him, "Didn't you have another wife in the part of the country where you lived before?"

"No, but my betrothed was there whom I was to marry."

"Prince, for two nights now we have heard a woman moaning

in your room and calling you husband, yet you were never awakened by her cries. Did you drink something from a glass?"

"Yes, every night."

"Well, do not drink it tonight. She is sure to come, and you will be able to answer her."

The third night the turkey girl showed her golden spinning wheel to the young woman. Again the girl agreed to let her go up to the Prince's room, in exchange for the golden spinning wheel. But the Prince, taking the maids' advice, poured away the contents of the glass next to his bed. Trembling, the young girl said to herself, "Oh dear, this is the last night I can speak to him, and perhaps he will be asleep again."

But the Prince was not asleep this time. They recognized each other, and they talked together all night.

The next day the young man said to his father, "Father, I still have something to ask you."

"Then what is it you wish, my son?"

"Order a great meal to be made to which all the castle servants will come. I want my wife next to me on one side and on the other the turkey girl."

The father agreed to this odd idea, and that day the turkey girl put on her best dress to appear at the Prince's side. In the middle of the meal the Prince spoke to the host, "Father."

"What is it you wish there?"

"If you lost the keys to your castle, would you have more made?"

"Yes."

"But if you found the old keys, which worked far better than the new ones, which would you take?"

"Well, the old ones, of course!"

"Ah well, it's the same with women. I was betrothed to a girl in another part of the country, and now I have found her again. From now on, I wish to live with her."

And the Prince took the turkey girl with him.

· JOHN OF CALAIS' FATHER was a shipowner of some importance. He had ships, and he loaded them with cargo in order to go and sell the merchandise in other ports. Now this man's wife said to him (when John was still quite young), "Find a ship for your son so that he may learn to work."

The father would not hear of it. "No, John is too young. If I give him a ship and the goods, he will spend everything and eat everything there is in the hold."

The wife insisted, and in the end the father looked for a ship for his son and loaded it with cargo for him to sell. He said to him, "You will go to such and such a port. You will sell your goods, and as soon as you have sold them, you will unfurl your sails and go off again."

So John of Calais left on his ship, and he reached the port mentioned by his father. He sold all his goods, but after that he went ashore in spite of his father's forbidding him and went and strolled about on land. He had not been given permission to do it, but he did it anyway.

While walking, what did he find but a corpse which had been thrown onto a heap of manure. "How did this happen? Don't they bury people round here?"

They answered him, "When people have debts, they have to be paid off first and then the burial must be paid for."

"Oh, did he owe very much?"

Then the voices started to shout, "He owes me so much!"

"And he owes me so much!"

"And to me he owes even more!"

There were some yelling around the corpse, and there were perhaps some to whom the dead man owed nothing, but there they all were, some yelling louder than others.

John spent all his money paying off the dead man's debts and also for his burial. By the time he reached his parents, at midday, he had spent all the money he had received for his father's goods. His father was not proud of him!

So another day his mother said to her husband, "You ought to get your son another ship so that he can learn to live by the clock to earn his living."

His father did not want to, but in the end he gave in.

There was John off again with a ship and goods to sell. He had got right out to sea when he heard frightful screams. "Who goes there?"

They were girls who were screaming, "Want to buy some?"

"Yes, I'll buy quite a lot of girls, I will!"

So then two girls appeared on the bridge of the ship, and John took one as his wife and one as his cousin Isabella. (Those voices were those girls yelling for someone to set them free.) So John had again spent all his money to buy himself a wife and a cousin Isabella. (The wife—can't remember what her name was—this girl he'd picked up there was the King's daughter).

He went home. On seeing his parents, he said, "I spent all the money again, this time to buy myself a wife and a cousin Isabella.

John's parents were not at all pleased, so they gave John and his wife the pigsty to sleep in. And so they were married there and they had a little boy.

John's mother never stopped saying to her husband, "Now in spite of everything he has done, give your son another load and let him go and sell it."

There was John of Calais off to sea again. His father had said to him, "You will drop anchor in such and such a port without permission. You will not ask anything of anybody."

He left with his wife. When they reached the port his father had told him to go to, someone yelled, "You are not allowed to disembark here."

So John of Calais was forced to go on farther. He started up the river. Now on the ship there was not only his wife but a friend of his, Don Jean, who wanted him out of the way because of his wife. And so this Don Jean gave John of Calais a shove with his elbow and threw him into the river. He drifted out to the open sea and found himself hanging onto a large rock, where he stayed seven years eating nothing but shellfish.

Well, by the time seven years had gone by, the corpse had appeared once before him in ghost form on the rock, saying to

him, "You are not in love just now, but your wife is much more
in love than you. She is going to marry again tomorrow!"

"If she is more in love than I am, I am not surprised. Look
at me. I have been on this rock all the time—for seven years!"

"What are you doing there?"

"Well, you see I am awaiting death!"

"You did me a good turn by burying my body. It is my turn
to do something for you. If you like, I will take you where your
wife lives."

"Ah!"

"However," he said, "what would you give me if you wanted
to be taken where your wife lives?"

"That which I hold most dear in this world, but are you going
to be able to take me there?"

"If you give me what is most dear in the world to you, I will
take you to your wife's dwelling place."

"Well," he said, "I have a child . . ."

"If you give me half of it, I will take you to your wife's dwelling place."

And to think that his wife was getting married the next day!

So his wife was still on the ship with Don Jean. She could go
on until she was blue in the face saying, "What have you done,
Don Jean? You have thrown my husband into the river," but
Don Jean had threatened to kill her if she spoke of what he
had done. He had come back on board with John of Calais'
wife, and then she had gone to her father the King. Don Jean
would not leave her alone. He courted her, but she did not want
to have anything to do with him.

So in the end the King said, "As your John of Calais has fallen
into the river (she could not say more, for otherwise Don Jean
would have killed her), "you ought to marry Don Jean."

The wedding was nigh. The corpse carried John of Calais to
the King's castle. He carried him from the island where he was
marooned to the castle, and then he said to him, "You have only
to ask if the King needs a woodcutter."

But for seven years John of Calais had neither shaved nor
cut his hair, and it goes without saying that he was still wearing

the same shirt. As they reached the castle, the guard stopped them, saying, "Where are you off to, *guenillu* (ragbag)?"

"Let him through. The King has said so."

The wedding was to be the next day. There was wood to chop before the feast. So John of Calais tried to split the logs, but he hadn't the strength. For seven years all he had eaten was shellfish. While he was trying to split the logs, he saw his wife, the King's daughter. She could no longer recognize him. It was seven years since he had fallen into the river, but he of course recognized her.

Now he saw his wife going by in the courtyard, and for seven years he had kept the embroidered handkerchief she had given him. So in front of her he drew out the handkerchief, and she recognized it.

The King's daughter went upstairs and asked her father, "Daddy, John of Calais is downstairs splitting logs—"

"John of Calais! It is seven years now since he fell in the river! How can you mean him?"

"I tell you it is."

She went down into the courtyard again. He was still trying to split wood, but he was tired. He could not manage it, and so he mopped himself with the handkerchief. The King's daughter hesitated no longer. She went upstairs again to her father.

"I told you John of Calais is downstairs."

"Well, if it is he, tell him to come up to my room with an armful of wood."

The servants would not let him through. "Hey there, you *barbu, peillu guenillu* (hairy, lousy ragbag)! What are you doing there?"

"I am going up to get to the King's room."

"Eh, what's that you're saying?" But the order was given. "Since the King has said so, let him through!" On each step of the staircase there were guards who shouted: "Hey there, you hairy, lousy ragbag! What are you doing there?"

"Let him through! The King has asked that he go up to his room." John of Calais reached the top. He put his armful of wood in a corner of the King's room. He was about to leave without saying a word when the King said to him, "How is it that you are here?"

He pulled out the embroidered handkerchief that she had given him. She threw her arms about him, saying to her father, "This is my husband, John of Calais."

The father could not get over it.

"So then you fell into the river and you survived?"

The daughter said to him, "No, Daddy. It was Don Jean who pushed him into the river."

"How is it that you never told me?"

"I could not tell you. I was not allowed to; otherwise Don Jean would have killed me."

And there you had Don Jean getting ready to marry the King's daughter. The wedding took place, at least the wedding feast as it had already been made, but it was not for Don Jean. The King said to the stokers, "Heat the oven. Let Don Jean be put inside!"

And so they had the banquet. John of Calais was by his wife, but the ghost interrupted the middle of the meal. The ghost had certainly told him when he was on his rock, "I will be next to you during the wedding feast but I shall not eat. Don't let anyone bother about me!"

So in the middle of the meal the ghost appeared. John of Calais remembered that he had promised him half his child.

The ghost said to him, "What did you promise me, John of Calais? What was most dear to you in the whole world if I carried you back to your wife's dwelling place. Will you give him to me?"

John of Calais said, "Yes, I promised you what is most dear to me in the whole world. Well, here he is!"

Then he took his child. He put him with his head down and his two legs apart, and he took a huge knife in his hand and said to the ghost, "I promised you half my child. Take one leg, and I will take the other."

"No, you did me a good turn. I did you one. Do you remember the dead body which was in the heap of manure? You had it buried. Well, I have brought you to your wife's dwelling place, and I shall let you keep your child!"

• THERE WAS a poor young lad who was one of many children of a large family. The others had put his eyes out so that he would go and be a beggar and they could collect the money he was given. For a few years they lived like this, making him hold out his hat, and as people were sorry for the blind boy, they put something in the hat.

Soon as he grew older the others decided to get rid of him and lose him in the forest. So they took him into the woods, and there they left him. The poor young lad might well walk along feeling the trees as he went, saying, "Where are my brothers? I want to find my brothers again!" The trees of the forest were not his brothers, and he had to get used to the idea that he had been abandoned there all alone. So he climbed to the top of a tree and stayed there to spend the night under shelter.

Well, now, some giants—three giants—came and sat under this great tree to eat their dinner and enjoy each other's company in comfort. Soon the young lad, who was still sitting in the branches, wanted to pee. He did. It fell in the giants' dish. One of them exclaimed, "Oh, how good the Lord is! He sends us vinegar."

A little later the young lad wanted to shit, and he did. Again it fell in the giant's dish, and this time one of them said, "Oh, now the good Lord sends us mustard!"

When they had finished they saw the young lad and told him to come down. "What are you doing there?"

"My eyes have been put out, and I have been left all alone in the forest."

The giants were sorry for him, and each one decided to make a wish for him. The first giant said, "I would like you to see again." The second giant said, "And I wish that you should soon meet a mule on your way." And the third giant said, "As for me, I wish that you should then find a golden feather on your way."

"No No! Don't wish that on him," said the two other giants to their brother. "It will bring him too much unhappiness."

"Yes," said the third giant, "I make that wish all the same."

After that the three giants left the young lad in the forest. But now he could see, and, oh, how straight he walked! Soon, just as the second giant had wished, he met a mule on the road and he mounted her. That was much better than walking! Suddenly at the edge of the road he saw a gold feather. "Stop," he said to the mule. "I want to pick up this gold feather."

"No, no," said the mule, "why ask for more worries?"

"Yes, yes. I want to pick it up." Anyway the spell cast by the first giant forced him to pick it up.

Shortly after, he got to the door of the King's farm and he was hired as a cowman.

The King became friendly with the young lad—with Golden Feather, if you like. The people around the King—the peers of France, you know what I mean—were soon jealous of his presence at court and decided to harm him in every possible way.

The King wished to gain the farms of the Queen of a neighboring country whom he had kidnapped and kept in his castle without, however, managing to make himself liked by her. He often begged her to accept him as a husband, but she always refused.

One day as he persisted in his advances, the Queen said to him, "I will not marry you unless you have my own castle, which is still in my part of the country, brought here opposite your castle." This was quite impossible. "Oh, I cannot have it brought here," said the King, "but, if you wish, I can have one built just like it."

"No, no," said the Queen. "It's my castle I want, not one just like it." The King was very put out.

Making the most of these circumstances, Gold Feather's enemies said to him, "Sire, Gold Feather, who is a friend of yours, has said that he could bring the Queen's castle here."

The King had the young lad brought to him. "You have said that you are able to bring the Queen's castle here. You shall do this."

"Oh, Sire, I did not say that."

"You said it and you shall do it."

Gold Feather was very downcast. When he went and found his mule, she said to him: "Ask the King to give you four ships

loaded with bulls and cows and sheep, and you will take yourself
off with these ships to the giants' island. They have lusty ap-
petites. When they have eaten everything, they will give you a
hand in getting the Queen's castle onto the four ships, and you
will take it to the King."

The King had four ships full of cattle made ready for Gold
Feather, and the young lad soon reached the giants' island. You
should have seen how they swallowed all these animals that were
being landed on their island. In the end their leader said, "Stop!
We have eaten enough." High time, too, for there was nothing
left to throw to them but a quarter of beef!

"You have done us a good turn, for we were famished, and we
are ready to do you one like it."

"Well, then, carry the Queen of England's castle to my ships!"
said Gold Feather.

The giants immediately did as he asked, and soon the castle
sailed for home, placed on the four ships, and the King was
somewhat surprised to see it. Gold Feather had managed to
save his own skin, but as for the Queen, she was very sorry for
herself, for she still would have nothing to do with the King.

As he still pressed his suit, she said, "I will not marry until
the keys of my castle have been found. I threw them overboard
when you brought me as a prisoner to your land." The King
said, "But why, when it is impossible to find them again, and
it is so easy to have some made just like them?"

"No, no," said the Queen. "I want the keys that I threw into
the sea to be found."

So the peers of France, more and more jealous of Gold
Feather's success, decided once more to get rid of him. They
went to the King. "Sire, Gold Feather has said that he could
find the castle keys which the Queen let fall into the sea." The
King had him brought before him. "You said that you could
find the castle keys which the Queen let fall into the sea. You
shall do it."

"But, Sire, I never said anything of the sort." However much
Gold Feather went on protesting his innocence, he had to obey
the King. And so he went again to his mule. She said to him,
"Do just as I say and you will find the keys. Ask the King to

give you four ships loaded with bread, and you will go right out to sea. You will distribute it to all the fish, and one of them will bring you the keys." So off went Gold Feather with his four ships loaded with bread, and he started throwing the bread into the water, and then more bread, so much and so well that all the fish came and surrounded the ships. The King of the fish even started to round them up so that each one could have his share of the banquet, but when the roll call was over there was still one missing, a little fish who was gallivanting heaven knows where. At last he was seen, arriving long after the others.

"Ah, I have caught you, you little ne'er-do-well," said the King of the fish. "What were you doing gadding about in the sea when I called upon you all to rally?"

"Well, I have found a rather odd thingumajig on the sea bed. I tried to pick it up to carry it, but it was too heavy. I didn't succeed." (These were the keys to the Queen's castle.)

All the fish gathered around, and all together they lifted the keys and carried them to Gold Feather's ships as a way of thanking him for the bread which he had given them so generously.

Thus the young lad came back triumphantly, bringing the castle keys to the King. The King was very happy, but the Queen of England was most vexed and still refused to marry the King.

The peers of France, more jealous than ever, managed to persuade the King that the Queen of England had set her cap for Gold Feather, whose success had gilded him in her eyes. The King decided to have Gold Feather burned in a pile of faggots set up in the square.

The poor young lad, who was really afraid this time, went to see his mule again. "Don't worry," she said. "I will save you again. Do everything I tell you to do. You will go and fetch seven *aunes* [1] of worsted, and you will cut out of it a piece of fabric folded over seven times—that is to say, you will need a piece which is seven times the thickness of one piece of fabric. Then you will take this piece and put it on my back as a saddle, and you will mount me and make me walk until the first six

[1] The measure used here is *aunes*. One aune = 118.3 cm. = 46.5 inches.

folds are worn through. Then you will take the seventh cloth and wrap yourself up in it on the day they want to burn you in the middle of the faggots."

Gold Feather did what the mule advised him to do. He put the seven *aunes* of fabric on her back, mounted her, and made her walk and walk so much that he took pity on her because he was crushing her under him as she toiled on and on.

But the mule went ahead, saying, "Go on! Keep walking. Don't take any notice of my weariness, for the fabric must be worn down to the seventh fold." At last there was only the seventh thickness left.

This was on the day the King had decided to burn Gold Feather alive in the square. The faggots were already piled up there. Wrapping himself in the fabric, he put all his faith in the words of his mule. And soon the fire was lit, the flames consumed the wood, but the higher they reached and the nearer they got to him, the more handsome Gold Feather seemed, and not one of the flames hurt him.

The King was stunned to see him not only survive the flames but grow more handsome. Giving up all thought of killing him, he asked him how he had managed to escape the flames, which had even made him better-looking than any other living man; for the King wished to become even more handsome than Gold Feather to please the Queen of England.

Gold Feather said to him, "Sire, I did not use any extraordinary means. I simply wrapped myself in seven *aunes* of fabric that I soaked in water first in order to resist the flames at the stake."

The King said to himself, "I shall buy fourteen *aunes* of fabric, as I can afford it, and I shall then be even better protected, and I shall become twice as handsome as Gold Feather. Then I shall have no rival to fear for the Queen's favors."

The faggots which were going to be set fire to and which were intended to surround the King with flames were soon seen piling up in the square. And soon the burning took place. Though the King had soaked his fourteen *aunes* of fabric in water, the fire did not take long to dry the stuff, and the King was soon turned to ashes.

And so there was an end to the misfortunes of Gold Feather. The Queen of England was at last rid of the King, whom she had always rejected, and as Gold Feather had become the most handsome man alive, it was he who married the Queen.

•*12* • *The Orange Tree*

• ONCE UPON A TIME there was a lord, a Marquis, who had three sons. In their garden there was an orange tree all covered with oranges. There came a time when, every morning as the Marquis was doing his round of the garden, he noticed that an orange had been pilfered.

Day by day and one by one the orange tree was losing all its oranges. "Soon there will be none left," said the Marquis to his sons. "One of you should go and keep guard at night at the foot of the orange tree so as to catch the thief."

The first evening the eldest went, but although he kept watch all around him, the night wore on without his seeing anyone coming. In the end he got tired of waiting and went home without having found out anything.

The next evening it was the second son's turn to go and watch, but he also became bored and went home to bed without having caught the thief.

The third day it was the youngest son's turn. He went off to the garden with a pack of cards, quite determined to spend the whole night at the foot of the orange tree and to play cards to while away the time while waiting for the thief.

He had played several card games all by himself when, in the middle of the night, he heard a rustling in the branches and he saw a bird. "Ah, there's the one who steals our oranges!" He immediately aimed at it with his gun, but the bird started to talk to him. "Don't kill me," it said. "If you like, we will play cards together." The bird then took on his human form again.

He played several games of cards with the young man, and then he said to him, "We'll bet like this, if you like. If you win, I will make you a castle all of ivory, and if it is I who win, you will come and join me without fail where I live."

The young man accepted the challenge. At the first go it was he who won. "You shall have your ivory castle," said the bird. "And now let's have another go." The second go was won by the bird. "Goodbye," he said to him. "I am counting on your coming to find me where I live. Ask everyone for the road that leads to the Bird King, and they will show it to you. You can bank on seeing the ivory castle rise in front of your house."

In fact, as soon as he awoke the next day, the young man could see that an ivory castle was rising opposite his home. So, as the bird had kept his promise, the youth really was obliged to keep his.

He set off, and wherever he asked for the way to the Bird King, he was answered, "Oh, you poor soul, don't go there. No one who has gone there has ever come back!" Anyway, in spite of everything, he went on walking. Soon he met a poor old woman who really looked most wretched. "Here, my poor old soul," he said, "here are two pennies. I can't bear to see you so wretched."

"Thank you, my lad," she said to him. "Good luck to you on your way but—where are you going?"

"I am going to the Bird King."

"It is here," said the old crone, "and I'll show you how to go about getting the upper hand with him. You'll see that near here there is a pond, and the King's three daughters just happen to be swimming there now. Creep closer to them, but very quietly. They have left their three girdles on the bank. There are two blue ones. Don't take them, but take the one that is green. It belongs to his youngest daughter, and it is she who will rescue you from her father. But listen carefully. You will take the boat which seems to have the largest hole in the bottom by the pond and you will row toward the three girls. They will be surprised to see you, and the one who sees her green girdle in your hands will claim it from you. Don't give it back to her before she has promised to be faithful to you. When she has sworn it, you will be sure of her and you can give it back to her. From then on, it will be her job to advise you on how to escape from her father."

The young man thanked the old crone and obeyed her to the letter. When he had taken the boat and rowed toward the three girls, showing the green girdle, one of them came toward him. "That's my belt. Give it back to me."

"Not until you have promised to be faithful," answered the young man. The girl was obliged then to swear she would be faithful. Then he gave the green girdle back to her. After she had come out of the pond, she took her things and accompanied the young man up to her father's house. "I am going to give you a piece of advice," she said to him. "My father is a very demanding man, and you'll have to put up a good fight if you want to gain the upper hand with him. When you go into his house, he will offer you bread saying, 'Be first to cut the loaf.' You will answer, 'In my part of the world it is the custom for the host to cut the bread first.' "

The young man took her advice. The old woman who was the wife of the host said to her husband, "You will have your work cut out with that one!" The host hired the young man anyway to work for him.

The next morning he led the young man into a grove and said: "You see this? It must all be cut down and made into faggots by seven o'clock tonight." And all he left him as a tool was an axe made of glass. The poor lad was very discouraged. How could he cut down a forest in one day with a glass ax? He broke his ax at the first blow, and so he sat under a tree feeling very despondent.

At noon the youngest of the King's daughters came to him with his dinner. "Well," she said to him, "aren't you doing anything?"

"What do you want me to do? I broke the ax your father gave me as soon as I started."

"Here," said the girl, "take this little knife. You will stick it into the largest tree you can find in all the forest and you will say, 'Through the magic of my little knife, let the whole forest be cut down and made into faggots by seven o'clock this evening.' " And she left him there.

The young man did what the girl had told him to do, and

that evening all his work was completed. When his boss came to see him, he could not get over it. When he told his wife about this, she said: "Ah! There you are! We haven't seen the last of him!"

The next day the boss said to his hired hand, "You see that bank over there? Well, it must be completely flattened and leveled by seven o'clock this evening." He gave the lad a pick made of glass. The youth did try hard to hack at the bank, but a glass pick, as you know, is easily broken. There he was, discouraged once again, and he sat by the bank not doing anything more.

At noon the girl arrived with his dinner. "Well," she said to him, "that's your job, is it. Don't worry. I know what my father has given you to do. Take this little shovel and dig it into the bank and say, 'With the help of my little shovel, let the whole bank be brought down and leveled by seven o'clock this evening.'" The same thing happened as the day before.

The boss no longer knew how to deal with this lad. It was all becoming more and more peculiar. His wife again said, "That workman is going to be hard to keep!"

The next day the King said to his workman, "I would like all the grains of sand on the sea bed counted, to know how many there are of each size, whether small, medium, or large." The poor lad kept asking himself what he was going to do, but the girl had not forgotten him. As she brought him his dinner, she said to him, "I shall give you a bowl [*roquille*] to empty the sea and sort out the grains of sand by size and to count how many there are of each size. You will simply say, 'With the help of my little bowl, let the sea be emptied, and let all the grains of sand that are therein be sorted and counted.' But be very careful to remember the number of grains of sand, whether small, medium, or large, that there are in the sea while the sea is emptied, for when it is full again it will be too late to find out."

Step by step the young man followed the girl's instructions. By evening the whole job was finished and he was able to tell his boss how many grains of sand there were of each size in the sea.

The boss was more than a little surprised!

"I'll tell you, you haven't seen the last of that one," his wife said to him.

The next day the boss led his workman to the foot of a glass mountain and said to him, "You must go and fetch three crow's eggs which are at the top of this glass mountain." He gave him a paper ladder. The poor lad was not able to climb very high with his paper ladder! He sat at the foot of the mountain feeling even more dejected than he had been on the other days.

This time the girl was at her window and she saw a crow fly by her. "Come this way, crow, and listen to me. You go off and fetch the three eggs you put on top of the glass mountain and give them to the one you find crying at the bottom of the mountain."

This was done.

"Aha," said the boss's wife, "I told you you would have trouble with that workman." The boss did not know how to get rid of such a man, and he tried to find some task he could still make him do.

The next day he said to the young man, "We are both going to have a drink, and we shall see who can drink the most without falling down drunk."

The girl again came to the rescue of her father's workman.

"Listen carefully," she said to him. "It takes three barrels of wine to get my father drunk. Be very careful, because he will pour you as much as he'll pour for himself. For each glass he fills for himself, he will fill yours, too. You will accept—this goes without saying—but you must not drink. When he takes a glassful, take one, too. Empty it into a flask that you'll have hidden in your ruffle, and while he's getting drunk, you will throw away the contents of the flask."

And so this took place. The barrels of wine were soon emptied, and the father fell down drunk. Then the young man went to find the girl to tell her. "Your father has now drunk the lot, and he has just fallen asleep."

"Let us leave together while my father is asleep," she said. "We will make the most of his slumbers to get away, for I know his plans against you. You will reach the stable. There are three horses there, Little Wind, Medium Wind, and Great

Wind. You will take the one who looks most worn out, and we shall ride on it."

The young man went to the stable. He saw the three horses, but one of them looked so tired out that he could not make up his mind to take him, and so he took the second one, who looked less tired.

The King's daughter arrived and said, "I'll mount the horse first. You get on behind." They left immediately. "What have you done!" said the girl. "You have taken Medium Wind. Now we are done for, as Daddy will rush after us, and he will take Great Wind." A few seconds later she said to the young man, "Don't you hear him coming?"

"I see a cloud of dust rising."

"It is he," she said. "And now let the horse turn into a mill, you into a mill's sails, and I shall be the miller."

The boss soon arrived on Great Wind, and he found the mill in front of him. The sails were turning so fast he could, however, find no way of approaching it. Furious, as he had by now lost all trace of the fugitives, he went back home and told his wife of his failure.

She said to him, "But haven't you understood? The mill was the horse, the sail was your workman, and the miller was your daughter." So off went the boss chasing them once more. But the mill was no longer there.

The young people had mounted Medium Wind again, and he was going full speed ahead. However, they heard something like a storm brewing behind them. It was Great Wind at their heels. So the girl said, "Let the horse become a chapel, you the altar, and I shall say Mass."

And then along came the boss, and he stopped in front of the chapel. "Haven't you seen anybody?"

"Amen," said the priest without turning round. That is all the boss could find out. Once home again he told his wife of his adventure.

"But you don't understand. The chapel was the horse, the altar was your hired hand, and the priest was your daughter."

This time the boss decided to take his wife with him, and both of them threw themselves into the chase after the young people.

When they saw them, they made a kind of barrier in front of them, an enormous fire, which was gaining in their direction. So the girl said, "Let the horse become a pond, and you shall be a drake, and I shall be a duck. But be very careful. When Mummy and Daddy reach the edge of the pond, they will have fun throwing us bread crumbs in order to trap us. Above all, don't eat any!"

There they both were, changed into duck and drake, on the pond. On seeing this, the people stopped making their fire and came to a halt at the edge of the pond. The old woman began to crumble bread to attract them, and the drake was tempted to catch it, but each time the duck stopped him by pecking [*pigossait*] at him.

In the end the old woman said to the old man, "Jump into the pond and catch him!"

"Oh, no, I would drown." And he wouldn't jump into the pond.

"Well, that's that," said the old woman. "You've lost your daughter now."

So the two young people were then free, and they went to the youth's parents' home. But soon the girl said to him, "I am leaving you to go and save my father, because otherwise he will be damned forever. You must be very careful that your parents do not kiss you, as then you shall remember nothing at all."

The young man was very careful about allowing anybody to approach him, but during the night his parents kissed him. When he woke up, he could not remember a thing, and when the girl came back he did not recognize her.

Now wasn't she clever! It was she who kissed him, and then they both recognized each other. After all this they were married, and they lived in the ivory castle which the youth had earned.

I was at their wedding feast. They gave me a piece of bread, butter and jam, and a kick in the arse, and after that I left.

·13· *March and April*

• ONCE UPON A TIME there were two brothers. The elder one was called March, and the younger one was called April. As they could no longer live with their old father, one of them had to get himself hired out on a farm. "Don't leave. You're too hotheaded," said April to his elder brother. "You will never stay with your master."

"It is my duty to leave," said March, "as I am the elder one." He went to work on a farm. The gentleman promised him three hundred francs a year as wages. That was good pay at the time. March was pleased. "Ah," said the boss," I must tell you something else. Here I hire my workers in this fashion. Whoever gets angry first, whether man or master, will have a strip of skin torn from his back by the other."

Anyway, that was what was said.

The next day the farm owner sent March to scythe the furze on the heath. When the lad reached the place, he began scything. As he went on and on working he became fed up with it, but there was not much chance of a rest. Every time he stood up, the dog from the farm went for him and bit him. Well, March was not very patient. In the end he left his work and went back to the farm in a fit of temper. "Boss, I cannot work under these conditions. Your dog keeps on trying to bite me!"

"And so you are angry?"

"Yes."

So, as was agreed, the boss tore from him a strip of skin. Much saddened, poor March went back to his brother.

"Ah, I knew you would not stay there long," said April on seeing him. "It is my turn. This time I'll go, and we shall see what happens."

"Listen," said March, and he told him about the business he had had with the farm owner.

"All right. You've told me all about it. I am going to your boss," said April, "and this won't happen again."

The farm owner imposed the same conditions on April, who accepted them.

The next day he was also sent out to scythe the heath, and the farm dog was with him. April worked all morning, and then the dog lay down to sleep. April then took advantage of this opportunity and cut his head off with his scythe.

At noon the hired man went back to the farm to have his dinner. The farm owner was very surprised to see him come back without the dog. "Hey, you have not brought back my dog!"

"Why should I bring back a mad dog? He bites everybody. I cut his head off with my scythe."

"What do you mean? You killed my dog?"

"Oh, are you angry?"

"No, I am not."

The next morning the fields were under heavy dew. The farm owner said, "You will take the mare out to graze in the field without disturbing the dew or knocking down the gate."

April went off with his ax on his shoulder, and he climbed onto the mare and cut off her head. Then he began chopping up the carcass and throwing the pieces into the field.

At noon the farm owner questioned him. "Have you done what I asked you to do?"

"Yes, don't worry. She will not be too glutted with grass to-night." The farm owner went and had a look. "What have you done, you wretch!"

"Well, you forbade me to disturb the dew and to open the gate, so I had to cut your mare to pieces to send her into the field."

The farm owner controlled his temper, because he was afraid of having a strip of skin torn from him.

The next day he said to his hired hand, "You will take the swine to the fair. You will drive them before you on the road. Later I will join you at the fair."

Now, on the way April met a swine dealer.

"Do you want some pigs to sell?" suggested April.

"If you like. Yes, certainly I would."

"Well, then, all right. I shall keep the tail of each one, and I shall keep the smallest pig as well. Look, you'll see. We shall bury him in the bog over there."

April sold the pigs, stuck all the tails in the mud, and he buried the smallest pig so that none of it was sticking out, but he made certain where it was.

Now then the farm owner came along the road. He was looking everywhere to see where his pigs could have got to. "Where are the pigs?" he cried.

"How do you expect me to herd them along? They are covered in mud. You see, only their tails are left."

The farm owner began to tug at the first tail. He pulled it up like a blade of grass. "Well, that's funny," he said.

"Then come here," shouted his hired hand; "the little pig is here, but I cannot catch hold of him." The farm owner raced up to him and helped him to free the only pig which was buried.

In the end he was red with anger. "You will ruin me, you will," he said.

"Are you angry?"

"No, no."

Sunday morning came. "As you killed my mare," said the farm owner, "you will carry us to Mass, my wife and me, on your back."

"Oh, well, we'll find a way. You will each sit in a basket, your wife in the front and you behind."

The hired hand started on his journey. As it was a long one, he got fed up with it. He stopped to kiss the woman in the basket.

"Oh, you wretch," shouted the farm owner, "you dare to kiss my wife?"

"Are you angry, boss?"

This made the farm owner well and truly angry, and he jumped out of the rear basket.

"If you are angry," said April, "give me my hundred francs, and I will tear a strip of skin from your back."

He got what he wanted, even the master's strip of skin. Then, later, he joined his brother.

Part III
Pays de Retz

.14. The Tale of La Ramée

• THERE WAS A KING with a daughter (I don't know her name.) He had a daughter, and she had never laughed in her life.

So the King said, "If a woman makes her laugh, I will give her a reward. If it is a man, I will get him to marry my daughter."

Now there was an old man called La Ramée who used to tramp across the fields with his bag on his back, earning a living as best he could.

One day he found a mouse.

"Where are you going, mouse?"

"I am going this way to make a life for myself."

"Climb into my bag. You'll come in useful. There is bread in there, and you can eat some of it."

So the mouse climbed into his bag.

After this he went a little farther and came across a small cricket, you know, the kind that goes "Cri-cri-cri." The old man said to him, "Cricket, where are you going?"

"I am going this way to make a life for myself."

"Jump into my bag. You'll come in useful."

So he went farther on, and he came across a beetle, you know, one of those little beetles you place on a stone saying (as you spit on your palm): "St. John's beetle, I give you white wine! You give me red."

"Where are you going, beetle?"

"I am going this way to make a life for myself."

"Jump into my bag. You'll come in useful."

Off he went with his three little creatures in his bag. He reached the King's door. In order to get his daughter to laugh, the King had lots of people trying all sorts of ways, such as putting little men up one way and then knocking them over the other way. They did all sorts of tricks. Suddenly La Ramée picked up his three little creatures in his hand and presented them to the King's daughter, whereupon she roared with laughter. "Oh, what pretty little creatures, all three of them!"

So, upon my soul, that was that. La Ramée was a poor old

codger, and it was not exactly an easy situation, as the King had promised to give his daughter to the first man who would make her laugh.

The others did not want it to happen. Then the King said, "Never will I have those two get married."

Now, there happened to be a huge elephant about. It was a fierce animal. Everybody said, "Give the old codger to him to eat, and we will marry the Princess to a handsome gentleman. (The King's daughter said nothing. She was not taking part in any of this.)

So they put the old codger La Ramée together with the elephant. But he popped the little cricket into the animal's ear, and it went, "Ti-ti-ti" in the elephant's ear and sent him to sleep.

So the others, they married the King's daughter to a handsome gentleman. Lord, I should say he was! When La Ramée saw what had happened, he took the beetle and shoved it up the gentleman's arse on the Princess's wedding night. Then the beetle (you know jolly well where it goes) scratched so much that the bed became all covered with diarrhea. The gentleman was unwell all night long. At the same time, the little mouse went and fed the cricket and the beetle where La Ramée had put them.

The King's daughter no longer wanted to be with the handsome gentleman, and as his discomfort went on for so long, they had to go and find La Ramée in order that he should take back his three little creatures.

What could be done with La Ramée? They had to let him marry the Princess. Then they put the handsome gentleman with the fierce animal, and this time the cricket didn't go, "Ti-ti-ti" to send the animal to sleep, so the elephant ate the handsome gentleman, and La Ramée married the King's daughter.

Part IV
Lower Poitou

·15· *The Goat Who Lied*

• ONCE UPON A TIME there was a man who used to send his little boy out every day with his goat so that she should graze. He had to take her grazing by Bois-Breton.

Every morning the little beggar used to leave with the goat, and he led her along, saying:

> Graze, my goat, graze
> By the Bois-Breton.
> Eat up the thistles,
> And when you're quite full up,
> You'll have milk
> For your little kid.

But this little goat would not behave herself. She refused to graze when the little beggar led her. In the evening when the little beggar came home to his father's house with his goat, she hadn't any milk.

"What have you done?" his father asked the little beggar.

"I really did take her to graze, and I really did say to her:

> Graze, my goat, graze
> By the Bois-Breton.
> Eat up the thistles,
> And when you're quite full up,
> You'll have milk
> For your little kid.

"Well done, my little beggar. That is just what you had to say to that goat."

The next day the little beggar led his goat to Bois-Breton to graze and said once more:

> Graze my goat graze, etc. . . ."

However, that naughty goat would not eat thistles. When she came back that night to suckle her little kid, her master asked her:

> Have you good milk
> In your udder
> To feed your little kid?

The father was very surprised. "Where did you take her?" he asked his little boy.

"I really did take her to Bois-Breton," answered the little beggar.

Oh dear! that goat just would not eat thistles. After a while, the goat's master was angry when he saw she had no milk, at least that she had barely enough to let her kid suckle even a little. What did he do? He broke the goat's leg and left her all alone in the Bois-Breton with her broken leg. The goat stayed there. She made herself a nook, or, better still, a little shelter, if you prefer to call it that, and then she would go and graze wherever she felt like. However, she had to go to the bonesetter to have her leg seen to. She carefully told her little kid:

> I'm off to St. Jacques
> To set my leg,
> To set my hammy ham.
> When I come back,
> I'll show you my white paw.

The goat went off to see the bonesetter, but a wolf who had heard her go, went into the goat's shelter and managed to slip his paw under the door, saying:

> I'm off to St. Jacques
> To set my leg,
> To set my hammy ham.
> When I come back,
> I'll show you my white paw.

The little kid answered, "You have a black paw. You are not my mother."

So the wolf went away and dipped his paw in flour to whiten it. This time when the little kid saw the white paw, well of course he opened the door of the shelter. Thereupon the wolf leaped on the kid and ate it. Then he went to sleep right there. When the goat came back after having had her leg set, she said at the door:

> I've come back from St. Jacques,
> Where I had my leg set,
> Where I had my hammy ham set;
> When I come back,
> I'll show you my white paw.

In the end the goat pushed open the door and went in. Alack! She saw that the wolf had eaten her kid. So she put a kettle of water to boil on the fire, saying:

> Boil, boil kettle mine,
> So that I may scald my wolf!

When the wolf woke up, the water was hot. The goat unhooked the kettle from the pot hook and placed it on the floor. Then the wolf said to the goat, "Will you jump over this kettle of water?"

The goat answered, "Where I come from, it is not the women who jump first." So the wolf was the first to jump over the kettle, but as he was made heavy by the kid being in his belly, he missed and fell into the kettle and was scalded to death.

· 16 · *Boudin-Boudine*

• ONCE UPON A TIME there was a little boy. His father and mother had killed a sow. The mother had sent the child out to take some black pudding and *fristure* (pork stew) to some of their neighbors, and then he was to go on to his grandmother's.

The little beggar left with his basket on his back. This was a basket in which his mother had put black puddings and pork stew. First he went to their neighbor, saying:

> Good day to you, my neighbor and your wife,
> I bring to you some black puddings-puddeous
> From our sow Courtine
> And a little bone from a trotter.
> But if you do not want it,
> I shall take it back.

The neighbor accepted it, as you can well imagine! And so off went the boy to his grandmother's, but it wasn't exactly next door. He had to go this way and that. His mother had said, "Make quite sure that you go by the Grand Veurdé so as not to fall in the ditch."

Now it so happened that the child was followed by a wolf, who asked him what he was carrying. "I am going to my grandmother's to take her some black puddings."

"Which way are you going?"

"I'll take the path through the woods."

The wolf went through the woods the shortest way possible, that is to say, by the short cut, in order to be the first to get there, and then he waited for the child.

When the little lad reached the old woman, he shouted through the door:

> Good morning, grandmother, godmother.
> I have brought you black puddings-puddeous
> From our sow Courtine,
> And a little bone from a trotter.
> But if you do not want it,
> I shall take it back.

The grandmother, however, was not listening.

"Knock! Knock! Open up, Granny. It's your grandson bringing you black puddings."

"Show your white paw."

The child slipped his little hand through the peephole in the door, and then the old woman said, "Draw the wooden bolt, and then the latch will fall."

Oh, what enormous white teeth that wolf had! He was all ready to catch the little beggar by the calves. And do you know he had great big ears that stood straight up!

"Open up as quickly as you can, Granny, because the wolf is right next to me!"

"You mustn't be afraid, boy. The door will be open for you before the wolf reaches it."

At last the boy drew the bolt and let fall the latch.

So the wolf hid near the door and waited until the little beggar had gone in.

Then it was his turn to knock on the door.

"Knock! Knock!"

"Don't open the door, Granny. It's the wolf."

"Where did you pick him up?"

"At the corner of Bois-Bené. That's where he caught up with me. He asked me where you lived, so I told him."

Now the grandmother was better-hinged than the little lad. As the wolf was knocking at the door, knock, knock, she answered, "Show your white paw!"

The wolf slipped his paw through the peephole. But the wolf showed her a black paw, and the old woman did not open the door. The wolf went away. He then dipped his paw in a dish of *bouillie bordelaise* (white semolina), which had been placed outside to cool, and he even upset the dish. Anyway, he buried his paw in it and went back to show it through the peephole.

The grandmother was still not very sure. Supposing it was the wolf? As she stood there wringing her bonnet in her hands, while the wolf waited, her grandson said to her: "Granny, you're afraid. You are wringing your bonnet." The old woman looked through the peephole, and then she saw the porridge on the ground.

> That's pork stew which has spilled.
> Then the wolf has lapped it up.
> I'll take up my broom.

The wolf was near the door. The old girl closed the door behind her and went after the wolf with a broom. She sent him flying, whisking him away with her broom.

After all that the little beggar was really very frightened and he did not want to go back to his parents. He was hiding in his grandmother's petticoats. Meanwhile his parents found that it was all taking a very long time and that their boy was still not back. The father went off to the grandmother's house, but he stumbled in the ruts on the road to Bas-Galioux, where they lived, and he fell down.

Well, the little lad had left his grandmother's to go home, hoping to reach it before nightfall, and the wolf made him run fast. But the boy met his father on the way, and they went back together. Then the father took a cleft stick, hit the wolf with it, and killed him.

They made a coat for the boy out of the wolf skin, and he was so happy after all that to have that wolf skin on his back. Lord, he had been so terribly frightened when he was taking his Granny those black puddings-puddeous!

·*17*· *The Iron Pot*

• ONCE THERE WAS a fairy who put a girl in an iron pot. Would you believe it! In an iron pot! So there the girl was, shut up in an iron pot under a rosebush.

Along came a gentleman out hunting with his dog. He saw the castle where the fairy lived and went in, hoping to be able to ask for food and drink. However, this house was somewhat unusual.

The gentleman met an eagle there. It was a great big bird. What on earth was it? Then he said to himself, "What shall I do?" The eagle said he liked him and that he would become the gentleman's master. Then the eagle went on to say, "In this castle lives a fairy who has shut a girl up in an iron pot." (The eagle must surely have been a man changed by magic. Perhaps he was a relative of the girl's whom the fairy had turned into an eagle.)

The gentleman found the fairy. When she saw how things stood, she said, "You've got work to do. There's a girl to set free."

By trying again and again, he finally set her free, but it took all of a month. The girl was buried under the earth, and she appeared only between eleven in the morning and noon, so the gentleman had to work hard during that hour to see her and set her free.

The fairy had said to him, "If you set her free, you will have won her and you may even marry her."

The gentleman had a little dog who went hunting with him every day. One day he met a woman on the road (I suppose it was the Blessed Virgin), and she said to him, "Would you like me to give your little dog a piece of bread?"

"Yes."

"Be on your way. Wherever you go, luck will follow!"

So luck followed him, and he rid the girl of the iron pot where she was imprisoned. He worked and worked every day between eleven and twelve to set her free. During the last days she could talk to him a little. Lor', when he began to work to set her free she was so far underground! To lift the girl up and the dog and the gentleman was the eagle's job. He said, "I'll lift all three of you, but you must feed me; otherwise, I'll never have the strength to reach the top."

The gentleman went hunting with his little dog. He killed some animals to feed to the eagle, and the first time the girl was lifted up to the top. The second time it was the little dog's turn to be lifted. But the third time the gentleman was still down there. The eagle said to him, "Go out hunting and kill some bulls and some sheep to feed me." The gentleman killed these animals and fed them to the eagle. The eagle then lifted him up. When he reached daylight, he said to the gentleman, "I'm all in. I'm going to let you drop." The eagle dropped him, but the gentleman had a box with all the necessary ointments in it, and he rubbed himself and recovered from his fall.

The next day he went back to his hunting and he killed animals to feed the eagle. That time the eagle lifted him to the top.

The girl and the little dog were waiting for him in the castle. They stayed there together, and the gentleman married the girl whom he had freed from the iron pot.

.18. The Little Lad Who Became a Bishop

• HE WAS a very intelligent little lad. His parents had only the one child, but his father did not understand a thing about the boy. He was sent to school, and his father asked the schoolmaster if his son was doing well. The master always replied, "There is nothing one can teach your son."

So the father began to beat the little lad, thinking that the boy did not want to learn anything at school, but of course the boy hadn't anything to learn from the master, because he understood everything. The father went on beating his son. When his father beat him, the boy would say, "One day, Father, you shall pour water over my hands." The father then beat him even harder, saying, "You miserable failure, there is nothing one can do with you except beat you and then kill you."

One evening he took him to the forest to lose him. He had tied him to the foot of a tree. Then the little lad saw some priests going by on the road. They were on their way to a town where a bishop was being ordained. So the little lad called out, so that they would set him free, "Brothers, Reverend Fathers, save my life!"

Well, the first one did not hear him. Then another group went by, and they heard him. They set him free and took him with them. After that they went into an inn to eat, I expect. There was a girl there who was very ill. The little lad said to the innkeeper's wife, "If you will make me robes like the priests have, I'll save your daughter."

In the doorway was a large stone. Well, then the little lad said to the lady, "Get a good fire going." Next he lifted up the large stone in the doorway. There was a big toad underneath. At once the toad was placed in the fire, and the girl found herself cured. She said, "I feel a millstone has been taken off my shoulders!"

In this way the boy had the robes he wanted, as it was just, and he left with the priests to go to the town where a bishop was being ordained. When they reached the door of the church, the boy began playing marbles with some urchins who were around the church.

When it was time, he went into the church and up to the altar. Actually there was a dove in the church and she was supposed to land on the head of the future bishop. The boy was wearing his robes like the priests, and the dove made its way toward the little lad's head. Then all the priests shouted, "Hail, Monseigneur!"

Later the Bishop (by now the little lad had become a bishop) wrote a letter to his parents without saying who he was. He let them know that the Bishop asked them to come to such and such a place. The mother said to the father, "You know what the Bishop is going to say to you. You went and abandoned our little lad in the forest. We shall certainly be reprimanded."

And so the parents came to the said place, but they wore the costumes of that particular spot so as not to show the clothes of their own village. When the Bishop saw them, he said to them, "Those are not your clothes you are wearing. Go back home and fetch your own clothes before you appear before me."

The mother and father went back to their village to fetch their clothes. The mother said, "You see, you abandoned our boy. What will the Monseigneur say to us?"

They came back to the place and went to bed in the Bishop's house. The Bishop said to the fellow, "Tomorrow morning you will serve the Mass, which I will say." He said to the old girl, "Tomorrow you will assist with the Mass."

So he said the Mass, and when it was time for Communion and the father had poured out the bottles, the Bishop said, "I told you, Father, that one day you would pour water over my hands."

At that the fellow was so overcome that he died! He fell down stone dead! As for the old girl, she lived happily ever after with "her" Bishop.

·19· Tom Thumb

· TOM THUMB was so very very small that he could turn up anywhere.

One day he went to his aunt's house. As she wasn't there, he climbed into the cheese basket. In those days it was hung from a beam in a storeroom. He tasted several of the cheeses, and then he ate the best ones. After that, he hid in the straw under them.

When his aunt came back she brought down the basket to take out the cheeses.

"Oh," she said, "who has been tasting my cheeses?" Tom Thumb, who was in the straw in the basket, kept quiet.

Off went the aunt to the cow barn. She put the straw from the basket into the manger. At that moment Tom Thumb's uncle came along. He put a cabbage on top of the straw in the manger. Tom Thumb hid in the leaves. The cow ate a leaf and swallowed Tom Thumb whole.

Then the aunt came in to milk the cow, and what should she hear but the cow talking!

"What on earth am I doing in here!" shouted Tom Thumb (imprisoned in the cow's belly).

The aunt was afraid. "Is this cow under a spell?"

Whereupon the cow raised a leg and pushed the aunt over. "All is lost!" cried the aunt.

The cow wanted to shit. She produced Tom Thumb in a cowpat, and as there was a bucket of water quite close, he jumped in and washed himself.

In the end the aunt believed that the cow was under a spell good and proper, and she told everyone about it.

·20· The Tale of Jean-le-Sot

· JEAN-LE-SOT WAS the son of a poor woman from near here. He wasn't very bright.

One day his mother said to him, "You will go to market and take this pot of butter to sell."

"Oh yes, Mom."

"Then you will go to the dealer. You will sell the butter to him and bring the money back to me."

"Yes, Mother, I'll do that."

So off he went with his pot of butter. He had to cross the fields of our Vendee marsh. As it was summer, the earth there was dried up. (You know in these parts the marshlands are under water in winter, and then in the summer the water withdraws and the earth splits into little cracks.)

Jean-le-Sot noticed how the earth had great cracks in it, so he said out loud, "Oh, poor earth, when I have cracked skin on my fingers it is very sore." Then he took his pot of butter and he put some in the cracks in the earth to make them better. He soon used up his pot of butter in this way. So home he went with an empty pot.

"Home already, Jean?"

"Yes, Mom."

"Ah! You sold the butter?"

"Oh, no. I did not sell it." he said, "I saw that the poor earth there in the marsh was so split up with cracks that I put butter in them to make them better."

"Ah, poor Jean! You'll always be Jean-le-Sot."

"Oh, well, Mother. I couldn't leave that earth all split up like that . . ."

Another time his mother said to him, "I can't go to market. You will go and sell the eggs there. Take them to the egg seller and bring back the money."

"Yes, Mother."

So once again he went over the marsh. It was the time of year when there are frogs. They were going, "coâ, coâ" in the ditches.

Jean-le-Sot soon had enough of this.

"Ah, there you are!" he said (he saw some frogs looking up at him). "This is the way you make fun of me, is it?" He picked up his eggs to throw them at the frogs. Soon his whole basket of eggs had been used up, and so he had to go home empty-handed.

"Well, Jean, you managed to sell the eggs?"

"Oh, Mother, don't talk about it. The ditches were full of

frogs, and they were making fun of me, so I threw the eggs at them."

Well, that was another of Jean-le-Sot's mishaps.

Then one day Jean-le-Sot was wandering along when he met a priest, and he said to him, "Oh, Monsieur le Curé, you are a happier man than I, for I have to work."

"You are happier than I, Jean!"

"Shall we exchange our clothes, Monsieur le Curé?"

"I don't mind if I do."

They exchanged clothes. Jean wore the priest's habit and let the other have his suit.

"Well. Tomorrow there is a burial to look after. How will you cope, Jean?"

"I'll get through." However, he said to himself, "What shall I do? I don't know any Latin. And here I go trying to speak Latin."

He saw an old girl going to market with a jug of milk on her head. She started to dance about, and the jug fell and the milk was spilled on the ground.

Jean-le-Sot started with his Latin there and then:

> Milk is spoiled! Jug broken! Amen!
> I've seen your arse? Amen!

(The old girl had fallen over and was showing her buttocks.)

Later Jean saw a magpie at the top of a tree, and at the foot of the tree, a quail sang.

> The magpie has her nest high!
> The quail has her nest low! Amen!

Following this he met a dead she donkey under a bridge. It didn't smell good, and Jean was soon started on a psalm:

> Under the bridge stinks the she donkey! Amen!

After that, as he went back to his parish, he stopped to spend the night at an inn. He went into the dining room and saw a dresser with plates on it, so he started to count, "Ten glasses!

Six cups!" That night he slept in a square bed without curtains or canopy, and he said, "Bed without a canopy!" Next to the bed there was a little table. Jean-le-Sot had a look at it. There was nothing on it.

So he started to sing, "Bed without a canopy and without a pisspot!"

Jean reached the church. The people had come to receive their new priest with all the pomp at their disposal. Came the time for a burial.

One man said to him, "You see, my father is dead . . ."

"We shall bury him. What was his name?"

"Well, his name was Pierre."

"Shall we bury him tomorrow? You may be a little surprised by my Latin but it is the Latin spoken nowadays."

"Yes, Monsieur le Curé."

The next day Jean-le-Sot put on his vestments and went up to the altar.

He began singing slowly, "Pierrot, Pierrot! Poor Pierrot!"

The chorister answered in spite of this, "Amen!"

The curé started up again, "Bed without a canopy and without a pisspot?"

The chorister answered, "Amen!"

The curé: Ten glasses, six cups."

The chorister: "Amen!"

The curé: "Under the bridge stinks the she donkey!"

The chorister: "Amen!"

The curé: "The magpie builds her nest high. The quail builds her nest low."

The chorister: "Amen!"

The curé: "Milk is spoiled! Jug broken! Arse seen!"

The chorister: "Amen!"

The burial ended like that. People asked each other what sort of priest this was.

After two or three burials, the parishoners were really worked up. "What a strange kind of priest! We must catch him out."

"One of us will pretend to be dead and get into a coffin. We'll soon see what happens. That will soon rid him of this whim."

They did as they had planned. One of them hid in a coffin.

(He was perhaps hard put not to laugh.) Now Jean-le-Sot started up his burial service singing. At a given moment the "deceased" lifted the lid of the coffin. The parishioners burst out laughing and they all came out of the church.

"What is happening?" asked the priest.

The "deceased" also popped his head out to see what was going on.

"Aren't you dead?" said the priest. "And here you are now wanting to get up!" Jean-le-Sot grabbed the candle snuffer and bashed the so-called dead man with it.

"Ah, so you don't want to die?" Then he took the cross from the choir boy's hands and he killed the "deceased" with it.

"Come, come!" he shouted to his parishioners. "He wasn't quite dead, but now he really is!"

And so the burial was over.

In the end Jean-le-Sot said to himself, "I really was better off at my old job. I shall give back my priests' robes and take back my clothes, and I'll be a sight more happy!"

Part V
Upper Poitou

.21. *The Wolf and the Soldier*

• THERE ONCE WAS a wolf around here near the Fontaine-blanche. This wolf had heard it said that no one could compete with a creature called man.

This wolf was roaming along just off the road to Areney. He was going by there when he reached the Croix-cassee and met an old woman. This wolf stopped and told the old woman what he had heard. "I would like to fight a creature called man."

The old lady answered, "You will go to the Fontaine-blanche, where you will see a soldier. You will ask him if he wishes to fight."

So this wolf went off. Having reached the Fontaine-blanche, he found a soldier who was returning from the wars with his uniform, saber, and musket.

The wolf stopped. He had only just met the old woman when he caught sight of the soldier and said, "Well, it's really happened!" And all at once he said to the soldier, "So there you are. Well, if you wish to fight, I am ready."

"Ah," said the soldier, "all right, if you wish it, just the two of us."

The wolf said, "Throw something in my eyes to make me angry."

The soldier had a loaded musket. He said to him, "Stand back a bit!" Then the soldier shot him in the eyes.

"How badly you spit!" said the wolf.

The wolf turned round, and that second the soldier drew his sword and sliced off his thigh.

Another wolf, who was only a few steps away at La Chausse-en-l'air, saw him coming back limping and asked him, "What has happened?"

The wolf who had wanted to fight the creature called man came along holding his severed thigh in his paws.

"What happened to you?"

"Oh, my poor old friend, I wanted to fight with a creature called man. He spat in my face. After that he hit my body with a stick. Oh, my friend, what will become of me now?"

"Well," said the other, "you would have been far better off if you had kept quiet."

·22· *The Little Elves of La Chausse-en-l'Air*

• AT LA CHAUSSE-EN-L'AIR there lived an old man and an old woman. In the winter when the old woman had a moment to spare, she would spin in front of the fire. She wore a cape—you know what I mean, with a kind of hood—which she drew over her head when it was too cold.

During the winter evenings the old woman would do her spinning by the light of a resin candle, which smoked. It smoked so much that one could hardly see the people in the room. When the old man was in bed, she drew the flax off her distaff to make thread from it.

Now one evening a *fadet* (elf) came down the chimney and started laughing. He came right up to her, saying:

> You spin and you spin,
> To your spindle roll it in!

This old woman complained to her old man after she had had this visit. (The elf used to come back every evening.)

"Oh, well, don't worry. It won't be long before I rid you of him," he said, and he added, "This evening I will change into your clothes, and I will sit and spin in your usual place.

The old man took his wife's cape and sat in her place by the fire with the distaff and spindle, which he started turning. Almost at once the elf came down and settled next to him. Then he said:

> Ah, but you spin and you spin,
> To your spindle nothing roll it in!
> This is not yesterday's lady.
> The spindle it turned,
> And onto that spindle she rolled it.

Then what did the old man do? Well, he had been careful to place a poker in the fire in order to make it red hot. As the elf's call was over and he was going up the chimney, the old man slammed the poker on his backside.

The elf, who was busy going up, began to scream, "Burned buttocks! Burned buttocks!"

The other elves said to him, "Who did that to you? Who did that to you?"

The old man, who was busy spinning, replied, "Me. I did it."

The other elves, thinking it was the scorched elf answering them, all said, "Oh, so it is you who did it. Well, then, keep it to yourself."

•23• *The Piece of Cloth*

• THERE WAS a Prince with three children who also had a niece whom he cared for as well. Now the three brothers came to love their cousin as they grew older. All three wanted to marry her, so there wasn't a moment's peace between them. The two eldest brothers were always teasing the younger one, who was a bit simple and whom the father looked upon as a fool.

One fine day their father said to them, "He who brings me the largest piece of cloth shall be the one to have my niece."

The two elder boys left at once to find carriages and horses and attendants—the whole lot—and then off they went!

The father said to his youngest son, "You're not budging, I suppose?" As I have already told you, the boy was a bit simple.

Well, he went. He went, too, but on foot. After a long walk he reached a ruined castle. He could not see the actual castle, but he noticed a fenced-in paddock where a horse was grazing. Meanwhile, his brothers in their carriages were already miles ahead. "What can I do?" the poor devil said to himself, and he went toward the horse. The horse looked at him. The youth was about to stroke it when the animal said, "Get up on me." He had never mounted a horse and there he was climbing onto it. The horse cantered off, but the young fellow was not afraid and did not fall off.

The horse took him before the ruined castle. Just an ordinary cat lived there. The poor devil went into this castle, and then the cat led him through several rooms. She made him twist and turn in that castle of hers. There was nothing but gilt and mirrors everywhere. Then she gave him a meal with her claws. He was having rather a good time, what with the cat being on his knees and her bringing food to him.

Just then he heard his brothers going home with their carriages filled with pieces of cloth.

"My brothers are going home, and I have nothing to take back there!" Well, then the cat gave him a tailor's box.

"Off you go with that box!" she said.

The youth unfastened the lid of the box. There was a little piece of cloth showing at the top.

"Someone must pull on that end, and the whole cloth will come out," said the cat. "Above all, don't show it to anyone. Put your hand in your pocket and the box also."

The poor devil climbed back onto the horse which had led him to the cat's castle, but he was the last to reach his father's house. His brothers had brought back magnificent pieces of cloth. They were very long but they had seams.

Their father was watching them. He caught sight of his third son and said to him, "Well, boy, what have you brought back?"

"A tailor's box."

Now, without showing them the box, he called his nurse.

"Nurse, I want you to pull on that."

The nurse began to pull on the little piece of cloth which was only just showing. She pulled and pulled. The cloth came out of the box. There was not a seam in it, and the more the nurse pulled, the more cloth came out.

Their father crossed his arms. "Where did he get that?" He was not at all pleased, and he was saying to himself, "There I was treating him so badly, and it is he who has won!"

The other two were dumbfounded to see what had happened to their brother. Then the father said, "That's not all, you know. You have brought back fine pieces of cloth, but that's not all." And to the youngest he said: "It is impossible for me to give you my niece. You are the youngest. Your brothers have the right of seniority."

Then the father thought this over, and at last he said, "You are all three going to go off once more. He who brings me the finest hunting dog will be the bridegroom." (The father was probably master of the hunt.)

And so they hit the road once again. The three brothers were searching for hunting dogs. The two eldest left with their horses, and that same evening they came back with dogs of all sizes, enormous ones and tiny ones.

The youngest? Well he went back to the cat, riding the horse he had found near the castle. He heard his brothers on their way back to their father with all their dogs. "Oh," he said, "my brothers will soon be home."

The cat gave him an egg.

"Here," she said, "here's an egg for you. You are not going to say a word about it. You will keep it in your pocket and hold your hand over it, but don't let anyone know."

The boy stroked the cat before leaving.

"See you a week from today," said the cat.

He went home to his father. When he got there, there were all kinds of dogs in the courtyard.

"Come on," he said (that was the father talking to the youngest son), "my boy, what have you brought home?"

The lad pulled the egg out of his pocket. The cat had also said to him, "When it's your turn, put your thumb on the egg, and you shall see what will come out."

He put his thumb on it. Out of the egg popped a little green dog who yapped and ran ahead of the others. He outran all the other dogs and, better still, he jumped back into the egg when the fellow placed his thumb on it. You should have seen how that dog obeyed!

"Ah," said the father, "it is the youngest there who has brought me the best hunting dog."

The father did not know what to do. In the end, he said, "I have had enough of this. All right, off you go, all three of you. The one who brings me the prettiest wench shall be the one to have my niece."

Once again the three brothers were off. The two eldest were

in the lead, and they brought back all the girls they could find. There were girls with raw, red hands who milked the goats, and old cooks—a hodgepodge of women of all kinds.

The lad went to the cat.

She said to him, "You must do me a favor and do as I say. You will get a good fire going. Now listen to me carefully. This is the last trick."

"Yes," said the fellow.

"You'll get a chopping block ready near the fire."

The fellow looked at her. He was scared stiff.

"Go on. Do as I say," she said.

He was so afraid that he was whimpering.

"This is your last trick, and don't bungle it. I shall put my neck on the block. You must cut through it with one blow." (How he shook, the poor fellow!)

That cat put her neck on the block, and her head flew into the flames in the hearth. The lad turned his head and saw a lovely maiden dressed in gold and silver who asked him to take her to his father's home, to the Prince's castle in fact.

When they had gone (there was no more cat; her head had been chopped off), the lad took the girl by the arm.

The horse was still grazing in the meadow. They went and found him, both of them together, and they rode on him and they got there in that way to the courtyard of the castle. There were ladies and maidens of all kinds brought there by the two elder brothers. The lad arrived on his horse with the beautiful young girl dressed in white satin trimmed with precious stones and diamonds.

The father could not get over it. In the end he said, "Well, you can marry my niece, if you wish."

"I don't want her," said the lad. "One is enough for me."

"Well then," the lovely girl said, "Come on, let's go! Off to my castle!"

And so the fellow married the cat. The horse was waiting for them. They mounted him and went back to the castle.

The cat was a fairy. She helped that fellow because his father and his two elder brothers had always despised him.

·24· The Three Gold Hairs from the Devil

• ONCE THERE WAS a little boy born of poor folk. There was also a King who was jealous of this little boy. He did not want him to live, for he had heard said, "That child shall one day become king."

So what did the King do? One night he went and knocked on the door of the poor people's house and asked, "Could you take me in to live in your house?" There was not much room in the house. "I shall sleep near the cradle," said the King. But during the night he jumped out of the window with the basket in which the little boy was sleeping, and he put it on the river. The little boy floated along until he reached an old house where some kind folk lived. They rescued him and brought him up until he was twenty years old.

The King who had placed the little boy on the water heard he had been rescued. He went to the old house where the boy had been taken in and said to the young man, "I am going to give you a letter. You will go to my country with this letter for my wife."

"I'll go there and take it to her," replied the young man.

So off he went taking the King's letter with him. The evening closed in. He did not know where to spend the night. In the end he landed in a house where there were three girls. They agreed to put him up, and then he said to them, "Above all, do not touch this letter."

He left the letter on the table and went to bed. But the three girls were inquisitive. They wondered what was in the letter. In the end, they unsealed it. In the letter it was stated that the young man, the bearer of the letter, should be killed.

"Oh," said the girls to themselves, "this young man is so kind and polite. We must not let him take this letter."

They rewrote the letter saying at the end of it that the young man should marry the King's daughter. (This letter was intended for the Queen.) Then the three girls tore up the King's letter after having forged the writing, and they then put in the envelope the letter which they had written.

The next day the young man picked up his letter from the table and took it with him. He was to take it to the Queen.

He walked for a long time and showed up in front of the castle. The Queen opened the letter and read it. Thinking that this was a message from her husband, the King, she did her best to make the young man welcome. Shortly after, she said, "Well, as you are to marry my daughter, we shall have the wedding at once."

The wedding took place, or at least the preparations for the marriage ceremony went ahead. Then the King arrived and was very astonished to find all this going on.

He asked, "Why? For whom are all these preparations being made?"

"Why, this is for your daughter's wedding to the young man you sent with a letter to the Queen."

The King exploded in a frightful rage.

"This is impossible. In the letter it was stated that he should be killed."

"No, no. In the letter it said that your daughter should marry the young man."

The King could contain himself no longer. So the young man toyed with the idea of running away alone, and then he thought of his betrothed and came back. The King said to him, "You shall marry my daughter on one condition only. You must first go and fetch three gold hairs from off the Devil."

Then the young man wondered what to do to please the King. Off he went walking and walking and walking. He crossed great forests, and one morning he reached the shore. There was a man there who took people from one side of the river to the other, and he was very fed up with his job. He asked the young man, "Have you any idea what to do in order not to carry on with this job?"

"Take me over first. I shall give you an answer when I return."

The young man crossed the river. He walked and walked and walked and arrived in front of the Devil's house. The door was guarded by an old woman. The young man introduced himself to her, saying, "I have come to take three of the Devil's gold hairs."

The old girl answered, "That is going to be very hard, but to help you, I shall turn you into an ant, and you will put yourself in my apron so as not to be seen by the Devil."

At that time the Devil was asleep. The old woman plucked one hair from him.

"Ouch! Why have you woken me up?"

"I was looking for a louse on you. I have killed it."

"If you start that again, watch out, or I'll give you something you didn't bargain for."

The old girl gave the gold hair to the ant hidden in her apron. A moment later the Devil was asleep once more. The old girl plucked another hair from him.

"Ouch! What are you doing to me?"

"Oh, I've squashed a great big flea!"

"Any more of this and you'll get the stick a hundred times over."

The old girl gave the gold hair to the ant. Not long after, the Devil fell asleep again. The woman plucked yet another hair from him.

"Ouch!" said the Devil, waking up. "I smell fresh flesh here."

"No, no, no. No one can come in here."

The old girl slipped the third gold hair to the ant. They left the room where the Devil was asleep, and the old girl turned the ant back into a young man.

So there he was on his way again and very pleased with himself, as he had the three gold hairs from the Devil to take to the King. He went along to find the ferry man on the river bank.

"Have you found out what to do so as not to go on with this job of mine?"

"Take me over, and then I shall tell you."

Having reached the other side of the river, the young man said, "Well, now, to get out of this job, you will hand over the boat to the first man who comes to you to cross the river."

The young man went off and hastened to take the Devil's three gold hairs to the King.

The King showed great surprise. He took the three gold hairs saying, "Fine, fine! This is well done."

He, too, had the idea of going to the Devil's house. "I shall try and get in there," he said.

The King went the same way as the young man, and he met the ferry man, who was still there on the river bank with his boat.

"Would you take me over?" The ferry man took the King aboard his craft and leaped onto the bank, leaving the King alone on the river.

Since then the King has been the ferry man, going endlessly back and forth.

One fine day a hurricane swept by. The waves toppled the King into the water, and he fought there in vain and was drowned.

Since these days the young man who married the King's daughter became king of that country.

·25· *Puss in Boots*

• A MILLER HAD three boys. When he died he gave the mill to the first boy, the donkey (who carried the sacks) to the second boy, and to the third boy he gave the cat (who used to catch the mice). The third boy was very downhearted. He said, "What shall I do when I have eaten my cat?"

But the cat said, "I am very intelligent. Ask of me what you will, and it will be granted to you." The boy had nothing to eat. He said to the cat, "I am hungry."

The cat went and stole four or five fat sausages and black puddings and a roast from a butcher's shop. Then he ran and took them back to his master.

"Which do you like best?" the boy asked the cat.

"Black puddings," said the cat, putting his paw over his tummy.

The boy gave him the black puddings and ate the sausages and the roast himself. "Now I am thirsty," he said.

"All right, I'm off," answered the cat.

He took a bowl and went to find some Anjou wine from a hotel and brought it back to his master. The boy drank the wine and gave some of it to the cat. "Now I want some work," said the boy. "I should like to be placed with a rich man. I'll work hard and then I shall be satisfied."

What did the cat do? He went to the King and asked him, "Would you be needing a fairly capable young man to help you?"

"Why do you ask me this?"

"Well, because I have a master who is out of work, and he would like to have something to do."

"All right, I'll take him on. He shall serve all the dishes and he shall eat a quarter of what he serves. Off with you! Your master shall be rich."

Oh, how happy the cat was!

"Will I, too, live with my master?"

The King said, "Yes, yes, yes."

So the cat went and found his master and told him what had happened. "I have found just what you need. You will be rich. You will eat well. You are to serve the King, and a quarter of the dishes served shall be yours."

Then the boy said to the cat, "And where will you live?"

"Well," he said, "I asked the King, and he said that I could go with you."

The cat and the boy went straight to the King at once.

The King had three daughters. The boy served at table, and the King was very pleased with him.

Somewhat later the King said to the boy, "If you wish to marry, you will have to choose one of my three daughters."

There was the eldest, the next one, and the last. The boy wasn't quite sure what he should say. "Well," said he, "I'll choose the eldest . . . Oh, no, I'll choose the next one . . . No, the third! Oh, I don't know!" he said, throwing up his arms.

"Choose whichever one you wish," said the King.

The boy said to the three girls, "Well, all three of you shall dance. The one who dances the best shall be mine."

At once the three girls danced before him, and it was the

second one who was the best dancer. The boy said to the King, "Right! I'll take your second daughter."

So the following Saturday the wedding celebrations took place. Now the two sisters were jealous, and they did not want to be present at the wedding. The King was very angry. He had people looking for them everywhere.

"If they are found," he said, "I'll chop their heads off!"

So the boy said, "Oh, no! This cannot happen today, nor can it happen tomorrow or the day after that, as the wedding celebrations will not yet be over." And then of course the bride was very fond of her sisters. She said, "Never shall they have their heads chopped off!"

Then the King said, "All right, all right. In order to please you, I shall not have their heads chopped off."

Now the cat was still with his master, even at the wedding. He, too, went and found one of the girls, and as he looked for her he thought, "Why shouldn't I get married, too?" At that moment he saw a big rat (at least it was a large female rat). "Oh ho!" said he, "I'll get married to that one, I will!" Then at the same time he took the female rat in his arms and started running about everywhere, under the tables and over the guests' feet and all over the place. Oh! If the King had seen this! (But he was still busy looking for his two other daughters.) Then the cat and the female rat went to the place where the cat was eating at the banquet table.

The cat said to the rat, "You will eat from my plate."

But the rat was too small. She had to climb up onto the table, and the King saw her. Ah, well, he killed the rat.

So the cat said, "Now I have lost my wife, but why shouldn't I marry a young girl?"

There and then he turned into a young man, and he went and found a young girl at the wedding and asked her, "Where is the King's youngest daughter?"

"No one knows where she has gone."

"I shall run after her." And he ran after her (as a young man still) and found her crying and crying and crying.

"What is the matter, Mamôselle?"

"Oh, I have lost my elder sister."

"Oh, poor Mamôselle. Perhaps you would like to get married, too?"

"Oh, yes," said the girl.

"Well, then," he said, "take my arm."

The cat (still as a young man) and the youngest of the three sisters both went and found the King.

"Who is this newcomer?" said the King, looking at the young man (who was none other than the cat!).

"Oh, well," said he, "I want to marry the youngest of your daughters."

The King was perhaps a little encumbered with his three daughters. Anyway he then said, "Well, while we are at it, we shall go on and have another wedding after this one."

Meanwhile the eldest of the King's daughters was listening at the doors and said, "What a handsome youth! Why shouldn't he take two wives. I shall go and ask him."

At the same time, the young man came out. The eldest daughter asked him, "Would you like two wives?"

"All the girls in the world!" said the young man.

"Well, will you have me?"

The cat (that is to say, the young man) took the two girls by the arm. That made three weddings at one go, or at least two, but the cat had taken two wives.

Now, it happened that the eldest noticed that the young man stopped looking after her and did not talk to her anymore. Then she said, "I would be better off dead." (Well, I would have thought so, too, if I had been in her place, I can tell you that.) So she hanged herself.

Then the cat stayed with the youngest of the King's daughters while his master had the second one (the one who danced best of all).

Well, that is about all I know!

.26. *The Pea*

• THERE WERE a fellow and his wife who were so poor that all they owned was one pea, and so they planted it in the earth, and the pea started growing. It grew so tall that it looked like a tree.

So the woman said to her husband, "Climb up this pea plant there. Climb up, right up high, and go tell St. Peter we have nothing more to eat!"

The man climbed from branch to branch and reached the top of the pea stalk. There he knocked at the gates of paradise.

St. Peter opened them and said, "What have you come to look for here?"

"I would give anything to have something to eat."

"Well, listen to me carefully. You will go back to earth, and then, when you are home, you will say to your table, 'Table, table, lay yourself!' and you will see on your table everything you could wish to eat."

The fellow came down from the top of the pea stalk and explained to his good wife what St. Peter had said to him.

At once they said, "Table, table, lay yourself," and they saw on the table all sorts of good things to eat.

The fellow and his wife now had enough to eat their fill, and they spent some time in this way.

Then the old girl said to her husband, "If we had a few crowns, we'd be a lot happier."

"Well, yes."

"Then up the pea plant you go, and ask St. Peter to give us some crowns."

The fellow climbed back up the pea stalk from branch to branch, and he reached the top, and there was paradise. St. Peter opened up for him.

"Now what do you want, my good fellow?"

"My old woman would like you to give us some crowns."

"Go right down again, and as soon as you get home, you will say to your chest, 'Chest, chest, be filled,' and the chest will fill itself with crowns."

The fellow came down from the pea stalk.

"What did he say to you?" said the old woman. "Did he give you anything?"

"I have to say to our chest, 'Chest, chest, be filled,' and we shall have plenty of money."

"Then go ahead. Try at once," said the old woman.

Immediately the fellow went to his chest and said, "Chest, chest, be filled." And when they opened the lid of the chest, it was full of crowns.

Well, by now this fellow and his wife were rich. They spent some time with their chest full of crowns. Then the old woman said to her husband, "Now we have plenty to eat and lots of crowns, but we ought to have a house, too. Go on up our pea plant and ask St. Peter."

The fellow climbed up the pea plant again from branch to branch, and he reached the top. He knocked on the door. St. Peter opened up for him.

"Well, now," said the fellow, "we have plenty to eat and lots of crowns. We should now like a lovely house."

"Go down again," said St. Peter. "You will find that by tomorrow you and your wife will be living in a lovely house."

The fellow went down to the ground.

"What did he say to you?" asked the old woman.

"He said that by tomorrow we would have a lovely house."

"How?" she said.

"You'll see right enough."

The next day when they awoke they were in a lovely house with all sorts of furniture and what have you and servants to look after them.

"Madam desires something?" said the maid.

"Would you like to go out, Sir?" said the coachman.

And so on. The fellow and his wife lacked nothing, but as a result of living in a beautiful house and being served like a king, they became arrogant and despised the world about them.

One day a beggar came and asked for a piece of bread at the door of their house. The old woman was there. "I shall give you nothing," she said, "and even if you don't ask, I'll send the dog after you."

As the beggar asked again for a piece of bread, the old woman set the dog on him, and that was the end of it.

But the next day when the fellow and his wife awoke there was neither a fine house nor any servants left. They were in their hovel as poor as they had been before planting their pea.

Part VI
Lower Marche

·27· *The Black Hen*

• ONCE UPON A TIME there was a beggar who was at the crossroads, at the spot they nowadays call the Crêpe-au-lait. It was nightfall and very dark. Our beggar had pulled down his hood so as not to feel the cold, and could see nothing but the hedges ahead of him. Just then the man heard something rummaging around in the night. He looked around, of course, but saw nothing except the hedges along the path. Midnight drew closer, but our man was not afraid to be there. Then he saw a black hen scratching and scratching at the soil. He went a little nearer and saw that she was unearthing gold, lots of gold coins with her claws.

Our beggar did try and pick up a few gold coins, but then the hen beat her wings three times. Next she sang, "Cocorico!" three times. She had looked at our man straight in the eye, and he was so frightened that he fled without having been able to pick up the gold—that is, apart from a few coins. He ran off as fast as he could and only stopped when he reached the castle of a squire, perhaps the castle of Barres. As soon as he saw this castle, he went into it to hide. Then he dropped to the floor of the grange and fell fast asleep.

The next day the squire asked him what had happened. Our beggar told his story, but the squire said, "This isn't true."

However, the next day the squire went to the crossroads of the Crêpe-au-lait. It was winter and the moon was full. The same thing took place as had happened to the beggar. At midnight the black hen appeared, and she started scratching at the soil, and the squire saw that she was bringing out gold.

Perhaps the squire loved gold more than our beggar did, for when he saw the gold coins on the earth, he stretched out his hand to pick them up. He picked up as many as he could, and there and then the coins turned to soot. They were nothing but little burned out embers.

The squire just saw the black hen beating her wings three times and he heard her sing out, "Cocorico! Cocorico! Cocorico!" The black hen gave him such a look that he was terrified. He fled as fast as he could to the castle, and there he fell fainting to the ground.

He lay there like a corpse all night long and all the next day. No one could bring him back to life. When midnight struck, the iron gates of the castle were heard to squeak. The walls creaked. The shutters banged, and then something in the earth could be heard rummaging around. It was the black hen, who had appeared in front of the squire's castle. She could not be seen, but everyone heard her sing out, "Cocorico!"

Well, then, the squire gave a sigh and sat up in bed and asked for a drink, and then he said to them, "When the old beggar told me he had found a black hen at the crossroads stirring up some gold, I wanted to go there and pick some of it up, but the gold coins turned into embers as I was about to carry them off. I tell you that black hen is the Devil!"

At that the men made the sign of the Cross, and the old women took to their rosaries.

Since that night time went by, but the black hen came every night and sang out before the squire's castle as midnight struck. She was seen by no one, but everybody heard her. From midnight on, the village could no longer get any sleep. The squire of the castle realized that he had sinned in wanting to pick up that gold.

He said, "I must go barefoot to the Holy Land as a penance."

So off he went on foot to the Holy Land. He was dressed in rags and took no money with him. Winter went by. Everybody in the village was waiting in the hope that the squire would soon reach the Holy Land. But the black hen still came and sang at midnight before the squire's castle, and no one around there could sleep. The master sent no news to the castle.

When spring came, it so happened that the whole village awoke to a morning of sunshine after having slept right through the night for the first time. That black hen had not come to sing at midnight before the castle.

"This means our squire has reached the Holy Land!" said an old woman.

It was true. The squire had entered Jerusalem at midnight.

Since then no one has ever heard the black hen of the Crêpe-au-lait sing again.

·28· *Jean of Bordeaux*

• JEAN OF BORDEAUX WAS a poor boy who used to go out to the fields in his wooden clogs to mind the hogs. He was a wretched lad and not very bright.

One fine day he went off. He left his parents and went to start a new life. He reached a country where everyone seemed melancholy. It was England. The King of that country had a daughter who was held prisoner by the Devil in a crypt below the altar of the church. The King of England had proclaimed, "He who frees my daughter shall be her husband." Many had tried to set her free, but none had come out of the church, because the Devil had eaten them.

Jean of Bordeaux said, "I shall try and set her free."

The King gave him a gun and a bayonet. He also had a cake brought to him for him to eat and a bottle of white wine to drink during the night he was to spend in the church. He was not to touch it until midnight. In actual fact, every night toward midnight something made a most frightful noise, but no one was any the wiser, for no one had ever come out of there.

Thereupon, one night Jean of Bordeaux went round the church and met an old woman there. She addressed him.

"Well, what do you know? So you are here, Jean of Bordeaux?"

The boy answered her, "How is it that you know me, old lady?"

The old woman replied, "I am going to give you some advice. If you go into the church tonight, the Devil will eat you, but here is what you have to do so as not to be eaten like the others. You will hide by climbing into the priest's pulpit. He won't find you there before midnight, and when midnight strikes, the Devil will be powerless against you."

Jean of Bordeaux took the old woman's advice. He hid in the

pulpit and waited. Eleven o'clock, half past eleven—there was the Devil beginning his round.

"Where are you, Jean of Bordeaux? I am so hungry tonight, and I haven't eaten yet."

The Devil went all over the place. He broke a chair, then another; he even lifted the pews. Nothing stood up to him. In the end he caught sight of Jean of Bordeaux in the priest's pulpit, but the first stroke of midnight rang out.

Then Jean of Bordeaux left the pulpit and ate his cake and drank his wine. Then he walked about the church awaiting daybreak.

The next morning the King had the door reopened for him to find out how he had protected himself with his gun and his bayonet. When he saw Jean of Bordeaux coming out of the church alive, he said to himself, "This lad is worth something more than the others. I shall trust him."

All day long Jean of Bordeaux lived as a free man. He ate and drank at the King's expense and did exactly as he pleased.

That night he had to go into the church again to face the Devil. The King of England gave another cake and another bottle of wine to Jean of Bordeaux.

That night the lad went in front of the church and met the old woman, who said to him, "Ah, you know, Jean of Bordeaux, tonight you will have to hide inside the statue of a saint. You will saw off the head of the statue, then you will slip into the body of the statue, and you will not move your head or even look around. When the Devil sees you, it will be too late for him."

Jean hid there. Eleven o'clock, half past eleven—there was the Devil coming out, and he climbed into the pulpit where he had seen him the day before, but this time he was nowhere to be seen. The Devil in a fit of temper shook and broke everything he came across, shouting, "Where are you then, Jean of Bordeaux? I tell you I am so hungry. This is the second night I have not eaten."

Midnight struck just when the Devil saw Jean's head sticking out of the statue. The lad came out of his hiding place and ate his cake and drank his bottle. Then he waited for daybreak.

The King was delighted with him. He said to himself, "This lad will manage to rescue my daughter from the Devil's clutches." And during that day again Jean drank and ate anything he wished at the King's expense.

The third night the old woman said to Jean, "This time the Devil will find you, but midnight will strike and he will not be able to eat you. Hide behind the altar in such a way that only your feet are showing. As after midnight the doors of the crypt will remain open, the King's daughter will say, 'Give me your hand, Jean of Bordeaux.' You will say to her, 'If you wish to take the end of my bayonet take it, but if you do, do not let it go.'"

Eleven o'clock, half past eleven—the Devil appeared in a frightful rage.

"Where are you, Jean of Bordeaux? For three nights now I have had nothing to eat. This time I shall find you." But then he saw the tip of Jean's foot which was sticking out from under the altar. Midnight struck. Ah, the Devil had not been able to eat him like the others.

This time Jean got up, but, instead of eating the cake and drinking the bottle of wine, he opened the door of the crypt where the girl was closeted. She was there, but she could not get out by herself.

"Give me your hand, Jean of Bordeaux," she said.

"If you wish to take my bayonet, take it, but if you do not wish to, leave it." (Actually Jean of Bordeaux could not draw her out by taking her hand.)

In the end the girl touched his bayonet and she was safe. She came slowly out of the crypt. So then Jean of Bordeaux took the cake and the bottle. They both had something to eat and drink, and then they began talking of love.

The next morning the King of England was there to open the door of the church. The King had to marry his daughter to Jean of Bordeaux, and really king though he was, the match delighted him. The wedding festivities lasted some time. Then one fine day Jean felt he wanted to go and see his parents in Bordeaux.

His wife gave him one hundred horsemen as an escort. They

were all mounted on fine horses, and she also gave him one hundred thousand francs to make the journey. As for him, he was dressed as marshal of England. What gorgeous clothes he had!

He was off. One night he reached an inn, which was in fact run by the old woman who had given Jean such good advice. He asked for rooms for himself and all his following.

"Ah, so there you are, Jean of Bordeaux! We shall give your escort something to eat. As for you, you shall sup with me, and we shall play cards."

Jean of Bordeaux stayed and played with the old woman, and then she won the lot. The hundred horses, the horsemen, the gold, and even his uniform of marshal of England went to her. He had nothing left. The next day the old woman sent him away dressed only in his old clothes.

So he went off feeling foolish and sheepish with his two wooden clogs on his feet. He reached his parents in Bordeaux in this state. There, in spite of his telling them all that had happened to him, no one would believe him.

His wife, who was anxious, as he did not seem to be coming back, left to search for him. She took with her two hundred horsemen and two hundred thousand francs, and she started on her journey.

That evening she drew up in front of the inn run by the old woman, and she asked for rooms. She received the same welcome.

"Let's play cards," said the old woman.

"You will give back my hundred horses, my hundred horsemen, my money, and my husband's uniform, which you stole from me, or else I shall kill you."

In the end the old woman did have to give back everything to her, but they killed her just the same.

There was an escort, therefore, of three hundred horsemen to lead the daughter of the King of England to Bordeaux. To everybody's surprise, she asked where the little inn owned by Jean's parents was. She then had her escort lodged at the large hotel, and she made for the little hotel.

"Oh, Madam, you cannot stay there—it's just a little inn."

"I wish to go there."

Anyway, she went into the inn and asked, "Madam, would you give me something to eat?"

"We haven't much to offer you . . ."

The King of England's daughter sat down at a table.

"Is it your son who serves the meals?"

"Oh, not on your life! With his wooden clogs on, he is so clumsy he might break the dishes."

"I wish him to serve me at my table."

Jean was sitting in a corner in his old clothes looking very unhappy. Anyway, he brought in the first dish and slipped on the waxed floor by mistake. He fell to the floor and broke the dish.

"It doesn't matter," said the Princess. "I would like him to bring me another."

Jean of Bordeaux stood up and went to fetch another dish. He had to be very careful in order to carry it without falling.

Just then the King's daughter said to him, "Don't you recognize me, Jean of Bordeaux?"

"Oh, yes, I recognize you."

So then the King's daughter took him to the barber to have his hair cut, for it was that long. She had him put on his gorgeous uniform of marshal of England. Then they went strolling round the town of Bordeaux in their fine wedding clothes, and after that they went back home and lived very happily.

•29• *Golden Hair, or The Little Frog*

• ONCE UPON A TIME there was a little girl. She was so pretty that she was called Golden Hair. The Holy Virgin was godmother to this pretty girl, and she often came to see her. Now she had given her a parrot, and this parrot talked sometimes and had his little say.

One fine day the Holy Virgin went off to visit her godchild, but by now of course Golden Hair had grown up and was a young girl, and she had a suitor, a good-looking young man who was very much in love with her and came to see her in secret. (He may well have been a king's son.)

The Holy Virgin knocked on the door, so Golden Hair quickly made her lover hide in the space between the bed and the wall. After that she said out loud, "Come in." The Holy Virgin opened the door. Then the parrot started to say out loud, "Madam, the gentleman is hiding behind the bed."

"Oh!" said Golden Hair, "the naughty little devil! It was my broom that I put there this morning."

The Holy Virgin left. She often came to visit her godchild, but this time she did not stay long.

Two or three days later she came back to see her godchild. This time Golden Hair saw her through the window.

"Let's get out of here," she said, and ran off through the garden with her lover.

Then the parrot began to screech, "Madam, the gentleman is taking her very far off into those woods!"

The Holy Virgin took the path through the woods to find her godchild. She went faster than the girl, and she found her all right. Golden Hair was on the bank of a small stream, and she could not cross it.

Her godmother said, "Golden Hair, where are you off to?"

But Golden Hair wanted to leap over the stream to follow her lover, who had already set off on the other side.

The Holy Virgin really scolded her. "Don't say another word. You shall become as ugly as you are pretty now."

And so in this way Golden Hair turned into a frog. She was a little frog in this stream.

This did not stop her lover from coming to see her every day. Then he would talk to his little frog.

This young man was the third son of a king, and his brothers, who went out a lot with girls, said to him to tease him, "Go on, go and see your little frog!"

The Holy Virgin also went to see her on the bank of this stream, but Golden Hair remained a frog all the same.

Now then the King said to his three sons, "I shall give my castle to the one who brings me back the finest horse."

Off went the two eldest to look for horses at the fairs. Now, then, the youngest went to find his little frog, and then he told her what the King had promised his sons.

"Go on, ask your godmother whether I can have the finest horse, for then I shall have the castle."

When the Holy Virgin came to call on Golden Hair, the latter made a point of asking her, and then a fine horse was discovered on the banks of the stream.

Now, then, the brothers reached the castle with the horses which they had bought, but they were nothing compared with the fine horse which the Holy Virgin had found.

The brothers were terribly jealous. They said, "Go on! Keep on going to see your little frog!"

So the King said, "I shall give my castle to the one who brings me the finest dog." (I think it was a dog this time.)

Off went the two eldest looking for dogs. The youngest left again to find his little frog, and the same thing happened. The Holy Virgin found the finest dog in the whole world for him, but the eldest were still teasing the youngest, saying, "Go and see your frog!"

Now then the King said, "I shall give my castle to the one who brings me the prettiest girl."

The elder brothers went off to see the girls they knew, but the youngest went to the bank of this stream and said to his little frog, "Go on and ask your godmother to make you as pretty as you were before!"

This King's son could not forget his Golden Hair, and he had never left her after she had been turned into a frog.

Now, then, the Holy Virgin forgave her godchild, and the little frog turned into Golden Hair again.

Along came her lover. He reached the bank of the stream. "Come on, Golden Hair. My brothers are arriving in the courtyard of the castle with their girls. You should see how ugly they are. I shall certainly be the one to win my father's castle."

Then the King's son took Golden Hair by the hand, and they left the little stream to go to the King's castle.

The King said to the others, "There can be no doubt about this. It really is your young brother who has won my castle. He deserves it more this time than the two other times."

The young man married Golden Hair, and then he was given his father's castle.

• A FAT GENTLEMAN had found a louse. He put it in a pot of fat. He then said, "When this louse is big enough and fat enough I shall skin it, and I shall have gloves made for my daughter from its skin. I shall wed my daughter to the man who guesses what kind of skin these gloves are made from."

There was a Prince round there who was much loved by this fat gentleman's daughter. He was called the Comte de mes Comtes. And so the girl whispered in his ear that the gloves were made of louse skin.

Sunday came. The gentleman was to give his daughter to the one who guessed what skin the gloves were made from. It would have been a poor man who would have said it; it would have been a poor man who would have seen it if he had found out what kind of skin it was!

A lot of people came to see those gloves, and many hoped to win the girl—but nobody guessed correctly!

Now, then, a little coalman appeared. (He was the Comte des mes Comtes, who had changed into a coalman).

He said to the fat gentleman, "It isn't a flea skin?"

"No."

"It isn't louse skin?"

"Yes."

This little coalman had won, and the daughter of the fat gentleman was awarded to him. Then, believe me, he took her by the hand and led her away with him, as was to be expected. It wasn't yet marriage, but the girl was his!

The little coalman made the girl climb onto his donkey, and left with her for the countryside. The poor girl kept saying, "Oh, I can see the farms owned by the Comte de mes Comtes.

"Keep the donkey moving, Mademoiselle," said the coalman. She could well grieve at the Comtes de mes Comtes! Then he took her into his little house or, that is, his barn. There was nothing but straw to sleep on.

The next day he said to her, "Guess what? Tomorrow they are doing the big *bugée* (annual wash) at the castle, the house of the Comte de mes Comtes. You will go there to help. We have no linen, nothing at all for our home. You will try to steal a few napkins to set us up."

When the washing was done, it was time for some fun in the evening. The little coalwoman was asked to dance, but she had put some napkins in her pocket. She had to dance with everyone from the farms, and soon the napkins fell out on the floor, and the people shouted, "The little coalwoman is a thief!"

She ran off home covered in shame and said to her coalman, "You know I had taken some napkins, and they fell out of my pocket, and it has put me to shame. I shall not steal any more."

"Oh, that's nothing," said the little coalman.

A few days later he said to her, "Ah, tomorrow at last they are making black puddings because it is the day they *firent boucherie* (slaughter the pig) at the castle. They will not count the black puddings, so you'll take a dozen and slip them into your pocket."

"Oh!" said the little coalwoman.

"Well, now, do you really think they are going to count the black puddings? That will give us both something to eat," said the coalman.

The next day the little coalwoman again went to the castle to help. She managed to get hold of a few black puddings, and she slipped them into her pocket. But in the evening there was merrymaking. She had to dance again. She skipped and skipped about so much that the black puddings fell out of her pocket.

"Oh, the little coalwoman is a thief! Now she has pinched the black puddings!" you could hear them saying loudly.

Once again she left, quite ashamed of herself, and she did not take the black puddings with her.

"Oh! Oh!" she said to the little coalman, "I was so ashamed of what I had done."

A little later the coalman said to her, "Guess what? The Comte de mes Comtes you are always talking about is getting married tomorrow, but the bride comes from far away. They need someone with a good figure up at the castle to try on the bridal gown. Well, go on up there. They need you."

"What do you mean?" said the little coalwoman.

"Don't you see? Your Comte de mes Comtes is getting married. He is having his bride's dress fitted for her. You try it on and keep it. Then you shall be the bride."

The little coalwoman went to the castle to try on the bride's dress. Her Comte de mes Comtes was there. They dressed her in the bridal gown and led her to the owner of the castle. Well, now she was the bride!

However, the little coalwoman did not want this.

"Oh, no, I do not want him. My daddy gave me to my little coalman. I shall not go as bride to the wedding of my Comte de mes Comtes."

So then the Comte de mes Comtes had to change back into a little coalman in order that she should agree to be his bride.

· 31 · *The Woman with Her Hands Cut Off*

· ONCE UPON A TIME there were a brother and a sister left living alone together. They loved each other very much. They had promised each other that they would never marry, neither one nor the other, so as not to leave each other.

Now the brother found someone to marry. One fine day he said to his sister, "Guess what, sister? I have found someone to marry."

"If she is right for you, this is marvelous. Get married, brother."

However, this woman was spiteful.

The sister went and lived in a house farther away, and the brother and his wife lived in the father's house.

Now the woman said to her husband, "You've no idea what's happened. Tonight I dreamed of your wicked sister. She had strangled your mares."

Her husband got up and went to look in the stables. The mares were dead. "Oh," he said, "it's really true."

The next night his wife said to him, "You've no idea what's happened. I dreamed again that your wicked sister had knocked over your wine barrels and that all the wine was spilled on the floor."

The husband got up and went to look in the cellar. All the barrels were knocked over, and the wine was spilled on the ground and in the cellar. But the brother said nothing of this to his sister. Every day he went to see her at her house.

"Good day, sister!"

"Good day, brother!"

Five or six days went by.

The woman said to her husband, "I dreamed tonight that your wicked sister had come here. She had killed our child. The knife was under the door."

The husband got up.

"You have only to look at the knife," said his wife.

The husband went up to the door and found the knife. It was covered with blood.

He went and found his sister. Anger forced him to speak. "Ah, you spiteful wretch! So you want me dead. You have killed my mares. You have knocked over my barrels, and I have said nothing. Now you have killed our child with this knife. Look! I have brought you the knife."

The sister said nothing. Then her brother grabbed his sister and cut her hand off at the wrist to punish her. So she said to him, "Don't say anything, wicked brother. When you jump over the hedge with the help of a ladder, you will get a splinter in your knee. Only I will be able to take it out."

Her brother, who was on his way home, lost his temper and cut off her other hand at the wrist. So the poor girl was walking around like that. She could no longer eat, as she had no hands. It so happened that as she walked she found herself in the King's garden. In it there were beautiful apples and pears. She hid herself, and then during the night she tried to catch them in her mouth as best she could, to eat them. The next day she hid in the garden during the daytime. This happened several times running.

The King said to his mother, "I am going to hide in order to see the creature who is eating my apples and pears."

So the King hid in the garden. At midnight he saw the young

girl who had come to catch the pears and apples in her mouth. She was all in rags. Her clothes barely covered her. The King went off without making any noise.

The next day he said to his mother, "Do you know? I have found the creature who is eating my apples and pears. You will give me dresses to clothe her in. She has no hands."

The King brought the clothes the Queen had given him to her, and then he took the young girl home with him.

A few days later he said to his mother, "I want to marry her." The mother did not wish this at all, but her son wanted the girl so much! In the end they got married.

Not long after, a great war took place. The King went off with his armies to make war and do battle. The King's wicked mother still refused to see her daughter-in-law, so she had her led into the woods by servants, and when the poor girl found herself there alone, it was only to give birth to two little boys.

At that moment the Holy Virgin and St. John and St. Paul appeared at her side to help with the birth.

Later the Holy Virgin was godmother to the two little twins, and each one had a godfather. Then St. John and St. Paul christened the two children.

The Holy Virgin said to St. John, "What are you offering your godchild?"

St. John said, "I, well, I offer him a fine castle in these woods."

The Holy Virgin said to St. Paul, "What are you offering your godchild?"

"Ah, well, that the castle should lack nothing, neither furniture, personal belongings, nor even servants," said St. Paul.

So the Holy Virgin said, "Well, then, I ask that the mother be given back her two hands."

The mother's hands were restored. In front of her was a fine castle, and nothing was lacking in this castle, and so she stayed there with her two children.

Seven years later the war was over. The King went home. He asked to see his wife. His mother answered, "She went off into the woods and has never been seen since."

The King left to find his wife in the woods. He reached the woods near the castle, of which he knew nothing. He saw two

little boys playing there. (They had grown tall, those twins.)
He asked them, "Where is your father?"

"We have never known a father."

"And Mummy?"

The twins' mother appeared. Naturally the King found himself staring at her. He asked her whether she had seen a woman (his poor wife, of course) who had no hands. She answered, "No."

"You look like her," said the King.

"You say she has no hands," she said. "I have some."

The young woman talked to the King for a while, and then she made herself known to him. The King was very happy.

Then she remembered that she had promised her brother she would go and look after him once she had her hands back. She had a horse saddled, and then the two of them, she and her husband, were led to her brother in their finest coach.

There must have been at least ten children in the courtyard, each dirtier and more ragged than the other. Even the threshhold of his house was filthy. A woman who was all dirty and in rags came and asked them what this coach was, stopping at his house.

The sister got out of it and said to her, "How do you do, Madam?"

"Ah, how do you do, Madam?"

"Is your husband here?"

"Oh yes, Madam. It is seven years today that he is lying in bed. He is still in bed, and no one can cure him."

"May I see him?"

"Yes, Madam." Then she went into the wretched room where her brother was in bed.

"Can you get up, Sir?"

"I cannot get up."

"Just a little, that's all. Let me see your leg."

There was a splinter imbedded in his knee, which was all swollen up.

The sister put her hand on the knee. The splinter flew up into the air, and so the brother recognized his sister. He started to cry and beg her forgiveness, and then he explained to her,

"My wife is to blame for my cutting off your hands. It is she who made me think you were the cause of all my misadventures."

His sister told him her story, and in the end they burned the spiteful sister-in-law.

• *32* • *Souillon*

• THERE WAS a mother with two little girls. This mother loved one of them and made the other one do all the unpleasant jobs. They called this one Souillon, because she always wore a big apron to do household chores and farm work.

The other one, the mother's favorite had nothing to do. She acted as lady's companion to her mother. Her mother always approved of what she said or what she did, and yet I assure you the girl did not work at all.

Souillon had to feed the poultry and sweep out the hen coops. She had to take away their droppings and give them fresh litter. Not satisfied with making her into a farmyard servant, her mother made her do the washing every week and wash the dishes every day.

Then came a time when both girls were grown up. Souillon was proposed to by a potter. She left with her husband, who plied his trade in another village.

The other one married, too, but her husband did nothing but drink and lead the gay life, squandering all his money.

A few years later the mother went to visit her two daughters, who lived with their husbands in different villages.

Souillon's husband was a potter, as I have told you. Every day he worked shaping his pots of clay, and every morning he prayed to God and asked him, "Lord, give me fine weather so that my pots can dry out and I can sell them and be able to feed my children."

When their mother reached Souillon's home, she saw a bunch of children clustered round their mother like a brood of newborn chicks. Then she noticed that her daughter had a lot of poultry in her backyard and that in the pigsty she had some very fine young pigs.

Souillon asked her into her house, which was spick and span. There was nothing missing, because she knew how to do every kind of work, as she had had to do all the most menial tasks ever since she was a child.

After having spent a few days with Souillon, who had welcomed her and given her everything she could possibly want, the mother said, "Now I shall go and see your sister, and I hope that she is as happy as you are."

"My sister, Mummy? Do you mean to say that you don't know how unhappy she is?"

"I thought as much," said the mother.

Souillon said to her, "My sister came here the other day to beg from me, saying she hadn't any money left to buy food."

The mother went to her favorite daughter's house. Before going in, she noticed that the house looked neglected. There was no poultry in the courtyard. The pigsty had fallen to pieces (perhaps that was why the hogs were dead!).

That woman was not surrounded by children but was alone and sad because her husband had abandoned her, preferring to lead a merry life with other girls.

When her mother went in to see her, the poor girl was crying. There wasn't even a chair in her house to give to her mother to sit in, not even a piece of dry bread to make her some soup.

The mother understood then that she had not helped to make her daughter happy by letting her do nothing. She went back to Souillon, who lived in comfort, and said to her: "Now I understand how I behaved toward my two daughters. Stay happy with your husband and promise me never to have favorites among your children as I had with you and your sister."

·33· *The Devil and the Good Lord*

· THIS HAPPENED when the earth had not yet been cultivated. The Devil and God were both there, so they set out to sow some wheat.

The Devil was a man who seemed as strong as a donkey, and

God looked like a weak man, but you'll see that he was one up on the Devil every time!

And so the wheat was sown.

"Which will you take? That which grows in the earth or that which grows in the air?"

"I want what grows in the earth."

So at harvest time the Devil had the roots, and God had the grain.

The following year they planted potatoes. "Which would you like to have?" God asked the Devil.

"I want what grows in the air."

This time when they were harvesting, the Devil had only the old leaves from the potato plants, because God had taken the roots.

The third time they sowed maize. God said to the Devil, "Come on now, I do not want to trick you. Which will you take this time?"

"I'll have both ends of this maize."

When the maize was ripe, God picked off the corncobs (you know how the cobs grow in the middle of the maize plant), and the Devil had only the stalks and the tassels of the maize.

So the Devil went away. Winter had come, and the Devil built himself a castle of stone, but God built himself a castle of ice.

The Devil thought this ice castle was so beautiful that he wanted to exchange his stone castle for the castle of ice.

So God made the ice castle melt in the sun. Then the Devil had no castle at all and he had to go elsewhere.

• *34* • *The Rat and the She Rat*

• ONCE THERE WAS a rat who used to go and work in the woods cutting furze. (In the old days furze was used as litter and cut with a scythe.) Now at soup time—that is to say, at noon—this rat did not see his she rat bringing him his food. In the end he started home. And when he got there, what did he find? No she rat. He looked in the soup tureen. The she rat had fallen into it and had drowned.

So then he began to weep. He bumped himself on the bench. The bench said to him, "You poor rat, why are you weeping so much this morning?"

"Oh, my she rat has drowned, and I am all alone!" So then the bench started to leap around. It bumped against the table.

The table said to it, "Oh, you poor bench, why are you leaping around so much this morning?"

> Oh, if you knew, you'd be dancing!
> The she rat has drowned!
> The rat is weeping!
> And I leap because of it!

And the table began to dance. It bumped into the door.

The door said to it, "Oh, you poor table, why do you dance so much?"

> Ah, if only you knew, you'd fall to pieces!
> The she rat has drowned!
> The rat is weeping!
> The bench is leaping!
> And I am dancing because of it!

And so the door began falling to pieces, and as it did so, it bumped into a cart which was standing in the courtyard, and the cart said, "Oh, you poor door, what are you doing, falling to pieces this morning?"

> Ah, if only you knew, you'd roll!
> The she rat has drowned!
> The rat is weeping!
> The bench is leaping!
> The table is dancing!
> And I am falling to pieces because of it!

And so this cart, rolling away, bumped into an oak. And the oak said, "Oh you poor cart, what are you doing, rolling away this morning?"

Ah, if only you knew, you'd uproot yourself!
The she rat has drowned!
The rat is weeping!
The bench is leaping!
The table is dancing!
The door is falling to pieces!
And I am rolling away because of it!

Now on this oak there was a magpie who had made her nest,
and this magpie said very angrily to the oak, "Oh, you wretched
oak, why did you uproot yourself like that?"

Ah, poor magpie, if you knew, you'd molt!
The she rat has drowned!
The rat is weeping!
The bench is leaping!
The table is dancing!
The door is falling to pieces!
The cart is rolling away!
And I am uprooting myself because of it!

The magpie molted near a fountain, and the fountain said,
"Oh, poor magpie, what are you doing molting this morning?"

Ah, if you only knew, you'd flow because of it!
The she rat has drowned!
The rat is weeping!
The bench is leaping!
The table is dancing!
The door is falling to pieces!
The cart is rolling away!
The oak is uprooting itself!
And I am molting because of it!

Yes, but just as the fountain began flowing, a woman who was
about to make her bread came along with two pitchers to fetch
water, but the water was running on the ground.

"Oh, poor fountain, why are you flowing like that when I
am so much in need of water?"

Oh, if you knew, you'd break both your pitchers!
The she rat has drowned!
The rat is weeping!
The bench is leaping!
The table is dancing!
The door is falling to pieces!
The cart is rolling away!
The oak is uprooting itself!
The magpie is molting!
And I am flowing on the ground because of it!

And so the woman broke her two pitchers. As she did not seem to be coming back, her husband went to see what had happened to her, and of course he said to her, "Oh, my poor wife, what have you done?"

Ah, if only you knew, you'd bash the oven to pieces!
The she rat has drowned!
The rat is weeping!
The bench is leaping!
The table is dancing!
The door is falling to pieces!
The cart is rolling away!
The oak is uprooting itself!
The magpie is molting!
The fountain is overflowing!
And I have broken my two pitchers because of it!

Then the man bashed his oven in. A man went by taking a horse to drink at the pond, and he said, "Oh, what are you doing to your oven, you poor man?"

Ah, if you knew, you'd slash your horse's belly!
The she rat has drowned!
The rat is weeping!
The bench is leaping!
The table is dancing!
The door is falling to pieces!
The cart is rolling away!
The oak is uprooting itself!

The magpie is molting!
The fountain is overflowing!
My wife broke her two pitchers!
And I bashed in my oven because of it!"

Thereupon the pond spread over everything, over the dead as well as everything else.

The child asked his grandmother, "And then?"

"And then? The dogs are off! Run after them!" answered the grandmother.

•*35*• *The Little Hen*

• IT WAS harvest time, and there were a little rooster and a little hen who had gone to glean in a freshly harvested field of wheat. Now, then, the little hen was always forging ahead of the little cockerel. In the end the little cockerel said: "Don't eat the lot, little hen. If you go in front of me again, I'll pierce your ruffle." However, the little hen went on gleaning in front of him, so the little cockerel leaped on her little ruffle with one blow from his beak. How could she get her ruffle to heal?

The little hen, who was very put out, went and found the tailor and asked him, "Poor tailor, would you sew my little ruffle, which the cockerel has pierced?"

Then the tailor said, "I'll sew on your ruffle, all right, but you must bring me a nice piece of bacon."

How was she to find bacon?

The little hen went and found the sow. "My poor sow, will you give me a piece of bacon, so that I can take it to the tailor, and he can then sew my little ruffle, which the little cock has pierced."

The sow said, "I cannot give you any bacon until I have eaten acorns."

"How shall I find acorns?" asked the little hen.

"It has to be windy," replied the sow.

The little hen went under the oaks and said, "Let there be wind. Let there be wind to make the acorns fall, so that I can take them to the sow, so that she can give me bacon, so that I can give some to the tailor and he can mend my little ruffle."

Now the wind began to blow through the oaks. Loads of acorns fell down.

The little hen picked up the acorns. She carried them to our sow, who fattened into bacon. She took the bacon to the tailor, and the tailor then sewed the little hen's ruffle, which the little cockerel had pierced.

Part VII
Angoumois and Ruffecois

The Goat, the Kids, and the Wolf

• THERE WAS a nanny goat who had broken her leg. She had to go and have it set at Saint Jard. She had to leave her little kids behind, and she said to them, "I am going off to have my leg set at Saint Jard. Don't open the door to anyone. When I come back I shall say to you:

> Little kid and she kid,
> Open the door for your mother,
> Who comes from St. Jard,
> Where she's had her leg and ankle set.
> Up you get, as if straw tickled your bottoms!

And then I shall show you my white leg. You'll know it's your mother, and you will open the door."

The kids knew quite well that they mustn't open that door. However, the wolf heard what the nanny goat said to her kids. He came to their door and said to them:

> Little kid and little she kid,
> Open the door for your mother,
> Who comes from St. Jard,
> Where she's had her leg and ankle set.
> Up you get, as if straw tickled your bottoms!

But the nanny goat had said to her kids that a white leg must be shown.

The little kids shouted through the door, "Show your white leg!"

The wolf put his leg through a hole, perhaps it was through the cat hole. (You know, of course, that there were cat holes in the doors in the old days.)

The kids saw that he had a black leg. "Oh," they said, "you have a black leg! You are not our mother."

The wolf went and dipped his leg in flour, which was nice and white, and he came back and knocked on the little kids' door, saying once again:

> Little kid and little she kid,
> Open the door for your mother,
> Who comes from St. Jard,
> Where she's had her leg and ankle set.
> Up you get, as if straw tickled your bottoms!

The kids said, "Show your leg!"

So then he had a beautiful white leg. The little kids opened the door, and the wolf was in their home.

"If you have something to eat, give it to me at once, or else I shall eat you."

The kids were so frightened that they did not know what to do. The wolf asked them if they had any *froumajhé* (cheesecake) in the dough bin to give him to eat.

Now it so happened that the nanny goat had just made cheesecake, which she had put into the dough bin next to the cheeses so that the cakes would keep cool. Well, now, you won't believe this. The wolf leaped into the dough bin, the greedy thing, intent on eating the cheesecake. So then the little kids had closed the lid of the dough bin, and the wolf was so busy eating that he took no notice.

When the nanny goat arrived, she knocked at the door, saying:

> Little kid and little she kid,
> Open the door for your mother,
> Who comes from St. Jard,
> Where she's had her leg and ankle set.
> Up you get, as if straw tickled your bottoms!

The kids ran to open the door for her.

"Do you know, the wolf came. He showed us a white leg, so we opened the door, and then he wanted to eat cheesecake. He went into the dough bin, so we closed the lid on top of him."

The nanny goat said they had done the right thing. "Wait a minute! We must put some water on to boil in the stewpot."

The wolf began yelling, "Open the lid of the dough bin!"

"Make some holes in the dough bin," said the nanny goat to her kids.

The little kids pierced the lid, and the wolf was able to breathe more easily. As soon as the holes were finished, the water began to boil over the fire. Then the nanny goat took the handle of the kettle and poured water through the holes in the lid.

The wolf tried to get out of the way, first one side then the other, but he could not escape. Try as he might, in the end he was scalded by the nanny goat.

When they had poured out the whole kettle, the nanny goat lifted the lid of the dough bin and the wolf hurled himself out.

Then the nanny goat stood on the threshhold and shouted:

> The running wolf is on his way!
> Watch out, shepherdesses in the hay!
> The scalded wolf is on the run!
> Watch out, shepherdesses every one!

·37· *The Sleeping Beauty*

• WHILE HUNTING with his guests one day, the King's son, who was after a stag, went astray in the forest. Dusk was approaching, and he was wondering what the night would be like out in the very heart of the woods, when he saw a light shining in the distance.

He followed it and saw a great castle surrounded by high walls. He pulled the doorbell, and the gate opened at once, but he nearly swooned with fright when he saw who was watchman at the gate. It was a monster with seven heads and as many paws, with claws like a lion. She did not harm him. On the contrary, she said to him, "Go to the castle. They are waiting for you. The fairy who made you lose your way did it on purpose so that you would come here."

He went on into the castle and entered a fine banqueting hall, where his place was laid. Footmen holding torches stood behind the chairs. At the end of the table was a girl as fair as the dawn, who said to him, "Come on, it's about time. A hundred years have gone by since my dear godmother promised me that a king's son would come and take me out of this castle and marry me. Is it you?"

The King's son looked at this girl who was so pretty and said to himself, "If she has been here one hundred years, how old must she be?"

He went up to bed, and every day he would eat at her table, as she was mistress of the castle. Afterward he would walk in the great park.

One day as he was thinking how anxious his father, the King, must be not to have seen him again, he saw, coming toward him, a woman with a crown on her head. She said to him, "I am the godmother of the pretty girl you see every day and I know that you love her, but to take her away, you will have to kill the monster who guards the gate. There is no other way out. You must go through the gate; all those who have tried to go through it have been eaten by the monster. I know that you are called the brave Prince, and tonight I shall bring you a sword. You must cut all seven heads off at once, for as soon as a head is cut off, another will grow in its place."

The King's son went up to the monster, whose seven heads rose ready to devour him as she saw him approaching. However, the fairy who had given him the sword was Queen of the fairies, and she made the sword lengthen by at least two meters when the King's son stretched out his arm to protect himself. This allowed him to reap all seven heads with one blow.

At the same time a rook, a very black one, came down from a great oak and squawked, "Long live King Arthur's son, who has set our Princess Yolande free and who shall have her as his bride!"

It took over a month to get the dresses ready. Never had there been such a gorgeous wedding. All the fairies were there, and after the banquet they brought in the monster's seven heads set on a great dish. Ah, yes, but now they were all of gold, and they said that seven children would be born and each of these children would have a ball of gold as a christening present.

That is what happened, and when the seven balls had been given, no other boys or girls were born, but the King and the Queen died in time surrounded by many grandchildren.

The castle of the seven-headed monster still stands in the middle of a great forest, but one can see only part of the high wall, all ruined and crumbling.

·38· *The Three Innocents*

• THERE WERE a girl and a youth who were about to get married. The girl's mother and father had invited the youth to a meal. They were about to eat when they saw that there was no wine on the table. They sent their daughter to draw off enough to drink from the barrel. A few minutes went by and she did not come back. All three wondered what she was doing.

The wife sent her husband off. "Go and see what our daughter is doing since she left to draw the wine from the barrel."

When the father reached his daughter, he found her standing in front of the barrel dreaming.

"What are you doing, Daughter?"

"Oh, Father! I have been thinking,

> If I marry, how do I do it?
> If I have children, how shall I have them?
> And what names shall I give them?
> All the names have been used!"

And the wine went on running out of the barrel.

Then the father said, "Well, you are right, Daughter. We shall both think this out together."

Then the mother, who had been alone with the youth all this time, said, "I do not know what those two innocents are up to. They aren't coming back. I, too, am going to go and fetch them."

Off she went, and when she reached them she saw them both standing in front of the barrel.

She said to them, "What were you up to, you two fools, while we have been waiting for you all this time?"

The fellow said to his wife, "Our daughter is far more clever than we are! She is thinking that if she gets married, how does she do it? If she has children, how does she have them? And what names shall she give them? All the names have been used."

"You are quite right, my poor dear. She is far more clever than we are."

And still the barrel flowed.

So then the youth, who was at the table all alone, stood up, saying to himself, "What are those three innocents up to? Aren't they going to come back? I had better go off and see."

Then when he reached them he found them all three standing like that, thinking.

He said, "What are you up to, you three silly fools?"

Then they told him their stories. They began their chorus, "Our daughter is far more clever than we are. She said to us, 'If I marry, how do I do it? If I have children, how shall I have them? And what names shall I give them? All the names have been used!' "

And the barrel still flowed. The youth bunged the barrel, and then he said to them: "I'm off. If I find three people as crazy as you are, I'll come back to fetch your daughter and marry her."

·39· *Coué or Couette*

· ONCE UPON A TIME there was a ram called Coué (or, if you prefer, a goat called Couette). When his mistress wanted to lead him to the fields, Coué did only as he wished. Coué ate as much grass as he could, but in the evening he did not want to go back into the pen.

"No, no. My mistress has done nothing but make me run all day long. I shall not go into the pen."

So the mistress called the dog.

"Coué does not want to go into the pen. Dog, go and yap at Coué!"

The dog said he did not want to yap at Coué.

The mistress said to him, "Well, Coué does not want to go into the pen. The dog does not want to yap at Coué. Stick, go and beat the dog!"

She stick said that it did not wish to beat the dog.

"All right," she said to him. "Coué does not want to go into the pen. The dog does not want to yap at Coué. The stick does not want to beat the dog. Fire, come and burn the stick!"

The fire said it did not wish to burn the stick.

"Well," she said to him, "Coué does not want to go into the pen. The dog does not want to yap at Coué. The stick does not want to beat the dog. The fire does not want to burn the stick. I shall tell the water to come and put out the fire!"

The water said it did not want to put out the fire.

"All right!" she said to it, "Coué does not want to go into the pen. The dog does not want to yap at Coué. The stick does not want to beat the dog. The fire does not want to burn the stick. The water does not want to put out the fire. I shall tell the ox to come and drink the water. Ox, go and drink the water!"

The ox said, "I'll go and drink the water."

The water said, "Well, I'll go and put out the fire."

The fire said, "All right, I'll go and burn the stick."

The stick said, "All right, I'll beat the dog!"

The dog said, "All right, I'll yap at Coué."

And Coué said, "Oh, well, I'll go into the pen!"

> The ox goes and drinks the water.
> Water goes and puts out the fire.
> Fire goes and burns the stick.
> Stick goes and beats the dog.
> Dog goes and yaps at Coué.
> Coué goes willingly into his pen.

Part VIII
Limousin

·40· *The Gold Ball*

· I AM GOING to tell you the story of the gold ball.

Once there was a girl who lived all alone in a castle. A young man came to see her every day with the idea of marrying her later on. Every evening the old women came to spend the evening with the girl. They said to her, "Oh, Mademoiselle, when you are married we'll come and see you in bed."

On the wedding night these old women wanted to go and see the young woman in bed. Yes, but this did not please the bridegroom. So he left the castle, going by the crossroads. Away went the husband—far away! And she, the poor girl, was very upset and sad about it all. She also left to find her husband, but she did not know where to find him.

Now on the way she met the Holy Virgin, who was her godmother.

She said to her, "Where are you going, Goddaughter?"

"Ah, Godmother, I am most upset. My husband left on our wedding night. He went by the crossroads, and I do not know where he has gone."

"Right. You'll see. I am going to give you something that will enable you to find your husband. I am going to give you a golden ball, and you will throw it. This ball will lead you straight to the place where your husband is. And then I shall also give you a hen with her chicks, all of gold, and finally I shall give you a skein winder made of gold. That will be very useful to you."

The young woman was on her way. She had thrown the ball, and it took her straight to a castle where her husband had settled. Her husband had remarried a certain lady.

The young woman with the gold ball thought of using the things given to her by the Holy Virgin. She brought out her golden skein winder.

The second wife was thrilled with it.

"Madam, if you allow me to spend a night with your husband, I shall give you the golden winder."

And in the end the second wife said, "Yes." However, as she

was cunning, she gave her husband a draught of opium. This drink put him to sleep. The next day he was not able to leave with his first wife. The following morning, as soon as he was awake, they had a talk, he and his first wife.

She said to him, "Tomorrow you will not drink any opium, and we shall both go away together."

So what did the young woman with the gold ball do? She went and stood once again under the castle windows, and this time she brought out her gold hen with its little gold chicks.

The second wife was even more thrilled.

"Oh, Madam, if you allow me to spend the night with your husband again, I will give you my gold hen and all the little chicks."

So once again the lady ended up by saying, "Yes." This time the husband did not drink any opium! Neither of them slept at all, but they left in secret. They took with them the gold skein winder and the gold hen and her gold chicks.

They were careful not to forget the gold ball. They gave it one blow so that it would direct them, and the ball led them to their castle.

And the next morning when the lady found nobody—neither husband nor gold hen nor gold chicks nor gold skein winder —she was most upset, but it was too late.

And now my story is over.

> I passed through a rat hole,
> And my story is whole.

· *41* ·   *The Brother Who Was a Lamb*

· ONCE THERE WERE three children, two brothers and a sister. They had lost their parents. They left home and walked and walked in the woods without ever coming to a fountain. In the end they were thirsty.

Then they met a man, and they asked him, "Where can we find water?"

He said to them, "There are three fountains over there. Do not drink from the first or the second but drink from the third."

When they reached the first fountain, the little girl tried to stop one of her brothers from drinking, but she was unable to and so he disappeared.

She brought her other brother there, but the boy drank from the second fountain and he was turned into a lamb.

As for the little girl, she drank only from the third fountain and she was turned into a beautiful princess who was well dressed.

Every day this little girl went to the fields to watch over her brother, the lamb. One day the King's son went by and found her so attractive he saw a lot of her. And then he asked her to marry him.

"No. I do not want to leave my little brother, the lamb."

"If you come with me, he will not be unhappy at home. He will have the courtyard and the room in which to play and run about in."

In the end she accepted, and both of them came to live in the King's castle. War broke out and her husband had to go off and fight. Now the mother-in-law was not very fond of her daughter-in-law, nor was she fond of the little lamb, who ran about everywhere. She wanted to kill them.

So she had the idea of drowning them in the well. The young woman was pregnant. She caught hold of her and threw her down the well. That is where her baby was born, on a fine white bed which happened to be there.

As for the lamb, even though they made every effort to catch him, he went on running round the well.

As for the King, the mother-in-law wrote to him that his wife was a flirt and that she was now pregnant.

Now the husband came back from the war. The mother-in-law was in bed. She was making herself ill saying, "The only thing that will make me well is to kill the lamb."

The husband said to his servants, "Catch the lamb."

But the little lamb began saying as he jumped about:

> Thérèse, Thérèse, my friend,
> Here are your husband's servants
> Coming to kill me.

The young woman's voice answered him from the depths of the well:

> Jump and skip, my friend,
> Make them run hard!

The servants had to withdraw without having caught the lamb.

Then the husband sent his maids, but the same thing happened. The little lamb ran to the well and said to his sister:

> Therèse, Therèse, my friend,
> Here are your husband's maids
> Coming to kill me.

And the sister's voice answered again from the depths of the well:

> Jump and skip, my friend,
> Make them run hard!

And the lamb escaped again. Neither valet nor maid was able to catch him.

The husband said, "I'll go myself."

The lamb again ran to the top of the well and screamed:

> Therèse, Therèse, my friend,
> Now here's your husband
> Coming to kill me.

But this time the young woman did not answer, and the lamb stayed on the edge of the well.

The husband came nearer, and then the child, who had been born at the bottom of the well, cried out, "Papa!"

The King saw his wife at the bottom of the well sitting on a beautiful white bed. He pulled her out of the well and the child also.

To end off, instead of burning the lamb, they burned the mother-in-law.

·42· *The Ogre*

• ONCE THERE WERE two little boys. Their mother was just about to have another baby. They said, "We do not want a sister. If our mother has a girl, we shall take off for the woods."

The mother died after her little girl was born, and the father married again.

The stepmother did not like the poor little thing. The little girl got to hear from neighbors that she had two brothers much older than she was. The Holy Virgin was her godmother. One day she thought that she would try and find her two brothers; then she started to cry, so the Holy Virgin appeared.

"Why are you crying, Godchild?"

"I want to go away and find my two brothers."

The Holy Virgin gave her a little ball. Perhaps it was even a nut. Then she said to her, "I am going to give you this little ball. You will throw it down in front of you on your way. It will lead you to the place where your brothers are."

The little girl walked along for a while in the woods. Then she ate her bread and walked a little farther. It was beginning to get dark. Now, the Holy Virgin had told her, "You will give your ball a tap, and it will bring you a *ponne* (laundry vat). You will sleep under that laundry vat for the night."

The next day, as soon as she came out from under the laundry vat, the ball was once again there to show her the way.

She tapped the ball again. This time she found herself in front of a *gabiote* (little shack). Her two brothers had built this shack, and they would go out all day to cut wood in the forest.

The Holy Virgin had said to the girl, "You will do the housework for your two brothers. You will sweep the floor and make some soup for them."

So when the girl had finished the housework, the soup was ready to eat. From her ball came a laundry vat so that she could lie under it and sleep there.

That evening her two brothers had come back from the forest. They found the soup ready and everything nice and tidy in their house. They were most astonished.

The first one said, "I am going to have a good look and see if anyone has been here." (He could not see the laundry vat.)

But the boy who was keeping watch fell asleep.

The second one said, "Now I'll watch, and I will not go to sleep."

Then the girl came out from under the laundry vat and she began sweeping the floor. The boy woke up his brother. Then he said to the girl, "What are you doing in our shack?"

She said, "I am your little sister. I have come here to live with you."

The two boys were very glad to see their little sister. They said to her, "You shall stay at home to do the work, but be careful. We have a neighbor and he's the *malbrou* (ogre). Be sure not to go into his home. Be very careful of the fire. If the dog peed on the fire, you wouldn't have one any more and you wouldn't know where to go for one other than going to the ogre's house."

One day the little girl did not want to share her bread with the dog, so the dog peed on the fire. Then the fire died out. How was she to cook the soup? The girl went to the ogre's house. The ogre's wife was there.

"What have you come to fetch, you poor little wretch?"

"I come to ask you for some fire."

"I would willingly give you some, but my husband will come along and he will eat you up."

In the end she gave her some fire. Then the ogre arrived. He could smell fresh flesh. Then he was in front of the shack. He said at the door, "I let you have some fire. You shall give me your little finger to suck every day at such and such a time."

So the girl had to put her little finger under the door, and then the ogre would suck it.

In the end she was getting thin and becoming quite pale because the ogre was sucking her blood.

So then the two brothers asked her why she was getting so thin. She told them that the dog had put out the fire and that then she had gone to fetch some from the ogre. After that the ogre came to the door every day to suck her little finger.

The boys said, "The next time he comes back, tell him to

shove his head forward through the cat hole because you cannot stretch your hand to reach him."

So when the ogre came once more to suck their sister's little finger, she said just that, and then the two boys cut the ogre's head off.

After that, of course, the ogre's wife could no longer find her husband. The boys sold the ogre's head to her. So his wife made combs out of the bones from his head and then she sold them, but even then the combs were traps. Those who combed their hair with them fell sick and could never get well again.

43   *Cinderella*

• ONCE THERE WAS a widower who remarried, and the stepmother did not like the husband's daughter by his first wife. This stepmother had a daughter of her own.

As for the husband's daughter, the stepmother called her *la Cendroulié* (Cinderella) because she was always to be found in the ashes in the hearth. Now the stepmother's daughter was called "Ram's balls" by everyone because she was so ugly.

The old woman and her daughter did not like the husband's daughter. The stepmother was always cross with Cinderella, and the other girl was no better to her.

One day the stepmother had said to her, "Go on off and look after the milking cow." Cinderella led the milking cow into the meadows to graze, but she had been given only dry bread to eat, so the Holy Virgin, who was this girl's godmother, gave her a hazel wand and said to her, "Give your milking cow a tap with this hazel wand, and she will give you something to eat." Then Cinderella took the hazel wand, tapped the cow's behind with it, and out fell bread and cheese.

From then on, Cinderella was well fed. The stepmother was very surprised. "How is it that Cinderella always has such a fresh complexion? All I give her is dry bread."

So then the stepmother's daughter watched to see what Cinderella did with the milking cow and then one day "Ram's balls" also took a wand to hit the milking cow, but the cow only presented her with a cowpat!

The Holy Virgin came along. So then what did the old hag and the girl do? They had the milking cow killed.

Poor Cinderella had no more bread and cheese. This time the Holy Virgin had an apple tree brought to Cinderella so that she could eat apples off it. The stepmother said once more, "How is it that Cinderella still has such a fresh complexion? She certainly hasn't any milking cow to give her food now."

So the stepmother's girl watched Cinderella once again. She saw her picking up apples. The apple tree would lower its branches to give her fruit, and then it would spring back up again. In this way the stepmother's girl could not get hold of these apples, and Cinderella went on having a lovely complexion. But the stepmother said, "You will not leave the house."

She gave her a mixture of millet seed and ash to sort out, but poor Cinderella had nothing to pull them out with. The old hag and her daughter went out for a walk, leaving her, by way of amusement, the ashes to sort out.

So the Holy Virgin brought her a hazel wand to sort out the ashes, and, quick as a flash, the millet seeds were separated from the ash. That evening the stepmother was more than surprised to see the ashes sorted out and the millet seed set aside.

Another time there was a ball in that part of the country. The old hag and her daughter went to it, but Cinderella looked after the house. She wished, however, that she could have gone, too.

So the Holy Virgin gave her a carriage drawn by two shining horses and a coachman to take her to the ball, and Cinderella had a beautiful dress and beautiful shoes. She climbed into the carriage and soon she went past the old hag and her daughter, who were on foot.

There was a Prince at this ball. When he saw this lovely girl, he wished to dance with her.

When the old hag and her daughter were still on their way home on foot, Cinderella had already reached the house in the carriage.

They told her, "If you only knew what a beautiful girl there was at the ball!"

"No fairer than Cinderella," said the girl.

Another time there was again a ball. Once more the Prince danced with the beautiful girl, but this time he wanted to know her name. So then Cinderella tried to run away, and one of her shoes slipped off her foot. The Prince was quick to pick it up while the beautiful girl was on her way home.

The next day the Prince said, "The girl who can slip this shoe on shall be my bride."

When the old hag and her daughter saw the Prince coming to their home, the woman said to her daughter, "Trim your foot, for heaven's sake! Then you will be able to slip the shoe on."

However, although "Ram's balls" tried hard to trim her foot, she could not slip on the shoe. Then the Prince noticed Cinderella, and he wanted to make her try it on. Well, the shoe was hers. She slipped it on at once.

When the stepmother saw that the Prince wished to marry Cinderella, she had her put in an attic, where she was locked up and no one could see her anymore.

Now there was a little dog who started yapping because Cinderella was shut up in this attic.

The Prince followed the dog and let Cinderella out of the attic.

Then the hag and her daughter were turned into stones. There was one on each side of the stairway in that house.

And so Cinderella married the Prince.

·44· *The She Donkey's Skin*

• THERE WAS a gentleman who had a very beautiful wife. His wife said to him before she died, "Do not marry again unless you find a woman as beautiful as I am."

When the gentleman became a widower, he looked everywhere for a wife as beautiful as his first but he could not find one.

This gentleman had a daughter. As she grew older, she looked much like her mother, so the father wanted to marry her. The girl would not listen to her father. She went to find her godmother, who was a *fado* (fairy) and who said to her, "Before you decide, ask your father for the most beautiful dresses in the whole world and wait and see what he does."

The father had people hunting everywhere for the dresses his daughter longed for, but the more she had, the more she asked for. In the end he said to her, "You'll bring me to ruin!" Still he pressed his suit.

The girl went to her godmother again, who said to her, "You are to run away from your father. I shall give you a chest, which goes underground, and a wand to make it do your bidding. You shall hide under a she donkey's skin (*peu d'anisso*), bringing the ears down over your face, and you'll leave your father's home."

The girl took the wand and the chest. When she said to the chest, "Open up!" the chest opened and she put her lovely dresses into it.

She dressed herself in rags and, hiding under the she donkey's skin, she fled during the night.

The next day she showed up at the King's farm. She was hired as turkey girl.

She looked so poor and dirty under her she donkey's skin that at first she was left to sleep outside with her turkeys. Poor Peu d'anisso! The turkeys came and rubbed against her, and this made her even more dirty. The Prince used to watch her going by and teased her because she looked so poor and so dirty.

When she was asked her name, she just replied, "I'm called 'Peu d'Anisso.' "

" 'Peu d'Anisso'? What a gorgeous name for a turkey girl!"

The owner of the farm asked her, "What can you do while you look after your turkeys? Do you know how to sew or how to knit?"

Peu d'Anisso answered, "I know how to make lace." Now this was true. Peu d'Anisso made the most beautiful lace in the world. Seeing that she worked so well, the owner of the farm gave her a room to sleep in. Then Peu d'Anisso took her chest and touched it with her wand, saying, "Open up!"

The chest opened. All the lovely dresses were there, and every evening Peu d'Anisso would wash and comb her hair and try on one of her dresses.

One winter's day Peu d'Anisso was keeping warm in a corner of the hearth. The Prince went by there, and he picked up a poker and gave her a poke with it to keep her at arm's length.

The next day there was a big ball in that part of the country. The King's son went to it, like everybody else. When everyone had gone home, Peu d'Anisso came into her room and opened her chest and took out one of her loveliest dresses. Then she ordered her chest to lead her underground to where the ball was being given. As she came in, everyone stared at her. The King's son went over to fetch her to dance with him. When the dance was over, he asked her her name.

"I'm called 'Poker Poke.'"

"Ah-ha!" said the King's son. "'Poker Poke' is a good name. I'll remember that, all right!"

The next day the King's son called at the farm and talked of the ball and the lovely girl who had been there. He started to tell them, "I danced with the most beautiful girl I have ever seen . . ."

"No more beautiful than I! No more fair!" Peu d'Anisso began saying as she warmed her ragged clothing by the fire.

"Shut up, Peu d'Anisso!" said the King's son, teasing her, and he took the bellows and gave her a puff from them to shame her.

A little later on, another ball was being held. The same thing happened. The King's son begged the beautiful girl to come and dance with him. She had an even more gorgeous dress on and she looked so lovely.

"What is your name?"

"I am called 'Bellows' Puff.'"

"Ah! 'Bellows' Puff' is a good name. I'll remember that, all right!"

The next day he found himself once more with Peu d'Anisso and he talked of his meeting this beautiful girl again.

"No more beautiful than I, no more fair!" she said very softly as she stirred up the ashes in the hearth.

"Shut up, Peu d'Anisso!" said the King's son, who was irritated by all this. He picked up a *friquet* (stick) and stuck Peu d'Anisso with it.

Not long after, there was another ball given. The King's son met the lovely girl again. She was wearing yet another dress. He asked her her name.

"I'm called 'Blow from the Stick.'"

"Ah ha! 'Blow from the Stick' is a good name. I'll remember that, all right."

Without being any the wiser, the King's son went home while Peu d'Anisso, thanks to her chest, fled underground.

Some time later the King's son fell ill. He took to his bed because he was so sick with worry. By constantly thinking of the pretty girl's name, he had got to the stage of asking himself whether she had anything to do with Peu d'Anisso. Had she not said to him, "No more beautiful than I, no more fair . . ."? He was so sick with worry that he refused to eat any of the food brought to him. One fine day he said, "I don't want to eat anything but soup made by Peu d'Anisso."

"Oh, poor Peu d'Anisso! Surely you won't ask her to make you a soup?"

"I will eat only soup made by Peu d'Anisso."

The turkey girl was asked to make the soup for the King's son. She washed herself and combed her hair and put on one of her loveliest dresses so as to be clean to make this soup. The King's son got up without anyone knowing and looked through the keyhole. He saw the beautiful dresses spread all over the room. They shone like gold. As for the girl, she was surely the one he had seen at the ball.

"Open up! Open up, Peu d'Anisso!"

The girl opened the door, but she never again wore her *peu d'anisso* because the King's son did not want her to any more. I don't know whether he ate the soup made by Peu d'Anisso, but what is certain is that he married her and they both were very happy.

·45· The Two Brothers, or The Fox, the Wolf, and the Lion

• ONCE UPON A TIME there were two boys. They were off looking for a job. They were hoping for a few days' work, but they could not get themselves hired. So they said to themselves, "We have nothing left to eat. One of us must blind the other, and then he will lead him around begging for money from people who will take pity on him."

Then the two boys drew lots, each one hoping to draw the lot that would mean he would lead the other. The one who was led had the thin edge of the wedge; there was no doubt that the other ate much better and only gave him dry bread.

One day the one with good eyes said to the blind one, "Guess what? I'll go first in order to cross the ditch, but do keep an eye on it."

And then he left the blind youth at the foot of a tree and ran off after saying to him, "Get a good start and jump!" The blind man jumped and then he reached the foot of an oak tree. So what did he do? He climbed into the branches of the oak tree. When he reached the top, what did he see? A wolf arrived with a roast lamb, then a fox with a goose, and then came the lion with a barrel of wine. All three came under this oak tree to have supper. They ate, and after that they drank all the wine.

"So," said the wolf, "what's new? Over to you, little fox."

"There is a gentleman who has a girl friend. She is very ill. She could soon be well if they knew that by bleeding their old white mare and getting the girl to drink the blood they could cure her. She might even become a beautiful woman."

"Yes," said the wolf. "I know something else. You see this oak tree. Well, whoever, one-eyed or blind, tears off the third layer of bark and rubs his eyes very hard with it will see again."

How the youth listened to what the wolf said about the manner in which his sight could be restored!

In the end the lion said, "At this gentleman's home people go and fetch water from far away. If only they knew that by dig-

ging in their own fields they would find a spring which would
yield enough water for the whole town!"

After this the fox, the wolf, and the lion left the place. The
young man looked in his pocket. He said to himself, "Have I
still got my knife?"

At last he found his knife at the bottom of his pocket. He dug
into the oak, lifted the first layer of bark and took it off. Then
he lifted the second layer of bark and took it off. Finally, he
lifted the third layer of bark and used it to restore his eyesight.
He took out the splinter of oak bark and rubbed it on his eyes.
He saw a bit more clearly. He rubbed again, and then he could
see perfectly. So he waited for daybreak to go and warm up in
the sun. He walked right into town and asked a man for something to eat. Some people gave him bread. He asked for water
to drink. "Oh, we'll give you gold aplenty, but no water. You
have to go too far to fetch it."

So then he said, "If you will dig a hole in this gentleman's
field, you will find a spring."

So great was their need that the people began looking for
water by digging in the field, and they found it. What a miracle! A spring spurted up!

Then the young man went to this gentleman. He asked to go
into this gentleman's house. Then he found himself at the door
of an old oven. He found a servant and asked how the young
lady was.

"Our young lady is very ill."

The young man said, "If they bled your old mare and gave its
blood to the young lady to drink, she would soon recover."

The servant ran to tell his master, "A young man says that
he could cure your daughter."

A fortnight later the young lady was convalescing. By the
end of the year she was completely cured, and these people who
had had to go so far to fetch water now had it in their homes.

This gentleman said to the young man, "You found a spring
in my field to give us water, and you have also saved my
daughter's life. Well, if you like her, I give you my daughter."

The other lad heard what had happened to the blind boy. He
retraced his steps and went and found his friend to find out how
he had recovered his sight,

"Ah, well, you must climb this oak where you left me all alone. You'll soon see what I found there."

A year went by. The fox, the wolf, and the lion came to see each other. Now the lion said: "One of us has given away the secret. It's you, little fox. You're nothing but a fool!"

"No," said the fox.

"Yes," said the lion, and he jumped on the fox, but the fox turned away with his foot up in the air. Then he saw a man in the tree and shouted, "Friend lion, take a look at this spy!"

So the lion cut the roots of the oak, and the oak crashed to the ground, and all three ate the man.

·46· *Little Fourteen, or As Strong as Fourteen*

• THERE ONCE WAS a very poor couple who lived in a shack close by the forest. They had a little boy, but they were so poor that no one wanted to be godfather or godmother to this child, and his parents just called him Petit.

The father died, and the mother was ill. There was so much missing in the shack, even wood for the fires. Petit was not at all strong, but he wanted to go to the forest to gather a small bundle of wood to make a fire and warm his mother. While he was gathering his twigs, a gentleman came toward him and said, "What are you doing there?"

"I am picking up a little kindling to start the fire and warm my mother, who is ill."

"What's your name?"

The boy answered, "As they could find neither godfather nor godmother, my parents call me Petit."

The gentleman said (this was God, by the way), "You will tell your mummy that from today on you shall be called Fourteen. I am your godfather, and the Holy Virgin is your godmother. From now on, you shall eat like fourteen. You shall work like fourteen, and you shall be as strong as fourteen!" Whereupon the gentleman disappeared.

Then as Little Fourteen wanted to lift his small bundle of

wood, he disappeared into the clouds. So he began again, making a huge pile of wood this time. There were oak trees and staddles, which he carried back to the shack on his shoulders. So in this way his mother had a good fire.

Little Fourteen wanted to learn a trade. He went to a smith, who took him on as apprentice, but he was so strong that he even broke the iron. The smith wanted to dismiss him. "Forge me a walking stick weighing five hundred pounds, and I'll go," said Little Fourteen.

He went far, far away with his iron walking stick. He had himself hired as a servant in a great house belonging to a timber merchant. He was sent to the forest with the other servants to gather wood. The others were used to eating a crust of bread before going to work. He swallowed half a loaf, and even then he had not had his fill. At last he went off tucking the other half of the loaf under his arm.

"He eats hearty," said the others. "Let's see if he works as well."

Each of them chose a team of oxen to saddle to a cart. For him they left two oxen who never walked in step. When he stung them with his goad, one would go this way and the other that way. He was very late in reaching the hedgerow. The two other servants were together loading a cartful of wood.

"It's my first time," said Little Fourteen, and, having watched how the other servants did it, he loaded his cartful of wood all by himself. Oh, he didn't take long loading it, but the oxen could not get the cart to budge.

"You'll never manage to take all that wood, will you?" shouted the other two.

"Yes, I will."

"Well, then, go on and try!"

There was no way of making his oxen work. So he unharnessed them. He led them up into the cart, and up onto his back went the whole load—cart, oxen, and all.

When they saw him arriving, one of the servants said to his master, "That's the Devil you've hired as a servant! If he's going to stay here, I'm off."

The second servant said the same thing. Then the master said to Strong as Fourteen, "You may leave."

Little Fourteen went on his way. A little farther on, he met a man making up faggots in a clump of oak trees. He used a whole oak to make the binding thongs.

"Hey, Oak Twister," said Little Fourteen, "come with me. We will not be afraid of each other."

They walked on together. What did they find? A miller was playing *palet* [1] with millstones.

"Hey, miller," shouted Strong as Fourteen, "come on with us. We'll walk along together."

After a good walk, all three came to a castle. They went in. There was no one there. They said to themselves, "We'd be all right here if only we had something to eat!"

When they had really had a good search, they found enough to make a supper. Then Little Fourteen said, "Let's stay here for a few days."

The others were a little afraid of staying in this empty castle. "Why not stay? No one interferes. If only we had a gun apiece, we could go hunting."

They made a thorough search and found two guns.

"We are three," said Little Fourteen. "Two will go hunting with the guns, and the third will make the soup here."

The first time no one wanted to stay alone in the castle.

"Who will stay?" said Little Fourteen.

"I don't want to!" shouted the miller.

"Oak Twister, you stay then and make the soup."

Willy nilly, Oak Twister ended by accepting. When the others had gone, he began to think. There was a big hole in the square in front of the castle. Little Fourteen had said, "Be careful not to fall into the hole."

The two hunters were far away. Oak Twister saw coming toward him an old man with a stick. He had come out of the hole and seemed angry.

"What are you doing here?" he said to Oak Twister.

"Nothing."

"You wait and see what'll happen to you. How could you allow yourself to come into my castle! I shall get you into the hole."

The other did not trust him very far. He fought as hard as he

[1] Game resembling bowls played with flat stones.

could, but he was beaten by the old man and thrown into the hole.

And what about the soup? Oak Twister was to ring the bell to tell his friends that it was ready. The bell did not ring, however. The two hunters were quite surprised. The day was coming to a close, and still nothing rang.

"Let's go home and see whether he has made the soup!"

The table was laid. The plates were there, but there was nobody to sit down at the table.

"Where can he be?"

"Let's eat the soup. After that, we shall see."

As they ate the soup, they heard the other one sighing in the hole. He was crying out as if he had been hurt. Strong as Fourteen came to the edge of the hole and said, "What's the matter with you? I told you to be careful!"

"I went very close to the edge of the hole, and here I am in it."

Strong as Fourteen went into the hole to pull him out.

"Why did you fall so far in?"

The other would not say. A man capable of twisting an oak could not let himself be beaten by an old man!

That evening Little Fourteen said to the miller, "Miller, you will stay at home tomorrow to make the soup. Oak Twister and I will go hunting."

It was never Little Fourteen's turn to stay at home. Once the hunters were away, the old man came out of his hole. He caught the miller and beat him as he had beaten Oak Twister, and then he threw him into the hole.

However, the other one did not boast to Strong as Fourteen about what had happened to him the day before. Now they were waiting for the time when the bell would ring to tell them to go home and eat their soup, but it never rang. They decided to go back home. They saw the table laid but no one there.

Once again Little Fourteen had to go and pull the miller out of his hole, but he would not say a word about it. A man able to spin millstones could not allow himself to be beaten by an old man.

The two confederates, Oak Twister and the miller, said to

each other very quietly, "Tomorrow it will be Fourteen's turn."

The next day Little Fourteen said to them, "Go off hunting both of you! I won't fall into the hole." The others said to themselves, "You'll do the same as we did. The old man will come and find you."

Once the hunters were away, the old man came along. "What are you doing here? Do you want to be beaten and thrown into the hole like the other two?"

"Not I. You'll see."

Strong as Fourteen took his walking stick weighing five hundred pounds. It was the one the smith had forged for him. He beat the old man and threw him into the hole. "Well, now, don't you dare come out again."

After that he went home to put the bread in the soup, and then he rang the bell. The others arrived looking very surprised. It was then that Little Fourteen started teasing them. "Hey, you cowards! You wanted to see me caught like you two, but I did not let myself be beaten, I didn't. I even beat the old man and put him back in his hole. Now, let's eat."

When Little Fourteen dug his walking stick weighing five hundred pounds into the hole, the earth fell away under the surface. The chasm was so great there was no way of reaching the bottom. Then he said to the other two, "You must use a rope to reach the bottom of the hole." Neither the miller nor Oak Twister, however, wished to go down.

Fourteen said to them, "You shall stay up at the top to hold the rope, and I will go down."

When he reached the bottom, Fourteen left the rope and walked underground. He walked so far that he found three lovely girls whom the old man was holding captive, having kidnapped them from their parents. As the old man had been beaten by Little Fourteen, he hadn't enough strength left to hold onto the three girls, and he did not stop Fourteen from setting them free.

"You are going to go back up there," Fourteen said to them, and he shouted to his friends: "Hold onto the rope! I am sending a young girl up to you. She has been held captive by the old man."

When the two confederates saw the girl coming up, the first one said, "I want her for myself."

The other said, "No, she shall be for me!"

"Wait," said Fourteen, "I am sending another one up to you."

When they saw the second girl, who was prettier than the first, the two friends exclaimed, "She is for me!"

"No, I want this one!"

After that, Fourteen sent up the third girl, who was the prettiest of all. The two confederates, scorning the first two girls, both exclaimed, "That one is for me!"

"No," shouted Fourteen, "that one shall be mine." So then the other two cut the rope so that Fourteen would not get the prettiest girl, and they fled with the three girls.

Little Fourteen was underground. He could not get out of the hole. He said to the old man, "If you do not tell me how to reach the top, I shall kill you."

The old man said to him, "Listen. I have a creature who will take you up to the entrance of the hole. You will sit astride it, and each time the creature goes 'Coua', you will give it a lump of meat to eat."

The old man gave him some meat to take with him.

"That will not be enough," he said to Fourteen. "When you are nearly there, the creature will go 'Coua', and you will have no more meat. So you will cut off a piece of your leg and you will give it to her to eat. She will end by taking you up to the top. Take this little pot of fat to grease your leg where you will have cut the end off."

Little Fourteen did as the old man told him, and he recovered at once. The creature left him at the entrance to the hole. He was above ground again.

So then he went searching for his two companions, and he found them with the three girls. After that, I do not know what he did with the miller and Oak Twister, but it is certain that Little Fourteen married the prettiest of the girls for whom his friends had left him at the bottom of the hole.

The Master and the Tenant Farmer

• THERE WERE once a master and a tenant farmer who made a bet.

The master said to the tenant farmer, "We are going to make a bet on who will tell the biggest lie. The one who tells the biggest lie shall win part of the other's harvest."

"Oh, I don't want to," said the tenant farmer. "I need my share of the harvest to live on."

"Oh, well, it doesn't matter. Perhaps you will win."

In the end the farmer had to accept the bet. The master said to the farmer, "You speak first. Tell me your lie first."

So the farmer began like this, "Well, Master, one day I had a lot of work to do. I felt like being idle, so I began to count our bees. Well, Master, I found out how many bees we had, but I could not find a single one. I looked and looked for them. I went in the gorse bushes and then I found them. There were seven wolves busy eating them. Well, Master, I threw my ax at the wolves to send them packing. They had already swallowed half our bees. The other half gave me enough to feed the other bees for seven years. After that I tried to find my ax again. I looked for that ax without ever finding it. In the end I set fire to the gorse bushes. It burned them down and my ax too, but the fire left the handle intact for me. Well, Master, after that, so as not to waste the ashes from the fire, I looked in my pockets and found a bean, and I planted it in the ashes. Master, that bean grew so well. It was such a fine bean plant and so tall that I felt I must climb up it to see how far it went.

"Well, Master, I climbed and climbed from branch to branch and on and on from branch to branch again. In the end I went up and found God busy flaying oats. However, once having climbed up there, I couldn't come down again, so I had to make myself a stout rope. I asked God whether he would give me some oat husks to make into a rope. 'Ah,' said God, 'all right. If you wish it.' Well, Master, I knotted and reknotted oat husks. When I had made my rope of oat husks, I wanted to go down. When I reached the end of the rope, I saw that it was not long enough to touch the ground. Well, I let myself fall on a

rock and I sank into it up to my armpits. At that moment some
women were going to market with their eggs and their cheeses.
They broke the rock, and here I am. Well, Master, now you tell
your lie."

"Oh," said the master, "you've won my share of the harvest.
I can never match that!"

·48· *Fanfinette and the King's Son*

· A GENTLEMAN had three daughters. The youngest was called
Fanfinette. She was also the prettiest. The others were called
Catissou and Martissou, if you like it that way. Their real names
were Catherine and Marthe.

This old gentleman wished to go off on a journey, but next
door to them there also lived the King's son, who wanted to see
Fanfinette.

So the father went on his journey, but before leaving he said
to his three daughters, "Now you won't let anyone into the
house, will you?" Then he gave each of them a rose, saying:
"This goes without saying. Be very careful that they do not
wither."

The father left. It was a long journey. Now the King's
son always wanted to seduce Fanfinette. He said to himself, "Now,
how do I get into her house?"

The first time the three sisters sent him flying. So he dressed
as a beggar. He put on old rags. Now, maybe it was cold. Maybe
it was raining. At any event, he went to their door and he was
shivering—br, br, brr.

They gave him money, but now the King's son wanted to
come in and warm up by the fire. So the eldest of the three
sisters said, "We can let this old man in. He will do us no harm."
However, Fanfinette insisted, "Better let him go on his way."
(She felt he was up to something.)

So the King's son warmed himself for a while. He caught hold
of a piece of his suit and threw it into the fire, thus ridding himself of some of his rags.

"What are you doing, you poor old man?" asked the girls.

"Oh, it's only a bit of my suit that has got scorched!"

By repeating this performance, he ended up by throwing all his rags into the fire, and then he was revealed as the King's son in his proper clothes.

By evening he said, "This time I've got you. I'm going to sleep with Fanfinette."

But Fanfinette replied, "I should not have that honor. It should go to my eldest sister first."

Thus Catissou went to bed with the King's son that night.

Came the second night, and the King's son still wanted the prettiest of the girls. "It's going to be your turn, Fanfinette."

She answered, "Ah, no, the honor is due to my sister, Martissou."

During those nights when the King's son was with her sisters, Fanfinette lost no time. She broke up the floorboards under the bed. As for the King's son, he spent the night with Martissou, of course.

After the second night it was Fanfinette's turn. The King's son was looking forward to this so much, saying to himself, "This time I'll have you."

She said to him, "As you are so happy, I want you while in this happy state to leap into the air." The King's son leaped with such abandon that he went through the loose floorboards and fell into the cellar on top of some barrels, and so Fanfinette was rid of him.

So some time later the King's son, who was very put out, was still saying to himself, "I'll have you! I'll have you!" and now he wished to kill her.

With this goal in mind, he had lined a barrel with nails. Inside it was bristling with them, and he wanted to put Fanfinette in there to die. At the bottom there was one pointed nail which stood out above the others. So then she said to him, "I am quite ready to get into this barrel, but that point is so long it will prevent me from dying."

So then the King's son decided to get into the barrel to remove that nail. Fanfinette made the barrel roll right, left, and center, so that the points would prick the King's son all over.

He was bleeding from all his wounds. Then he wrenched himself out of the barrel as best he could.

Fanfinette went home. So then for a good long while the King's son stayed in bed, all swollen up. The servants wondered what was the matter with him, for he had told nobody about it.

Meanwhile, Fanfinette's two sisters each had a little boy. So then Fanfinette said to them, "You must feed your children well and keep them clean."

Then she made a bundle of the two babes. She dressed as a man and, disguised as a doctor, she arrived at the King's house. Then she said to the servants, "I have come to see your master. I heard that he was ill. I am a doctor. Even if you hear someone cry out, do not move. I will not need you."

Then she went into the room where the King's son lay in bed. She brought out a whip and she hit him good and hard. And did he yell! Fanfinette put the babies on each side of his bed. Then the servants came (she had finished her job). She went away. The two babies started bawling. The servants thought it was their master.

"It's not surprising that the King's son is so swollen. He has just given birth to two babies."

Then their master said to them, "Go and get nurses to suckle these babes and get them out of here!"

So they then did what they wanted with them.

As for Fanfinette, she went home. Soon after, her father came back from his travels. So then each of his three daughters had to show him her rose. Fanfinette's was the only one which had remained fresh. She handed it to her eldest sister, and then the eldest handed it to the second one, and then the second sister returned it to Fanfinette.

Then after this the father said, "This is all very well, but I would like to see all three of your roses at the same time."

Then their father saw that the eldest sisters' roses were faded, but he said nothing.

When the King's son was well again, he went and asked the old father for his daughter. By heaven, it was Fanfinette he wanted!

Yet she would have none of him. He wanted to marry her and kill her because she had made him suffer too much.

She did not want to accept. She took her time answering. Her father kept saying to her, "What have you got against him? He is rich. He is good-looking."

She ended up by saying, "Yes."

Now there was an old nurse who had brought up this son of the King's, and she had never left him. On the wedding night Fanfinette was not at all at ease. The nurse said to her, "My poor Fanfinette. You do not seem happy, and yet you are so pretty and so ready to please."

"Ah, yes! Tonight I shall die," replied Fanfinette. So the nurse answered, "Wait a bit now. I shall go and prepare the room."

She took an enormous marrow and filled it with honey. Then she dressed the marrow and put it in the bed as if it were a person with a nightcap on.

Then, when the King's son came into the room, he took his great sword to kill Fanfinette. He came forward. All at once— Pouf! Right in his face! He tasted a little of the honey which had fallen on his lips. He sucked it and said, "Unfortunate man that I am, I have killed Fanfinette, and she had such good blood." Then he cried and made an uproar in the room. The nurse came. He told her, "I am unfortunate. I have killed Fanfinette, and she had such good blood. Couldn't you bring her back to life?"

The real Fanfinette was hidden under the bed. She had gone, "Ha-ah . . ." when the King's son had pierced the marrow.

The nurse told the King's son to go away. "I'll do everything in my power to bring her back by breathing over her.

The King's son went out. The nurse said to Fanfinette, "Come on out, Fanfinette. I need your help."

So Fanfinette came out from under the bed. Together they took off the sheets full of honey, and they remade the bed.

The nurse said to her, "You will get into bed. If the King's son asks whether he hurt you, you will say, 'Yes.' "

The King's son came up to sleep next to his Fanfinette. Now he was happy to find her.

He said to her, "I hurt you so badly, Fanfinette."

"Oh, yes." She pretended to be suffering and spoke only in a whisper, as if she were in pain.

Then in time they made a good couple. The King's son did not wish to kill his Fanfinette any longer, as she had such good blood.

Part IX
Massif Central

The Bear and the Beetle, or The
War of the Animals

· I AM GOING to tell you the tale about the animals at the time
when they made war on each other.

Once upon a time there were a bear and a beetle at the foot
of a tree. The beetle climbed up the tree and fell off. Then the
bear lifted his paw and put the beetle under it and held it there
a good long time. Then he let him go. So then the beetle said
to him, "You squashed me, and I declare war on you."

"Well," said the bear, "we'll make war by and by. Make up
your army, and I'll gather mine." And they left each other.

The bear went and fetched the panther, the fox, and the wolf,
but the beetle fetched the bees, the hornets, and the other insects. Then they all gathered at the bottom of a valley. When
they arrived, the wolf was not yet there, and the bear said to the
fox: "*Castafi!* Go and see if you can see them coming."

The fox galloped off and went and found the insects. When
the creatures saw him coming, they jumped on top of his head
and stung him all over. The fox had just time to throw himself
in the water in order to get away from the insects, but later he
was very careful not to let on that he had been stung by the
bees.

When the other animals—the panther, the wolf, and the bear
—saw him arrive soaked to the skin, they said to him, "Tell us,
now. What did you get up to?"

"Oh, I am perspiring. I have walked so far my big toes are
so exhausted I can stand up no longer."

"And did you find the insects?"

"Yes. They are up there and they are waiting for you."

"Up with you. Come with us, and we'll go and find them
together."

"Yes, all right. I'll be ready to bite, but you go first and I'll
follow."

When the other animals reached the insects, what did these
creatures do? They did the same as they had done to the fox.

They stung them all over their bodies, and the great big animals lay beaten on the field.

• 50 • *Jean and Jeannette*

• ONCE UPON A TIME there were a man and a woman who had two pretty little children called Jean and Jeannette, but they were as poor as church mice.

One evening the children were in bed, and their father and mother were keeping warm by the fire. Suddenly the woman said, "My poor dear, there is nothing left in the cupboard. We can no longer feed our children. I have only a handful of flour left at the bottom of the basket. I'll make a little round bun, and tomorrow you'll take it with the children. You will go out and let them get lost. Someone is sure to take them in." Jean was not asleep. He heard his mother and saw that she was crying.

The next day their father put the bun in his pocket and, taking the children by the hand, he went off to the woods. On the way, Jean bent over and picked up some small stones, one here, one there, and put them in his pocket. No sooner was he in the forest than he began to drop his pebbles on the moss without his father noticing. When they were in the thick of the forest, their father climbed onto a height and then he said, "You see this bun. I'm going to let it roll down this slope, and it will be for the one who catches it." He did just that, and the bun rolled deep into the woods, and the children ran after it, laughing and shouting.

Jean got there first and picked up the bun. He brought out his knife and split it down the middle and gave half to his little sister, who had only just reached the foot of the slope. This was by a stream. There were lots of birds and butterflies, mulberries and raspberries to pick if they wished. They set to it and ate as many as they could. When they were satisfied, they looked for birds' nests and made whistles and picked flowers and had a lovely time.

After quite a while, the little girl said, "It will soon be noon.

We had better go back to our father." They hurriedly climbed up the slope again. When they reached the top, they began shouting, "Daddy! Daddy!" From all sides came the echo, "Daddy! Daddy!" but no one answered. They roamed around the woods all evening shouting, but search as they might, roam as they might, there was nobody anywhere. Then Jeannette started to cry.

"Don't cry, little sister," her brother said to her, "our father has lost us, but I'll find our way again." He did so by finding his white stones, and by going from one to the other, they came out of the woods. It was about time the sun was setting, and they saw their house far, far away at the end of the world.

When they reached the house, it had been dark quite some time, for the little girl's feet were cut and so she could only walk slowly. When they got there, they looked through the keyhole without anyone seeing them. The oil lamp on the table shone dimly. Their mother and father were eating their soup in silence. Drying her eyes, the woman suddenly spoke. "Who knows where my little children are now?"

"Perhaps they are hungry," said their father.

"Perhaps they are crying," said their mother.

"Perhaps the wolf has eaten them," said their father.

And they began to sob.

The children, who were hiding behind the door, could hold back no longer. They ran in and threw their arms round their parents. They were all crying and gobbling each other up with kisses.

All went well for three weeks, even a month—but the longer it lasted, the less they had to eat. Once more the wife said to her husband, "After all we have done we cannot let them starve to death. Go and lose them again. Perhaps some rich person will take them in." This is what they did.

The next day the father took the children out to pick up pine cones. This time, however, he cut straight through the fields. "Let's take the shortcut," he said.

When they had gone quite far, Jean thought that his father might lose them again, but what could he do? There wasn't a single stone on the grass, and they soon reached the edge of the woods. As Jean looked in his pockets, he found a piece of bread, and he began crumbling it little by little until it was finished. So they picked up pine cones from one side of the woods to the other, but after a while the little girl said, "I'm thirsty, Daddy."

"Me, too," said the boy.

"Don't worry," said the father. "I know a spring over there at the bottom of this gulley. There's fresh water there to slake your thirst." He pointed it out from afar, and while the children were running to it he slipped away. They did not delay long, however, and soon they were on their way back, but when they reached the spot where their father had been—no more father!

"He must have lost us again!" said Jean. "We must get home before nightfall. I'll find the way again." He set about looking for the bread crumbs, but he could not find them. The birds had pecked up the lot. Then Jeannette started to cry.

"Don't cry, little sister," said Jean. "I am going to climb this tree. Perhaps I shall see the house." In three leaps he was up in the middle of it.

"Can't you see anything, little brother?" said Jeannette.

"No, little sister."

"Climb up a little farther. Perhaps you'll see something. Can't you see anything, little brother?"

"No, little sister."

"Climb to the top of the tree. Can't you see anything now, little brother?"

"Yes, little sister. I can see a red house and a white house."

"Throw your knife at the red house and your hat at the white one."

Jean did this, but the wind carried his hat to the red house. "Then it's there we must go!" said the children.

Now the red house was the Devil's house, and the white one belonged to God. As they went into the red house, they saw a woman as ugly as sin sitting by the fire. She had a hooked nose and long teeth. Her hair was like a mare's mane. Her bonnet was all crushed with two little horns sticking out on each side.

"Good evening, woman," said Jean. "Would you let us sleep in your hayloft tonight?"

"I'll make a point of not letting you do any such thing," she said cantankerously, "for you'd set fire to it, no doubt. Hide under the bed, if you like, for my husband is the Devil, and if he finds you, he'll eat you." They quickly slithered under the bed. The Devil's wife threw them a crust. That was all they had for supper.

In the middle of the night, the Devil came home. They heard him dragging the chains through the house and grumbling like a tinker. Suddenly he began to scuffle around. "I smell . . . I smell . . . I smell . . . fresh flesh," he began saying. He picked up the oil lamp and looked under the table, in the cupboards, under the stairs, and in all the corners. At last he found them under the bed, and he pulled them out, one by the leg, and the other by the arm.

"Well, look at this! It couldn't be better. Here's a girl who can become my servant, for my wife's legs can barely hold her up, poor dear. And here's a boy who's a bit on the thin side, it's true (he was feeling his hips), but I'll shut him up in the pig-sty, and I'll eat him when he's fat."

What he said came to be. Jean was shut up in the pigsty, and the Devil's wife kept the key in her pocket. Jeannette worked as the maid and was given a terrible time, as the Devil's wife was a fierce creature.

Every morning and evening she made the pig's meal and took it to her little brother and passed it to him through the cat hole. Sometimes she took him something a little better, like an apple, or a pear, or something else. From time to time, the Devil would slip his hand through the cat hole and touch Jean's little finger to see if he was fat enough. One day Jeannette found a rat's tail as she was sweeping the floor. She took it to her brother. "Take this rat's tail," she said to him. "When the Devil comes, you will get him to touch it. In this way he will never find you fat enough and he won't kill you."

All went well for a time, but one day the boy lost his rat's tail and he could not find it anywhere. He was obliged to let the Devil feel his little finger when he came. This time he found him fat enough. He sharpened an enormous ax and said to his wife, "Now that our meat to be preserved for winter is ready, I'm going to travel. You'll kill him, and when I come back I shall eat him." The Devil's wife was very uneasy about this because she had never done it before. She told Jeannette so.

"Is that all?" she said, trying to stop herself from crying. "I'll show you. Put your head on the block."

The other one did this, and with one blow of the ax Jeannette sent her head flying out in the middle of the house. She took the key and went and opened the pigsty. Then they both hastened to wash away the blood. They carried the Devil's wife to her bed and arranged the blankets to make it look as if she were asleep. Then they went to the stable and harnessed the white horses to the coach and the cart and galloped away.

When the Devil arrived, he was famished, and he saw his wife in bed! He was as angry as a horsefly. "Well, well, well! What do you know? You keep your old carcass in bed while I split my gut going miles across the country!" He went over to the bed to beat her. He took her by the hair, but the head came off in his hands.

"*Fichtre!*" he said, "what is going on here?" He ran to the stables. There were no horses there. In the shelter there was no carriage, in the pigsty no boy. Then he understood, and he lost no time at all! He took to the road like greased lightning. After a little while, he met some haymakers, and he shouted to them, "Have you by any chance seen my Jean and Jeannette with my carriage and cart and my horses with shoes of gold and silver?"

"What are you saying? Is the hay ready?"

"I am not talking about that!" Off he ran like a man demented.

He met a shepherd a little farther on. "Tell me, shepherd," he shouted, "have you by any chance seen my Jean and Jeannette with my carriage and my cart and my horses with shoes of gold and silver?"

"What are you saying? Is my flock at rest?"

"I'm not talking to you about that!" He began running again.

He found three washerwomen by the side of a river. "Ladies, have you by any chance seen my Jean and Jeannette with my carriage and my cart and my horses with shoes of gold and silver?" he asked them.

"Well, yes!" all three answered. "In fact they were galloping so fast that the cobbles were throwing off sparks. They went this side of the river. If you want to catch them, then cut off your legs and put them round your neck."

The Devil cut off his legs and put them round his neck. Then he fell into the river and was drowned.

The cock crowed, and the tale ended there.

·51· *The Magic Napkin*

• THERE WERE two children who had lost their mother and father. It was their stepfather and stepmother who brought them so much trouble. Because of them, they did not have enough to eat and they were crying in the middle of the woods. Suddenly a fairy appeared carrying a napkin.

She said to them, "What are you doing here, children?"

"Oh, we are crying because we haven't anything to eat and we have no money to go and buy food."

"Well," said the fairy, "here is a napkin. When you are hungry, you will spread it out on the ground and you will say to it, 'Napkin, do your stuff!' Then the napkin will bring out stew, bread and butter, and salt meat and fresh meat. When you have finished eating, you will say to the napkin, 'Napkin, do your stuff.' The napkin will then be empty. You will fold it up and take it with you."

The children took the napkin the fairy had given them, and that evening they went home and talked of the meeting they had had. Then the parents hurried the children off to bed and said to the napkin, "Napkin, do your stuff!"

Immediately the napkin brought out stew and salt meat and even fresh meat. After that the parents said to the napkin, "Napkin, do your stuff!" The napkin folded itself up again and looked all clean and neat.

The next day the children left, taking the napkin with them, but it wasn't the one given to them by the fairy. So they went once again to the woods and found the fairy. She asked them, "Well, doesn't the napkin give you anything to eat?"

The children said, "We are not the ones who have the napkin."

So then the fairy said to them, "Well, go to this donkey here, and when you need something, say to him, 'Donkey do what you know how to do!' The donkey, instead of shitting, will give you some five-franc pieces."

The children hastened to try the donkey that the fairy had given to them. The donkey shat five-franc pieces—you want some? Here they are! They quickly went back home to tell what had happened to them. So then the parents told them to go to bed in order that they could make the donkey do its work.

When the children were in bed, the parents said to the donkey, "Donkey do what you know how to do!" The donkey made as many five-franc pieces as they wanted. They kept them and went and found another rather weak-looking donkey to give to the children.

Then the children again went to the woods, but this donkey could not give them five-franc pieces. He could only pour out a few droppings. At that moment they once more saw the fairy who had already given them the napkin and the donkey. She asked them, "Well, are you pleased with the donkey, children?"

"Oh, no, this donkey doesn't give out five-franc pieces any more. He only gives droppings."

"Ah, well, children, here's a stick. When you reach home you will say to it, 'Stick, do what you know how to do!' and it will do this and that."

So when the children took the stick home, and once again they told their parents what had happened. The parents hurriedly took the stick and said to it, "Stick, do what you know how to do!"

However, the stick, instead of giving them five-franc pieces, gave them many a whack!

And now my tale is at an end.

Part X
Forez

• "Cric-crac, clog, kitchen spoon—walk today, walk tomorrow, by walking and walking we cover a lot of ground."

Once, on the day of Saint Sylvester, there was a little white goose who had quite a headache. She decided to go to Cervières in order to get better. To tell you the honest truth, I don't know why. Anyway, whichever way you take it, she was off up the stony paths and climbing, always climbing up toward the mountains. Now, it wasn't until some time later that a tiny cat, who was black as midnight, came out from under a bush and said to the little goose as he politely took off his hat, "A very good day to you, Friend Goose, and where are you going?"

"Good day, Tiny Black Cat. I am going toward Cervières to get rid of my dreadful headache."

"Would you like me to go with you? I'd like a change of air."

"All right. As you wish."

So up the stony path went our two little friends. A bit farther on, they met a smart, curly little lamb, who made a deep curtsy to them. "A very good day to you, little ones. Already up and on your way so early in the morning? And where are you going?"

Little Friend Goose answered, "Good day to you, Curly Lamb. We are going toward Cervières. I'm going to get rid of my dreadful headache, and Tiny Black Cat is going to get a change of air."

"Do you want me to come along with you?"

"Please yourself," purred Tiny Black Cat.

And there they went all three of them climbing up toward Cervières.

They went by a great meadow where a fine heifer was about to birth to a calf. She put her snout over the hedge and said to them politely, "A very good day to you, you three beasties. It's a steep climb. Why don't you stop for a little while to get your breath back? And where are you going?"

"Good day, dear Heifer-Ready-to-Deliver. We are going off

in the direction of Cervières. I am going so as to get rid of my dreadful headache. Tiny Black Cat is going to get a change of air, and Curly Lamb is going along with us just for the walk."

"Would you like me to come along with you all? That would make four of us."

"Just as you like, dear Heifer-Ready-to-Deliver," said the cat, raising his tail.

"It's a great honor for us," bleated Curly Lamb.

By dusk they reached a shabby-looking house. They were rather keen to take shelter to avoid Mr. Wolf. They went to the little window where a light was shining. My dear friends, this was no castle. There was a tall bed with two puffed-out pillows and a neatly tucked red blanket. There were also a chair, a bench, and a big table. A chest in which to store clothes stood in the corner, and that was all. In the fireplace a lifeless little fire threw out a thin flicker which didn't look very hot. An old woman was sitting on the bench, and she was talking to herself out loud.

"Ah, my friends, what haven't I been through! To think that there are people who have bacon to eat and they complain. Ah, what a world! I don't even have a goat to give me milk, nor do I have a sheep to give me wool, so that I could spin and knit myself some nice warm woolens. I always have to drag about in rags. I don't even have a little hen to lay an egg for me. All by my lonesome self, all alone I live without even a cat to listen to me. Life is much too long for me."

Outside Friend Goose, Tiny Black Cat, Curly Lamb, and dear Heifer Ready-to-Deliver were all ears. All at once little Friend Goose said, "I haven't a headache any more. Let's go in."

She put up her foot and scratched gently at the old woman's door.

"Come on in," said the old woman, turning away slightly.

"Good day, old mother," said Tiny Black Cat, putting his hat under his arm.

Then he coughed, and while Friend Goose was putting her head on one side and tying her bonnet, and Curly Lamb was drying his eyes, and dear Heifer-Ready-to-Deliver stretched out her neck to see better—as she had stayed outside so as not to dirty the house—he spoke. "We are four friends, and we were on our way to Cervières. But we still have far to go, and the night is pitch black, so you shall put us up for the night. Friend Goose will go in the hen house. Dear Heifer-Ready-to-Deliver and Curly Lamb will go to the stable, and I'll stay by the kettle and keep an eye on the fire."

Did the old woman ever welcome all this! She kissed Curly Lamb and scratched dear Heifer-Ready-to-Deliver's forehead. She stroked Friend Goose and led them all to their beds. Then she picked up Tiny Black Cat in her apron and sang him a lovely song to send him to sleep.

They all lived together very happily. Never was the old woman hungry or thirsty again.

Little Friend Goose never had another headache, and never again did any of them want to climb to Cervières.

·53· Half Chicken

• ONCE THERE WAS a tiny little hen, so thin and so weak the mother hens called her Half Chicken. And what a life they led her! Those beaks were busy, believe me! Poor Half Chicken's head was quite bald because of it, and her wings were all plucked. Even at night the rooster and the hens gave her no peace. She had to go and crouch under the perch, and droppings would fall on her comb. The other hens were doing it on purpose.

So much so that one morning Half Chicken had enough. She took the little bit of grain the others had left. She put it in a small bag under her right wing and, as the door of the barnyard was open, she went away without saying goodbye to Tchouca or to Faverotte or to Rita or to White Jau.

The road was good and flat. The sun warmed Half Chicken's sticky feathers, and she felt so fit she began singing, "At Essertines at Chambest the hens crown the roosters!"

Well, then, as she was full of beans, she thought she would

go to the King. So off she went as fast as she could. The wee hen's feet were steaming, she was going so fast. Every so often she rearranged her small bag of grain under her wing and then she was off again. As she went along by a pine wood she heard someone calling her.

"Help, Half Chicken, help!"

The kind little hen left the path and began looking under the junipers.

"Here, here on the right."

In the end she found the wolf lying on his side, and he looked so tired it made Half Chicken sit up.

"Half Chicken, I am all in. Take me with you or else I shall die."

"Come on, Sir Shaggy Wolf, come with me. Climb into my neck, and I will carry you." Panting hard, Shaggy Wolf slipped into the little hen's neck.

She went on her way just a little bit more slowly.

After going through another hamlet and another copse, Half Chicken reached the bank of a river.

"Half Chicken! Half Chicken!" said the water, "I am quite exhausted because I always have to flow in the same direction. Take me with you."

Half Chicken took pity on Fair River, who was so bored. "Draw in your claws a little," she said to the wolf. "The river is coming in next to you. Come on, Fair River. Come along with me. Climb into my neck, and I will carry you."

Fair River made haste and in a flash she went into Half Chicken's neck, and Half Chicken started off again just a little more slowly.

At four o'clock in the afternoon, they saw in the distance a big city with golden tiled roofs and chimneys of finest silver.

"This must be His Majesty the King's city," thought Half Chicken. She stood on the crown of the road to shake off the dust on her wings. And then she made a face. "I smell something jolly, like burning!"

In her neck Shaggy Wolf began to cough. A bonfire of couch grass was smoking so much it was difficult to see through the smoke.

"Half Chicken! Half Chicken! I am tired of burning and smoking. Take me with you and carry me."

Half Chicken flapped her wings a bit and said that before doing anything else she would put the wolf in the middle of her neck. Think of it—water and fire! What a life they would have led side by side! And also the river being on the right and Shaggy Wolf in the middle, the little hen turned to the fire and said, "Let's go, Burning Fire. Come along with us. Climb into my neck, and I will carry you."

Burning Fire was soon ready. He crouched in the hen's neck and, as he had good manners, he made himself very small so as not to heat Half Chicken or roast Shaggy Wolf or make Fair River have the vapors. So Half Chicken, who by now was heavily loaded, moved off very slowly.

Just as the sun was setting, Half Chicken reached the King's house. She scratched at the great door. A footman dressed in greenish silk opened it, and without further ado the little hen headed for the King's room. My dear children, you should have seen it. My, it was something! On the wall hung masses of huge embroidered cloths. Sheepskins and hides of all sorts of strange animals lay scattered on the floor. A table was loaded with ham, roast rump of veal, little suckling pigs with mustard under their tails. The King, seated on a glittering throne, wore a great red cloak, and he had a nice new hat on his head.

Half Chicken came in carefully lifting each foot so as not to get tangled up in all the skins lying there as carpets. She made three curtsies before His Majesty the King, and, stretching out both her wings, she said, "A very good day to you, Your Majesty. I have come on foot from near Poncins to see you. I was so weak the other hens tore my feathers out. I come to ask you for a new coop and a handful of grain and some clear water. In return I shall lay one egg for you every morning."

The King started to laugh. He did not reply at all, but he beckoned to a long tall weed of a servant, who was looking his way, and Half Chicken found herself in a hen house with mother hens ten times larger than Tchonca and a golden rooster like one I saw as a weather vane some time ago. Think of it! The King's hens!

Yes, only these hens were as mean as they were large. As soon as Half Chicken had settled on her perch and was getting out her little bag of grain to eat, they began to shove her about with their wings and with their claws and made her take that on the head and take that on the rump. Filthy words showered down on Half Chicken. Suddenly she said, "Shaggy Wolf! Shaggy Wolf! Shaggy Wolf! Come out of my neck now, or I am a poor lost chick!"

The wolf came out, and in a minute all the hens fled.

The next morning when the footman came in he found all the hens with white combs and stiff legs, and Half Chicken was all alone on the perch.

"You spiteful fool of a hen! Look at your handiwork. Don't you budge, my little friend. You'll see how you get roasted!"

The screams from Half Chicken's throat were enough to deafen one. It wasn't long before the poor little hen was thrown before a roaring fire with her feet tied. This was a fire worse than the one used to boil the Devil's cauldrons.

The little hen thought the end had come, and in a tiny voice, which was all choked up, she said, "Fair River, Fair River! Come out of my neck, or else I am a poor lost chick!"

And here came my Fair River, murmuring softly as she flowed on and on. She put out the fire and upset the kettles and threw down the servants in the kitchen. She rose and rose, drowning everything except the King, who had climbed on top of a cupboard with his wife, and Half Chicken, who was stuck atop a dresser. Only the water was still rising and was going to spoil everything, so, with all the power she could muster, the little hen said, "Burning Fire! Burning Fire! Come out of my neck, or else I am a poor lost chick!"

Burning Fire came roaring down worse than the wind in the great pure forest. Things soon dried up, believe me! Half Chicken flew down to the ground and shook herself. She put up a small ladder and made the King come down. He put out his hand for his wife, so that she, too, could get out. They were all there on the ground. The King said, "My little Half Chicken, you have caused me a lot of trouble, but you were no coward and you saved both of us, my wife and me. I shall

give you a fine house. I shall give your wolf a forest, and your
river shall have a country, and your fire shall have all the
chimneys."

The King did as he said, and they lived to such a ripe old age
that no one in their lifetime could tell my great-grandmother
about the end of their lives.

Part XI
Franche-Comté

·54· *The Wolf and the Fox*

• THERE WERE once a fox and a wolf who got together. They bargained for a field of grain, which was to be harvested. As they cut it down, the fox had an awful backache—so much so that he stood up and yelled, "Excuse me, please!"

The wolf said to him, "So, what's the matter with you?"

"Oh, I think I'm being called upon to be godfather."

"Oh, well," said the wolf, "you'd better go. One can't refuse a christening."

By golly, that fox picked up three sheep's droppings, rolled them in flour, and then he dipped into the butter in the pot, and after that, believe it or not, he went back to the wolf and said to him, "Look, here are three *dragées* [1]. We haven't bought any. You see, we are not well off. Well, what d'you think of them?"

"Well, they're not so bad. What kind of name did you give him?"

"Gobbled."

"Oh," said he, "that'll do."

Anyway, they went back to work. The fox's backache came back. He started to yell, "Excuse me, please!"

The wolf said, "Well, now, what's the matter?"

"Well, I'm needed to be godfather once again." Then the fox went on to say to the wolf, "You ought to go."

"Oh, indeed no. It's better if you go. You walk better than I do."

So the fox went off. He picked up two or three more sheep's droppings and then he ate half of what was in the butter pot. Back he came to the wolf and he gave him the sweets. "I just can't buy any as I am godfather so often."

"What sort of name did you give him?"

"Half."

Back to work they went, and they scythed more of the harvest.

---

[1] Sugared almonds, a traditional sweetmeat offered at christenings.

Then about an hour later the fox began to yell again, "Excuse me, please!" The wolf did not listen. He was making haste. Then the fox yelled again, "Excuse me, please!" and said to the wolf, "They want me to be godfather again. Go on, Wolf. You go, Wolf. You ought to go. Run along and give yourself a bit of a rest."

"No, indeed not. I don't want to go. I can't read or write. What should I go for? Go there, Fox. You go once more."

So, by my faith, off he went, that fox. When he got there, he licked the butter pot clean and he didn't bring back any sweets.

Then the wolf said to him, "What name did you give him?" "Well-Licked."

Well, when evening was coming, the wolf was dead tired. The fox said to him, "Wolf, you don't know it, but you've got to go and make the soup, and you're dead tired."

The fox worked on till night and then he came home. The wolf was in bed. The fox said again, "What you doing in bed? You haven't made the soup, then?"

"What would I have put in the soup, I'd like to know, seeing as how you've eaten everything. Three times you went off to be godfather—some godfather! You came after the butter pot. You gave it a name all right—Gobbled, Half, and Well-Licked. Fox, I've got to eat you."

Fox said to him, "No. The one who feels like going to bed will be the one who's eaten the pot of butter."

"Fine!" said he. "I don't want to go to bed. I haven't eaten anything. I haven't had any supper. This time I've got to eat you."

"Wolf, I know you like meat. A butcher comes by there on the road every Tuesday. You ought to go out there and pretend to be dead. Then, when the butcher goes by, he'll say, 'Oh, I won't skin him just now. I'll throw him into my cart like that.' You'll grab the pieces of meat and run off."

Well, now, the wolf went away and pretended to be dead. The butcher came along and stopped his cart. Then he said, "Here's a dead wolf. What shall I do with him? Well, I'll take my knife and I'll skin him." When the wolf felt that the knife was pricking him a bit, he ran away. He came back to the fox, and this one said to him, "Then you didn't do as I said?"

"Oh, yes, I did, but, instead of just chucking me in his cart, the butcher wanted to skin me, so I ran away," said he. "So I've got to eat you this time."

"Well, no, Wolf. There's going to be a wedding in the village nearby. Now that means we'll both go there while they're all at the Mass. We'll have a good tuck in, and then we'll run away."

So off they went. They got to the wedding. The windows were open. They slipped through the bars. They got through those for sure. Then the wolf dived into one dish and made a pig of himself—that's for sure! The fox would grab something and eat it and then jump out again. That wolf really set to it and stuffed himself.

Then after a long stretch the fox came out and yelled at the wolf, "Get out of there, Wolf. Here come the wedding guests."

The wolf tried to get out, but he'd eaten so much he couldn't slip through the bars this time. When the guests came in and saw all the dishes knocked over, they grabbed some clubs and they hit the wolf. The wolf came out quite exhausted, and the fox said to him, "Well, Wolf, did you dine well this time? Did you really have a good feed?"

"Yes, I had a good feed but I've had quite a bash."

"Should have done the same as me, Wolf. You should have come through the bars. I kept taking a piece, and then I would come out to see if I could still get through."

"But, Fox, you ought to have told me. This time, Fox, I must eat you."

"No, Wolf, no. I know you like fish. We'll go on a night when there are lots of fish. You put your tail in the water, Wolf, and when you feel them biting, we'll pull it out and then you'll have a fish."

So there he was putting his tail in the water, and it froze solid. When it was good and frozen, he pulled out his tail, but it was all skinned.

"This time, no fooling, I must eat you."

"Well," says he, "no. Look here, Wolf. Tonight I know where there's a lovely bit of cream cheese. I know you like it."

So then he was off that night. It was a lovely moonlit night. The moon was full. He led him to a well and said, "Wolf, you take a look and see if there isn't a fine cheese? Now you need to go down in a bucket. I'll let you down, and then when you reach the cheese you jump onto it."

When the fox heard the wolf jump onto the cheese, the fox brought up the bucket and the wolf drowned. So be it.

·55· *The Wolf and the Fox in the Well*

• THE WOLF FOUND the fox and said to him, "Ah, here you are. Well, you'll make two nice mouthfuls for me."

"Oh, I do beg your pardon! I do beg your pardon!"

"Well, find something for me."

"I'll find something."

"Now, what are you going to find for me? I want you to find me a whole cheese."

"Oh, I'll find that for you."

"Agreed."

They crossed three orchards and went round Benjamin's place (the Faivret used to live there), and then they crossed the garden belonging to the Chalandre (between Benjamin and Fortunat). Then they were in Fortunat's yard. There was a well there with coping stones around the edge. It was a well with two buckets and a chain and pulley.

"I can't see anything there."

"Yes, wait a bit. It's here at the bottom. There is something. There's cheese there, I promise you."

Now the moon was shining down directly into the well, so the fox said to him, "Look!"

"Well, then, go on down."

"Oh, what a millstone of a cheese! Look how big it is! Look at that millstone of a cheese!" he shouted from the bottom. Then he said to the wolf, "Climb into the other bucket."

As the wolf was heavier than the fox, he was soon down at the bottom, and the fox was overhead.

"Well, you wanted to eat me. This time you come up. I'm safe!"

The wolf kept saying, "Draw me up. When I reach you, I'll gobble you up."

But he didn't reach him. He drowned instead.

• 56 • *The Black One, the White One, and the Plucked One*

• ONCE UPON A TIME there were three ewes. There were a black one, and a white one, and the plucked one. They had been together in the same pen for a long time. They went to the fair—the Gendrey fair—and when they reached the corner of the wood, there was the wolf waiting for them.

"Oh!" said he to the black one, "Black ewe, you black one, I must eat you!"

"Oh, poor wolf, help yourself to the white one who is behind me, for I am too thin!"

"White ewe, you white one, I must eat you!"

"Oh, do eat my sister who is behind me!" (This was the plucked one.)

"Oh, plucked one, plucked one, I must eat you!"

"Oh, poor wolf, eat me if you like! I am nothing but skin and bone."

"Oh, really? Well, I'll wait for you to come back."

So they went off and reached the fair at Gendrey. There they began browsing in a field of clover. Oh, they really ate well for eight long days! They were much more plump than when they had set off.

Now they were on their way back. They were no longer thinking of the wolf, but he still had his mind on them.

"Hey, black ewe, I must eat you!"

"Oh, wolf, let me by! Eat my sister who is behind me!"

(The narrator stops at this point, and the audience asks, "And what about the plucked one?")

"Kiss her on the backside so her feathers will grow back again!"

Part XII
Dauphiné

·57· *The Girl and the Thief*

• A FATHER and mother with a daughter had gone to the fair. They had asked a neighbor to come and sleep with her. As she bent down, this neighbor saw a man lying under the bed. She said to the girl, "I must go and get my bonnet and I'll be back."

As she did not seem to be coming back, the girl said her prayers and went to bed. Now the man came out from under the bed and said to her, "You must give me everything you own in the house."

After that they made bags out of the linen. When he was ready to tie up the bags, he asked her for some string.

She answered, "Oh, I haven't any string. When my father wants to tie up a bag, he climbs up the tree outside and cuts off little twiglets that bend easily."

He said, "All right. Come and give me some light." The girl lit the lamp and went out to give him some light. When he was at the top of the tree, she put out the lamp and went in. She locked herself in and barricaded the door. He came down from the tree and began scrabbling under the door. He said to himself, "I'm getting my hand through. I'll manage the rest."

As he put his hand under the door, the girl cut it off. When her parents came home she was so scared that she did not want to open the door to them. But they made themselves known, and as soon as they were in, she explained to them what had happened.

A few years later a boy showed up and asked to marry her, but the girl recognized him. He had one gloved hand and the other was bare. She said to her parents, "Next time he comes, ask him to take off his glove."

So when he came back, the father said to him, "I wish you would take off your glove."

The other answered, "It isn't the fashion in my part of the world. When you ask a girl to marry you, you keep your gloves on."

In spite of this, the father wished his daughter to marry this man at any price.

When they were alone together, he took off his glove and said to her, "You see this one is sister to that one—you cut it off but you'll be sorry."

As soon as they were back in his home, he tied her to the foot of the bed and he said to his mother, "Keep an eye on her and see that she does not get away. In the meantime I shall get the knives ready to bleed her."

Then the girl started begging her mother-in-law to let her go.

"Here are some pins. Scratch your face with them and say that it is I who scratched it and that you could not hold me back any longer."

Well, after that, she went away and reached home, saying, "I told you he was the one. He wanted to kill me."

Her parents kept her in their house. Then one Sunday she was with her mother and father at Mass. The girl turned round and saw the thief at the foot of the church. She told her father. The father went out to warn the police, who then arrested the thief. The girl then went on living with her parents. That is the end.

·58· *The Devil's Boot*

· A LANDOWNER'S SON had used up every penny of what his father had left him. When he discovered he was bankrupt, he made the acquaintance of a young lady who owned a castle and was of his class. So he went to her father to get permission to marry her. Her father said to him, "How can I give you my daughter—you who got through a fortune in such a short time! But as you love each other, I'll give you my daughter if you manage to remake your fortune within the next year."

So the landowner tried to get a loan to show he had done something, but as his credit was bad, he found no one who was ready to lend him anything.

One day as bankruptcy approached, he was standing on top

of his castle pulling his hair out, when he shouted, "Only the Devil can get me out of this one!"

That very minute he smelled sulphur, and a man dressed in red appeared before him. He had horse's feet. He said to him, "You called for me? What do you want me for?"

So the landowner explained his situation. He said that it was gold he wished for. Only gold would save him. The Devil answered, "You wretch! We make all the gold where I come from. I'll give you as much as you like and more!"

"Yes, but what will I have to give you in exchange?" he retorted.

The Devil said, "Not much. There is nothing you need give me during your lifetime. Only, after your death, you shall give me your soul."

So then he thought and said to himself, "I would like his gold but I would not like to give him my soul forever." He said to the Devil, "Come back at the same time tomorrow and I shall give you the right answer."

So then he thought again. He took a boot and punctured the bottom of it and he placed it at the top of his castle, having first pierced the floorboards and emptied the rooms. When the Devil appeared, he said to him, "If you fill my boot in one hour you shall have my soul, but if at the end of one hour the boot is not full I shall keep your gold and my soul."

The Devil answered, "That's a deal. Tomorrow at the same time I shall be here with the gold."

The next day the Devil arrived with several of his minions, each of whom carried a bag of gold on his shoulders, and he made them empty them into the boot. However, at the end of an hour, the boot was still far from full, as it was punctured. My grandfather used to say that it was a riding boot.

So after that the Devil went away swearing stormily, and the landowner kept his soul, and with the help of the Devil's gold, he was able to marry the girl.

Well, now, that really is the end.

• A YOUNG married couple, who were not very rich, had, during the first few months of their wedded life, to borrow a small kettle for boiling their soup. Then later when they had to return it to its owners, neither husband nor wife could make up his mind to go. The wife would say, "Well, then, you go and give it back!"

Then he said to her, "Look, we'll do this. The first one to speak shall take back the kettle. You can sing as much as you like, and I can whistle."

This man was a shoemaker, and his wife was a weaver. They spent their days singing and whistling. She sang as he wove, and he whistled as he drew the awl.

Now it so happened that the King and his following came out hunting in the vicinity. Night came upon them in the wood. Suddenly their lantern went out. Then they saw light coming from this house, and the King sent his servant there to get a light for the lantern. The servant went into the house and spoke to the woman, saying, "Would you allow me to light my candle from your lamp, Madam?"

The woman showed him her lamp, singing. The servant said to himself, "Either that woman is crazy or she is mute." And he turned toward the man and asked him, "Would you allow me to light my candle from your lamp, sir?"

The man pointed at the lamp with his awl, whistling. The servant went to the King and said ot him, "Those poor people must be out of their minds. I can't understand it. They don't speak!"

So then the King came to see to satisfy himself. He asked the woman, "Would you allow me to light my candle from your lamp, Madam?"

The woman began to sing as she pointed at the lamp with her finger. Then the King said to the shoemaker, "Allow me, Sir, to light my candle from your lamp!"

Now the man pointed at the lamp with his awl, whistling. The

King said, "Poor wretches! We must have them taken away from here!"

He started by taking the woman on his back, but when the shoemaker saw his wife going off, he wept and said, "Oh, Sir, please, Sir, give me back my wife, and I'll return the kettle!"

·60· *The Fearless Shoemaker*

• IN THE OLD DAYS people were very much afraid of having to keep watch over the dead.

There was a shoemaker who was not afraid, though. So a man said, "I am going to scare that shoemaker, I am."

He pretended to be a dead man, and the shoemaker went and watched over him, having brought some of his work with him. Now, during the night the other man sat up and said, "When one watches over the dead, one does not work!"

However, the shoemaker replied, "When one is dead, one does not speak!"

He gave him a blow on the head with his hammer and really did him in.

It was the other man who got caught!

Part XIII
Savoy

• THERE WAS an old woodcutter who lived with his wife at La Fraissette. Now his wife was called Jeannette. They were the only ones to live there all the year round. They would spend the winter there.

One night they were going to have their soup. The woodcutter was making up a basket. As it was hot, they had opened the door. Coming back to the table to put down her pot, Jeannette let out an "Ah!" of surprise as she stared through the half-open door. Her husband turned round, and what did he see? There stood a wolf, a huge one. This wolf was a big as a donkey. Jeannette was standing there with her tureen in her hand. Her husband shouted at her, "Pour away, Jeannette!" So then his wife tipped the pot over the wolf. The animal gave one howl and fled into the depths of the forest. He was steaming all over. They quickly closed the door, and that night they went without soup, but they were only too happy to have rid themselves of the wolf.

Some time later, when it was fine, our woodcutter went off to the forest. He went to the Replat to make a few faggots. His wife had packed his game bag. He began making a faggot, and he did not notice the time going by. Dusk came and he found he had strayed a bit in the forest. It took him quite a while to find his game bag. Well, by the time he had finished roaming around looking everywhere, night had fallen and he could hear the howling of the wolves. He set off for home as fast as he could, but the howling began again and he climbed up a fir tree. Now what did he see coming out from a corner of the clearing? There was a huge wolf. It was their wolf, the scalded one! The woodcutter recognized him. His coat had not yet grown back. The wolf stopped at the foot of the tree. He sniffed the air and he, too, recognized the woodcutter, and with his wolf's brain he worked out: "This is it. This time I have him." He let out a terrifying howl and called his brothers. A few seconds later the whole pack arrived. There were ten, fifteen, twenty. There was a whole pack! They formed a circle round the tree. Then at a given moment the wolves stood aside and held a meeting. After a minute or two they came back to the foot of the tree. The scalded one placed himself at the foot of the tree, and the wolves made themselves into a ladder. One climbed up, then another, then a third, and a fourth. The woodcutter, who could see them coming, climbed higher, too. In this way they reached the top of the fir tree. Our poor woodcutter felt that he was caught, and he saw the wolf climbing and climbing and knew that he could be reached. Then the woodcutter shouted, "Pour away, Jeannette!" The scalded one, remembering the words referring to the tureen of boiling soup, took off at once, but it was he who was holding up the column of wolves, and so down they all came. They fell at the foot of the fir tree and, limping as they went, they ran back to the depths of the forest. The woodcutter went home.

Soon it was Christmas, and there was a little snow. One day Jeannette said to her husband, "Next week it will be Christmas. We must go down to Chambéry to buy some food. You'll take the small sledge to cross the Col des Prés, and you'll put a small barrel on the sledge."

She gave him a snack and a little wine, and the woodcutter left, drawing his barrel along on the little sled. He went by the Col des Prés and went down the other side. When he reached the Croix de Fornet, he met half a dozen brigands, who asked for his money. Afterward they said, "What are we going to do with this man?"

The leader said, "We've only to bring him down and throw him into the ravine." But one of the younger brigands said, "After all he is an old man. We are thieves, not murderers. We must let him live."

Then the leader said, "We've only got to put him in his barrel and then we'll run away."

They took out the bottom of the barrel and put the woodcutter into it. They put back the bottom and the bands, and then they left it. The leader sent the barrel rolling down into the ravine.

The barrel came to a halt against a bush, and our woodcutter came to. He wondered how he was going to get out of the barrel. He tried calling through the bunghole, but no one

answered. Night fell. He felt cold, but luckily he had his little
bottle of wine to keep him going. The night was followed by
another day spent in the same manner. A second night fell.
Our woodcutter felt all was lost. He said to himself, "This time
this is the end."

There was a moon, and the cold was even more intense. Now,
in the middle of the night he heard a noise. He glanced through
the hole, and what did he see? The scalded one!

The scalded one came up to the barrel and sniffed at it, and
then he began to scratch around it a little, growling. In the
end he went right round it. Now at one point the wolf stopped,
and the woodcutter saw the wolf's tail swinging in front of the
hole. He put his hand through the hole and grabbed the end
of the tail and pulled it in. Then he shouted, "Pour away,
Jeannette! Pour away!" Our wolf at once imagined the kettle of
boiling soup hanging overhead. He set off as fast as he could,
dragging the barrel and the woodcutter after him. He climbed
up the ravine in this fashion, and helter-skelter they went over
the Col des Prés again. Then he reached the chalets of La
Fraissette.

When the woodcutter saw the smoke from the chimney of his
house, he let go of the wolf's tail and came to a halt in front of
his home. He called his wife, "Jeannette!" Jeannette!" Jeannette
came up to the barrel. She saw that it was her husband shut up
in there and she set him free.

The scalded one was never seen again.

•62• *Princess Elisa*

• THERE WAS once a beautiful Princess called Elisa. She wished
to marry a man who could stay hidden either in the heavens or
on earth or in the sea, and she gave him only three days in
which to hide.

Now there was a man who had found an eagle fallen from
its nest. He put it back in its nest, and then he went and found
the Princess. She said to him, "I am quite willing to marry you,
but do try and hide well."

So then he went away to hide. He met the eagle whom he had helped. The eagle said to him, "Well, now. You are going to climb onto my back and hang onto one of my feathers. I shall fly so high up into the sky that the Princess will not find you."

So then off went Princess Elisa to look for him, and she began shouting, "Earth, give him back to me! Heavens, give him back to me!" Right then the man came down on his eagle and appeared before the Princess.

Now another man found a fish dying out of water as he was coming to see the Princess. He took it and put it back in the water. After that he went to see the Princess. She said the same thing to him, "You will have to hide so that I can find you neither in the sky nor on the earth nor in the sea."

So he left to hide. He went by the seashore and said to himself, "Where could I hide really well so that the Princess cannot find me?"

The fish leaped out of the water and said to him, "You will come down with me, and I shall take you so deep down in the sea that the Princess shall not find you."

After three days Princess Elisa began saying, "Heavens, give him back to me!" But nothing came. "Sea, give him back to me!" And he came up to the surface and he had to appear before the Princess. She was stronger than he was.

So, then, a third man came forward. On the way he had helped a drowning ant. He said, "Oh, poor little thing!" Now he took the ant and put it back in the ant-hill. Then he appeared before the beautiful Princess, saying he wished to marry her. She said to him, "I shall marry you on condition that I find you neither in the heavens nor on earth nor in the sea."

He left. He too had only three days in which to hide. He said to himself, "So, where can I hide then?"

Now he met an ant, who said to him, "You helped me. You will take me in your hand and you will turn into a little ant like me. You shall climb into the Princess's garter and she will not find you."

The Princess went away. She began saying, "Heavens, give him back to me!" Nothing came. She turned toward the sea. "Sea, give him back to me!" Still nothing happened. Then she shouted, "Earth, give him back to me!" Ah! Always nothing. She said to herself, "That one really does know how to hide."

Well, when the three days were up, the man came down from the Princess's garter, and she said to him, "As you know exactly how to hide, I shall marry you." And they were duly married.

63 *The Little Devil of the Forest*

• THERE WAS a mother once who had a dinner to prepare, and she had wanted to make some cakes. She had made five cakes and she had placed them in the room next door.

She said to her little girl, "Go and see if the cakes are cool."

As they smelled so delicious, the little girl ate one. She came back and said, "No, Mother. They are not yet cool."

A little later the mother again said, "Daughter, go and see if the cakes are cool yet."

The little girl ate them all, and came back and said, "No, they aren't cool yet."

Then her mother lost her temper and said: "It's impossible. They must be cool by now."

Then the girl said, "No, Mummy, they aren't cool."

Her mother, who could tell that she was lying, went to see and found no cakes left, which made her furious. She went out onto the balcony and shouted, "I am going to tell everybody about you, you greedy girl!"

She sang in her anger:

My daughter has eaten five cakes today!

Then a handsome young man went by on the road. Her mother changed her tune. "My daughter has spun five spindles of wool today!" He asked her what she was saying, and she repeated:

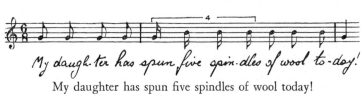

My daughter has spun five spindles of wool today!

"Oh, she must spin well, your daughter, to have spun all that. And my mother, who has so much wool to spin!" (You see in those days there weren't the machines we have now.)

"Well, come on up. She'll go with you." Now the girl whispered to her mother, "You know well that I can't spin!"

Her mother answered, "That will teach you to be greedy."

It was time to go. Without further ado, she left with the young man. They reached a lovely castle standing at the edge of the forest. He said to his mother, "Here you are, Mother. I have brought you a girl to spin your wool. Apparently, she can spin five skeins a day."

His mother said, "Ah, well, my girl, I'm thrilled. We shall put you in the room behind the castle so as not to disturb you."

They got the spindle ready and the five lumps of wool to spin. They gave her her tea, and her supper, and her bed, and they left her there.

Now once she was alone, she began to cry, as she did not know how to spin. She tried to place the spindle correctly for spinning, but she could not manage it. Then she heard someone scratching at the window pane. She went up to the window and saw a little devil. Now it didn't say what this little devil looked like. It was one of those little devils of those times!

The little devil said to her, "I'll spin for you, I will." Then she said, "You know how to spin!" He could not talk very well. He said to her, "You'll have to guess my name, and then I'll weave the lot. When I bring you the wool in the evening, you will have to guess my name, or else if you have not guessed my name on the last night, I'll take you off to the woods."

She had eight days in which to spin that wool, and every evening the little devil would appear with his five spindles all spun, and well spun at that. Then he would say, "What's my name?" The girl had nothing else to do all day but find a name for him. She would say, "Tonight I'm going to say François." When he handed her the wool through the window he would say, "What's my name?"

"François."

"No, no, no. I am going to catch you and carry you off to the woods."

The week went by like this. For five days, every evening she would say a name like that—"Auguste"—Now on the sixth evening the young man came up to bring food to the girl. He said to her, "I went for a walk in the woods. Guess what I saw there."

"I don't know."

"I saw a little devil spinning there. He spun and spun saying:

> You'll never know my name.
> I'm called Mimi Pinson, Mimi Pinson.

Then the girl, who was very surprised, said to him, "What did you say, Sir?"

"Yes, yes. I saw a little devil spinning and singing:

> You'll never know my name.
> I'm called Mimi Pinson, Mimi Pinson.

And so she began trying out "Mimi Pinson" so that she would remember it clearly when the little devil came and asked her for it.

There was another evening, when she was going to use another name, Robert. So there you are. At last the final evening was at hand, and the little devil entered the house through a window instead of scratching on the window pane. He gave her the remaining wool, saying, "What's my name?"

"Mimi Pinson."

He gave an awful groan and fled into the forest. Well, since then the mother was thrilled with the gorgeous wool in the end, the son married the daughter, and as for me, they left me here.

Part XIV
Pyrenees

.64. *The Charcoal Burner*

• THERE ONCE WAS a charcoal burner up in the mountains. One day during the winter, when snow was falling and it was very cold, he had made a good fire. During the night he heard someone knocking at the door—bang, bang, bang. The charcoal burner did not want to open the door. He asked, "Who's knocking? I am not opening for anyone." It was a bear knocking.

"Open the door for me, I beg you. I'm cold and shivering. I want to warm my paw."

"Who are you?" asked the charcoal burner.

"The bear."

"But, my poor friend, if I let you in, you would eat me up."

"No, I wouldn't eat you. Please let me in." He let him in. The bear lay down near the fire. He was cold and he dozed off. After a while someone knocked at the door with a stick—Bang, bang.

"Who is there?" said the charcoal burner.

"It's me, the wolf. I see you've made a fire. If you want me to get warm, please let me in."

"No, I won't let you in. You would eat me."

"No, I won't eat you. Let me in, I beg you, for I am shivering with cold," said the wolf.

In the end he let him in. When he was inside, he lay down next to the bear by the fire and there he lay dozing in the warmth.

After a while there was a knock at the door.

"Who is there?" said the charcoal burner.

"Me," answered the fox. "I am the fox, and I would like to get warm."

The charcoal burner answered, "No, you would eat me up."

"Of course not. I wouldn't eat you up." So then the charcoal burner let her in. She settled by the fire and she dozed off next to the wolf and the bear. There were all very happy. A few minutes later someone was knocking at the door again—Bang, bang. It was the hare. "Open the door! I'm so cold!"

The charcoal burner asked, "Who's there?"

"It's the hare."

"You would eat me up," said the charcoal burner jokingly.

"No, I wouldn't eat you up. Let me in." So the hare came in and settled by the fire to get warm. Then the charcoal burner saw that they were all sleeping there because the fire was giving a good blaze. After a while they all woke up and said to him, "As you let us get warm, let's all have a good meal together."

"I know where there is a young calf on a farm. I'll go and fetch it," said the bear.

The wolf said, "I know of a fine, fat little lamb. We'll go and get it."

"And I," said the fox, "I know of a lovely pair of fowl. They are plump and juicy. I'll go and get them."

"And I know of a fine cabbage with a big heart," said the hare. "I'll go and get it." So they all went off at the same time. Very soon the bear was back carrying the calf. He had killed it, and now he put it down there on the floor of the shack and warmed himself.

Soon after, the wolf arrived carrying a fine lamb. He put it down and warmed himself.

Shortly after this the fox arrived. He was carrying a pair of chickens. He put them down and did as the bear and the wolf had done. He warmed himself.

Very soon the hare arrived. He carried a gorgeous cabbage with a big round heart. He put it on the ground and he, the hare, warmed himself, too.

When the charcoal burner saw that all these animals were falling asleep because they were tired out and cold, he thought to himself, "If I killed the bear, the wolf, the fox, and the hare, I could have a feast. I would have the calf, the lamb, the chickens, and the cabbage." So in a flash he took a great club—really a big hammer—and he put it in the fire to make it red hot. When the tip was red hot, he gave the bear a blow on the head with it, and the bear fell to the floor half dead. He gave another fast blow to the wolf. He was in a hurry. The wolf fell to the ground like the bear. He could not stand up. Then he put the tip of the hammer up the fox's arse and he gave the hare a blow on the head which killed him. When the hare was dead, he opened the door, and the bear, the wolf, and the fox went out. They could not walk very well, but nevertheless they made their way out, and as he fled the bear was groaning. "Aï, aï, aï! Help! He gave me a blow on the head which is making me go dingdong."

The wolf was saying, "Help me, too! He gave me a blow on the back and the head which is making me go dingdong."

"And I," said the fox. "He put the tip of the red hot iron up my arse. It will never be the same again."

Would you believe it? The charcoal burner had the calf, the fine lamb, a couple of chickens, the hare, and the cabbage, and so he had enough to eat the whole year long.

And so, tric-trac, my tale is at an end. [*Et tric-trac, Moun counte es acabat.*]

.65. *The Three Deserters*

• ONCE UPON A TIME in a village there was a family who got their living from the soil. They were father and mother and three small boys.

After some time, the father decided to leave, as he could not even support his family by his hard work. One fine day they all left together in the direction of Paris. After a long journey they reached Paris, where they had a great deal of trouble finding shelter. At last, after having looked for work just about everywhere, they ended up by tagging onto a family of rag-and-bone men. Two years later the wife died, and he remained a widower with his three boys, who were now much older.

The eldest, François, was eighteen years old. The other, Jean, was sixteen, and the youngest, Paul, was fourteen. The job of rag-and-bone man did not appeal to them very much. So the eldest said, "Father, I would like to join up." His father ended up by consenting, and he enrolled with the Twenty-fourth Colonial Regiment, which was at Perpignan. At the end of six months, he was made a corporal. At the end of a year, he became a sergeant. With his sergeant's pay he was able to send some money to his father. At the end of two years, Jean was eighteen, and he asked his father whether he, too, could join up. By golly! The father didn't really want it, but in the end he agreed to his going. So then he enrolled in his brother's regiment. He left to join the Twenty-fourth Colonials. He was made a corporal. Meanwhile, the eldest had been made quartermaster sergeant.

After another two years Paul, the youngest, wished to join up. His father would have liked to keep him. He saw himself growing old alone. He did not want to give his consent, but in the end he let him go. Paul chose his brothers' regiment, the Twenty-fourth Colonials, and after six months he was made a corporal. Meanwhile, his elder brother was made sergeant major. His brother Jean became a sergeant, and he, by golly, became a corporal! When they received their pay they sent some money to their father every month. Thinking himself wealthy, he gave up the job of rag-and-bone man and made the most of being a small stockholder.

By the time two years were up, the eldest began gambling and having a wild time. He got himself into bad company, and it brought out the bad side of his nature. He started to gamble, and one evening he gambled away all the money he was supposed to pay his whole company. When he got home, he found he was in trouble. He tried to borrow money from his friends. No one was ready to lend him any. He wanted to kill himself, but he thought, "What are your brothers going to say?"

So he went and found his brothers, and he told them what had happened to him. His brothers saw that it would be wrong of him to commit suicide. They said that it would be much better to become a deserter. So at dusk on the following night they left the barracks and set off dressed as soldiers. They walked all night, and at daybreak they hid in a wood.

The next morning the captain of their company wondered what had happened to them. He did not yet report them as deserters. This allowed them to make good their escape. Only on the third day did the captain report them as deserters. Meanwhile, the three brothers had gone quite a long way, keeping hidden as much as possible. The eldest was surviving well, but the second one was hungry, and the shoes of the third one were hurting him so much that he could hardly walk. At last, by nightfall, they reached a huge castle, and they said, "Let's knock."

They knocked on the door, but no one answered. There was no light, nothing at all. They skirted the castle grounds and went a little farther on, when they saw a small cottage, where there was a light. They knocked there, and a nice old woman came and opened the door to them. When she saw that three soldiers had come her way, she was not afraid, and she asked them what they wanted. The eldest said: "Dear lady, we are three soldiers from the French army. We went astray during maneuvers, and we would like to ask you whether we could spend the night here tonight."

The good woman answered, "Come in, you fine soldiers."

And the good woman made them come in and said to them, "My husband will be here soon. He is gamekeeper for the castle."

After a while the gamekeeper came in, and when he saw the three soldiers, he asked them to join him at table and share their meal. As they were eating, the sergeant major said to them, "We knocked on the door of the castle, but no one answered us." Then he said to them, "You see! One is received far better by the poor than by the rich!"

But the gamekeeper answered, "Let me put you right, men. The reason why no one answered at the castle is that it is haunted and nobody can live there."

Then the sergeant major said to him, "But hasn't anyone been in to see what's going on?"

"There have been some who have tried, but they were so frightened that no one could get anything out of them."

"Well," said the sergeant major after having talked to his brothers, "if you will accept our help, we shall keep guard at the castle."

His two brothers answered, "Yes," and the old people, too. They decided to begin their watch on the castle that very night. A cold meal was prepared for them with a few bottles of good wine, and they were given a long key to the front door of the castle. With this and a packet of candles, the three of them left after having wished the old folk good night.

They left for the castle. They opened it and locked it again.

They lit a candle and had a look at some of the inside and, after having started a good fire in the kitchen hearth, they sat down again at the table to eat their cold meal. After a couple of drinks, they began to talk. The eldest said, "You think this castle is haunted! I don't believe it."

"Oh, well, perhaps," said the others, "perhaps."

"Never mind."

"Ah, well," said the eldest, "it is not worth all three of us staying up. I shall be the first to keep watch. Each of you two can go into a room and go to bed."

The two brothers went to bed comfortably. Meanwhile, the sergeant major filled his pipe, and while he waited he took the odd swig from the bottle. At about midnight a great storm gathered. The wind blew and someone knocked at the window. He asked, "Who is there?"

The answer came, "You are bragging, you poor deserter from the French army. You want to stop me coming in. You are a poor good-for-nothing without a penny to your name. If you let me in, I'll make you rich. I shall give you a purse in which you will always find one hundred francs wherever you are and whenever you like."

He said, "Come on. Give me the purse so that I can try it."

"No. Let me in."

"No, no, no. Give me the purse, then we shall see."

So the Devil slipped the purse through the window. It was the Devil himself! The sergeant major climbed onto the table. He opened the purse and spilled out the contents. A hundred francs, another, and another came pouring out. There was a pile of hundred-franc notes, and more one hundred franc notes. He was rich! He said to the Devil, "I accept." And he opened the window. The Devil came into the castle. After a while he again heard a loud noise and then nothing more. He fell asleep on the table until the following morning.

At daybreak his two brothers came and found him in the kitchen. After having said good morning to each other, they asked him, "Well what happened? Did you see anything? Did you hear anything?"

"No, nothing. I went to sleep. They're just tall stories. There is nothing."

They closed up the castle. All three went off again to the little cottage, where the old people were waiting for them wreathed in smiles. They gave them coffee and asked them what had happened. They said that they had gone to bed and that the eldest had seen nothing. The old folk said to them, "Would you mind keeping watch one more night?"

They accepted, and that evening they left for the castle again. That evening it was the second one's turn. The sergeant, Jean, was to keep watch. The other two brothers went to bed. Like the other one, he had a swig or two as he waited by the table keeping watch. At midnight torrential rain hit the window panes of the castle, and he heard a tapping on the pane. He was a little afraid. He asked: "Who is it? Be careful. Don't move, otherwise I shall shoot through the pane and do you in."

The answer came, "Poor deserter from the French army, you are dying of hunger and you make believe you are strong. I want to reward you. If you let me in, I'll give you a magic napkin which has the power to lay the table. You've only got to say 'Napkin lay the table!' and the table is laid. The best wines and the most delicious dishes appear on the table."

"Let's see. Give me the napkin."

"No. First let me come in."

"No, no. Give it to me. Then I'll think about it."

So the Devil passed the napkin to him through the window. He said, "Napkin, lay one hundred places at this table!" In a flash the table was laid for a hundred.

The sergeant said, "All right. I'll let you in. I'm keeping the napkin."

The Devil came in. He went all round the castle and disappeared with a bang. After having kept watch all night, the sergeant fell asleep. The next morning his two brothers came to find him, and after wishing each other good morning they asked him what had happened.

"Oh, nothing at all. I saw nothing. I heard nothing. Those were just stories. It is quite possible to live in the castle."

They went back to the little cottage, and the old folk asked them to keep watch a third night. They accepted once again. On the third night they settled once more in the castle, and it was the youngest, Paul, the corporal, who took the watch. His brothers went to bed after a hearty meal, and he began his watch. At midnight a hurricane blew up and snowflakes fell on the window panes of the castle.

"Well, well! So you are the unlucky one!"

Paul said, "Who is it?"

"You also make out that you are strong, you poor deserter from the French army. You can no longer walk, but still you want to confront me."

"Go back, or I shall bust your gut with my bayonet."

So then the Devil said to him, "You are a strong man. Calm down. Look, as a reward for letting me in, I will give you a magic coat which has the power to carry you wherever you like."

"Let me see. Hand it to me."

The Devil handed him the coat through the window. He put it over the shoulders and said. "Coat, make me go round the room!" He began whirling around, and in the twinkling of an eye he had been round the room over a hundred times.

"Well, well," said he, "that's not bad."

"So, will you let me in?"

He said to him, "No."

"And why not?"

"I wish to know what you are up to in the castle. I have the coat and I'm going to keep it."

"And suppose I don't tell you?"

"You shall not come in. I'll bust your gut!"

"Well, I'll tell you. In the castle cellar where it says number nine there is a treasure hidden inside. It is my job to look after it. That is why every night I come and make sure nothing has been tampered with. This money does not belong to me. It will not become the castle owner's property until the treasure has been blessed, and once it is blessed, then they will be able to make good use of it. I shall not came back any more then, and the castle will be a pleasant place to live in."

"Is that all?"

He said, "That's all."

"All right then. Come in."

The Devil did his work and went away. The next morning the

brothers met once more, and they wished each other good morning and the youngest was asked whether he had seen anything. He said to them, "No. I neither saw nor heard anything at all. The castle can be lived in."

So they went back to the old folk. They told them, "The castle can be lived in. We have seen nothing there."

The old fellow said to them, "I can no longer keep you here. I thank you."

And so they left. As they reached a crossroads, the sergeant major said, "As we are three deserters and they are looking for us, it would be better if we separated. Each one must find his own way to Paris, where we shall meet at our father's house."

They said, "Yes," and they separated. After a day's walking, the youngest came back to the castle. He had put his coat over his shoulders and said to it, "Coat, take me back to the castle which I have left." Sure enough he landed like a tornado in the courtyard of the castle. He folded his coat and went to the cottage where the old folk lived. He knocked on the door, and the old folk opened it. They had thought the lad knew something, but had seen that no one would let on. Then Paul told them what had happened between them and the Devil. He explained the whole thing to them.

At once they sent for the owner of the castle, who arrived by coach and went to find the treasure and bless it. Then the owner shared it with everybody. He gave it as a gift to the poor. He wanted Paul to stay in the castle, but Paul would have none of it and he went away. When he was at some distance from the castle, he put his coat back over his shoulders and said to it, "Coat, take me to Paris!"

That very evening he was in Paris. He came back to the place where his father lived. The latter, as he had no longer received any money from his sons, had been forced to become a rag-and-bone man again. He had left the place, and Paul did not find him. Paul went looking for a job, and he stayed in Paris. His brothers, by golly, also came to town.

This was at the time of Louis Philippe, and the King announced publicly that he wished his daughter to marry the richest man in the world. Well then, by golly, plenty of suitors showed up. François, too, came forward with his magic purse as the richest man in the world. He was asked for his credentials and he said, "My credentials are this purse."

"What do you mean, this purse?" They teased him.

"Well, have you a big room?" he said. "Now, I'll fill it with hundred-franc notes." He took his purse and opened it. He began emptying it out. One hundred francs and more and more and more. Still they came, those hundred-franc notes. When he saw this, the King said, "Well, yes. He is the richest man in the world. He always has one hundred francs in his purse."

So he dismissed everybody, as he had now found the richest man in the world. He introduced him to his daughter. "Here you are, Daughter. He is the rightest man in the world."

When she saw him, she made a face and whispered in her father's ear, "I don't like him."

Then the King answered, "Well, you know what you have to do."

"All right."

She summoned him and said: "Ah, how d'you do, Sir, how d'you do. It seems that you are the richest man in the world because of the magic powers of your purse. Well, while we wait to get married, you shall stay at the castle. You shall take a room, and, as proof of your friendship, you can in the meantime leave me your purse." By golly, the unsuspecting François handed it over to her. She called a servant and said: "Take this gentleman to room number twelve. See that he has everything he requires." He was led to his bachelor's room, and, after having spent a whole day in the castle, he went to bed. At one o'clock in the morning a spring was released, and he found himself flung into a drainage ditch. Having run along a sewer for most of the night, he then found himself at the opening, where there was an old fellow who pulled him by the shirt tail. It was his father. He said to him, "Well, what sort of place are you working in now!" He took the lad back to his apartment, and he went back to working as a rag-and-bone man for his father.

Well, some time after all this had happened, the King proclaimed once more that he wished to marry his daughter to the man who was the best cook. Having the magic napkin, Jean came forward as the man who was the best cook. He was tested by being asked for his credentials.

"My credentials," he said, "here they are—this napkin."

"What do you mean, this napkin?"

"With the help of this napkin I can be responsible for laying the table for two hundred or one thousand people, as you wish."

"Well," said the King. "Here is a dining room where one thousand places may be laid. Get to work."

Jean took his napkin and said to it, "Lay the table for a thousand people. Do not forget a thing." To the King's great astonishment, all this was done like magic. The King said, "All right, young man. You are the finest cook in the world." He said to the others, "You may go. Here is the finest cook in the world." He said to his daughter, "There you are. Let me present you with the finest cook in the world." She made a face and whispered in his ear, "I don't like him." Her father said to her, "You know what you have to do now."

She played the same trick on this man as she had played on the other one. She asked him for the napkin, and at one o'clock in the morning he found himself in the sewer. Once again his father fished him out of the opening of the sewer. He said to him, "But you all work in the same place!" He again worked for his father as a rag-and-bone man.

After some time the King proclaimed that he wished to marry his daughter to the best horseman in the world. Then the youngest Paul came forward as the best horseman in the world. And, by golly, he bought a horse which was an old nag. The other competitors started laughing when they saw him. He kept mum, by golly! When they gave the starting signal, he put the cloak on his shoulders and said to it, "Cloak take us on this horse to the end of the field and back as fast as possible—flat out!"

As quick as a flash, the horse set off and he came back at a terrific speed. The others could not get over it. In fact, by golly, he became the best horseman in the world. So much so that an Englishman wanted to buy the horse from him, and he sold it to him at a fantastic price.

"I am going to win all the races in England!"

"Yes, you will win them."

When he witnessed this, the King said to his daughter, "That is the best horseman in the world." The King suspected something. "As you are to marry him, here he is."

She whispered to him, "I don't like him."

"Well, then, come to some arrangement with him." So she took him to the castle. In her room she said to him, "Why did you sell your horse?"

He said, "My horse had nothing to do with it. It wasn't the horse who won the race!"

"I should have liked to keep an animal like that."

"Oh, no! That had nothing to do with it. What won the race was the cloak."

"How?"

"You'll see. Open your window." Then he said, "Come here next to me."

They stood at the sill like this. He put his cloak over his shoulders, and then he placed a fold of his cloak over the shoulders of the Princess. At the same time he said to the cloak, "Cloak, take us to the most secluded island in the world!"

Well, the cloak actually took them to such an island. They stayed there. Night fell and they lay down one next to the other. He put the cloak under his head so that she could not steal it from him. The next morning they went all over the island. They found some apple trees and they picked apples from them and bit into them. As soon as they had eaten some apple, their noses grew longer, and in the end they could reach anywhere with their noses. They reached into all the streams all over the place.

When night fell, they again lay down and he put the cloak under his head. Only the Princess stayed awake and for so long that he fell asleep, and she stole the cloak from him. Then she put it on and said to it, "Take me once again to my father's castle in Paris."

The next morning she was back in the royal castle. Her father recognized her as soon as he saw her, but she had a nose which reached all over the place. She told him what had happened.

The next day, when Paul woke up, he found himself alone and with an elongated nose. Well, by golly, he went over the island, and as he was doing this, he found a pear tree. His hunger made him taste the pears. As he began eating one, his nose shrank, and finally fell off. So then he said to himself, "This is a cure. The apples make one's nose grow, and the pears make it drop off. So be it!"

He brought in a store of apples and pears. He went along the shore and was rescued as a castaway by a ship. He landed in France again with the apples and pears and came back to Paris.

The King called for the most famous doctors in the world to come and cure his daughter. Then Paul showed up as an American doctor. He made some apple ointment and pear ointment smartly presented in labeled pots. He arrived at the castle disguised as a doctor. He said to the King, "I wish to cure your daughter."

"Good! But where are your medicines?"

"I have them here."

"You must be just another quack!" But he brought him to his daughter, who did not recognize him. He said to her, "Now I can see that what ails you is serious. You must have done a few wicked deeds during your life. If you don't tell me about them, I don't know whether I shall be able to cure you."

The girl said to him, "Yes. My father wished me to marry the richest man in the world. He had a purse, and I stole it from him."

"Is that all?"

"Yes. That's all."

"Right! Well you must give it back to me." She gave it back to him. He said to her, "Try this ointment." It was the apple one, and her nose grew longer still. So then he said to her, "You see you must have done something else which was bad."

"Well, yes. In the same way my father wished me to marry the best cook in the world. He had a magic napkin. I stole it from him."

"You must give it back to me. We shall try." He took the purse and the napkin and put them in his pocket. Again he tried the apple ointment. Her nose grew even longer. So then he said to her, "You must have done some other wicked deed."

She said to him, "Yes. Some time ago my father wished me to marry the best horseman in the world. He had a cloak, and after the adventure which earned for me this long nose, I stole it from him."

"You must give it back to me." She gave it back to him. Then he said to her, "Is that all?"

"Yes."

"Well, we'll try the experiment again."

He rubbed her nose with pear ointment, and her nose grew smaller again. He gave her a little more to eat, and it grew still smaller. Then he made her eat some of the apple paste and rubbed her with it. Again her nose grew so long that she could not turn round in the room any more. She began to cry. He left her just like that, promising her he would come back.

The King, who was waiting to hear whether he had cured her, received this answer, "I'll come back and see her, but I am not certain that I can cure her."

He was able to leave the castle, and the King's daughter kept her long nose. He never went back there. Finally, after a long search, he found his father and two brothers again. He gave back to them what was theirs, and the two brothers were very surprised. However, he explained everything that had happened. As for him, he came back to the magic castle. The owner greeted him with open arms. He had a young daughter, and Paul married her. They had a magnificent wedding celebration, which his father and his brothers attended. They lived happily for a long time and had many children, who brought him much happiness.

As for the King's daughter, she died, having kept her long nose all her life.

Cric-crac. My tale is at an end.

·66·   The Laurel Flower

• THERE WAS ONCE a father who had three sons. He said to the eldest, "If you bring me the laurel flower, you shall be my heir." His mother did not want to let him go. "You will not find it! You will not find it!" She was very sad to have to let him go. Her son wanted to leave in spite of her. So his mother packed a game bag for him and gave him bread, wine, and an omelet. He picked up his walking stick and left. He went far, far away from home right into a large forest to go and look for the laurel flower.

When he was in the forest, he was walking along a little path when he felt very tired and he had a rest there. While he was eating, a lady came along and this lady asked him for a little bread, for she was hungry.

He said to her, "No, no, I don't want to give you any. I have just enough for myself."

The Holy Virgin did not reveal herself. She said to him, "What are you doing there, my lad?"

The lad answered, "My father has told me that if I bring him the laurel flower he will make me his heir, and I cannot find it anywhere."

He had looked for it all over the forest. She thought to herself: "You shall not find the laurel flower. You are a bad boy."

He started to go home, as he had looked everywhere without finding it. There his father said to him, "Did you find the laurel flower?"

"No, I have not found it."

The younger brother said, "Father, I want to go. I believe I shall find it!"

He left. He found the lady, just as the first had done, and he would not give her any bread, either, and he, too, did not find the laurel flower. He went home and said to his father, "I looked all over the forest for it, and I have not found it!"

So then the third and youngest brother said to his father and mother, "I want to go and find the laurel flower."

His mother said to him, "Don't go, child. You see your brothers have not found it, and you won't either."

However, the youngest insisted. "Mother, do let me go. I want to go and find it. Let me go."

So she packed a game bag for him, as she had done for his brothers. She put in bread, wine, and sausage. When he found himself in the forest he came across a fountain, and he sat down next to the fountain to eat his snack, as he was tired out. He ate the lunch he had brought with him. Then a lady appeared before

him, and she came and stood next to him. This lady asked him,
"What are you doing there, child?"

He said to her, "I have come to get the laurel flower because
my father has told me that if I brought it back, I would become
his heir."

She said to him, "Won't you give me a piece of bread, child,
as I am so hungry?"

The youngest answered, "Yes, Madam. If there is enough for
one, there is enough for two."

The youngster gave her some bread and sausage.

"Here you are, Madam."

She answered, "Thank you, my child. I can see that you are
very polite and good and you think well of the poor. Thank you,
my child."

She did not take any.

"I am the Holy Virgin. You are kinder than your brothers. I
asked them for bread, and they did not give me anything. As
you are so kind, I shall show you the laurel flower. Look at that
flower at the foot of that rock next to the fountain. Take a
sprig of that."

The boy went and cut a sprig of it, and he went home singing
this song:

> Tran la la,
> Tran la la.
> I've found the laurel flower,
> I shall be the heir.

As he came nearer to his home, he was going down hill. His
brothers heard him singing:

> Tran la la,
> Tran la la.
> I've found the laurel flower,
> I shall be the heir.

They said to themselves, "He's carrying the laurel flower. He
will be the heir, and we will have to leave home!" The two
brothers then said, "We must go and kill him!" They met him

later in a meadow. They went up to him, and they killed him and they buried him under a heap of stones. Then they came home with the laurel flower.

Later, one fine day, there was a shepherd looking after the sheep. He went up to the pile of stones and noticed an instrument like a trumpet or something like a bone. They said that the Holy Virgin had had something to do with this. He took this flute or this trumpet and put it to his lips, and the trumpet began saying:

> Oh, shepherd,
> Oh, dear shepherd,
> It is not you who killed me
> To get the laurel flower.

Then this shepherd came down to the village, and he made the trumpet sing out wherever he went. Good Lord, everyone was anxious to hear this man! There was a merchant in the village who said to him, "Do you want to sell the trumpet, Sir?"

He answered, "No, I don't want to sell it. I want to keep it for myself."

The other insisted. "Do sell it to me. Sell it to me!"

He wanted it, so he said to the shepherd, "I'll give you six hundred francs for it." Six hundred francs was worth a fortune in those days, so the shepherd sold it to him. The merchant put the trumpet to his lips and the trumpet said to him:

> Oh, merchant,
> Good merchant,
> It is not you who killed me
> To get the laurel flower.

The merchant went from village to village, always playing the trumpet. It always said the same thing, "Oh, merchant . . ."

So imagine what happened. This merchant went to the youngster's village. He began playing the trumpet, and it was still saying, "Oh, merchant . . ." So then this boy's father and mother and sister heard this and said to themselves, "What is the meaning of this?" They said to the merchant, "Would you by any chance like to sell us that trumpet?"

"Oh, no, Sir."

The father and mother said to him: "You must sell it to us! You must sell it to us!" They went on, "How much do you want for it?"

He said to them, "I want two thousand francs." He gave them the trumpet. Once the sale was over, the father put the instrument to his lips, and the trumpet began to sing:

> Oh, father,
> Good father,
> It is not you who killed me
> To get the laurel flower.

Good Lord! When the mother heard this, she said to him, "Lend me the trumpet." She put it to her lips, and the trumpet began to sing:

> Oh, mother,
> Good mother,
> It is not you who killed me
> To get the laurel flower.

Well, you should have seen the father and mother when they heard this.

"What is the meaning of this? What does it mean?"

Then the sister said, "Mother, hand the trumpet to me."

She put it to her lips and the trumpet began to sing:

> Oh, sister,
> Good sister,
> It is not you who killed me
> To get the laurel flower.

That trumpet said the same thing over and over again. So then the brothers who had killed him said to their sister, "Lend us the trumpet."

("This is it. Now we have it," warned the teller of this tale.)

One of the brothers put the trumpet to his lips, and it began to sing with a dark and angry voice:

> Oh, brother,
> Wicked brother,
> Yes, it was you who killed me
> To get the laurel flower.

The same thing. Always the same thing. Then the other brother said to him, "Let's see what happens if you lend it to me."

It sang again even more angrily:

> Oh, brother,
> Wicked brother,
> Yes, it was you who killed me
> To get the laurel flower.

Imagine the father and mother's reaction when they heard that! They said to them, "It is you who killed your brother! It is you who killed him! Scoundrels!"

The father said to them: "So that's the way you thought you would become the heir?" He got hold of one of them and beat him up. He hit him in the face and threw him down the stairs, and he died. He did the same to the other one. And now it's over.

Part XV
Corsica

·67· *The Legend of the Oxen's Pass*

• AT THE FOOT of the Rinuccia at the edge of Lake Nino is the Oxen's Pass, which is also called Forge Pass. Now this is why it bears that name.

One day the Devil was plowing near the pass with a wooden plow drawn by a pair of oxen like the ones still seen around here sometimes. At one point the Devil wanted to adjust the blade of the plow with a hammer, and he gave his fingers a blow with it. Enraged, he flung the hammer through the mountain we now call Cabu Tafonatu; that is to say, Pierced Peak. After having gone through the mountain, the hammer fell on the sands of Calvi beach.

Since then, too, they show you the furrows drawn by the Devil. In the direction of Rinuccia you can see them engraved in the stone. As for the oxen, two enormous stones of their shape can be seen silhouetted in the distance. From afar it looks like a mountain plowed with long lines.

As for the Devil, if he was turned into stone like the oxen, he was not to remain visible! On the other hand, one can still see the floor of the forge where he mended his tools. There are pieces that look like lumps of coal in that place. So they sometimes call that Forge Pass, and sometimes the Oxen's Pass.

·68· *The Fox and The Blackbird*

• ONE FINE MORNING a blackbird sang cheerily from her perch on the branch of a tree. A fox happened to go by and, speaking to the blackbird, he asked her why she felt so happy.

"What makes you so happy, friend blackbird?"

This one answered, "I am so happy, friend fox, because I had three young last night."

"May I see them?" added friend fox.

"Oh, no," said the bird, "you are quite capable of eating them."

"I swear to you I will not touch them."

Trusting the fox's oath, the blackbird showed him her nestful.

Friend fox looked at the little birds and said to himself, "That could make a good mouthful."

The first time the blackbird flew away, he made the most of it. He ate them up. When the blackbird came back to its nest with a bit of food it had gone to get, it found the nest empty. A few days later a dog went by and, seeing the blackbird crying, asked her what had happened, and the blackbird told him of her misfortunes. Friend dog promised to avenge her. "To accomplish this," he said, "this is what you must do. You have noticed that every morning the shepherds go along this path carrying cheeses. They take them to the caves for them to dry out there. Among these shepherds there is a boy you can entertain somewhat. Place yourself in his path and pretend to limp. Then he will put down his cheese-draining board and try and catch you. Meanwhile, I'll eat his cheese, and then I shall pretend to be dead in the bushes. When friend fox goes by once more, you will sing like last time. When he asks you why you are singing, you will say to him, " 'The dog who has eaten my young has been killed by a shepherd because he had eaten his cheese.' "

And the fox actually did go by once again, and, seeing the blackbird singing, he said to her, "Friend blackbird, have you had more young to be as happy as that?"

"No, friend fox, but the dog who ate my young has been killed by a shepherd whose cheese he had eaten."

"Serves him right!" said the fox. "If that is true, I knew the varment. He was a greedy one. I wonder where he is now. I would go and spit in his face."

"He is lying in the bushes," the blackbird said, and she showed him the path.

The dog was there with his four feet sticking up. The fox stood over him to carry out his threat, but he did not have time to spit in the dog's face. The latter grabbed him by the throat and killed him.

So in this way the blackbird found herself avenged.

·69· *The Shepherd and the Snake*

• ONCE THERE WAS a shepherd who took his sheep to graze in the meadows. On his way there he came across a fire. A little farther on, he suddenly heard a whistle, and he tried to find out where it came from. He saw a snake. It was a large one, and it was burning. So what did the shepherd do then? He pulled the snake out of the fire.

When the snake was out of the fire, he said to the shepherd, "I am a magician's son. Come and see my father. My father will be pleased that you have saved my life, and he will reward you generously."

"But I must look after my sheep."

"Don't worry about your sheep. Let's go to my father's. He will offer you a pile of gold, and a pile of silver, and a little box of notes. Don't take them; they would all turn into coal. Then be careful and answer him in this way, 'If you want to reward me, I wish to get to know the language of the animals.'"

The two took to the road. They reached the magician, and his son explained to him, "There was a fire, and this shepherd pulled me out of it. You must reward him, for he saved my life."

"What's that? This shepherd saved my son's life?" The magician showed him a room where there was a heap of gold, a heap of silver, and a heap of small change.

"Oh, no," said the shepherd, "I don't want that."

"What do I do now? Don't you want a reward?"

"If you want to give me a reward, then teach me the language of the animals."

The magician said to him, "All right, I'll teach it to you, but if you give away the secret, you are as good as dead."

"Right! I'll not talk about it."

And so he went off. The shepherd left. Goodbye! Goodbye! He went to join his sheep and ran far, far away. At last he lay down under a tree. A crow happened by who said as he turned to the shepherd, "You sleep now, but if you knew what treasure lies buried here under this chestnut tree you wouldn't sleep."

No sooner had he said this than the shepherd rose. He left his ewes to rest with their lambs and went home. Then he left home once again taking a pickax with him. He went back to the chestnut tree pointed out by the crow.

He started using the pickax there, and little by little he picked up the gold. Out of caution, he took the gold home only a little at a time. In this way he became rich, leading all the while his shepherd's life and looking after his ewes every day. He sold his animals and he set himself up as "the Frenchman." In the end, his wife grew astonished by all this wealth and asked him, "How is it that you have all this money?"

"Well, I earn it by keeping my ewes!"

"They couldn't bring you in all that money. Come on, you've got a secret."

"Well, I've worked hard, so I have sold my ewes."

"That isn't true. If you don't tell me where you got this gold, I shan't give you a moment's peace."

His wife never let him be after that. She grew more and more anxious as the days wore on, and she showered him with questions. Finally, the shepherd said to her, "If you want to know the secret, get my coffin ready, for if I tell you, I'm as good as dead."

Right then the shepherd heard the cock in the barnyard scuttling about among the hens saying, "Cock-a-doodle-do! Cock-a-doodle-do!" So then the dog said to the cock, "Our master, the shepherd, is about to die and you sing, rooster?"

"Our master need only do as I do. Look how many wives I have, and they have given themselves up to me."

So the man understood the lesson. He said to himself, "This rooster has given me an example. I've only to do the same thing."

And to his wife he said, "So you want to know. Well, go and fetch my whip."

The shepherd suddenly took his whip made of bull's tendons and began beating his wife. The blows showered down. He hit her as hard as he could. "Well, now do you want to know?"

"No. Now I have had enough."

They walked together up to the fork and nothing more was said.

Fola foletta   Fable, little fable,
Dide la vostra   You tell yours;
A mea è detta.   Mine is told.

·70· *The Child Promised to the Devil*

• ONCE UPON A TIME there were a husband and a wife. They had already been married ten years, but they had no children. The husband was upset because his wife gave him no family. Every day when he went home everything was set on the table, but there was no child at the table.

So, weary of seeing her husband's unhappiness, the wife would go off alone and, despairing, prayed to the Lord, saying, "Send me a son to satisfy my husband."

One fine day the Devil appeared. He was smartly dressed in a suit and a bowler hat, with a cane in his hand. He said to the wife, "What are you requesting?"

The wife answered, "Send me a son to satisfy my husband."

"If you want a son to satisfy your husband, promise to give me your son's soul when he is eighteen years old. You will be expecting a child, and in nine months' time you shall give birth to him."

The woman began her pregnancy. She said to her husband, "Oh, if only you knew, husband! You would be so happy!"

He said, "Well, what is all this about?"

"I've something to tell you. I am pregnant, and in nine months' time I shall give birth to a boy."

Nine months later a son was born. He was a fine boy. Every day the father would come home all happy because his son was there, and his wife was happy, too. They laughed to have him there with them. When the child was four or five, he began to go to school. When he was ten, he was already very learned, and everybody was pleased with him. When he was seventeen, the boy noticed that his mother's eyes would fill with tears as she looked at him, and then she would start crying. He asked her, "Until now you have shown me that you are proud of me, and I am proud of you. Now you are crying. Why?"

"It is because I am so happy to see you so handsome and learned," said his mother.

The next day, however, his mother began crying again, and the following day there were more tears. So, then, the boy could stand it no longer. As he could get no other answer from her, he ended up by saying to himself, "They are hiding something from me."

He went and found the schoolmaster to explain his parents' attitude.

The schoolmaster said to him, "You are sad. You are not as you were before."

"I've something to tell you. There is something wrong at home. My parents are in tears every day, and I cannot find out why."

The master said, "Well, buy yourself a dagger. Point it at your heart and say to your parents, 'If you do not tell me the reason why you are crying, if you have deceived me, I shall kill myself!' You'll see. Your parents will not deceive you."

The young man took his advice. He went and bought himself a dagger and held it to his chest. Once he was at home and everybody was sitting at table, he began eating, and his parents started to weep because it was nearly the end of the year and he was going to be eighteen years old. The young man said to them, "Why do you deceive me? Let me tell you. I have a dagger and I am going to plunge it into my heart. Yes, if you go on deceiving me, I shall kill myself."

Then the mother said to him, "Don't kill yourself. We shall tell you everything. As you wish to know, this is what happened. Your father complained every day because he had no son. So one day I went out begging God to give me a child, and the Devil appeared before me. Then he said he would send me a son but that he would come and fetch you when you were eighteen years old."

Now when the youth heard that his soul was to be the Devil's, he was not at all pleased. He went back to see his master.

"I took your advice and I have succeeded. I found out some amazing things. Mother and Father told me they had promised the Devil my soul when I reached eighteen years of age."

The master said to him, "You are freed from this agreement, as your parents accepted these conditions as far as your soul is concerned, but not your body, and so you shall go and fight the Devil." Then he added, "Take a large sword and a horse and go before the Devil as soon as you are eighteen years old."

The young man bought himself a large sword and put on his great cape. He mounted his horse and left when he was eighteen. On the morning of the day he reached his eighteenth year he met the Devil. The Devil said to him, "You belong to me."

The young man answered, "No. My mother agreed with you to certain conditions regarding my soul, but you had better know that I am going to fight you."

"How?"

"Let's fight a duel. The one who wins shall have my soul."

So, baring their chests, they flung themselves into the duel one against the other to find out who was to have the youth's soul. The Devil struck, and lost.

Then he said to the youth, "You are free."

The Devil went away in a terrible rage, and the young man went home. There his father and mother were already in mourning. They fell into each others' arms. Then they had a splendid meal, to which the schoolmaster was invited, and henceforth the young man went on with his studies and remained free.

Notes
to the Tales

PART I

LOWER BRITTANY

· 1 · Yann the Fearless

Type 326, *The Youth Who Wanted to Learn What Fear Is.*

Recorded in 1953 in the course of my research in the Trégor area in Prat (Côtes du Nord) from a sixty-seven-year-old peasant, Veuve L'Héréec.

The name of the hero—*Yann* (John) *heb aon* (without fear)—which has no connection with King John the Fearless, serves also as the title of the folktale type chosen by Paul Delarue for his *Catalogue des Contes Français* (Paris, 1957, p. 293), in which he uses a version found in Nivernais. Very popular among French storytellers, this theme seems to have spread throughout several provinces: Delarue cites sixty-three versions. It also occurs frequently among the French of North America, notably in Canada, in Michigan, and in Missouri. To this list could be added variants recently recorded in Corsica (*Le Neveu du Curé:* cf. my *Contes Corses,* No. 48, p. 116) and in the Lower Marche region (*Richard Sans Peur*).

Even though the first European version of this theme was given by Grimm at the beginning of the nineteenth century, Delarue calls attention to the fact that a direct allusion to it is found in France in the seventeenth century in the *Mémoires* of Roger de Rabutin, which appeared in 1640 (I, 76–77), and in which he writes: "I remember those tales that are told to children, of meals served by strangers, and then of arms, heads, legs, and the other parts of the body falling out of the chimney and forming people who disappeared after having taken a drink." In this passage can be recognized Motif H1411.1 of of Stith Thompson's *Motif-Index,* which is well represented in our version from Lower Brittany. The first two episodes of *Yann Heb Aon,* which end with the release of a soul in torment, relates this version of Type 326A. The final episode of the blackbird enclosed in a loaf of bread—a last attempt to frighten the hero—is also found in the Corsican variant mentioned above.

· 2 · Old Fench

Type 516, *Faithful John.*

Recorded in the village of Prat (Côtes du Nord) in 1954, from the same informant as the previous tale.

As in many of the tales of Lower Brittany, the hero, *Fench* [Francis], is a Breton (and, in this case, an old servant) who has

entered the service of the King of France. When questioned about
the nature of the three mysterious figures who gathered at the foot
of a tree at night in order to trade secrets, the informant stated that
she believed them to be *korrans,* or dwarfs, or *korrigans,* as they are
more often called, supernatural beings who enjoy playing tricks on
men and who especially enjoy luring them around the fire at night.

The theme is rather widespread in France, where it is associated
with several separate motifs, so that there is a great deal of variety
among the different versions. It is equally popular in the folklore of
the American French, and I have also recorded a version of it in
Corsica (*Contes Corses,* p. 277). German and Chilean versions can
be found in *Folktales of Germany* and *Folktales of Chile,* other
volumes in this series.

The final motif of the child sacrificed by his father in order to
bring a faithful friend back to life (cf. Stith Thompson, *Motif-Index,*
S268) appeared in the Middle Ages in the epic poem *Amis et Amiles.*
Amiles slits the throats of his two sons and uses their blood to heal
Amis, who has become a leper (cf. Gédéon Huet, *Le Conte Popu-
laire,* p. 148). In his tale of the *Corbeau,* Basile (*Pentamerone,*
Fourth Day, story No. 9) has Millucio kill his twin sons in order to
smear their blood over the body of his petrified brother.

·3· Ugly Yann

Type 675, *The Lazy Boy.*

Recorded in 1953 from the same informant as the two previous
tales. This old peasant woman—a rival of Marguerite Philippe, from
Plouaret, the famous informant of F. M. Luzel for his *Contes Populaires de Basse Bretagne*—knew by heart countless stories handed
down to her orally; she told me a good thirty of them during my
1953 and 1954 vacations. Most of the stories in her repertory belong
in the category of tales of magic, but they still include fiercely critical or sarcastic touches in the morals of the treated themes.

In this version, the initial motif of the hero doing a superior being
a service is missing. In a variant recorded in Upper Brittany, the
superior being is a fairy transformed into a snake by a jealous rival;
the hero takes pity on her, and is rewarded by having his wishes
granted. The motif of the bundle of firewood which becomes a
means of transportation because the young man is tired of carrying
it on his shoulders, is found in Corsica, associated with Type 851
(cf. my *Contes Corses,* No. 66, *Pedi Untu,* p. 145, discussed p. 320);
it can be compared to Motif D441.3.1, "faggots transformed to

chargers," which Thompson and Balys discovered in India (cf. Stith Thompson, *Motif-Index*).

This theme does not seem to be widespread in French folklore, since the last edition of Aarne's and Thompson's *The Types of the Folktale* lists only thirteen versions in France and eight among the American French.

·4· *The Tailor*

Type 1640, *The Brave Tailor*.

Recorded in 1953 from an old man in the forest of Loc-Envel (Côtes du Nord), François Thomas, who made wooden shoes and spoons.

This theme first became famous when the Grimm brothers published a version which went back to an old German book published in 1557 by Martinus Montanus of Strasburg. Motifs from Type 1045 (where the hero's mere threat intimidates the ogre) and Type 1060 (characterized by the episode of the "crushed" rock) are also included in the story.

This folktale type, categorized in the series of "Lucky Accidents," is rather popular in French folklore, in France as well as among the francophiles of North America, even though the last edition of the Aarne-Thompson type index does not indicate it. In 1961 I recorded several variants of it among the French of Nova Scotia in which the battle against the unicorn (Aarne-Thompson, Type 1640—III b) plays a prominent role. In our version from Lower Brittany, however, the plot is centered in the series of tricks used by the tailor, whose bluffs get the better of his adversaries, the giants. On the other hand, the episode of the tailor's marriage to the King's daughter is missing here.

Cosquin, in his *Contes Populaires de Lorraine* (II, 95–102), has studied this tale-type in great depth in relation to a variant recorded at Montiers-sur-Saulx, *Le Tailleur et le Géant*.

·5· *The Priest's Pig*

Type 1792, *The Stingy Parson and the Slaughtered Pig*.

Recorded from the same informant as the previous tale, the old shoemaker of Loc-Envel.

The 1961 edition of the Aarne-Thompson classification indicates that this theme is relatively little known in folklore, except in Germany. In France, eight versions have been recorded. Aarne-Thompson classify this Type 1792 among the jokes about "Parson and Sexton" (Types 1775–1799). In this variant from Lower Brittany, the initial motif which reveals the parson's stinginess is missing, and there is no sexton in the story; instead, the theft is motivated by the extreme poverty of a large family.

The little verse with which the thief's son mocks the victimized parson, and which he repeats in the pulpit, altered only so as to be slanderous, reflects an attitude commonly found among the people of Lower Brittany, for whom a deep attachment to traditional religion does not exclude a critical mockery of the members of the clergy when they are found to be at fault. This exchange of rhymed sentences can be compared to Type 1831, *The Parson and the Sexton at Mass,* in which the theft of a lamb is discussed in antiphony.

PART II

UPPER BRITTANY

·6· *The Devil and His Three Daughters*

Type 313, *The Girl as Helper in the Hero's Flight.*

Recorded in 1958 from a farmer, Jean Belliot, who had learned it from his father, Jean Belliot, known as Guineau, a basket maker who lived in La Chapelle des Marais, in Brière.

In the past the story must have been part of the vast repertory of the "basket makers' tales," described in a masterful way by my colleague Ariane de Félice in her *Contes de Haute Bretagne* (Paris, 1954, pp. i–xiv). As she points out (p. v), over a hundred years ago Gérard de Nerval, in his *Chansons et Légendes du Valois* (Paris, 1854), made this comment about a part of a tale: "Here is a folktale that I remember hearing the basket makers tell of an evening." Recently one of my colleagues from the National Center of Scientific Research, who is studying the old crafts of Limousin, shared with me his observations on the culture of the basket makers of this area, who have also inherited a rich folklore tradition.

The theme is a favorite among French storytellers, as my teacher Paul Delarue has pointed out, because it is one of those tales of magic that lend themselves the best to a stirring and vivid exposition and that at the same time combine motifs of magic inherited from the ancient past. In the first volume of the *Catalogue des Contes Français* (I, 199–241), Delarue lists 118 versions in French, to which must be added the Canadian collections—Luc Lacourcière lists eighty-one Canadian and Nova Scotian variants in *Mémoires du IVe Congrès des Investigateurs des Contes Populaires* (Kiel-Copenhagen, 1959, p. 148)—and those versions recently recorded in France. (I recorded five versions in Corsica and a sixth unpublished version has been given to me.) A version from Norway is contained in *Folktales of Norway,* another volume in this series.

Our version from Upper Brittany, which preserves fairly well the series of tasks, attaches to the episode of the flight that of the forgotten fiancée, which can also stand alone as a story in itself (according to the wife of the informant).

·7· *The Boy Whose Mother Wanted to Throw Him in Boiling Water*

Type 314, *The Youth Transformed to a Horse.*

Recorded in 1954 from a sixty-year-old housewife, Jean Broussard, in La Chapelle des Marais, Brière.

Like the previous tale, this story was part of the repertory of the basket makers, of whom the informant's husband was one of the last to know how to "spin a yarn." It includes a few motifs which do not properly belong to it. The coach carved from a turnip by a fairy and drawn by four white rats brings to mind the pumpkin transformed into a coach in Perrault's *Cinderella* (Type 510A). Delarue, in his commentary on the *Contes du Nivernais et du Morvan* (p. 279), points out that this motif of the transformation of animals and objects into a coach is frequently found in French folklore. And the three beautiful suits, the colors of the sun, of the moon, and of the stars, which the hero received from the fairy are reminiscent of the marvelous dresses in Perrault's *Peau d'Ane* (Type 510B).

In French folklore, the hero usually has golden hair, which he covers up under the pretense of having ringworm until the moment when its beauty is publicly revealed. The Brière version omits the magical episodes I, II, and III, and opens with episode IV, in which the hero is hired by the king to care for his animals. This theme has already been recorded in Upper Brittany by Paul Sébillot, the great folklorist of the nineteenth century (the versions numbered 26 to 31 by Paul Delarue, *Catalogue des Contes Français,* pp. 255–56) and by Ariane de Félice (*Contes de Haute Bretagne,* No. 2, p. 24); in one of the versions recorded by Sébillot, the reason behind the hero's departure is the cruelty of his parents, as in this story.

Other versions of this tale may be found in *Folktales of Japan* and *Folktales of Chile,* companion volumes in this series.

·8· The Seven-Headed Monster

Type 317, *The Stretching Tree,* Type 300, *The Dragon-Slayer,* Type 303, *The Twins or Blood-Brothers,* and Type 314, *The Youth Transformed to a Horse.*

Recorded in 1954 from an old farmer from Missillac (Loire-Atlantique), Jean Tobie, who had heard the story from his mother, a well-known storyteller; he told me thirteen of her tales.

This tale combines in an interesting way elements from the narrative defined by Delarue (*Catalogue des Contes Français,* p. 275) as Type 317, with a battle against the seven-headed monster—an episode belonging to Types 300 and 303—and with episodes reminiscent of Type 314. The hero goes back to his menial job in the service of the King, and reveals his identity only after having pranced about on three magnificent steeds, in contempt of the fences raised by the King in order to stop him.

Type 317 has only a narrow distribution in France as a whole, but it is well represented in the folklore of Upper and Lower Brittany and in that of French Canada. Kurt Ranke has pointed out in his monograph *Die Zwei Brüder* (FFC 114, p. 197) the frequent association of this theme with that of the seven-headed monster (just as in this case). Delarue (p. 279) notes that in France this theme serves rather often as an introduction for Type 300 (seven times), more rarely for Type 314 (once, in a tale recorded by Luzel, *Robardic le pâtre*) or for Type 530 (once, in a tale published by Cosquin, *Lorraine,* II, 89, *Le Petit Berger*). In his commentary on this latter story, Cosquin compares it to several versions from other parts of Europe (Tyrol, Hungary, Moravia, Italy) and points out the frequency of the motif of the "triple appearance of the hero in a tournament, on three horses of different colors" (II, 97).

·9· The Beast

Type 425, *The Search for the Lost Husband.*

Recorded from the same informant as the previous tale.

This theme, which was made famous by Leprince de Beaumont's adaptation, is also widespread in the oral tradition of French folklore, in France—where there are sixty-six versions according to the Aarne-Thompson type index, of which a few show traces of the eighteenth-century literary version, which was widely circulated by peddlers —as in North America, where forty-three variants have been collected. Additional versions may be found in *Folktales of Ireland, Folk tales of Israel,* and *Folktales of Japan,* other volumes in this series

Maurice de Meyer has brought to light the characteristics of French folklore in *Amor et Psyche, Etude Comparée de Variantes Recueillies en France, en Belgique et an Allemagne (Folk-liv,* II, 1938, 197–210). In our version from Upper Brittany, the motif of the three drops of blood that the wife lets fall from her finger onto the shirt of her husband when he is forced to leave her stands in opposition to the motif of the harmful drops of water which the jealous sisters-in-law pour on his pelt. In contrast to those spots of blood that Lady Macbeth thinks she sees on her hand, these indelible spots are the symbol of the wife's faithful love, and will enable her to later make herself known to her husband.

The expression *l'eau d'endormie,* which designates the sleeping potion used by the second bride to put the prince to sleep, is a vestige of Old French. Godefroy (*Dictionnaire de l'Ancien Langue Française,* III, 132) cites these medieval verses: *"Avez-vous beu de l'endormye / Que dormez si grant matinée?"*

·10· *John of Calais*

Type 506A, *The Princess Rescued from Slavery.*

Recorded from the same old basket maker of Brière as No. 6, *The Devil and His Three Daughters.*

This story was sometimes known as *John of Pontchâteau,* from the name of a small town close to the village where the basket makers lived, to which they went to sell their baskets at the fair. Type 506A, to which it belongs, was made famous in France by the version circulated by the peddlers under the name *John of Calais.* Our version from Upper Brittany reflects both the peddlers' booklets (the names of the hero and the heroine's cousin, Don Juan and Isabella, suggest the literary version) and traditional folklore traits: the seven-year sojourn of the hero on a desert island, the little scene in which he becomes a woodcutter and is referred to as *"barbu peillu guenillu,"* his recognition by means of a handkerchief embroidered by his wife, and so on. The reproach to the woodcutter cited above reflects the local speech, in which the term *peille* means "rag" and *peillu* means "ragged." Furthermore, the informant seems to want to suggest from the very beginning that the area around Saint-Nazaire, at the mouth of the Loire, a site close to Brière, is the setting for the story, when he says, "He sailed away on the river."

Marie-Louise Tenèze has devoted a praiseworthy study to "Jean de Calais (Type 506A) en France: Tradition Ecrite, Tradition Orale, Imagerie," in *Mélanges Archer Taylor* (pp. 286–308). Few French folktales have been so widely circulated by means of peddlers' booklets; of the 32 versions recorded from the oral tradition (and half of them are Breton), only six versions seem untouched by any literary influence. However, the majority have still preserved the episode of the buried corpse, a typical episode of the universal theme, which is missing in the French literary version written by Angélique Poisson Gomez, born in Paris in 1684.

· *11* · Gold Feather

Type 531, *Ferdinand the True and Ferdinand the False*.

Recorded from the farmer from Missillac (Loire-Atlantique) who provided me with the story about *The Beast* (No. 9 of this collection).

As often happens, the initial episode of this variant—in which a poor child's eyes are put out to make him a beggar, and who is then purposely lost—is not peculiar to this type; it is also found in association with Type 613 (see No. 45 of this collection). The same thing is true of the next episode: three figures with supernatural and even magical powers—in this case, they are three giants —gather beneath the tree in which the child has taken refuge, and they interpret even the blunders he makes while perched in the tree in a quaint way, and always in his favor (see also my *Contes de l'Ouest,* Paris, 1954, No. 21).

The story of *Gold Feather* has also appeared in the repertory of the basket makers of Brière: the oldest of my informants in this region, Pierre Thureau, who was eighty-eight years old in 1950, told me its beginning that year. It is interesting that my informant from Missillac, who owed his stories to his mother, had learned from her a "literary" version belonging to the same Type 531, *Avenant*. In this version the features characteristic of Mrs. d'Aulnoy's story are clearly repeated; but for this peasant storyteller, who was ignorant of the international classification of types, these stories—incorporated into the local folklore from different sources—were entirely distinct.

· *12* · The Orange Tree

Type 313, *The Girl as Helper in the Hero's Flight*.

Recorded from the same informant as the previous story.

This story belongs to the same type as No. 6, *The Devil and His Three Daughters,* but its moral is completely different, even though Missillac (the informant's home) is geographically close to Brière, the home of the basket makers. The initial episode of the golden fruit—oranges in this case—stolen from a lord is not peculiar to this theme, and is frequently found in France as the beginning of Type 301A. But in this story, the bird-magician who stole the oranges does not lead the pursuing hero underground; instead, he forces him to rejoin him in an ivory castle. The motif, which is unclassified, of the castle all in bone or ivory is also found in Lower Brittany: the tale of *Luduenn* which I published in *Rencontre des Peuples dans le Conte* (Munich: France-Allemagne, 1961, ed. G. Hüllen and M. L. Tenèze, I, 92–94) has as its hero a "Cinderella," the youngest of three brothers, who successfully performs the task of constructing a "castle all in bone"; in that story, a dragon surrounds the bone castle "with its tail curved around it like a golden ring."

This story, *The Orange Tree,* includes the episode of the bird's daughters bathing in the pond, which is missing in the version from Brière. On the other hand, even though after the performance of the series of tasks, and the transformations of the flight, there is indeed a kiss which makes the hero forget his fiancée, she immediately makes herself known to him; therefore the episode of the forgotten fiancée is not included in this story, as it is in the Brière version.

·*13·* March and April

Type 1000, *Bargain Not to Become Angry.*

Recorded from the same farmer of Missillac as the previous tale.

This theme is known in neighboring Brière by the title of *Premier Lassé* (cf. my *Contes de l'Ouest,* p. 98), and even of *Cendrillon* (cf. *Contes de Haute Bretagne* by Ariane de Félice, pp. 66 and 255). In this version the names of the heroes—who are two brothers, the eldest and the youngest—bring to mind two successive months at the beginning of the year, as in a variant that I recorded in Lower Brittany, *Janvier et Février;* this feature also recurs in other provinces of France.

This folktale type is usually associated with other themes of the series "Tales of the Stupid Ogre," as is noted in the latest edition of *The Types of the Folktale* (p. 340); however, in this version it is found in its pure form. The punishment reserved for the first one to become angry—a strip of skin will be removed from his back

—is the one that appears the most frequently in the versions from different parts of France; I also encountered it in a Corsican version, *Les Trois Tranches de Peau* (cf. my *Contes Corses,* Gap, 1963, No. 23, p. 53). But this annoying punishment can just as well be the loss of the loser's ear or nose, or even death, as Delarue has pointed out in his commentary on the work by Ariane de Félice mentioned above.

For a Chilean version of this tale type, see *Folktales of Chile,* a volume in this series.

PART III

PAYS DE RETZ

·14· *The Tale of La Ramée*

Type 559, *Dungbeetle.*

Recorded in 1958 from a seventy-one-year-old farm woman, Clémentine Lezin, in Sainte-Pazanne, in the Retz region. Lying to the south of the mouth of the Loire, this region forms a transition between the area around Nantes (which belongs to the ancient duchy of Brittany) and Lower Poitou, to which it is related by its dialect.

My informant had learned this story as a young child from an old basket maker. There are only a few versions in French folklore of Type 559, which is not widespread in the rest of Europe either, except in Ireland. However, Aarne-Thompson lists sixteen French versions in America. The motif of the suitor who must make the Princess laugh in order to marry her, which here is related to the series "Animals as Helpers" (Type 530–Type 559) within the category of "Tales of Magic," also belongs to Types 571–574, and is often enjoyed as a humorous tale by the storytellers and their audiences.

G. d'Aronco has devoted a paragraph in his *Fiabe di Magia in Italia* (Udine, 1957, pp. 78–79) to the theme of *La Principessa che non Ride.* A version of Type 559 appears in the *Pentamerone* (Third Day, Story 5, *La Sorece e lo Grillo*) in which the hero, instructed by his father to purchase some goods, buys for a hundred ducats each of the three helpful animals—a mouse, a dungbeetle, and a cricket. Our variant from the Retz region features as its hero an old man, or perhaps an old soldier (for the name "La Ramée" was a common nickname for a soldier under the *ancien régime*), who simply meets a mouse, a beetle, and a cricket on the road, and who welcomes them as companions, somewhat in the manner of

Demi-Coq (Type 715), a tale which is widespread in this part of western France.

PART IV

LOWER POITOU

·*15*· *The Goat Who Lied*

Type 212, *The Lying Goat,* and Type 123, *The Wolf and the Kids.*

Recorded in 1960 from Mme Pierre Péau, aged sixty-seven, in Saint-Hilaire de Riez, where the salt marsh borders on the freshwater marsh, close to the mouth of the Vie River.

Lying to the south of the Retz region, the Vendean Marsh (sometimes incorrectly called the Breton Marsh) is an area which is still strongly steeped in its old traditions, even now in the middle of the twentieth century. *The Maraîchins* (as the inhabitants of the Marsh are called) are especially well known as singers and dancers, and their gay spirit, sometimes touched with melancholy, lends itself more to these two popular media than to the folktale.

Type 212 and Type 123 are both found throughout western France (especially the latter), as well as in Upper and Lower Poitou, in Aunis, in Saintonge, and in Angoumois. They are frequently combined in the folklore of the rural areas: Ellenberger noted their association in Upper Poitou (cf. *Arts et Traditions Populaires,* 1960, No. 3, p. 139) and Maugard in the Pyrenees (cf. his *Contes des Pyrénées,* 1955, No. 26, p. 211).

In French folklore, the development of these two tales is marked out by means of set phrases, which are generally in either rhyme or assonance, and which are modified as the plot progresses. A great Walloon folklorist, Elisée Legros, has emphasized the importance of these formulas in her work, *Trois Récits de Lutins et de Fées dans le Folklore Wallon et le Folklore Comparé* (Liège, 1952), and especially in *Quelques Formules de Contes d'Animaux en Wallonie et en France* (Brussels: *Les Dialectes Belgo-Romans,* 1953, pp. 149–68). These formulas have generally been adapted to the dialect of each region in which they have taken root, and therefore sometimes contain archaic terms and symbolic allusions.

The Vendean folklore tradition is rich in stories studded with this type of short verse; some are simply rhymed (as in this case), while others are sung (see my *Contes de l'Ouest,* No. 12, *Les Brigands,* and my *Poésie Traditionnelle Enfantine* [Poitiers: *Bulletin de la Société des Antiquaires de l'Ouest,* 1958, pp. 540–43]); almost all can be beautifully adapted to stories suited for children.

A version of Type 212 from Germany may be found in *Folktales of Germany,* another volume in this series.

· *16* · *Boudin-Boudine*

Type 333, *The Glutton.*

Recorded in 1958 from Mme. Panetier, aged eighty-five, in Gué-de-Velluire.

The marsh of the Sèvre River, also known as the *Marais Feuillu,* is on the border of the present departments of Vendée and of Deux-Sèvres. Its inhabitants, who used to be called *huttiers,* lived in huts (*huttes*) on the islets of the Sèvre River, surrounded by its many channels, and conducted their agricultural affairs with boats as their sole means of transportation. Their speech, very different from the *maraîchin* used in the Vendean Marsh to the north, has preserved until the present some peculiarities which make its set expressions and short verses almost impossible to translate. I have therefore incorporated them in this story as they are.

This story is a local variant of the well-known *Little Red Riding Hood* (Type 333), which, like another version recorded in La Taillée in this same Marsh, features a little boy rather than a little girl. Furthermore, this little boy does not take his grandmother a cake and a small pot of butter as in Perrault's version, but instead, after the Vendean fashion, some black puddings from a freshly killed sow on his parents' farm. He also takes her some *fristure,* a local dish made with pork rinds boiled in a pot, for one local custom requires that when a pig is killed and butchered, the best pieces be shared with neighbors. The name Courtine for the sow indicates that she was *écourtée*—that is, that her tail had been bobbed. The informant sets the story in the marsh of the Sèvre River (just as her grandfather did when he told her the story, she said), which is alluded to in several place names: the Grand Veurdé, the Bas Galioux.

The motif of the wolf who dips his black paw in the semolina in order to whiten it belongs to another type, Type 123, *The Wolf and the Kids,* which was also discussed in relation to the previous tale. As to the term *bouillie bordelaise,* it seems to have been the name the informant's mother used for a white semolina probably made from wheat. The happy ending of this story is not unusual, for Paul Delarue (Paris: *Bulletin Folklorique d'Ile de France,* 1953, pp.

513–14) notes that this ending is found "in certain versions from France, Italy, and Tyrol, and in a tale related to the Far East, *Le Tigre et les Enfants.*"

A variant of this tale can be found in *Folktales of Japan,* in this series.

·17· *The Iron Pot*

Type 400, *The Man on a Quest for His Lost Wife,* and Type 401, *The Princess Transformed into Deer.*

Recorded in 1958 from an old peasant woman from the center of the island of Yeu, Eugénie Lacroix, aged seventy-five, who had heard it from her great-grandfather.

The island of Yeu, which is farther from the shore than Noirmoutier and which has also been more influenced by maritime life, has well preserved its traditional customs and its oral literature.

This story is an altered version of Types 400 and 401 (deliverance of the lost wife). Interestingly enough, another tale known by this same title, which I heard that same year in the unique village of the island of Yeu, is related by one motif to Type 401A (with the three nights of torture endured in silence) even though it belongs as a whole to Type 425, *The Search for the Lost Husband.*

In this version, the informant has emphasized the role of the eagle, which as the hero's guide helps him to identify and to deliver his future wife, who is enclosed not only underground but also in an iron pot. To this role has been added the motif of the hero pulled from the underground world up to the light by the eagle, which he must feed with the game he kills and then with a piece of his own flesh. This feature, which frequently serves as a conclusion to Type 301A in France, has in this case been altered in an ingenuous way: the hero's wound is simply due to his fall, and it is in another underground hunt that he kills the game which will give the eagle the strength to carry him back up to the surface. Here his delivered wife-to-be and his dog wait for him, for they had been carried up first.

·18· *The Little Lad Who Became a Bishop*

Type 671, *The Three Languages.*

Recorded in 1958 from Delphine Soupault, aged seventy, who worked in a sardine-packing house on the island of Noirmoutier.

In the universal theme, three successive episodes correspond to the three categories of animals—dogs, birds, and frogs—whose languages the boy learns. This folktale type is fairly widespread throughout the different provinces of France; a more complete version of it has been published in my *Contes de l'Ouest* (No. 4, p. 36, *Le Pape;* commentary by Paul Delarue, p. 249), and another one in F. Cadic's *Contes de Basse Bretagne* (No. 12, p. 133, *Le Pape Innocent*). The theme of animal languages appears also in my *Contes Corses* (No. 2, p. 4), but this variant clearly belongs to the related Type 670, as does another Corsican variant mentioned in my *Commentaires* (p. 268).

We know that the understanding of animal languages by a man is a motif that goes back to antiquity. Melampus, a Greek magician, raised some young snakes he had rescued. One day his snakes cleaned out his ears so well that when he woke up he was astonished to discover that he understood the languages of mammals, birds, and reptiles. Later, this motif appears in *Gesta Romanorum* and in the *Roman des Sept Sages;* the theme of Type 670 was itself treated by Morlini around 1520 in one of his *Novelle* (No. 71).

·*19*· *Tom Thumb*

Type 700, *Tom Thumb.*
Recorded in 1960 from Mme Bellion, aged sixty-five, from Brétignolles (Deux-Sèvres).

The name *Petit Poucet,* which Perrault gave the hero of his famous tale (derived from Type 327, *The Children and the Ogre*), actually belongs to a different theme, Type 700, which is that of *Tom Thumb,* the French *L'Enfant Gros comme un Pouce,* or the German *Daumesdick.* In order to avoid confusion, Paul Delarue has proposed the name Pouçot, which appears frequently in Nivernais, for the folklore versions of Type 700 (see his commentary on my *Contes de l'Ouest,* p. 269).

This tale is an example of this theme, which is widespread in western France, where the adventures of Pouçot are well known and are often interspersed with brief rhymed verses, smatterings of which quickly come to the minds of the old peasant women, even when they think they have forgotten the main content of the story.

A version of this tale may be found in *Folktales of Japan,* a volume in this series.

·*20*· *The Tale of Jean-le-Sot*

Type 1696, *What Should I Have Said (Done)?*
Recorded in 1958 from Mme Chevalier, aged eighty-three, a farm woman in Chaillé-les-Marais (Vendee).

This story is studded with chanted phrases in deliberate imitation of religious chants. Paul Delarue realized that his country's many versions fell into two categories according to the interpretations of the foolish young man: Type 1696A, "What should I have said?"; and Type 1696B, "What should I have done?"

Our Vendean version has the originality of taking place in this marsh of the Sèvre River, which extends into the departments of both Vendée and of Deux-Sèvres. The local setting is reflected in the episodes of the cracked ground, which the hero treats with butter, and of the frogs croaking in the ditches, which he bombards with eggs. This quick-moving story is also characteristic of the rebellious spirit and in particular of the sarcastic attitude toward the clergy which are typical of this small region.

PART V

UPPER POITOU

· 21 · The Wolf and the Soldier

Type 157, Learning to Fear Men.

Recorded in 1960 from Olivier Sennegon, a seventy-three-year-old farmer, in Martaizé (Vienne).

This type is widespread in the Nordic areas of Europe, and is also well represented in France. The informant, who had learned this variant from his grandmother, faithfully retained the old woman's local references, identifying the setting by referring to places allegedly in his own village: the Fontaine blanche, the Croix cassée, and La Chausse en l'air. This is a technique old people frequently use when addressing children, in order to bring an extraordinary story close to home.

An interesting aspect of this tale is the fact that the wolf, eager to fight "a creature called man," does not ask a fox for directions but, instead, an old woman, who sends him out against a soldier armed from head to toe. And after his unfortunate fight, the wolf relates his defeat not to a fox but to another wolf.

Sixteen variants of Type 157 collected by Richard M. Dorson from Negroes of the Southern United States are given in his article, "King Beast of the Forest Meets Man," Southern Folklore Quarterly, XVIII (1954), 118–28.

·22· *The Little Elves of La Chausse-en-l'Air*

Recorded in 1960 from Mme Brissaud, aged seventy-nine, in Martaizé (Vienne).

This legend is a "news item" about those evenings of long ago which is widespread in all of France. The original term used in this story, *fadet,* designates in the west of France those small elves who came down chimneys, as distinct from the *lutin,* those elves (who were no less mysterious) who used to haunt stables. Cosquin includes in his famous *Contes populaires de Lorraine* (II, 288–89) an analogous legend, *La Fileuse,* recorded in Montiers-sur-Saulx, and notes that a Basque tale and an Angevine are similar to it, except that the mysterious figure has become a fairy. The general meaning of the little verse, which is rhymed in the local speech and which provokes the anger of the man disguised as a spinner, is "Last night's spinner spun a lot better."

·23· *The Piece of Cloth*

Type 402, *The Mouse (Cat, Frog, etc.) as Bride.*

Recorded from the same informant as No. 21.

This type owes its fame in France to a literary version by Madame d'Aulnoy, *La Chatte Blanche (Contes Nouveaux ou les Fées à la Mode,* Paris, 1698, II, 89), but it is also well represented in French folklore, where it has been little influenced by the literary version. In our variant from Upper Poitou, the motif of the father promising his niece in marriage to his three sons also suggests Type 653, interesting versions of which have been found in Lower Brittany (cf. F. Cadic, *Contes de Basse Bretagne,* Paris, 1955, No. 13, p. 142, *La Fille du Sabotier*) in the Pyrenees (cf. Maugard, *Contes des Pyrénées,* Paris, 1955, No. 2, p. 7, *Le Rusé Voleur*) and in Corsica (cf. my *Contes Corses,* p. 139, No. 61). As I have noted in the commentary on the Corsican version, *La Fleur, le Miroir et le Cheval* (p. 315), this motif is found in *A Thousand and One Nights* in the first part of a tale entitled *The Story of the Prince Ahmed and of the Fairy Pari-Banou,* where the King's three sons are in love with his niece, Nourounnihar. But in Type 653 the three rare objects that the suitors must bring back later help to save the life of their fiancée, whereas in Type 402 the items found by the youngest of the three brothers enable the animal that helped him through his trials to return to human form; in the end the hero marries, not the original object of his desire, but the Princess (or the fairy) to whose deliverance he contributed.

For a Chilean version of Type 402, see *Folktales of Chile,* a companion volume in this series.

·24· *The Three Gold Hairs from the Devil*

Type 461, *Three Hairs from the Devil's Beard.*

Recorded in 1960 in Martaizé (Vienne) from a ten-year-old girl, Marie-Renée Baudouin, who had heard it from an elderly neighbor woman.

This variant contains the essential elements of the theme, but it does not include the series of questions the hero must answer, except for the last one, the ferryman's. However, the informant greatly elaborated the amusing dialogues between the hero, the old housekeeper, and the Devil over the pulling of the three golden hairs.

The initial motif—the King's jealousy of a poor newborn baby who, according to prophecy, would become king (cf. Motif M312— "Prophecy of future greatness for youth") is not peculiar to Type 461; it also appears at the beginning of the Corsican tale of *Tignusellu,* the rest of which belongs to Type 516. (Cf. my *Contes Corses,* No. 14, p. 31, commentary pp. 277–78; by mistake I wrote Type 314 instead of Type 461, Motif 321 instead of Motif M312, and Motif 461 instead of Motif M314.) Types 930 and 1525R also begin with a similar motif.

The basket in which the newborn child is placed is probably the Poitou *bourgne,* a basket formerly used by peasant women in the fields to lay their babies in.

Other versions of this tale may be found in *Folktales of China* and *Folktales of Germany,* additional volumes in this series.

·25· *Puss in Boots*

Type 545, *The Cat as Helper.*

Recorded from the same young informant as the previous tale.

This variant of Perrault's famous *Chat Botté* reflects in a fanciful way the story which is probably derived through many intermediate forms from the original literary version. The cat's first thefts for his master's sake and the sharing of the spoils (the cat gets the black puddings and a draught of wine) are touches added by the common people which are told with great zest. The transformation of the cat into a young man after his short-lived marriage to a rat is inserted into a scene which probably originated with one of the people in the line of those who handed down this story. On the other hand, the dialogue which characteristically enhances the Marquis of Carabas is lacking in our Poitou version. We know that oral versions of Type 545 are rare in France.

·26· *The Pea*

Type 555, *The Fisher and His Wife.*

Recorded in the spring of 1960 from an old farm woman from Marçay, in Vienne, Mme Fraigneau, who as a small child heard it in dialect form from an old woman who was a cowherd.

This theme was illustrated in Old French literature by the *fabliau Merlin-Merlot,* which corresponds to Type 555. The hero's benefactor (the hero is the head of a poor household) is often a fish, as in *La Petite Sardine,* in my *Contes de l'Ouest* (No. 18, p. 164); but the pea or bean which, when planted, climbs to the sky is an initial motif common to this folktale and to Type 563.

Paul Delarue, having published a charming Nivernais version entitled *Pourquoi les Chats Huants Sont des Personnes (Contes du Nivernais et du Morvan,* No. 10, p. 96), considered comparing it to a story of the *Pantachantra (Les Souhaits,* trans. Lancereau, p. 333; see his commentary on *Contes de Gascogne* collected by Perbosc, No. 7, p. 253). He had already counted thirty-three French versions of this theme and was thinking about commenting on it at greater length in relation to a variant recorded in Lower Brittany by F. Cadic (No. 8, p. 92), *Pourquoi le Hibou Fait-Il Hou! Hou! et la Chouette Ha! Ha!*

PART VI

LOWER MARCHE

·27· *The Black Hen*

Motif N555.1, "Between midnight and cockcrow best time for unearthing treasure."

Recorded in 1960 from Mme Bourot, aged twenty-three, who had learned it as a child from her grandmother.

The informant used landmarks allegedly in her native village of Bouresse (Vienne)—*La Crêpe-au-lait,* the *Logis des Barres*—as the background for this legend, which also strongly suggests the former

Poitou mentality. It contains some well-known motifs: the search for a mysterious treasure which appears only as midnight approaches, and the interruption of the search by the cackling of a hen at midnight; the lord's greed, which is greater than the beggar's; the punishment of the greedy lord; the diabolical nature of the apparition (the black hen). The expiatory pilgrimage to the Holy Land suggests the faith of the Middle Ages, which remained evident in the rural areas of Poitou up to the beginning of the twentieth century.

·28· *Jean of Bordeaux*

Type 307, *The Princess in the Shroud*.

Recorded in the fall of 1960 from M. Boutin, a farmer in his sixties, in the village of Asnières-sur-Blour (Vienne), on the northeastern border of the department of Charente. This village had preserved its folklore exceptionally well.

The story of *John of Bordeaux* is a variant of Type 307; Delarue has listed thirteen versions in France (cf. his *Catalogue des Contes Français*, Paris, 1957, p. 172). In French folklore, the Princess is not a diabolical creature but instead is simply enchanted, and the hero disenchants her at the end of three nights spent not in prayer but in undergoing trials. The version from Lower Marche does not feature a soldier, like most of the French versions, but a poor swineherd in wooden shoes who finds himself pursued by the Devil himself. (Uusually the hero is pursued by the enchanted person.)

The final episode is the hero's return to his parents, his loss of everything to an innkeeper after a card game, his successful search for his wife, and the final recognition scene. This episode is not included in the description of the theme in the international classification and in the *Catalogue des Contes Français* mentioned above. However, it is found in a less detailed variant recorded in Ariège by Charles Joisten in 1953, also known as *John of Bordeaux*.

A German version of this tale may be found in *Folktales of Germany*, in this series.

·29· *Golden Hair, or The Little Frog*

Type 310, *The Maiden in the Tower*, and Type 402, *The Mouse (Cat, Frog, etc.) As Bride*.

Recorded in the fall of 1960 from Mme Rouyer, a farm woman in her sixties, in Bouresse (Vienne). She had learned it from her mother, Mme Grelier, born in 1865, who had heard it as a child from an old woman who was a cowherd.

Like many French versions of this type, this story is contaminated
at the end by another tale, in this case Type 402. Delarue (*Catalogue
des Contes Français*, p. 181) notes that this merger and this ending
are brought about by the transformation of the heroine into a frog,
a motif common to these two types. He then points out an original
feature peculiar to French folklore—the parrot who spies on the
lovers. Our variant from Lower Marche also contains an adaptation
which is peculiar to it alone—the young girl's godmother, generally
a jealous fairy, is here the Virgin Mary, who, far from punishing her
goddaughter, comes to her aid by assisting her fiancé.

The theme of Type 310 was already known by Basile (*Pentamerone*, Second Day, Story 1) and by Mlle de la Force (the story of
"Persinette" *Le Conte des Contes*, 1698).

· 30 · *The Comte de Mes Comtes*

Type 621, *The Louse-Skin*, and Type 900, *King Thrushbeard*.

Recorded in 1960 from Mme Barbier, aged ninety, a farm woman
originally from Queaux now living in Luchapt (Vienne).

This strange title designates the hero of a popular theme of
French folklore, known notably in Vendée by the name of Monsieur
de Montanville (cf. *Arts et Traditions Populaires*, 1953, p. 111), a
member of the nobility who disguises himself as a poor man in
order to better test his beloved, and who reveals his true identity to
her after a series of trials. This combination of Type 621 and Type
900 is not unusual in France.

The suitor who correctly solves the riddle is sometimes disguised
as a beggar (cf. Vendée) and sometimes as a pilgrim (Charente);
here he is a coal merchant. In its Vendean form, this quick-moving
story is studded with disappointed remarks by the young lady as
she is led by the poor man through her beloved's property: "Oh,
how I loved Monsieur de Montanville!" Ariane de Félice has studied
these characteristic recurring remarks in a suggestive article (*Inter-
nationaler Kongress der Volkserzählungsforscher in Kiel und Kopenhagen*, 1959, pp. 93–97).

It is interesting that in my Limousin version the lord's name is
Marquis de Keraba. It has evidently been influenced by Perrault's
Chat Botté (Puss in Boots), in which an analogous stylistic motif
is developed in relation to the Marquis de Carabas. In our version
from Lower Marche, the peasant humor is given free rein in the
little scenes of local color where the disguised count enjoys making
his wife steal napkins on the day of the *bugée* (the large annual

washday), and then black puddings on the day of the *boucherie* (the slaughtering of the hogs), and all this takes place on the estate of his own castle.

· 31 · The Woman with Her Hands Cut Off

Type 706, *The Maiden without Hands.*

Recorded from the same informant as No. 29.

The medieval antecedents of this tale have been thoroughly studied, notably by Suchier and Puymaigre. This theme, which was included in Basile's *Pentamerone* (Third Day, Story 3) and in Straparola's *Facétieuses Nuits,* seems still to be greatly enjoyed by audiences of folktales throughout the different provinces of France. I recently recorded four versions of it in Corsica (cf. my *Contes Corses,* Nos. 59, 75, 81, and 104; commentary, p. 312) one in Lower Marche, one in Upper Brittany, and one in Lower Brittany, and also I found many variants in the course of my research among the French of Nova Scotia.

This story reflects the influence of Christianity, as do many stories recorded in this area, which was influenced by the Langue d'Oc civilization. The kindly figures who help the heroine during the delivery of her twins are the Virgin Mary, Saint John, and Saint Paul, who then serve as godmother and godfathers to the twins. The motif of the splinter driven into the leg of the executioner, which only the heroine can remove, is typical of French folklore. In Brittany, it is generally a thorn which takes root and grows in the foot of the guilty person.

Other versions of this tale may be found in *Folktales of Japan* and *Folktales of Germany,* volumes in this series.

· 32 · Souillon

Recorded in 1960 in Moussac from Mme Loiseau, aged seventy, born not far away in Luchapt (Vienne).

Paul Delarue noticed in the folklore of southwestern and midwestern France a theme not classified in the first edition of Aarne-Thompson, dealing with *La Soeur Propre et la Soeur Sale* (The Clean Sister and the Dirty Sister), for which he suggested the number 915B (see his commentary on Perbosc's *Contes de Gascogne,* p. 248). In the 1961 edition of Aarne-Thompson's *The Types of the Folktale,* the outline of Type 915, *All Depends on How You Take It,* is described, but in only one of the forms observed in France: the two different ways in which two daughters interpret their mother's precepts when they marry.

The variants that I recorded in France—one in Corsica, two in Lower Marche, three in Upper Poitou—correspond to Delarue's indexing of Type 915B rather than to the Aarne-Thompson form. However, this latter type is represented in Upper Poitou by an interesting version recorded by Ellenberger, mentioned by Delarue in *Contes de Gascogne* and published in *Arts et Traditions Populaires* (1960, No. 1, p. 115; commentary by Marie-Louise Tenèze, p. 138). Type 915B of Delarue's catalogue, like this story of *Souillon,* features a mother and her two daughters. The favorite daughter, who is lazy and spoiled, is not compelled to do any work, whereas her slighted sister is given the most tiresome jobs. The clean, hardworking sister manages her home very successfully, for she had the better training, whereas the dirty, lazy sister becomes poor.

·33· *The Devil and the Good Lord*

Type 1030, *The Crop Division,* and Type 1097, *The Ice Mill.*

Recorded in 1960 from Mme Faideau, a seventy-five-year-old farm woman who had heard it from her husband in Bouresse (Vienne).

This story joins the Devil and the Lord. It reflects both Type 1030, which is often associated with other themes, such as Type 9B (cf. my *Contes Corses,* No. 5, p. 10; commentary, p. 270), and Type 1097, which is well known in France as a separate story (there are nine versions). It is interesting that the Devil here plays the role of the stupid ogre, and God that of man, "weak," according to the informant, but intelligent (by implication). We have already seen in relation to tale No. 31, *The Woman with Her Hands Cut Off,* that the Christianization of the characters was a trait characteristic of the areas of midwestern France which were originally part of the Langue d'Oc country.

·34· *The Rat and the She Rat*

Type 2022, *The Death of the Little Hen.*

Recorded in 1962 in Pressac (Vienne) from Mme Boutant, aged fifty-two, who had learned it at the age of five from her grandmother, who was originally from Availles-Limouzine.

This *randonnée* is very popular among children. The story is developed through a series of enumerations, but is not summarized by beginning with the last verse and working backward, as in the

Chanson de Bricou, the song *Biquette A Tout Mangé Nos Choux,* and the following *randonnée* about the little hen.

Our version from Pressa is one of the most complete of its type. After telling of the drowning of the rat's mate and the rat's tears, it sets in motion the bench, the table, the door, the cart, the magpie, the fountain, the woman carrying pitchers, the man at his oven, the man leading a horse; then the water spreads over the body of the disemboweled horse, marking the end of the *randonnée,* and drowning out the "news story" originated by the tears of the unfortunate rat. The brief dialogue terminating this story introduces the usual set expression given in answer to children's requests for the sequel of a story.

·35· *The Little Hen*

Type 2032, *The Cock's Whiskers.*

Recorded in 1960 from Mme Benaîton, an eighty-two-year-old farm woman, in Adriers (Vienne).

The *randonnée* about the little hen and the little *jau* (rooster) is one of the favorite tales of children, who enjoy both its content and its form. These enumerations and then the summary, which are generally in rhyme or assonance form, enable the child to follow the evolution of a story, and even then to retrace it himself. When I watched in person the method used by a mother to transmit the story orally to her ten-year- old daughter, I noticed that she tirelessly had the girl repeat each fixed formula in order to have her memorize the progressive stages of a rather long *randonnée,* which she then had her recapitulate.

PART VII

ANGOUMOIS AND RUFFECOIS

·36· *The Goat, the Kids, and the Wolf*

Type 123, *The Wolf and the Kids.*

Recorded in 1959 from an old peasant woman, Mme Lavaud, aged seventy-nine, in Montjean (Charente), at the northern edge of Ruffecois.

This variant of Type 123 represents the form this theme most frequently takes. It is still very much alive in the folklore of western France, and is perhaps the animal tale country children enjoy most, with its rhymed verses, its rich dialectal resonant tones, and its mysterious rhythm, set by the grandmother's cane or her wooden shoes.

The heroine of the story is usually a nanny goat, but she is sometimes also a sow (in a variant from the island of Yeu) or a hen (in a variant from the Pays de Retz). The local customs are reflected in the description of the dishes enjoyed by the wolf: the *froumajhé* or *tourteau froumajhé* is a cake stuffed with fresh cheese, popular in a small area running through the southern ends of the departments of Deux-Sevres and of Vienne and the northern end of the department of Charente.

In the twelfth century Marie de France (in her Fable 90, *De la Chèvre et ses Chevreaus*) and later, in the seventeenth century, de la Fontaine (in his Book IV, Fable 15, *Le Loup, la Chèvre et les Chevreaux*) already put this traditional folklore theme in verse form in French.

· 37 · *The Sleeping Beauty*

Type 410, *Sleeping Beauty*.

Recorded in 1959 in Ambérac (Angoumois) from a farmer, M. Ganachaud, aged seventy-four, who learned it as a child from an old Vendean immigrant (a common case in Charente, where the immigrants of Vendean origin now constitute an important proportion of the rural population).

The beginning which properly belongs to Type 410 is missing here. The story begins instead with episode IV; owing to the initiative of a fairy, the beauty's godmother, a Prince arrives a hundred years after the young girl was put to sleep. Several traits characteristic of our story from Angoumois are not included in the "international" theme: the monster with seven heads and seven paws with claws (cf. Types 300 and 303), a magic sword which increases in length by two meters to strike the monster, the cawing of the crow to announce the breaking of the spell, the transformation of the monster's seven heads into seven golden balls which announce the birth of the seven children to the couple.

The strange motif of the sword which increases in length is found in the folklore of Armenia among the attributes of a *dève* (a seven-headed dragon), and the hero or heroine must seize it in order to kill the *dève* (cf. Lalayantz, *Revue des Traditions Populaires,* 1895, X, 193).

A version of this tale from Chile may be found in *Folktales of Chile,* in this series.

·38· *The Three Innocents*

Type 1450, *Clever Elsie.*

Recorded in 1959 in the Ruffecois area from Mme Latinois, aged seventy-six, in Villiers (Charente).

This story is widespread in Ireland and Sweden as well as in France, where it is frequently associated with Type 1384, *The Husband Hunts Three Persons as Stupid as His Wife.* In his commentary on a version of the *Three Innocents* recorded by Ariane de Félice (*Contes de Haute-Bretagne,* No. 21, p. 277), Paul Delarue expressed the opinion that the two associated themes (a combination represented in France by thirty versions) should be considered a distinct type (see also F. Cadic, *Contes de Basse Bretagne,* No. XV, p. 160, *Les Surprises de Jean le Rigodon*). It is interesting to note that in Charente, however, a version of Type 1450 has circulated in its independent form. We have already seen in relation to No. 30, *The Comte de Mes Comtes,* the frequency in French folklore with which two types are associated (in this latter case, Types 621 and 900 were combined).

Another version of this tale may be found in *Folktales of Germany,* in this series.

·39· *Coué or Couette*

Type 2015, *The Goat Who Would Not Go Home.*

Recorded in Montjean from the informant who told me No. 36.

This little *randonnée* is characterized by the final recapitulation of all the set phrases, only now inverted, beginning with the last one. Here, the initial motif—the attitude of the ram which refuses to return to the sheepfold—is explained by a trait suggestive of Type 212, *The Lying Goat* (cf. our No. 15): "My mistress has done nothing but make me run all day long." The local names Coué or Couette are probably related to the dialectal word *coué,* meaning "tail"; thus a sheep or goat with a long tail (a rather rare phenomenon).

PART VIII

LIMOUSIN

·40· *The Gold Ball*

Type 425, *The Search for the Lost Husband.*

Recorded in the spring of 1961 in the Limousin dialect in Chassenon (Charente) from an octogenarian, Mme Rougier, who had learned it as a child from her father, who was originally from the neighboring village of Saint-Quentin.

On the borders of the departments of Charente and Upper Vienne, a small region, centered in the two towns of Confolens and La Rochefoucauld, stretches along both banks of the Vienne River. Here they still speak the old Limousin dialect made famous in the Middle Ages by the first troubadour, Bernard de Ventadour.

This story does not begin with the usual initial motif for this type—an animal-husband—but instead with the indiscreet behavior of some old neighbor women, who surprise a newlywed couple in bed. The golden ball which the Virgin Mary gives the young wife, and which leads her to the spot where her husband has taken refuge, brings to mind a variant of Type 451, *La Boule Rouge* (The Red Ball; cf. my *Contes de l'Ouest,* No. 20, p. 175). It would seem that the golden ball became confused with the first of the three magic objects the maiden received to use in exchange for her brothers, the two others being a golden hen and her chicks and a golden bobbin. In French folklore the magic objects are usually a spindle, a spinning wheel, and a bobbin.

·41· The Brother Who Was a Lamb

Type 450, *Little Brother and Little Sister.*

Recorded in the spring of 1961 from Mme François Audonnet, a farm woman, aged fifty-nine, in Esse (Charente).

This type is represented by several versions in Lower Marche and in Limousin. The motif of the three fountains, the first two of which transform into an animal anyone who ventures to drink from them, while the third one transforms the young girl into a pretty, well-dressed lady, is particularly widespread in this area, where it is sometimes added on as an episode of Type 327. In this story, another woman is not substituted for the wife (cf. Type 450, episode IV), but instead the mother-in-law pretends to be ill in order to persuade her son to kill the lamb. It is at this point in the story that the rhymed verses are placed, exchanged at the edge of the well by the sister, a Queen, and the brother, a lamb. This final episode is frequently found in the versions of Type 451 which come from the western and midwestern parts of France.

A German version of this tale may be found in *Folktales of Germany,* in this series.

·42· The Ogre (Malbrou)

Type 451, The Maiden Who Seeks Her Brothers.

Recorded in the fall of 1961, in Alloue (Charente) from a spry eighty-three-year-old shepherdess, Mme Delage, who had learned it as a child from an elderly neighbor.

The local name for the evil figure—malbrou—suggests the Poitou term lebrou or brou, the ogre's name in certain versions of Tom Thumb (Type 700), and the Nivernais term loup-brou (cf. Paul Delarue and Achille Millien, Contes du Nivernais et du Morvan, p. 148).

Other local terms are the ponne (a large washtub) and the gabiote (a forester's cabin). The final episode of the brothers' transformation into animals because they ate vegetables growing on the ogre's grave is missing in our variant; but even so, the malbrou remains harmful after his death, since the combs made from his bones cause an incurable illness.

Another version of this tale can be found in Folktales of Germany, in this series.

·43· Cinderella

Type 510A, Cinderella.

Recorded in the spring of 1961 from a seventy-three-year-old peasant woman, Mme Joly, at Saint-Maurice des Lions (Charente).

This variant of Type 510A, which is generally known in France by the name of Cendrillon, is of this area.

The motifs of the food-providing animal—in this case, the milking cow which the little girl strikes with a hazel wand as the Virgin Mary, her godmother, told her to—and of the magic tree that bends down to feed the disinherited girl, are considered by Delarue characteristic of a related type which he calls Type 511A, while he reserves the classification Type 511B for another type, Le Petit Taureau Rouge (cf. his commentaries on Contes du Nivernais et du Morvan, p. 268). On the other hand, the ugly sister who trims down her foot in order to be able to slip on the shoe, and the animal which reveals the place where the pretty sister is hidden, are both typical of Type 510A. The transformation of the two jealous women into stones flanking the staircase or into doorjambs is found in other folklore themes as the punishment for jealousy: in our tale No. 9, The Beast, the two sisters who drenched the animal-husband's pelt are changed into coulombres (doorjambs).

Other versions of this tale can be found in *Folktales of Japan* and *Folktales of Chile,* companion volumes in this series.

·44· *The She Donkey's Skin*

Type 510B, *The Dress of Gold, of Silver, and of Stars.*

Recorded in 1960 from a seventy-eight-year-old peasant woman, Veuve Delage, a native of Le Lindois, who lived not far from there, in Vitrac-Saint-Vincent (Charente). She had heard this story from her deceased husband.

This theme, which is closely related to the preceding tale in the international classification, is characterized in French folklore, according to Delarue, by the motif of the Prince's three encounters with the heroine dressed as a servant. The Prince strikes the servant successively with three household objects; in this case, a poker, a bellows, and a *friquet*—the local name for the stick used to stir the meat to make *grillons* or potted minced pork. Interestingly enough, in spite of the local setting for this variant in which the heroine is a turkey girl, the story has assimilated a feature of literary origin—the chest which goes underground—probably a reminiscence of Perrault's famous tale *Peau d'Ane.* This story, which is still popular in the countryside, is one of the earliest recorded in French folklore. Noel du Fail mentions the tale *Cuir d'Asnette* (The She Donkey's Hide) in his *Propos Rustiques* (1547), and Bonaventure des Periers alludes to the story *D'une Jeune Fille Surnommée Peau d'Asne* (A Young Girl Nicknamed "Donkey Skin") in his *Contes ou Nouvelles Récréations et Joyeux Devis* (1557).

Another version of this tale may be found in *Folktales of Chile,* in this series.

·45· *The Two Brothers, or The Fox, the Wolf, and the Lion*

Type 613, *The Two Travelers.*

Recorded in 1961 from an eighty-eight-year-old peasant woman, Mme Dumaine, who told it to me in the Limousin dialect, in Esse (Charente). Another elderly person from the same village told me the same story, but with a different setting.

Thirty French versions of this theme have been recorded. Cosquin has pointed out how extremely old it is by comparing it to an ancient Egyptian tale (*Les Deux Frères,* fourteenth century B. c.; cf. *Contes Populaires de Lorraine,* I, Appendix B, LVI–LXVII), and yet it is interesting to see how alive this type still is in French folklore now in the twentieth century. I myself have recorded four variants in Corsica, all of them rather different from each other (cf. my *Contes Corses*, Nos. 43, 51, 82 and 88; discussed, pp. 299–300), and one in Upper Brittany which is contaminated by Type 300; Ariane de Félice has found in this same area a version which has merged with Type 531, *La Belle Kévale* (cf. *Contes de Haute-Bretagne*, No. 8, p. 87).

In the universal tradition, the heroes generally have symbolic names: Bien-Faire et Mal-Faire (Good-Doer and Evil-Doer; as in the case of our Corsican variant No. 43), Bonne-Foi et Mauvaise-Foi (Sincerity and Insincerity; *ibid.*, No. 82), Loyal et Déloyal (Loyal and Disloyal; the title of a Norwegian tale mentioned by Cosquin, *Contes Populaires de Lorraine*, I, 88). Delarue writes about a third-century Chinese version, the story of Fait-Bien et Fait-Mal (Does-Good and Does-Evil) in his commentary on the story *Secret des Bêtes* (cf. Perbosc, *Contes de Gascogne*, p. 254). In this concise story recorded in Esse, it is simply a matter of drawing lots: the one who loses has his eyes put out in order to solicit alms, which the other one gathers but does not divide evenly. We have already encountered this initial motif in the story of *Gold Feather* (No. 11 of this collection).

Other versions of this tale may be found in *Folktales of Israel* and *Folktales of China*, in this series.

· 46 · Little Fourteen or As Strong as Fourteen

Type 650A, *Strong John*, and Type 301B, *The Strong Man and His Companions* followed by *Quest for a Vanished Princess* (Type 301A).

Recorded in 1960 from a farmer from Saint-Christophe (Charente), Jean Chansigaud, aged sixty-seven, who had heard it from his mother, and who remembered the final episode during my second visit in 1961.

These two themes are frequently associated in French folklore, as Delarue has noted. The symbol of strength multiplied fourteen times is not peculiar to our version from Saint-Christophe. Sébillot recorded in Upper Brittany a story of *Quatorze* (Fourteen), which is more distinctly related to Type 301B (cf. Delarue, *Catalogue des Contes Français*, p. 125, No. 56).

The initial motif of this variant tells of a child so poor that no one is willing to be his godfather, but who in the end becomes the godson of eminent people (generally a king or queen, and in this case, the Lord and the Virgin Mary). This is a beginning common to several themes, notably to Type 531 (cf. *Motif-Index*, N811). Once again the characters have been Christianized, a trait characteristic of the Marche and Limousin areas.

·47· *The Master and the Tenant Farmer*

Type 852, *The Hero Forces the Princess to Say, "That Is a Lie."*

Recorded in the spring of 1961 in Esse (Charente) from an old farmer, François Audonnet, whose father was still famous as a storyteller at evening get-togethers.

This story belongs to the special category of "fibs," for Type 852 is usually about a Princess to whom her suitors must tell a story so preposterous that she says, "That is a lie." The central motif (Type 852, episode IIb) of a tree growing up to the sky overnight, which the hero climbs and then descends on a rope made from bales of oat husks, is preceded and followed in our variant by a series of original "fibs." In addition, and most importantly, it has a highly characteristic local setting. The story is not about a princess and a suitor, but a master and a tenant farmer who in a way is driven to tell these "fibs" in order to preserve his share of the harvest, which is at stake because of a bet imposed on him at his master's whim.

·48· *Fanfinette and the King's Son*

Type 883B, *The Punished Seducer.*

Recorded in the fall of 1961 from a seventy-seven-year-old peasant woman with a remarkable repertory, Mme Bertrand, in Saint-Claud (Charente).

The last edition of the Aarne-Thompson type index lists only one version of this theme in France, which became famous as Miss Lhéritier's story of *Finette ou l'Adroite Princesse* (published in 1696: *Revue des Traditions Populaires,* 1888, III, 275, and St. Prato, *Giornale della Società Asiatica d'Italia,* IX, 229).

The motif of the flower which fades (*Motif-Index,* E761.3), symbolizing the young girl's seduction, is replaced in a variant that I recorded in Upper Poitou by a distaff which breaks. Léon Pineau found in the same area a combination of the two traits: the father gives a rose to the two older sisters and a stick to the youngest (cf. *Revue des Traditions Populaires,* the tale of *Finon-Finette*). Pineau also ran across the motif of the cask lined with nails in which a person is rolled in this Poitou variant. However, I recorded this same motif in Vendee in association with a version of *The Giant Killer and His Dog* (*Bluebeard*) (Type 312: cf. my *Contes de l'Ouest*, commentary p. 259, No. 19, version C).

The giant gourd placed in the bed to look like a person and take the sword's blows is a trait found in another theme, where a poor young girl's guile is also set against a prince's seductions. This is *La Jeune Fille au Pot de Basilic*, not classified in the Aarne-Thompson index. Delarue has analyzed a version in *Incarnat, Blanc et Or* (Paris, 1954, p. 67; see also my *Contes Corses*, p. 37, No. 18; commentary, p. 280).

PART IX

MASSIF CENTRAL

·49· *The Bear and the Beetle, or The War of the Animals*

Type 222, *War of Birds and Quadrupeds.*

Recorded in 1951 in Crandelles, to the west of Aurillac, from an octegenarian, Mme. Fournier, and her forty-eight-year-old daughter, who had heard it from her mother as a child. It was recorded during the research done by the *Atlas Linguistique et Ethnographique du Massif Central,* and comes from the collection of its director, Pierre Nauton, made in the department of Cantal.

This story belongs to the category of animal tales, which are always enjoyed in the rural areas. The conflict is actually between the insects, offended in the person of the beetle which the bear held under his paw, and the quadrupeds, the bear's colleagues. The role given to the fox—that of a messenger who is careful not to admit that he was stung in order to let the others run the same risk—is consistent with his character as presented in oral French folklore. In his commentary on a Gascon variant of this theme (cf. Perbosc, *Contes du Gascogne,* No. 26, p. 271, *Le Loup et le Grillon*), Delarue notes that this theme was already well known in the Middle Ages, and that from it "Marie de France took her fable *D'un Loz è d'un Escarboz* (fable LVI, p. 241 of the Roquefort edition)." He lists thirteen versions of this type in France, almost all in the Langue d'Oc country.

·*50*· *Jean and Jeannette*

Type 327, *The Children and the Ogre.*

Recorded in 1941 from two elderly peasant women in Saugues (Haute-Loire), to the north of the Margeride mountain, by Pierre Nauton, the author of a remarkable monograph on *Le Patois de Saugues* (Clermont-Ferrand, 1948), and the director of the *Atlas Linguistique et Ethnographique du Massif Central.* Nauton heard this tale himself in Saugues around 1920, when he was a child.

He has specified that this is one of those evening stories which children were formerly told while their mother or grandmother was sewing or knitting. With his background as a linguist and dialectologist, Nauton is primarily interested in these dialectal tales because their content has not been suggested to the informants, and their style and syntax present original forms often missed in direct questioning. Folklorists consider the story of *Jean and Jeannette* to be a version of Type 327, in the form which is characteristic of the center of France, but at the same time a little different from those already published by Paul Sébillot in his *Littérature Orale de l'Auvergne* (p. 33, *Les Enfants Égares* from Cantal; see *Revue des Traditions Populaires,* 1887, II, 146), *L'Almanach de la Lozère de 1928* (p. 42, le diable et la diablesse), and by Léon Pineau in *Les Contes de Grand-Père* (Paris, 1938, No. 6, p. 47; a variant from the Loire region).

We have already discussed the Christianization of themes in the Langue d'Oc country; in this case, the evil character is not the ogre but the Devil, in his "red house," and his pursuit of the fugitives gives rise to dialogues in verse form between the Devil and the haymakers, a shepherd, and the washerwomen who finally cause the Devil's drowning. The motif of the child considered too thin and placed in a pigsty to fatten up, as well as the pretense to help the Devil's wife, who must kill the child, are found in association with Type 327 as well as with Type 328.

The episode of the rat's tail which the child substitutes for his own finger when the Devil comes to feel it is an intrinsic part of Type 327 (cf. Delarue, *Catalogue des Contes Français,* p. 311, Episode III, Motif F3), but it also suggests Type 451, in which the ogre comes and sucks through the cat hole the finger of the little girl, who is wasting away (cf. No. 42 in this collection).

·*51*· *The Magic Napkin*

Type 563, *The Table, the Ass, and the Stick.*

Recorded, in June, 1952 in Lozère, in a hamlet close to Mende, from a seventy-year-old woman who had learned it at fifteen, by Pierre Nauton in the course of his research for the *Atlas Linguistique et Ethnographique du Massif Central*. Like the two preceding tales, this one was recorded in dialect form; though the informant knew French, she was used to telling stories in her local dialect. The following text, like the preceding ones, is a translation by Nauton.

The theme is here prefaced by a brief introduction describing two hungry children abandoned by bad parents (cf. Type 327). A fairy brings objects to the children that will relieve their misery, somewhat in the same way she helps the orphan who, in the folklore of the central France, is the heroine of local forms related to Type 510A (*Cinderella*) and Type 511 (defined by Delarue according to the motif of the food-providing animal). In this version a particularly cruel trait should be noted: the first two magic objects are not stolen by an innkeeper but by the two children's foster parents.

Other versions of this tale may be found in *Folktales of Israel* and *Folktales of Germany,* companion volumes in this series.

PART X

FOREZ

· 52 · *The Four Friends*

Type 130, *The Animals in Night Quarters*.

Recorded in Poncins, in Forez, from an old miller's wife, by Marguerite Gonon, who collaborated on the *Atlas Linguistique et Ethnographique du Lyonnais*.

This story is preceded by the peasant storytellers' favorite introductory rhyme.

The departure of the four animals on a trip the night of Saint Sylvester is generally motivated in French versions by their master's or mistress's plan, overheard by one of them, to kill them for the New Year's banquet (usually Christmas, and they leave on Christmas Eve). Friend Goose, Tiny Black Cat, Curly Lamb and Heifer Ready-to-Deliver are the four companions of Type 130, forty-five versions of which have been recorded in France, according to the latest edition of the Aarne-Thompson type index; the rest of the story seems to have been altered, perhaps in order to arrive at a more peaceful ending. In this version the four friends do not encounter thieves in the house in which they take shelter but a poor old woman who is very happy to receive them and to keep them with her.

·53· Half Chicken

Type 715, *Demi-Coq*.

Recorded by Marguerite Gonon shortly before 1939 in Poncins (Forez).

Aarne-Thompson list seventy-two versions of this theme in France, where it is one of the most popular among the peasants, plus five among French-speaking Canadians and one in the French West Indies. In his discussion of this story's fame in France, Delarue quotes from Destouches' *La Fausse Agnès* (1759), in which a young girl, when asked what she knows about fables, answers: "I know the tale of *Peau d'Ane* of *Moitié-de-Coq* (Half a Rooster) and of Marie Cendron." In addition, he points out that Restif de la Bretonne gives a Burgundian version of it in *Le Nouvel Abailard* (1779).

The initial motif of this folklore theme is missing in our Forez version. Usually an egg is divided in two and from one of the two parts Half a Rooster hatches, with only one leg and one wing; or two neighbors divide a rooster in two; Half a Rooster finds a money purse, which is then stolen from him, and he leaves in search of the thieves. In this story, Half Chicken goes to the King to seek justice —in other words, a henhouse where she would be respected by the poultry; and in spite of the ups and downs of her stay at the King's court, she finally gains protection for herself and her friends, Shaggy Wolf, Fair River, and Burning Fire.

A German version of this tale may be found in *Folktales of Germany,* another volume in this series.

PART XI

FRANCHE-COMTÉ

·54· The Wolf and the Fox

Type 15, *The Theft of Butter (Honey) by Playing Godfather;* Type 2, *The Tail Fisher;* and Type 34, *The Wolf Dives into the Water for Reflected Cheese.*

Recorded by Jean Garneret in 1950 from Louis Mouchotte in Burgille-lès-Marnay (Doubs) in Franche-Comté.

This story is related to these three universal themes which are based on the legendary rivalry between the wolf and the fox. There are sixty versions of the first theme in French folklore, according to Delarue. In general the fox is after a pot of butter, of fat, or of honey, and while the names the fox gives his godson vary between regions, they all describe the state of the pot—in this case, Gobbled, Half, and Well-Licked.

The next trait (the wolf sent to the butcher) could be considered an alteration of the end of Type 1. The episode of the wolf fishing in a pond with a pail attached to his tail is represented by twenty-four variants in France, and was made famous by the *Roman de Renart;* in folktales it is sometimes followed by another episode in which a new tail is manufactured for the tail-less wolf (Type 40B).

The concluding episode of the wolf mistaking the moon's reflection in a well for cheese is less widespread in France (there are four versions).

Additional variants of Type 15 may be found in *Folktales of Ireland* and *Folktales of Germany,* volumes in this series.

·55· *The Wolf and the Fox in the Well*

Type 34, *The Wolf Dives into the Water for Reflected Cheese;* and Type 32, *The Wolf Descends into the Well in One Bucket and Rescues the Fox in the Other.*

Recorded by Jean Garneret in 1950 from Charles Pepin in Lantenne (Doubs) in Franche-Comté.

The second episode is represented by five versions in France, and was also made famous by the *Roman de Renart.*

·56· *The Black One, the White One, and the Plucked One*

Type 2300, *Endless Tales.*

Recorded by Jean Garneret in the winter of 1960–61 in Etrabonne (Doubs).

This little Franche-Comté story belongs to the family of those tricks used by tired storytellers when their audience urges them to tell another story. The form of these "endless tales" is also suitable to an audience of children, like the joke of the *Rouge-Cochet,* also known as the "ricochet fable," or of the *"sourneto* of the white lamb" (see my study "C'est la Fable de Ricochet," *Le Français Moderne* (Oct., 1964), 286–95). Underlying the story is the eternal theme of the wolf duped by weaker animals, in this case ewes—his natural prey—as in Type 122C, *The Sheep Persuades the Wolf to Sing* (to alert the dogs). The names of the three ewes call to mind another animal fable recorded by the same man in Franche-Comté,

La Blanche, la Noire et la "Depoilée," which belongs to Type 124.
For an "endless tale" from Japan, see No. 14 in *Folktales of Japan,* in this series.

PART XII

DAUPHINÉ

·57· *The Girl and the Thief*

Type 956B, *The Clever Maiden Alone at Home Kills the Robbers.*

Recorded in 1954 from a farm woman, Marie Arnoux, aged sixty-one, in Abriès, in the Queyras area (Hautes-Alpes), by Charles Joisten, a young disciple of Paul Delarue who visited even the smallest villages of this department, where he gathered a collection of over five hundred folktales.

In Dauphiné this tale seems to be particularly appreciated in the Queyras and Briançonnais areas, where it is represented by five versions. Joisten writes, "The high valley of the Queyras, close to the Italian border, is one of the richest centers we have discovered in the French Alps."

Aarne-Thompson does not list any versions of Type 956B in France, though it mentions twelve Franco-American versions. However, some good variants have been recorded throughout different provinces as far apart as Lower Brittany and Corsica. The theme usually appears with more highly developed hardships than in this story. Usually there is a whole band of thieves and not just one, and the heroine's flight gives rise to a series of incidents: in Trégor, she hides in a wagon full of hay, into which the thieves stick their swords, and then she runs to a washhouse and from there goes and hires herself out to some farmers. Just as in this Dauphiné story, one of my Corsican versions also contains the motif of the mutilated hand hidden with a glove (see the commentary in my *Contes Corses,* Nos. 24 and 68, pp. 287–88).

·58· *The Devil's Boot*

Type 1130, *Counting Out Pay.*

Recorded by Charles Joisten in 1960 from a farmer, Joseph Genon-Descotes, aged fifty-five, in Miribel-les-Echelles, in the department of Isère (Dauphiné).

This theme is widespread in the Nordic areas of Europe (two

hundred variants have been listed in Finland, forty-five in Estonia) as well as in the western areas, notably in Germany (twenty-six versions) and in France (eight versions). The initial motif—a ruined young nobleman calls up the Devil, who proposes a bargain for his soul—is also found in France at the beginning of certain versions of Type 313. The appearance of the Devil with the smell of sulphur, red clothes, and horse's feet, is consistent with his traditional representation.

·59· He Who Speaks First

Type 1351, *The Silence Wager.*
Recorded by Charles Joisten in 1959 from an eighty-five-year-old peasant woman, Mme Octavie Jail, in Saint-Jean d'Hérans, in the Isère region.
This theme is the subject of a study by W. N. Brown, "The Silent Wager Stories: Their Origin and Their Diffusion," *American Journal of Philology,* XLIII (1922), 289–317. It fits into the cycle of domestic quarrels over some insignificant detail, such as closing the door or bringing back an object. Seven versions have been found in France, two among the Walloons, and one among the American French.
An English version of this tale may be found in *Folktales of England,* in this series.

·60· The Fearless Shoemaker

Recorded in Isère by Charles Joisten.
This story about a shoemaker who watches over a dead man does not fit under a type classified in Aarne-Thompson. It can be compared to an episode of Type 326, *The Youth Who Wanted to Learn What Fear Is,* in which the hero is not afraid of ghosts. In a Corsican variant of this theme (published in my *Contes Corses,* No. 48, p. 116), the hero is lured one night into a cemetery, where a sacristan hidden in a tomb speaks to him; far from being frightened, the hero instead gives him a sharp answer and throws him over the wall. This Dauphiné story, however, is about a man who pretends to be dead and who is caught in his own trap, for the hero takes him at his word and strikes him as though he were a ghost, thus making him as silent as a real corpse. This brings to mind the final episode of our Vendean version of *The Tale of Jean-le-Sot* (see No. 20 of this collection).

Charles Joisten calls to our attention two published versions of this unclassified theme: one recorded by him and published by M. L. Tenèze and Georg Hüllen in *Begegnung des Völker im Märchen* (Frankreich-Deutschland, Münster, 1961, I, 134); the other recorded and published by Yvonne Sévoz in "Contes Populaires Recueillis à Villard-Reculas, Canton de Bourg d'Oisans," *Bulletin de la Société Dauphinoise d'Ethnologie et d'Archéologie,* XX, 2–3 (April–June, 1913).

PART XIII

SAVOY

·61· The Scalded Wolf

Type 121, *Wolves Climb on Top of One Another to Tree* (Motif J2133.6), and Type 1875, *The Boy on the Wolf's Tail.*

Recorded by Charles Joisten in 1958 from a thirty-seven-year-old farmer, Gaston Trépier, in Aillon-le-jeune, a mountain village of the department of Savoy.

The landmarks of this village—La Fraissette, the Replat, the Col des Prés, the Croix de Fornet—provide the setting for the story, which presents Types 121 and 1875 as though they were the successive episodes of a true narrative. The episodes of Type 1875 are preceded by an anecdote about the scalded wolf which recalls the final motif of Type 123 (see Nos. 15 and 36).

Aarne-Thompson does not mention any versions of Type 121 in France. However, Delarue cites a charming variant from French Lorraine in the journal *Arts et Traditions Populaires* (1953, pp. 42–43). The story Joisten recorded in Savoy also bears witness to the fact that this theme, which is rather common in Nordic folklore and which is also known in Spain (including Catalonia) is found in southeastern France. Delarue has written several commentaries on Type 1875 (see his *Contes du Nivernais et du Morvan,* No. 21, p. 292; the *Contes de Gascogne* by Perbosc, No. 45, p. 289), for which twenty-nine versions are listed in France; and he has devoted a comprehensive study to it in the journal *Arts et Traditions Populaires* (1953, pp. 33–58), in which he remarks on how often this theme is presented as an authentic adventure, especially in literary adaptations, notably that of Mistral.

·62· *Princess Elisa*

Type 329, *Hiding from the Devil.*

Recorded by Charles Joisten in 1958 from Léonie Clerc-Pithon, aged fifty-eight, in Jarsy, in the Bauges mountain range in Savoy. The informant had learned it as a child from an old woman nicknamed La Pesoule, who died in 1918, famous for having inherited from her father the art of telling stories for an entire evening.

Until now only one version has been recorded in France, the Lower Breton version published in F. Cadic's *Contes de Basse-Bretagne* (No. 1, p. 17). It was reproduced and discussed by Delarue in his *Catalogue des Contes Français* (pp. 342–45), who reports that this theme is also found in the French West Indies (Guadaloupe) and in Canada, where until now thirteen variants have been recorded. The Savoyard version seems to fit the definition of the universal folktale type better than the Lower Breton version, but it has not preserved as well the motif of the characteristic magic gifts. The three successive heroes are helped through their test by grateful animals: the eagle, the fish, and the ant (cf. Motifs H982 and B500), like the hero of Type 302, *The Ogre's (Devil's) Heart in the Egg* (see my *Contes de l'Ouest*, No. III, p. 25).

A Chilean version of this tale may be found in *Folktales of Chile,* another volume in this series.

·63· *The Little Devil of the Forest*

Type 500, *The Name of the Helper.*

Recorded by Charles Joisten from a sixty-three-year-old farm woman, Françoise Dupérier, in Jarsy (Haute-Savoie).

This story is greatly enjoyed by storytellers and their audiences because its formulas are to be sung; thirty-nine versions of it have been recorded in France. The initial motif of the mother's deceitful boast, which is based on a play on words, is common to both Types 500 and 501.

The Devil's picturesque name, which the heroine has to guess, varies among the different regions: it is Tirlemiton-Tirlemitaine in Franche-Comté, Fanfimois or Ropiquet in Lorraine, Mirloret in Bourbonnais, Ricouquet in Guyenne, Racapé or little old man Ripopé in Poitou (cf. *Arts et Traditions Populaires,* 1960, p. 139). In a tale by Miss Lhéritier which was inspired by this theme, the Devil's name is Ricdin-Ricdon (*La Tour Ténébreuse et les Jours Lumineux,* 1705), and in a Norman folklore version it is Rindon. It is odd that in Savoy the heroine's diabolical helper has the feminine name of Mimi Pinson, which suggests the famous song by Alfred de Musset, "Mimi Pinson is a Blonde." Cosquin (*Contes Populaires de Lorraine,* No. 27, I, 268–272) has discussed several French versions of this theme in relation to one recorded in Montiers-sur-Saulx.

An English version of this tale may be found in *Folktales of England,* in this series.

PART XIV

PYRENEES

·64· *The Charcoal Burner*

Type 159A, *Animals Warm Selves at Charcoal Burner's Fire.*

Recorded in 1953 by Charles Joisten from a seventy-one-year-old farm woman, Veuve Marie Rouzaud, in Montgailhard, Vaut par Nalzen, in the district of Lavelanet (Ariège).

This is a very rare theme which has been found only in southwestern France and in Catalonia. It is a kind of antithesis to Type 130, *The Animals in Night Quarters.* In this case, it is the cold which drove the bear, the wolf, the fox and the hare to the charcoal burner's hut in the mountains. In opposition to Type 130, at first they are well received and are able to warm up at their leisure. But the food they bring their host by way of acknowledgment arouses his greed, and they are the ones who are attacked in contrast to the four associates of Type 130, who throw the owners out of the house and take it over. This theme can also be compared to Motif W154.8, *Grateful Animals; Ungrateful Man.* Delarue has made a record of the French versions of this tale (see his commentary on Perbosc's *Contes de Gascogne,* p. 273) and has proposed the number 162 for this theme, which is also found in Joan Amades' *Folklore de Catalunya* (Barcelona: Rondallistica, 1950, No. 278, I, 586).

·65· *The Three Deserters*

Type 566, *The Three Magic Objects and the Wonderful Fruits (Fortunatus).*

Recorded by Charles Joisten in 1953 from a farmer, E. Bonnet, aged sixty-three, in Luzenac, in the district of Cabannes (Ariège).

Twenty-seven versions of this theme have been recorded in France, thirteen among the American French, and five in the French West

Indies. The great folklorist Cosquin discussed this theme at great
length in relation to a variant recorded in Montiers-sur-Saulx, *La
Bourse, le Sifflet et le Chapeau* (cf. his *Contes Populaires de Lorraine*, No. 11, I, pp. 121–132). In his commentary on a Nivernais
version (cf. his *Contes du Nivernais et du Morvan*, pp. 281–285),
Delarue states that "in France, the recipients of the gifts are usually
three soldiers, sometimes brothers, either discharged or deserters,
sometimes three brothers to whom their father leaves the magic
objects; or finally, a young girl imprisoned in a castle gives these
objects to the soldier who releases her after three nights of trials."
Interestingly enough, in our Pyrenees version the three magic objects
—the purse which is always full, the napkin which lays the table,
the coat which carries you wherever you want to go—are furnished
by the Devil when the three soldiers keeping watch in the haunted
castle allow him to come in to look after a treasure. The motif of
the nose which grows longer or shorter does not appear as often in
folktales as does the motif of horns sprouting on the dishonest
Princess' head.

·66· *The Laurel Flower*

Type 780, *The Singing Bone.*

Recorded by Charles Joisten in 1953 from the same informant as
No. 64.

The little verses in rhyme or assonance—sometimes sung—which
link the different episodes of this theme give it a certain charm, while
they also help to fix the story in the listeners' minds. It is therefore
one of the themes that are told to children in spite of its cruelty.
Thirty-six versions of it have been counted in France. There are
three brothers in our Pyrenees version, the youngest of whom is
polite and kind, and therefore succeeds where his older brothers
failed. This motif, which is widespread in French folklore (Luzel
has grouped a whole series of his *Contes de Basse Bretagne*, II,
cycle VII, 123–250, under the "cycle of the three brothers"), serves
as a beginning for variants of rather different folktale types (cf.
Motif-Index, Q2, "Kind and unkind"). The desired wonderful
object, in this case the laurel flower, is almost everywhere a rare
plant: the *Rose de Pimprenelle* (see my *Contes de l'Ouest*, p. 157,
No. 16), the *Rose de Montperlé* (Maugard, *Contes des Pyrénées*,
No. 4, p. 25; he also cites the *Rose de Pimperlé* or the *Herbe de la
Salogne*).

PART XV

CORSICA

·67· *The Legend of the Oxen's Pass*

Recorded from Jeanne Alfonsi, from Albertacce, in Corsica.

Corsica is not lacking in mountain legends, for it is a mountainous island where the shapes of peaks and rocks and the lake beds give rise to popular explanations. The most famous is undoubtedly the legend of Spusata, in the Sartene region, which explains how a young hard-hearted wife was turned to stone, for she took everything away from her poor mother, even down to the little scraper from the family kneading trough. An old storyteller from Niolo, who came from the same village as the informant, told me a much more complicated story on the same subject of the pass, in which Saint Martin's presence is placed in opposition to the Devil's senseless anger (see my *Contes Corses,* No. 53, p. 129; commentary, p. 307). The legendary explanation for the hole through the *Capu Tafonatu,* and for the rocks in the shape of petrified oxen, already appeared in Saint-Germain's *Itinéraire de la Corse* (1868) and in Mortillet's *Rapport sur les Monuments Mégalithiques en Corse* (1893), and in the works of still other more recent authors.

·68· *The Fox and the Blackbird*

Type 56B, *The Fox Persuades the Magpies into Bringing Their Young into His House.*

Recorded from a shepherd, Henri Rossi, from Albertacce (Niolo), in Corsica.

I have already published a Corsican variant of this type, *Le Chien Cippone,* from Castagniccia (cf. my *Contes Corses,* No. 6, p. 12; commentary, p. 271). The emphasis on the blackbird's revenge, which is legitimate since the fox cruelly deprived her of her offspring, is in keeping with the Corsican mentality. The universal theme can be compared to a little scene from the *Roman de Renart* in which the sparrow Droïn, tricked by the fox, who offered to guard her young, asks the dog Morhout to help her gain revenge. In the Corsican story, the blackbird pretends to limp to attract the shepherd's attention; in the *Roman de Renart,* the sparrow flutters about in front of a peasant's cart, and their trick has the same result. The dog takes advantage of the man's diverted attention to steal his food; his strength thus increased, the dog grabs the fox by the throat and avenges the wronged bird.

·69· *The Shepherd and the Snake*

Type 670, *The Animal Languages.*

Recorded in 1955 from a ninety-year-old shepherd, François Castellani, originally from Rutali (Nebbio) in Corsica.

Aarne-Thompson lists only two variants of this theme in France; however, I have already recorded two versions, one of which has been published in my *Contes Corses* (No. 2, commentary pp. 268–69).

In these Corsican stories, the episode of the hero learning about the existence of hidden treasure from the crow is perhaps borrowed from Type 673, *The White Serpent's Flesh,* in which the rooster's example incites the man to punish his wife for her curiosity about his secret. However, the motif exists independently of this theme: Straparola (*Facétieuses Nuits,* VII, Fable 5) tells the story of "three poor brothers, the youngest of whom learned the birds' language, and thus found out the existence of a hidden treasure"; and before him, Morlini (*Novella* 80) tells the same story.

The basic content of the theme of Type 670 already appears in the Middle Ages in the *Gesta Romanorum* and the *Roman des Sept Sages,* and among the Italian storytellers of the Renaissance, Morlini (*Novella* 71: *Du Pouzzolan Qui Entendait le Langage des Bêtes*) and Straparola (XIIth Night, Fable 3: *Histoire de Frédéric du Petit Puys*), who attribute similar adventures to imaginary heroes.

Other versions of this tale may be found in *Folktales of Germany* and *Folktales of Ireland,* companion volumes in this series.

·70· *The Child Promised to the Devil*

Type 811A, *The Boy Promised (or Destined) to Go to the Devil Saves Himself by His Good Conduct.*

Recorded in 1955 from a housewife in the suburbs of Bastia.

In my comments on another Corsican tale recorded in Castagniccia, *Ambrunu* (cf. my *Contes Corses,* No. 21, p. 47; commentary, p. 283), in which the theme of *The Boy Promised to Go to the Devil* precedes Type 400, I have already mentioned a third variant, *L'Enfant et les Croix d' Asphodèles,* recorded by Charles Giovoni in the Taravo valley. Whether the story is about a fisherman in despair because he cannot catch any fish, or a compulsive card player, or a wife distressed over her sterility, the child, promised to the Devil either before or after his birth, makes up for his parents' rashness or sin by his valorous conduct. In this story, the young man gets rid of the Devil through a real duel with swords.

Bibliography

AARNE, ANTTI, and STITH THOMPSON. *The Types of the Folktale.* (Folklore Fellows Communications, No. 184.) Helsinki, 1961.

ARONCO, GIANFRANCO, D'. *Le Fiabe di Magia in Italia.* Udine, 1957.

Arts et Traditions Populaires. Paris, since 1953. (A continuation of *Mois d'Ethnographie Francaise.*)

BASILE, GIAN ALESIO ABBATUTIS. *Lo Cunto de li Cunte, overo lo Trattenemiénto de' Peccerille.* Naples, 1637. (Known as the *Pentamerone* since the edition of 1674.)

CADIC, FRANÇOIS. *Contes de Basse-Bretagne.* Paris, 1955.

Collection de Contes et Chansons Populaires. 44 vols., Paris, Leroux, 1881–1930.

COSQUIN, EMMANUEL. *Contes Populaires de Lorraine.* 2 vols., Paris, 1886.

DELARUE, PAUL. *Catalogue des Contes Français.* Vol. I, Paris, 1957. Vol. II was prepared by his associate, Marie-Louise Tenèze. Paris, 1964.

———. *Contes Merveilleux des Provinces de France.* 7 vols., Paris, 1953–56. Published under the general editorship of Paul Delarue, as follows: Nivernais-Morvan (A. Millien-P. Delarue); Ouest (G. Massignon); Gascogne (A. Perbosc-S. Cezerac); Pyrénées (G. Maugard); Auvergne (M. A. Meraville); Basse-Bretagne (F. Cadic); Haute-Bretagne (A. de Félice). (Issued in two editions, with and without notes.)

FÉLICE, ARIANE DE. *Contes de Haute-Bretagne.* Paris, 1954.

HOEPFFNER, ERNEST. *Les Lais de Marie de France.* Strasbourg, 1920.

HUET, GEDEON. *Les Contes Populaires.* Paris, 1923.

Les Littératures Populaires de Toutes les Nations. 47 vols., Paris, 1883–1903.

MASSIGNON, GENEVIÈVE. *Contes Corses.* Aix-en-Provence, 1963.

———. *Contes de l'Ouest.* Paris, 1953.

———. *Contes des Teilleurs de Lin du Trégor.* Paris, 1965.

MAUGARD, GASTON. *Contes des Pyrénées.* Paris, 1955.

Mélusine, 11 vols., Paris, 1877–1901.

Mémoires de IVe Congrès des Investigateurs de Contes Populaires, Kiel & Kopenhagen, 1959. Berlin, 1961.

MERAVILLE, M. A. *Contes d'Auvergne.* Paris, 1956.

Les Mille et Une Nuits. trans. Galland. 12 vols., Paris, 1704–17.

MILLIEN, A., and PAUL DELARUE. *Contes du Nivernais et du Morvan.* Paris, 1953.

MORLINI, GIROLAMO. *Novelle.* Naples, 1520 and 1524.

OESTERLEY, HERMANN (ed.). *Gesta Romanorum.* 2 vols., Berlin, 1872.

PERBOSC, ANTONIN, and SUZANNE CEZERAC. *Contes de Gascogne.* Paris, 1954.

RANKE, KURT. *Die zwei Brüder.* (Folklore Fellows Communications, No. 114.) Helsinki, 1934.

Revue des Traditions Populaires, succeeded by *Revue d'Ethnographie et des Traditions Populaires.* Paris, 1886–1919; 1920–29.

Le Roman de Renart. Edited by Mario Roques. Paris, 1948.

ROOTH, ANNA BIRGITTA. *The Cinderella Cycle.* Lund, 1951.

STRAPAROLA, GIOVANNI FRANCESCO. *Le Piacevole Notte.* Venice, 1552–53. In French, *Les Facétieuses Nuits.*

THOMPSON, STITH. *The Folktale.* New York, 1946.

———. *Motif-Index of Folk Literature.* 6 vols. Rev. ed. Bloomington, Ind., and Copenhagen, 1955–58.

VAN GENNEP, ARNOLD. *Manuel de Folklore Français Contemporain.* Vol. IV, Paris, 1938. (Bibliography, pp. 654–715, nos. 3720 to 4279.)

NOTE: See "Foreword" for additional titles on French folklore.

Index of Motifs

(Motif numbers are from Stith Thompson, *Motif-Index of Folk Literature*
[6 vols; Copenhagen and Bloomington, Ind., 1955–58].)

E. THE DEAD

F. MARVELS

G. OGRES

H. TESTS

X. HUMOR

Z. CUMULATIVE TALES

Index of Tale Types

(Type numbers are from Antti Aarne and Stith Thompson, *The Types of the Folktale* [Helsinki, 1961].)

III. JOKES AND ANECDOTES

IV. FORMULA TALES

General Index